Old Testament Narrative

green press INITIATIVE

Westminster John Knox Press is committed to preserving ancient forests and natural resources. We elected to print this title on 30% post consumer recycled paper, processed chlorine free. As a result, for this printing, we have saved:

8 Trees (40' tall and 6-8" diameter)
3 Million BTUs of Total Energy
756 Pounds of Greenhouse Gases
3,643 Gallons of Wastewater
221 Pounds of Solid Waste

Westminster John Knox Press made this paper choice because our printer, Thomson-Shore, Inc., is a member of Green Press Initiative, a nonprofit program dedicated to supporting authors, publishers, and suppliers in their efforts to reduce their use of fiber obtained from endangered forests.

For more information, visit www.greenpressinitiative.org

Environmental impact estimates were made using the Environmental Defense Paper Calculator. For more information visit: www.edf.org/papercalculator

Old Testament Narrative

A Guide to Interpretation

Jerome T. Walsh

WESTMINSTER JOHN KNOX PRESS
LOUISVILLE · KENTUCKY

© 2009 Jerome T. Walsh

First edition
Published by Westminster John Knox Press
Louisville, Kentucky

10 11 12 13 14 15 16 17 18 19—10 9 8 7 6 5 4 3 2 1

All rights reserved. No part of this book may be reproduced or transmitted in any form or by any means, electronic or mechanical, including photocopying, recording, or by any information storage or retrieval system, without permission in writing from the publisher. For information, address Westminster John Knox Press, 100 Witherspoon Street, Louisville, Kentucky 40202-1396. Or contact us online at www.wjkbooks.com.

Scripture quotations from the New Revised Standard Version of the Bible and copyright © 1989 by the Division of Christian Education of the National Council of the Churches of Christ in the U.S.A. and are used by permission.

Book design by Sharon Adams
Cover design by Mark Abrams

Library of Congress Cataloging-in-Publication Data

Walsh, Jerome T., 1942–
　Old Testament narrative : a guide to interpretation / Jerome T. Walsh.
　　　p. cm.
　Includes bibliographical references and indexes.
　ISBN 978-0-664-23464-5 (alk. paper)
　1. Bible. O.T.—Criticism, Narrative.   2. Narration in the Bible.   I. Title.
　BS1182.3.W36   2010
　221.6'6—dc22

∞ The paper used in this publication meets the minimum requirements of the American National Standard for Information Sciences—Permanence of Paper for Printed Library Materials, ANSI Z39.48-1992.

Westminster John Knox Press advocates the responsible use of our natural resources. The text paper of this book is made from at least 30% post-consumer waste.

To the memory of my parents
Thomas and Madeleine Walsh
Let their works praise them
at the city gates
and of
William Payne Rogers
(1942–2009)

Contents

Preface	ix
Introduction	xi
Chapter 1: Two Theoretical Preliminaries	1
Chapter 2: Plot	13
Chapter 3: Characters	23
Chapter 4: Characterization	33
Chapter 5: Point of View	43
Chapter 6: Manipulation of Time	53
Chapter 7: Gaps and Ambiguities	65
Chapter 8: Repetition and Variation	81
Chapter 9: Voice(s) of the Narrator	97
Chapter 10: Structure and Symmetry	107
Chapter 11: Responsibilities of the Reader	121
Appendixes	131
1. The Jeroboam Story	133
2. The Elijah Story	159
3. The Ahab Story	183
Notes	209
For Further Reading	247
Scripture Index	251
Subject Index	256

Preface

This book was begun in the midst of some serious medical issues. I am more grateful than I can say to friends who helped me during those weeks and months, and whose friendship has continued to sustain me ever since: Dr. Kathleen Burk of the University of Dallas, Steve Hopkins, and especially Jeff Marlatt and Al Stewart. And many friends and colleagues have helped me in the formulation of the ideas and words of these chapters. First and foremost, I am grateful to students here and abroad who were the guinea pigs for my early attempts to offer a practical introduction to narrative criticism. I have learned much from their successes, their failures, and their feedback. Next, several colleagues at the University of Dallas, particularly Dr. Mark Goodwin, Dr. John Norris, and Dr. Brian Schmisek, have patiently and carefully worked through much of the text and exercises, catching my mistakes, clarifying my obscurities, tweaking my prose, and generally suggesting great improvements to the book on every level. Finally, but far from least, I thank the Lady of Orcas Island, Alice Logan, for insightful discussions, more insightful challenges, and most insightful editing. Alice, our conversations have been a joy! Thanks—and long live the Internet! The flaws and infelicities that remain I claim for my own.

Introduction

"It is not the voice that commands the story: it is the ear."
Marco Polo to Kublai Khan
in Italo Calvino's *Invisible Cities*[1]

Storytelling is a human universal. Stories help us preserve the past, explore the present, and extrapolate the future. The drive to give experience a narrative shape is no less urgent in the cultures that produced our biblical texts than in any others: over half of the Bible consists of narratives. Yet, surprisingly, scholars have only recently begun to attend to the *narrative* character of biblical texts. In both religious and academic biblical scholarship, the Bible has been investigated first and foremost for its "truth" (narrowly understood as historical accuracy or theological orthodoxy); and literary scholars, by and large, have defined the "classics" of Western civilization as beginning with literature written in Classical Greek and Latin and bypassed the literary legacy of other ancient languages and cultures.[2] Happily, this situation is changing, and the last generation or so has seen an explosion of biblical scholarship with an avowed and sophisticated interest in biblical stories[3] precisely as literary artifacts.

The goal of this book is to introduce some of the basic points of entry literary critics use to discover how narratives communicate to their readers and to equip you to pursue the same sort of narrative analysis on your own. I presume no technical knowledge of literary criticism on your part; I hope that my explanations and illustrations will be clear even to those who have no such background.

On the other hand, I do assume that great literature (and whatever else they may be, I am convinced the biblical stories we will read are great literature!) is worthy of careful, reflective, and self-critical reading.

Nor do I presume on your part a knowledge of biblical languages. I will assume that you are reading the Bible in English translation. I have chosen the New Revised Standard Version (NRSV) as the basis for most of my discussion. Unless I state otherwise, all citations of the biblical text in English are either from the NRSV or my own translations. On the other hand, I hope you will forgive me if I occasionally indulge in a detour to discuss some aspect of the Hebrew text. When I do so, it is because I find its specifics particularly interesting and I want to share them with you.

Finally, I do not presume on your part either a familiarity with or an acceptance of standard biblical criticism[4] (commonly referred to as "historical criticism"). The focus of narrative criticism is quite different from that of historical criticism. The latter seeks to get back behind the present text to earlier written and oral forms, in an attempt to recapture its earliest form(s) and determine what the original author(s) intended to communicate. Narrative criticism, by contrast, accepts the text in its final form—that is, the form in which we currently possess it—and asks what it communicates to its readers in that form. (In chapter 1 we look more closely at this difference and the theoretical ideas that underlie each approach.)

Two principles will guide our exploration of narrative criticism; both of them can be summed up in a single phrase: "making sense." First, narrative texts attempt to evoke responses from readers. That is, such texts are not limited to—or even primarily concerned with—the transmission of information. Narrative's appeal goes beyond the intellect to the emotions (we *like* or *dislike* stories and their characters) and the will (we are moved to accept or reject the values we perceive at work in the stories and to make moral judgments about characters and their deeds). By our responses we *make sense* of the story—that is, we experience its power and come to know the ways in which that power is operating upon us. Much of our time in this book will be spent examining the means authors use to elicit such responses from readers and the sorts of responses those means typically invite.

The second principle is that readers are not unworked clay that authors can sculpt into any shapes they choose. We are individuals with personal and communal histories and cultures—histories and cultures unimaginable in the days when the biblical authors wrote their texts. We bring all that we are to our act of reading, and the unique blend of personality and experience that each of us is inevitably influences how we read and how we respond to the story. In other words, our responses—that is, the *meaning* the story has for each of us—are shaped not only by the power of the text but also by the stories of our own lives. In this stronger signification too, a reader *makes sense* of a story—that is, *constructs* its meaning in dynamic collaboration with the words of the text.

Together these principles point to a right way and a wrong way to undertake our study. The wrong way is to learn a catalogue of narrative techniques, search for their presence in the text, and in that way figure out what response the author is seeking to elicit from a reader. If we do that, we fail in a fundamental way: we have not been *readers*. We have been detectives ferreting out clues, but we have not let ourselves be moved by the narrative power of the text. The right way to do narrative analysis with integrity is to read with openness to the text's power, to allow ourselves to respond as spontaneously as we can, and then, reflectively, to become aware of what our responses are and to seek to identify precisely what it is in the text that has evoked them. In this way we can both discover how the text shapes our reading experience and distinguish the ways in which we ourselves contribute to shaping that experience. This is how great literature accomplishes its deepest good: it reveals *us* to ourselves. Or, as literary critics often say, "The text reads the reader."

A Note on Pronouns

A laudable development in recent scholarly writing is the recognition that individuals are either female or male and acknowledgment of that fact by the use of gender-inclusive language. I have striven to follow this principle in writing of authors, readers, and narrative characters. There is a class of personal figures, however, for whom that observation is not always true: analytical constructs like implied author, implied reader, narrator, and narratee. (I discuss these constructs in some detail in chapters 1 and 9, but they appear throughout the book.) They are personal but usually—at least in biblical narrative—ungendered. I have resorted to the conventional English masculine for these constructs.

Chapter 1

Two Theoretical Preliminaries

OF MEANINGS AND METHODS

A Parable

One warm, late-summer afternoon, three friends went walking through a state forest. They happened upon a large oak tree to which, years before, someone had nailed a sign. The sign was old and weathered, the trunk had begun to grow over its edges, its paint was faded and its words were only barely legible. When the men managed to make the sign out, they read,

> Trespassers
> will be
> persecuted

"Look at that," said the first hiker. "Whoever wrote that sign misspelled it. He meant 'prosecuted,' not 'persecuted.'" "Perhaps," replied the second. "But it might mean just what it says: 'Trespass here and you'll get shot at!'" Their companion laughed, "Not any more it doesn't! We can't trespass on state land. That sign doesn't mean *anything*!"

The field of biblical studies has been in unusual turmoil for nearly two generations. Whether one thinks of the turmoil as chaos or as creative ferment depends to a great extent on one's appreciation of some underlying issues. Foremost among these is the question of "meaning." Our three hikers can help us unravel some of the complexities of this issue.

A written text, such as the sign on the tree, is an instance of a "communication act"—in other words, of an event in which a sender (here, the "author" who painted the sign) produces a message (the sign itself) that reaches a receiver (the three hikers who read it). The structure of communication via written text can be diagrammed:

$$\text{author} \rightarrow \text{text} \rightarrow \text{reader}$$

The question this simplicity conceals, however, is, Where in this diagram is "meaning" to be located?

Our first hiker identifies the meaning of the sign with what the author wanted to communicate to the reader. He recognizes that the author may not have expressed himself accurately ("He meant 'prosecuted,' not 'persecuted'"); but author's intention trumps textual imperfection. The sign's meaning is what the author intended to write, not what he actually wrote. One of the tasks of the interpreter is to identify such instances of disparity between intention and expression and to retrieve the former (the meaning) despite the inadequacies of the latter (the words).

Our second hiker also recognizes that textual expression may not coincide perfectly with authorial intention, but he is not willing to privilege one over the other as the unique meaning of the text. He entertains the possibility that the text as it stands, even though imperfect and inadequate with respect to the author's intention, may convey coherent and intelligible meaning to a reader ("It might mean *just what it says*"). Textual meaning then has autonomy as *one* (though not *the only*) possible meaning of the text. To put it another way, what the sign *says* and what the author *intended to say* can differ from one another, yet each can still be meaningful.

For the third hiker, the meaning of the sign lies in its contemporary impact. We might think of "relevance" or "significance" as synonyms for "meaning" in this sense. When it was originally posted, and for some unknown period of time thereafter, the sign no doubt warned its readers that their actions could trigger real consequences; it *meant* something. But now, since the sign has no contemporary relevance ("We can't trespass on state land"), it "doesn't mean *anything*." For this hiker, then, meaning derives above all from the circumstances in which the text is read, and that context determines meaning with greater potency than either the intention of the author or the words of the text itself.

Although it is something of an oversimplification, we might say that our three hikers each locate meaning at different points on the line of communication. The first hiker locates it in the author, the second in the text, and the third in the reader:

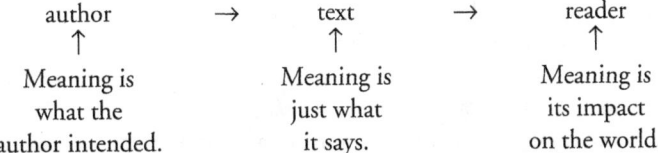

Now, the point of this parable is not to set up three rival definitions of "meaning" for the title of "*real* meaning," but merely to distinguish them as alternative objects of inquiry. Though they can be quite different from one another, each can be called "meaning" and each is worth investigating. Indeed, each is the central focus of attention for one or another cadre of biblical scholars today.

Biblical Studies Today

In the history of biblical scholarship, the centuries after the Enlightenment saw the gradual triumph of a single critical approach to the Bible, called "historical criticism." Its goal was to get *behind* the text to its origins, on the premise that the meaning of the text was what its (human[1]) author intended to communicate. Our first hiker is a historical critic: he wants to know what the author was thinking, even if the text fails to convey that thought perfectly.

The results of two or three centuries of historical criticism are rich and varied. Scholars have developed several precise and careful methods of analysis to afford access to the world behind the text. Textual criticism retrieves original wording when manuscripts differ because of scribal changes; source criticism reconstructs older written documents that were incorporated piecemeal into our present texts; redaction criticism reveals ways in which editors overlaid their own interpretations onto the materials they transmitted and manipulated; form criticism and tradition history even promise to penetrate the period of *oral* tradition that predated the written text and thereby to allow glimpses of the originating events themselves. And historical critics have collaborated with other disciplines—history, archaeology, ancient Near Eastern and Mediterranean studies—to coordinate data and integrate interpretations within broader horizons. What historical criticism has achieved is equally rich: the reconstruction of an Israelite history and culture much more complex and nuanced than we find in the Hebrew Bible; the identification of an immensely complex weave of oral traditions, written sources, and editorial hands in the extant text; the revelation of a vibrant and vital theological diversity in ancient Israel; and much, much more.

Historical criticism continues to flourish in the guild of biblical scholars. Excesses and oversights of the past continue to be identified and amended; gains of the past are refined and extended. In recent years, historical criticism has adapted new methods from the social sciences (particularly sociology and anthropology) in an attempt to discern in our texts clues to an ever more detailed and nuanced reconstruction of the society and culture of ancient Israel.

In the second half of the twentieth century, for reasons that would take us too far afield to investigate, some biblical scholars began to ask new questions—questions that focused not on the world *behind* the text, but on the text itself (sometimes called the "world *in* the text"), or on the text's effective presence in the contemporary world (the "world *in front of* the text"). In other words, our second and third hikers spoke up. It was soon obvious that methods designed to penetrate the world of the text's origin were not apt for answering these new questions; and so biblical scholars looked to other disciplines for methodological tools.

Those interested in the text itself found immediately to hand all the methods developed over the years by those who read texts for a living, namely, literary critics. Methods such as close reading (borrowed from Russian Formalism and the New Criticism), structuralist analysis (rooted in the mid-twentieth-century European philosophical movement), narrative criticism, rhetorical criticism, reader-response criticism,[2] and others enabled interpreters to focus on the final, extant form of the text as having coherent meaning even in the face of historical criticism's demonstration that the text is the end product of an enormously complex array of oral traditions, written sources, and editorial manipulations.

Today these methods, under the umbrella term "literary criticism,"[3] are producing important new insights into ancient Israelite literary conventions and opening our eyes to an unprecedented appreciation of their literary aesthetic. We are learning the stylistic and psychological subtleties of Israelite poets and storytellers, and we are beginning to perceive the unique genius of their literary craft.[4] In the course of this book, we will explore one small province of this vast terrain: How do ancient Hebrew prose narratives work their magic on a reader?

Those who, like our third hiker, were most interested in the text's societal effects found theoretical inspiration in such movements as the critical theory of the Frankfurt School and practical direction in the increased attention to and concern for minority rights that emerged in the West in the 1960s and subsequent decades. Methods were developed to read the biblical text for its power of societal emancipation, particularly in base communities of South America; and these methods and readings received theoretical systematization from liberation theology. Subsequent decades saw the liberation model extended to a wide range of oppressed minorities along classic lines of gender, race, and class, under the general heading of "ideological criticism." Perhaps the best known of these liberation or advocacy methods is feminist criticism, but gender-oriented approaches today also include gay and lesbian readings, gender-sensitive readings focused on male spirituality, and others. Under the heading of "race," African American, Hispanic, and Asian readings are the most prominent but by no means the only ethnically oriented approaches. The original liberation theology remains the clearest example of a class-oriented approach, but postcolonial reading is rapidly emerging as a rich new source of insight, particularly in countries in Africa and Asia.

Summary

The ferment in biblical studies today, then, is not so much the result of competing opinions about what the text means as it is of confusion about which meaning we are looking for. That confusion is only compounded when we fail to distinguish the different meanings that are all subject to legitimate inquiry. Once that is recognized, then it becomes possible to see that the field is, in fact, orderly and that beneath the apparent chaos it is simply growing more complex. Elaborating our earlier diagram, we might map the current state of affairs something like this:

author →	text →	reader
Meaning is what the author intended.	Meaning is just what the text says.	Meaning is the text's effect on society.
Methods: (historical criticism) source criticism redaction criticism form criticism tradition history sociological methods anthropological methods and others	Methods: (literary criticism) formalism close reading structuralism narrative criticism rhetorical criticism reader-response criticism and others	Methods: (ideological criticism) feminist criticism gay and lesbian criticism African American criticism Hispanic, Latino/a criticism liberation exegesis postcolonial criticism and others

Our task in this book is specific and narrow: to explore, in a practical fashion, the method of narrative criticism. As the diagram above shows, this focuses us on a text-oriented definition of "meaning." We will not then need to argue that our interpretation was "intended by the author" (although, as we shall see in the next section, there is a way to accommodate author's intention in a text-oriented analysis). Frankly, the only way such a claim could be verified is if the author left us, separately, a commentary on his or her own writings; for better or worse, that is not the case in biblical studies.[5] What we must do is identify elements *in the text* that plausibly ground our interpretations. And since, as we shall see, the reader too is a contributing factor to the creation of meaning (and, like the author, can be accommodated in a text-oriented analysis), our approach will incorporate elements of reader-response criticism as well.

THE WORLD IN THE TEXT

The Structure of Narrative

Let's return for a moment to the simplicity of our earlier diagram:

author → text → reader

One of the results of several centuries of critical biblical scholarship's concentration on the author was the discovery of the immense complexities hidden in that simple word. Precritical scholarship held that the Pentateuch, for instance, was the work of a single author, Moses. By the time historical criticism reached a near consensus on the matter, that unity had been fragmented into a veritable mob of four major and several minor narrative source documents; at least four distinct legal corpora, each with its own origin and transmission history; several originally independent poems; and enough editors to weave all these sources together one by one—not to mention the uncountable host of oral storytellers that lay between the originating events and their first reduction to writing. In the face of such a multitude, it is no wonder that historical criticism generally avoided any attempt to deal with the final form of the text as a meaningful and coherent literary unity. Without a singular author it is difficult to speak of a singular author's intention.

Somewhat ironically, one of the results of a literary critical focus on "text" has been the realization that it too is a surprisingly complex reality. In what follows, I shall restrict myself to narrative texts, though no doubt something comparable could be elaborated for poetic texts, and perhaps even for legal ones. I have taken the diagram below, with only slight modifications, from Terence J. Keegan's excellent *Interpreting the Bible*.[6]

Between "author" and "reader" (here specified as "real author" and "real reader") lies a "text" that comprises a series of nested boxes, each with its own contents. This diagram, with its various components, is not to be understood as a template consciously used by authors to compose stories, but as an analytic tool that offers the literary critic a number of access points to identify and trace

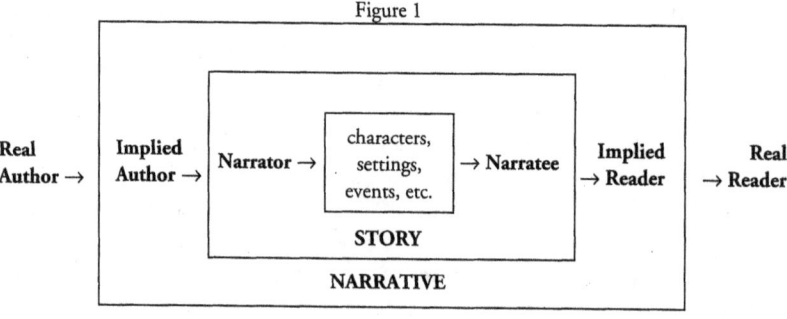

Figure 1

the dynamics of narrative. We will examine each of the components here, some at greater length than others; in the chapters that follow we will revisit many of them (particularly the narrator) in greater detail.

The World of the Story

We begin in the innermost box, the "story." It is most convenient to imagine this as a "world" (the world of the story), a realm where individuals live (characters) and things happen (events) in particular circumstances (settings). As an analogy, think of the staging of a dramatic production. From the point of view of the actors and their actions, the stage is a self-contained locus that has no relationship to the auditorium and audience that surround it. Similarly, this world of the story is to be carefully distinguished from our own world (the "real world," as we are prone to call it). This does not mean that it is necessarily dissimilar to our own world, but it *can* be. Let's call the world in which the real author and we, the real readers, exist the "primary world," and the world of the story the "secondary world."[7] The rules by which the secondary world operates may well be like those of the primary world. Historical narrative, for instance, ranging from true history writing to historical fiction, must attempt to duplicate the primary world's dynamics if it is to possess verisimilitude. On the other hand, the secondary world's rules may be entirely different from the primary world's. Science fiction has its spaceships, fantasy its sorcery, there are impossibly handsome heroes in romance novels and impossibly clever sleuths in detective stories, and even the Bible has its talking donkey and its talking snake. The key here, however, is coherence with the primary world on a deeper level: even when we accept the premises of the secondary world, we still expect that world to operate consistently, with causal connections linking its events.

Together, the characters of the world of the story and the events that take place in its settings constitute the plot of the story. In a sense, both "plot" and "story" refer to the same thing, though with a slightly different emphasis.[8] We will begin our practical study in the next chapter with a closer examination of plot.

The World of the Narrative

Encompassing the box called "story" we find a larger box called "narrative." The world of the narrative is identical to the world of the story (the "secondary world"), except that the narrative's events are chronologically later than those of the story. What happens in the world of the narrative is that a narrator *tells the story* to a narratee. We will discuss these terms in greater detail in later chapters. What is important here is to recognize that the *oral* nature of storytelling means that the narrator and narratee encounter one another without the mediation of a text. For both of them, the world in which they exist is the world in which the story took place in the past, and the narrator is recounting it to the narratee. Think, for instance, of a parent telling his or her adult child about how the child's parents met, or of a witness recounting the details of an accident to a reporter.

The World of the Text

Finally, there is the outermost box, the "text." This too can be understood as a world, but it is not the secondary world of the narrative and the story. It is our primary world, in which the written text we hold in our hands exists, just as we ourselves do. It is a limited subset of that primary world, however, because it incorporates only what is contained in the text, namely, the world of the narrative and two oddly named figures, the "implied author" and the "implied reader."[9] Just as the world of the narrative is one in which a narrator tells a story to a narratee, the world of the text is one in which an (implied) author *writes a narrative* about a narrator telling a story to a narratee, and an (implied) reader reads it. That narrative is in the text we hold in our hands.

Who, then, are the implied author and implied reader, and how are they related to the real author (that is, the flesh-and-blood person who penned the text) and real reader (that is, you or me, the flesh-and-blood person who reads it)? To begin with, the implied author and implied reader are not entities like the narrator and narratee; they are essentially *constructs made by the (real) reader*. In other words, they are names for parts of the process by which the reader makes sense of the text. Let me unpack that sentence. When an author writes a text, he or she inevitably stamps that text with aspects of the author's own personality (domains of knowledge and expertise; political, religious, or other ideological opinions; attention to detail; depth and bias of insight into human personalities; and so on); in other words, *implicit in the text* is a subset of the real author's characteristics. These are the clues the reader uses to construct an idea of what the real author might have been like. It is important to note that this is true *even when the text's real author is composite*, as historical criticism has shown to be the case in almost all biblical writings. In order to read a narrative as a coherent unity, the reader must *posit* a singular authorial mind to explain that coherence. This author, presupposed by the reader's readiness to accept the narrative as coherent, and constructed by the reader out of clues selected as meaningful, is the "implied author."[10]

The "implied reader" (some critics speak of the "ideal reader") is the reader who understands perfectly and precisely what the implied author is saying, and brings nothing extraneous to that understanding. Or, to put it another way, the implied reader has all and only those capacities that the implied author expects. This reader too is constructed by the real reader out of clues implied in the text. To take a simple example, the book of Kings is written in ancient Hebrew. That is, the implied author of that book expects its implied reader to be literate and to have a native fluency in that language.[11]

This last example illustrates one of the inferences we can draw: no real reader of the Bible (or of any other literary text, for that matter) is perfectly identical to the implied reader. First, none of us is an ancient Israelite (or a Christian of New Testament times), and so we cannot bring to our reading of the text all of the capacities—cultural, linguistic, social—that the text expects of us. Furthermore, we are all shaped by twentieth- and twenty-first-century experiences, both personal and social; and inevitably we bring those effects with us to the act of reading. This gap between the implied reader and us is why incorporating reader-response awareness into our interpretation is almost inescapable. Our differences *will* affect us. Attention to those differences gives us some limited control over the ways in which they individualize our interpretations and shape the meanings we realize; it will also enable us to celebrate the diversity of different readings of a text not as a contest to see who can find the "right" meaning but as a measure of the rich potential inherent in any great text.

Summary

The structure of a narrative text proves to have unexpected complexities comparable to those historical criticism revealed in the author. This, however, should not be considered a burdensome obfuscation, but an array of entry points for deeper insight and analysis of a narrative's meaning. There is, first and foremost, the story, with all the elements that make it up. What are characters? How are they created? How are we moved to respond to them? And events: What causes them and what are their effects? How are they recounted? How are we moved to make moral or other judgments about them? And settings: How are they described? How is our position in those settings established and manipulated?

Notice too that there are two separate communication acts taking place, both of which are grist for the interpreter's mill. First, the narrator is telling the story to the narratee. What result is the narrator aiming to achieve? Information? Entertainment? Moral judgment? Shock? Scandal? Answers to these questions depend not just on the *content* of the story—the characters, events, settings—but also on the *mode of telling*. The story is built out of *words*, and the narrator's choice to use *this* word rather than *that* word, and to organize the telling in *this* way rather than *that*, is not innocent: each of those choices evokes a response from the narratee.

Second, there is the implied author who writes a narrative for the implied reader, which recounts how a narrator tells the story to a narratee. What response is the implied author aiming to achieve in the implied reader? Is it the same as the narrator's purpose in telling the story to the narratee? Is the narrator simply the mouthpiece of the implied author, or might the latter have different values and biases? Since we construct the implied author from clues in the text, but the words and organization of the story come to us only in the narrator's voice, it is not always an easy task to discern clues that enable us to distinguish the narrator from the implied author—but it is by no means impossible.

These are the sorts of questions that will occupy us for the remainder of this book.

PLAN OF THE BOOK

The diagram of the complex structure of a narrative text also supplies us with a road map for the remainder of the book. In the next two chapters we will look at two constituent elements of the story: the connected events that make up the plot and the characters who live those events. Chapters 4 through 8 will concentrate on how the narrator *tells* the story by exploring some of the techniques he uses to communicate the story to the narratee. Chapter 9 will consider the narratorial voice itself and ways in which the narrator communicates with the narratee in addition to telling the story. Chapter 10 will concentrate on techniques most appropriately located in the *written* narrative, therefore more properly ascribed to the implied author than to the narrator. Finally, in chapter 11 we will discuss how the complexity of a narrative text calls forth comparable complexity in a real reader's approach to it.

Chapters 2 through 10 will each proceed in the same way. I will introduce you to some point of entry for narrative analysis in a mildly theoretical fashion: what it is; what its major varieties and variables are; how it is embodied textually; what sorts of responses it is likely to evoke from readers; and so forth. I will illustrate the issue with examples drawn most often from 1 Kings 1–11, the story of Solomon; you should familiarize yourself with these chapters, especially with chapters 1 and 2. (Occasionally I will have to cast my net a bit wider, when no satisfactory example is found in the Solomon story.) The complexity of the issue and the clarity of the example will determine how extensively I comment on each. When necessary, I will supply a translation of the passage I am analyzing; but basically I will rely on the NRSV, unless I explicitly mention another published translation. I will sometimes include in my discussion a statement about *how this text affects me*—I too am a reader, and my reader response is fair game, just as yours is. In these cases, I have no expectation that the same example will evoke the same response in all other readers. I share my response as plausible, and I will explain and defend it (sometimes vigorously, if it is not the common reading among critical biblical scholars); but I offer it as no more than that: *my* reading as an experienced reader, not a *normative* reading to be deemed the only correct one.

Following this, I will supply a set of leading questions for each of three narrative blocks (each about three chapters long) drawn from the second half of 1 Kings: the story of Jeroboam (11:26–14:20), the story of Elijah (17:1–19:21), and the story of Ahab (20:1–22:40). The questions will guide you to consider elements and passages in each story that illustrate some aspect of the issue under consideration. Not all issues will be present in all three stories, of course; but together the three stories illustrate just about everything I intend to cover.

Why 1 Kings? For several reasons. First and frankly, because this is the book of the Hebrew Bible that I know the best. I have been working my way through it for over thirty years now. Second, because it has traditionally *not* been treated as an object of literary art, but as a theologically tendentious recounting of history. If we can find evidence of high literary art in 1 Kings, how much more likely are we to find it in the clearly more creative tales of Genesis, Exodus, Judges, and so on? Finally, because my study of the book convinces me that it is indeed a superb example of literary art, and I hope to deepen both your understanding of a book I find enthralling and your appreciation for the unique genius of ancient Hebrew narrative art.

Then, in three appendixes I will give you some indication of what I think you might have found while working your way through the leading questions. I repeat what I said above: these are *my* readings—experienced, but not normative. (I have often gained insight into a text from something a student has seen that I have never noticed before.) If our readings converge, their plausibility is doubly demonstrated. When they do not (and they will not always, I assure you!), perhaps my reading will offer you an alternative that you overlooked. Or perhaps, on the other hand, it will remain unpersuasive to you even after I elaborate on it. It is up to you, then, to judge which of the readings presents a more adequate way of incorporating the passage under consideration into an overarching coherent and consistent reading of the whole story, or whether each offers unique insights into the text. This last possibility is more common than one might expect. Different—and sometimes incompatible—readings can often be equally plausible.

I urge you to choose one of the three stories, and focus on it as you proceed through the book. You will find that repeated reading of the same chapters can deepen your insights and reveal new possibilities, even with respect to issues that were covered in previous chapters. The truly eager student or study group, then, can work through the book three times, each time honing his or her skills on a different story.[12]

Chapter 2

Plot

THE DYNAMICS OF PLOT

We begin with *plot*, in order to get a sweeping overview of the story and a sense of how the story is organized. These first impressions will necessarily be tentative. Reading good literature is largely a dialogue between reader and text: The more deeply a reader penetrates a great text, the greater the response it evokes; this in turn enables renewed and deepened reading, and the dialectic continues. We are often drawn to repeated readings of books that move us deeply; we always seem to find something new in them. This is because we ourselves have changed since our last reading, and that in turn is due at least in some measure to the book's transformative impact upon us in earlier encounters (they "moved us deeply").

There are many ways to approach plot, of course. Plots can be analyzed and characterized by their genre (tragedy, comedy, quest, adventure, mystery, fantasy, and the like), by their length (from short story to novel), and in many other ways. Here, however, I am more interested in the dynamism that energizes a plot than in its classification. What makes a plot *move*? Aristotle opined that a plot has a "beginning, middle, and end." Banal as that observation may appear on the surface, its cogency is real. Plots move like an arc from a situation of (relative) stability, through a process of tension or destabilization,[1] to a new situation of (relative) stability.[2] *Tension* is what impels a plot: What happens next?

Similarly, individual units and subunits of a story—we might call them "scenes" or "episodes"—often exhibit the same dynamic, though of course the stability and destabilization are usually even more limited and relative, since their arcs of tension are subordinate to the larger arc of tension of the whole story.[3]

Tension: Two Simple Examples

The first episode of 1 Kings (1:1–4) supplies an example that is simple, though not without a couple of interesting twists. The initial, relatively stable situation is set out in 1:1: King David has grown old and is plagued, apparently, with circulatory problems. The next verses destabilize the situation by an elaborate attempt to improve the king's condition (1:2–4a).[4] The king, however, remains feeble (1:4b). One interesting feature of this brief scene points up a stylistic difference between Hebrew and English narrative conventions. As the Hebrew reads, there are *two* attempts to relieve David's ills, both of which fail. The first attempt is to pile blankets on the old man; the second is to supply him with a nubile maiden to keep him warm. The first attempt (1:1b) reads, "they covered him with blankets but he did not get warm." English style, however, does not take kindly to a piling up of short main clauses like this; and so many English translations reword the first attempt to include a subordinate clause ("*although* they covered him with clothes . . ."; see the NRSV). They thereby reduce what is in Hebrew a short arc of plot tension to background information. The result is not significantly different in content from the Hebrew, and conforms much better to fluent English narrative style; strictly speaking, though, it gives the English a slightly denser narrative structure than the Hebrew.

A second interesting feature lies in the relationship of the end of the scene to its beginning. The situation has changed little. In 1:1 David's failing health is a concern, and the intervening attempts to better it have no success; and so, at the end, he remains feeble. In the last words, we learn that "David did not *know* Abishag." In view of the sexually charged language describing their relationship (she is a virgin; she is beautiful; she "lies in his bosom"), there is no doubt the "knowing" of which David proves incapable is sexual.[5] But how does this final state of stability compare with the initial one? When we look at the two together, we may suspect the narrator of double entendre in telling us that "David could not get warm." His circulatory problems may or may not have been more generalized, but one type of heat he was unable to generate was sexual potency.[6]

The second example, 1 Kings 2:36–46a, is slightly more complex.[7] This brief story takes place in three stages. Stage one is a dialogue between Solomon and Shimei (2:36–38a). The arc of tension begins when Solomon summons Shimei and gives him difficult[8] commands: How will Shimei respond? The tension resolves when Shimei agrees to the king's demands. Stage two is a narrative about

Shimei (2:38b–41) that recounts an action he performed. The dramatic tension starts in 2:40, when Shimei leaves Jerusalem in violation of Solomon's command. (Verses 2:38b–39 supply background information about Shimei's long-term obedience and the circumstances that will eventually lead him to violate the king's order.) At least two arcs of tension begin here: What does Shimei plan—will he make a bid for escape under cover of trying to retrieve his slaves?[9] And what will Solomon do about Shimei's disobedience? The first tension is resolved at the end of the narrative section, when Shimei returns to Jerusalem (2:41). The development and resolution of the second arc of tension occur in 2:42–46a (stage three, a two-part monologue), where Solomon judges Shimei and has him executed.

Linearity: A Complex Example

One fundamental characteristic of narrative art must be kept in mind: it is a *linear* form. In other words, the reader encounters one word after another, one scene after another. (Contrast painting, for instance, where an entire canvas is open to view at the same time, or sculpture, where the observer can move around the object in any direction.) The linearity of narrative affords an author both limitations and opportunities. For example, self-referential allusions are more difficult to discern in narrative than in painting. In a painting, one may see clearly that the blue of the gentleman's waistcoat matches perfectly the blue of the eyes of the woman who gazes at him (and is, perhaps, his clandestine paramour?). In literature, even if the author described the blues in unmistakably identical terms (usually a very bad idea, stylistically), the reader would read the descriptions at some temporal remove from one another. On the other hand, linearity allows the author to guide the reader's journey through the text. Viewing the painting, I may be struck by the woman's eyes and follow her gaze to find the corresponding waistcoat; or I may be struck by the vivid color of the waistcoat first, be drawn by a pattern in the wainscoting toward the woman, and only then notice her eyes. And my view might take in anything else in the painting along the way. In prose, however, the author chooses which of the corresponding elements to tell me about first, and whether to tell me about anything else before introducing the second element. The author controls precisely *what* I observe, and the order in which I observe it. We will examine some of the important implications of linearity later, when we consider point of view and order of telling in the narrative. For the moment, however, let us concentrate on how this characteristic affects our sense of plot tension.

Because of linearity, we discern the particulars of any given arc of tension only gradually, as we move through the action. This gives the narrator the opportunity to add nuance to our focus, to sharpen it, or even to redirect it. For an example, look at 3:16–28. This is the famous story of the two harlots who appear before Solomon with two infants, one alive and one dead. Each claims the living baby is hers and the dead one the other woman's. That is the opening situation of relative stability. As the arc of tension begins (that is, as they present their case before the king), the question seems clear: Who is the mother of the live baby? This is what we wonder, and this is what Solomon wonders. But in 3:26 the narrator throws us a curve: he *tells* us which woman is the mother of the live baby. This gives us information that Solomon does not have, and shifts the question for us, the readers, from, Who is the mother? to, How does Solomon figure out who the true mother is?[10]

Sometimes, though rarely,[11] two related themes are interwoven almost inextricably through a narrative. Look again at the opening words of 1 Kings, which tell us that "King David was old and advanced in years." There are several possibilities for development here. The emphatic repetition of David's age, illustrated by the brief anecdote in 1:1b–4, inevitably raises the question, Is David dying? Perhaps this will be a story of David's last days and death, of efforts to prolong (or shorten!) his life, of a miraculous recovery of vigor, or the like. On the other hand, a king's old age and worsening frailty signal a time of upheaval for a kingdom, since succession to the throne is often uncertain. Perhaps this will be a story about the succession and the forces that struggled to determine it. Only as we make our way through what follows will we realize that *both* of these themes are developed in tandem.

The theme of David's last days begins in 1:1–4 and poses the question, Is David dying? That question is reiterated more forcefully with the remark in 2:1 that David's "time to die" had come and the report of his "last words" in 2:2–9.[12] It is finally and definitively answered in 2:10–11: "Yes, David is dead." Yet that is not the end of the theme's development. David's last words include advice to Solomon to kill Joab and Shimei, both of whom had, in David's view, offended him unforgivably during his life. So the thematic question modulates into, Will Solomon follow David's dying wishes? (To point up the continuity of the two questions, we might rephrase this second one: Even though David is dead, can he still achieve what he wants?) The last two episodes of chapter 2 answer that question positively: Solomon has Joab killed in 2:28–35 and he eliminates Shimei in 2:36–46a.[13]

The arc of tension from 1:5–53, however, does not focus on David's death but on the second theme, the question of who will succeed him. In terms of this theme, then, 1:1–4 appear to supply background information necessary for our understanding of what happens in the rest of chapter 1. The tensive question is, Who will succeed David? It is answered in part at several points in the narrative (e.g., 1:39), but is finally resolved definitively when Adonijah, Solomon's older brother and rival for the throne, submits to Solomon in 1:53. The theme resurfaces in a slightly different form in David's last words; in 2:2–4 he advises Solomon on how to achieve a long and successful reign. After David's death, the theme of the succession receives emphatic closure in 2:12. Surprisingly, this does not end the development of the theme. Even though his royal dominion "was firmly established" (2:12), Solomon proceeds to eliminate his rival, Adonijah, and two of Adonijah's main supporters, Abiathar and Joab. In the execution of Joab the theme of David's last words and death emerges again,

Figure 2
Theme: David's Last Days

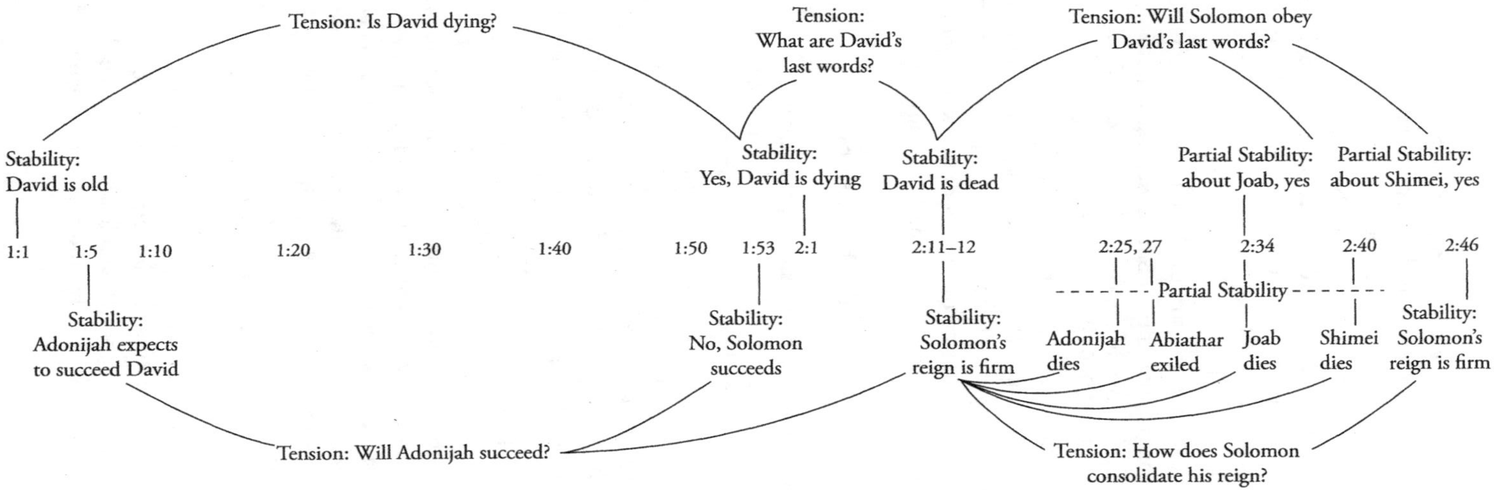

Tension: Is David dying? Tension: What are David's last words? Tension: Will Solomon obey David's last words?

Stability: David is old Stability: Yes, David is dying Stability: David is dead Partial Stability: about Shimei, yes

1:1 1:5 1:10 1:20 1:30 1:40 1:50 1:53 2:1 2:11–12 2:25, 27 2:34 2:40 2:46

Stability: Adonijah expects to succeed David Stability: No, Solomon succeeds Stability: Solomon's reign is firm Adonijah dies Abiathar exiled Partial Stability Joab dies Shimei dies Stability: Solomon's reign is firm

Partial Stability: about Joab, yes

Tension: Will Adonijah succeed? Tension: How does Solomon consolidate his reign?

Theme: Who Will Succeed David?

and the two themes converge: Solomon consolidates his hold on his kingdom by eliminating a supporter of Adonijah, and at the same time carries out David's dying request for vengeance against Joab. Similarly, the elimination of Shimei fulfills one of David's dying requests, and also eliminates someone whose curse on David's kingship (see 2 Sam. 16:5–14; 19:16–23) could appear to pose a continuing danger to Solomon's security. Solomon explicitly links the death of Shimei with *both* themes in 1 Kings 2:44–45. The closure of the theme of succession is repeated in 2:46b.[14]

At times an analysis of this sort can become overly complex, at least for our purposes. For example, the story of Shimei discussed above has its own arcs of tension, but also forms part of the development of several larger questions: Will Solomon carry out David's final commands? Will Solomon's throne be securely established? Is David dying? Who will succeed David on the throne? Our purpose here is essentially practical: to use the dynamic of tension and resolution as a way of getting a first sense of the story's themes and its organization. As you explore your chosen story using the questions below, do not attempt anything quite as ambitious as the analysis of 1 Kings 1–2 above.

Final Observations

Different arcs of tension can be successive, like the eliminations of Abiathar (2:26–27), Joab (2:28–34), and Shimei (2:36–45).[15] At times the point where they meet will resolve one tension and begin another. See, for instance, 1:22 (literally, "and there she is still speaking to the king and Nathan comes in"), which simultaneously brings Bathsheba's first audience with David to a close (she has said her piece, even though the larger issue of the succession has not been resolved) and opens Nathan's first audience with David, introducing the tension, What will he say? Will he convince David? At other times—although this is not common—separate arcs of tension can cross, when something that occurs in the middle of one scene becomes the starting point for a later thematic development. One could, for instance, analyze the minor theme of Joab's elimination in this way. The arc of tension for this theme (which is a subsidiary component of the question, Will Solomon honor David's last requests?) begins with David's words in 2:5–6, and ends with Solomon's explanation in 2:32 and Joab's execution in 2:34.

Obviously arcs of tension, at least subordinate ones, are often coterminous with scenes. Conventions for marking the beginning and the ending of scenes can therefore be a clue to the thematic and tensive organization of the story. Those conventions are similar to what we find in English prose narrative: the shift to a new location, a new time frame, or a new character or character group usually signals a new scene. Mention of an important character's departure—especially separate mentions of departure for *both* principal characters in a scene—often marks the end. Common types of simple scenes include dialogue (speech by one character, answering speech by another),[16] command and compliance or noncompliance (orders given by one character and either obeyed or not by the other), prophecy and fulfillment or nonfulfillment. There are, of course, many other types of scenes and many different ways of marking their boundaries; but that is a topic for chapter 10.

EXPLORING THE STORIES

Before we begin exploring the plot dynamics of the Jeroboam, Elijah, and Ahab stories, it is essential that you become familiar with the story you are going to concentrate on. Read through your chosen story in a single sitting. If possible, do so several times, on different days. Most of us—especially those of us whose primary mode of encountering the Bible is in liturgical readings—rarely read biblical stories as continuous narratives several chapters in length. Much more often we think of them as short, lectionary-sized vignettes.

If you are using this book for private study, and you intend to work through all three stories, I recommend that you do so successively, not simultaneously. That is, go through the whole book concentrating on the Jeroboam story, then go back through it a second time concentrating on the Elijah story, and finally go back again and focus on the Ahab story. You will find that narrowing your focus to one of the three stories will facilitate deeper reading and will enable you more easily to cross-reference the insights of one reading with the discoveries of another. If, on the other hand, you are part of a study group that has divided the three stories among its members, familiarize yourself with the other two stories by reading them through (again, in a single sitting); but concentrate most of your attention on your assigned story.

I have organized my remarks in the appendixes, one for each of the three stories (Jeroboam, Elijah, Ahab). In those appendixes, I treat one by one the exploratory questions found in chapters 2 through 10, and I suggest some of the things you may have found in pursuing those questions.

You may wish to begin by jotting down a few notes about your story after you have read it once or twice. What impresses you? What surprises you? What puzzles you? What do you think of the characters—do you like them, dislike them, have mixed feelings about them? Are there any points in the story where you have suddenly found yourself strongly engaged emotionally (whether positively or negatively)? Can you sum up in a couple of sentences any lasting impact you think the story may have on you? File these notes away not because they are a checklist of things to look for, but because they offer a benchmark. After working through the same story in each chapter that follows, you will be able to compare how you are reading the story then with how you read it now.

After you have familiarized yourself sufficiently with your target story and filed any preliminary notes you may have made, go on to the exploratory questions below.

The Jeroboam Story (1 Kings 11:26–14:18)

Simple Arc of Tension

In 1 Kings 12:21, Rehoboam, Solomon's son and successor, begins to respond to the dissolution of the Davidic kingdom that occurred in the preceding scene, 12:1–20. The situation of relative stability that ends 12:1–20 and begins 12:21 is that the leaders of the northern assembly at Shechem have rejected the authority of the Davidic line and have chosen the rebel leader Jeroboam to reign over the northern tribes. Rehoboam, meanwhile, has fled for his life from Shechem back to Jerusalem (12:18), where we find him in 12:21. How would you describe the arc of tension that begins in 12:21 and where do you find that tension resolved?

A More Complex Example

The scene of Jeroboam's encounter with a "man of God[17] from Judah" who condemns the altar Jeroboam has built at Bethel appears in 13:1–10. Where does the overall arc of tension that encompasses the whole scene begin and end? How many distinct tension/resolution arcs can you discern *within* the scene? Are any of the arcs of tension unresolved?

The Whole Jeroboam Story

How would you identify the *major* arcs of tension (that is, the major scenes, episodes, or "story units") in the whole Jeroboam story (11:26–14:18)? Do not attempt to refine your analysis too much; that is, do not look for short, low-level arcs of tension as you did in the previous question. Look instead for the larger arcs that eventually incorporate the whole Jeroboam story into a series of linked episodes. Remember what I said in note 16: monologues (such as those of Ahijah in 11:31–39 and 14:6–16) do not in themselves contain arcs of tension, since there is no action. They may, however, contribute to the development and/or resolution of larger arcs of tension of which they are components.

You may find it easier to begin with those blocks of text where dynamics of tension and resolution are most obvious (like those you have identified in the last two questions). Then work on the material that lies outside those blocks, asking where complications seem to begin, and where they seem to return to some sort of stability.

The Elijah Story (1 Kings 17:1–19:21)

These chapters mark the first appearance of Elijah the Tishbite in the Hebrew Bible, and initiate a series of hostile encounters between him and King Ahab of Israel.

Simple Arc of Tension

What is the main arc of tension in 18:1–6? Where exactly would you begin that arc of tension and where would you end it? Is the tension finally resolved? Other than characterization (which we will consider in chap. 4), does the narrator's lengthy description of Obadiah in 18:3b–4 contribute to the development of this arc of tension in any way?

A More Complex Example

How would you demarcate the arcs of tension in 1 Kings 17? Where would you start and end each arc? Are there any arcs of tension that are left unresolved in this chapter?

The Whole Elijah Story

How would you identify the *major* arcs of tension (that is, the major scenes, episodes, or story units) in the whole Elijah story (17:1–19:21)? Do not attempt to refine your analysis too much; that is, do not look for short, low-level arcs of tension within episodes. Look instead for the larger arcs that incorporate comparatively large blocks of the story into a series of linked episodes. Are there any significant parts of the three chapters that are relatively independent of the rest? That is, they are only loosely connected to the overall arc of tension within which they fall?

The Ahab Story (1 Kings 20:1–22:40)

In the Ahab story two chapters about wars between the kingdoms of Israel, under King Ahab, and of Aram, under King Ben-hadad, surround a chapter about a series of events internal to Ahab's kingdom. The setting is the last four years of Ahab's twenty-two-year reign (16:29).

Simple Arc of Tension

Two short, somewhat bizarre scenes in 20:35–37 end with the departure notice in 20:38a ("Then the prophet departed"). The following verses (20:38b–43) describe a hostile encounter between the prophet and King Ahab. How would you describe the arc (or arcs) of tension in that scene? What is the situation of stability in which the tension originates, and is there any state of (relative) stability at the end of the scene?

A More Complex Example

How would you demarcate the main arcs of tension in 20:1–11? Do you see one arc of tension that is entirely enclosed in another one?

The Whole Ahab Story

It is difficult to identify an arc of tension that would account for the presence of the story of Naboth's vineyard between the two stories of Ahab's Aramean wars. (This may explain why, in the ancient Greek translation called the Septuagint, the story of Naboth *precedes* both chapters about the Aramean wars.[18]) For this exercise, it is probably best to approach each chapter separately (though at the end I will pose a couple of questions that have a broader view).

Earlier questions have identified arcs of tension in 20:1–11 and 20:35–43. What are the major arcs of tension in the intervening verses, 20:12–34? Do not attempt to refine your analysis too much; that is, do not look for short, low-level arcs of tension within episodes (like those in 20:35–37). Look instead for the larger arcs that incorporate comparatively large blocks of the story into a series of linked episodes. Do the same for 22:1–38.[19]

Chapter 21, the story of Naboth's vineyard, is a bit more difficult. Notice that 21:1–16 can stand alone as a self-contained (though tragic) story, whereas 21:17–29 presume the events of 21:1–16. It is useful, therefore, to consider the first part of the chapter in isolation, and only then to see how 21:17–29 relate to the earlier material. Trace the main arcs of tension that structure 21:1–16. Are they consecutive, or is there some nesting of one arc inside another?

The second part of the chapter, 21:17–29, is even more problematic. It does not lend itself easily to an analysis of the sort we have been using. In these verses, see what possible arcs of tension you can identify. (Remember that a character's *speech* is simply a single action; it may form part of a larger arc of tension, but do not try to find arcs of tension *within* the speech.)

There are obvious connections and contrasts between the two chapters dealing with Ahab's wars with Aram (chaps. 20 and 22). Connections include not only the major theme of Aramean war and the two kings Ahab and Ben-hadad; also in both chapters Ahab is supported by some prophets and opposed by others, all of whom claim to speak in Yhwh's name. Among the contrasts is that, in chapter 20, Ahab seems to be a vassal of Ben-hadad, whereas in chapter 22 Ahab seems to be Jehoshaphat's overlord. (Compare the very similar sentiments expressed by Ahab in 20:4 and by Jehoshaphat in 22:4; note also how Ahab commands Jehoshaphat in 22:30 and Jehoshaphat obeys, as 22:32 shows.) There is little, however, that links the two chapters in a tension-resolution dynamic. I can find only one tiny detail that starts in the stable situation established by the treaty between Ahab and Ben-hadad in 20:34 and is destabilized by something in chapter 22. Can you find it?

Chapter 3

Characters

If the "story world" is a world, "characters" are the people who inhabit it. This is more than just a convenient metaphor. To read a narrative is to enter the story world as an observer of its people and events; that is, it is to treat the story world as *real*. Some literary critics speak of this as a "willing suspension of disbelief," but that double negative does not adequately capture the commitment good reading entails. J. R. R. Tolkien preferred the term "secondary belief"—a positive dynamic, rather than a negative one.[1] When we read, we treat the story world as real, even if only secondarily so, and thus we encounter the characters who populate it as real people. We like or dislike them, we contemn or admire them, we understand or are perplexed by them—just as we are by the people we meet in everyday life. In the next chapter we will examine techniques narrators use to evoke these responses from us. In this chapter we will concentrate on the sorts of characters that people the story world.

TYPES OF CHARACTERS

"Flat" and "Round" Characters

The great English novelist and literary critic E. M. Forster proposed to distinguish "flat" from "round" characters.[2] The former are one-dimensional, characterized by one or two traits that change little or not at all in the course of the narrative. The latter are more complex, manifesting multiple traits that develop and might, at times, be in tension with one another.[3] Forster's proposal is helpful, but it should not be understood as establishing two distinct categories of characters; rather, "flat" and "round" are two points on a continuum of complexity from highly developed, many-sided characters down to those so simply drawn as to be little more than animated props.[4] "Main" characters, naturally, tend to be more complex; supporting actors in the story are simpler, but may still have varying degrees of "roundness"; at the extreme of simplicity come figures that are more functions than persons. (Consider, for example, the nameless, faceless, actionless "young men" in Gen. 22:5. They are more like hitching posts than people, but somebody has to guard the donkeys!)

Less developed characters are equally essential to a good story. They act as foils to contrast with, or to highlight, the more important figures in the scene. Sometimes they function as stereotypes to represent particular viewpoints or qualities (such as "the bad guy"). Though secondary characters can often present interesting features in their own right, if they were as complex and intriguing as main characters, readers would be distracted and the effect of the story would be diluted. If everybody is important, nobody is important.

Narrators have several ways to signal a character's importance. Naming the character first or most often in a scene is one way. This is hardly surprising. To illustrate complexity, the narrator will usually foreground the character frequently, having him or her act or speak in a variety of situations and with a variety of people. Main characters will regularly do more, speak more, undergo more, or change more than secondary characters. However, multiple indicators like this allow for a complication: the character who acts more or speaks more, for instance, may not be the same as the character who undergoes or changes more. This suggests that it may not always be possible to identify a single, unique main character, and that the reader's own interests and responses may, in part, influence which character seems more important.

A lengthy story is made up of a series of units and subunits that can themselves range from relatively extensive (1 Kgs. 1:1–53, for instance, as part of the story of Solomon) to quite brief (1:38–40, Solomon's coronation at Gihon). It is no surprise that the overall importance of a character in a lengthy literary unit need not imply that that same character will be equally important (or even present!) in every scene the larger unit comprises. Character relationships will vary from scene to scene, and from low-level units like simple scenes to the larger narrative complexes that incorporate them.

Group Characters

Occasionally several people function as a group within a story. Individuals within the group are not differentiated and only the group itself has any real role. If the group is relatively unimportant, it will often be treated simply as a "they." Occasionally, however—especially if the group's role is a bit more substantial—one member of the group will act as representative of the whole. That individual is not really a "character" in his or her own right, but is only, so to speak, the face of the group.

Examples

The story we have already looked at in some detail, 1 Kings 1:1–2:11, gives us notable examples of the entire spectrum of character complexity. We saw in the last chapter that it is possible to read it as a story of David's last days or as a story of Adonijah's failure to succeed his father. David appears first in the story (and last, if we continue through to 2:11, though Adonijah gets the last word if we go any further). David is named sixteen times in 1:1–2:11 and Adonijah fifteen times. (David wins the day, though, with forty additional references to him as "the king.") David changes notably in the course of the chapter, but the change does not last. At first he is moribund, impotent, perhaps even a bit in his dotage; he rises to decisive and rhetorically impressive action at 1:33–35; but he sinks back, bedridden (1:47), and eventually dies (2:10). Adonijah, on the other hand, undergoes considerable and catastrophic change. From eldest son and heir apparent to the throne, he tumbles to find himself at the end of the chapter under a conditional death sentence.

Supporting characters include Nathan (named ten times) and Bathsheba (five), whose behind-the-scenes manipulation of events results in the success of their joint palace intrigue. Much about their behavior, however, makes them of interest in their own right. Did David really swear to Bathsheba the oath that Nathan cites or is it Nathan's fabrication? Is Bathsheba merely Nathan's tool, or does she have an agenda of her own? Note that, when she confronts David, she makes several modifications to the speech Nathan supplied her with. Are they innocent or manipulative?[5]

Still lesser characters, approaching one-dimensional stock figures, include Abishag, Joab (at least in this story), and Jonathan. *Abishag* is the femme fatale, the beautiful woman who represents danger. She is named twice, does little, says nothing, and usually just stands around looking beautiful. But this is precisely her function: her very presence at David's side means that Bathsheba, Solomon's mother, the woman for whom David had once committed adultery and murder, is no longer the king's favorite. The story goes out of its way to contrast and counterpose the two women; note the echo of 2 Samuel 11:2 in 1 Kings 1:4,[6] and how the narrator confronts Bathsheba with Abishag's presence at David's side in 1:15.[7] As the commander of David's armies, *Joab* has been a major supporting character throughout David's story in 2 Samuel. But in this chapter he is reduced to playing a stereotyped character. He is the old guard, standing for the past: he supports the expected successor; he is allied with the priestly representative of ancient lineage;[8] he emerges to speak on his own only once (1:41), when his battle-trained ears pick out the alarum of the trumpet and he wonders about the hubbub of the crowd. Like Joab, *Jonathan* is part of a larger story as well (see, for instance, 2 Sam. 15:32–37; 17:15–22); but in 1 Kings 1 he is a similarly stereotyped character: the "messenger who brings bad news."

Finally, there are figures on stage who are best thought of as extras: Adonijah's guests at his gathering at En-rogel, the "people" who follow Solomon's procession down to the Gihon and acclaim him king there, the "Cherethites and Pelethites," and the "king's servants" (i.e., courtiers) in 1:47.

Group characters also appear in this chapter. For example, in 1 Kings 1:2 "his servants" (as a group) speak, and in 1:39 "all the people" acclaim Solomon. The clearest example of a group character with an individual spokesman in 1 Kings 1 is found in 1:41, where Joab's question seems to represent the uneasiness of all of Adonijah's guests. Another example, outside 1 Kings, occurs in 2 Kings 1, where three times "a captain of fifty with his fifty" functions as a single character, and the attitude the captain expresses determines the fate of the whole company.[9]

Avoiding Clutter

Ancient literature (and much modern literature likewise) avoids cluttering up the stage with too many characters. By and large, no more than three characters are active in any given scene and, when circumstances require that more be present, usually some fade out, not to return, before others become active. As a rule, two active characters are the norm; three is a crowd, but a manageable crowd; more than three is too many. Even when there are only three active parties, usually two will interact with the third, but not with each other. Thus, A and B may converse, and B and C may converse, but A and C will not.

The reasons for this are not hard to understand. More than three active characters would require repeated and relatively ponderous identifications of who is speaking or acting in regard to whom at every step of the way, lest the reader (and, a fortiori, the narratee, who hears an *oral* version of the story) become hopelessly confused.

Consider, for example, the scenes in David's chambers in 1:15–37. Bathsheba approaches David and converses with him (Abishag is present, but remains silent and inactive). When Nathan enters in 1:22, Bathsheba fades into the background. Indeed, she leaves the room, although we do not learn that until David summons her back in 1:28. Once she returns, Nathan fades into the background (indeed leaves, only to be summoned back in 1:32). In the final scene, Bathsheba has once again disappeared, and David's interlocutor is a group character comprising Nathan, Zadok, and Benaiah, the last of whom acts as their voice.

Much modern popular literature conforms to the same convention, and for much the same reasons. However, one particular modern genre takes full advantage of the confusion engendered by ignoring the convention: frequently in trying to solve a detective story, the reader is hard put to juggle a multitude of suspects and picture what all of them are doing at the time of the crime.

Ironically, one of the rare Old Testament passages that make use of this confusion has also often been likened to a modern detective story. In 1 Kings 3:16–28 two women confront Solomon with a legal case concerning their babies, one of whom is alive and the other dead. There are only three active characters—Solomon and the two women—but the narrator cleverly transforms them into five. In the first half of the story, the two women are identified simply as "first woman" and "other woman." In the second half, they are "woman whose child was living" and "other woman." But it is impossible to tell which of the two "women" in the first part corresponds to which of the two "women" in the second.[10] Thus the reader needs to keep track of five separate personae, who address not only the king but one another as well. Trying to navigate this highly unusual complexity is one source of the absorbing fascination this tale has held for centuries of readers.

Anomalies

Given what has been said so far, you can easily imagine two ways in which the portrayal of a character can violate our expectations: it can underdevelop a main character or overdevelop a secondary one. In other words, the narrator can present us with a character whose importance is obvious, but whose portrait is very sketchy; conversely, he can present us with a character whose presence is relatively inconsequential, but whose portrait is drawn with unusual attention to detail. Both are useful strategies for narrators, because each elicits the reader's curiosity.

An underdeveloped main character poses a puzzle. Since the character is, or at least promises to be, important in the story, we (the readers) want to know as much as possible. Indeed, most readers unconsciously assume a right to know a good deal about the main characters. We have something of a sense that the narrator, by telling the story, has contracted to supply us with whatever information we need to enter the story world effectively. When a main character remains insufficiently delineated, we feel that the narrator is holding out on us.

Solomon is a clear example. In 1 Kings 1:1–53 he is named twenty-five times (nearly twice as often as Adonijah), and his destiny changes more than anyone else's: from ostracized lesser son (see 1:9–10) to crowned king. Yet what do we really know about him? Until 1:52, he says nothing, and he appears on stage only in 1:38–40, where the only thing he does is ride a mule, and even that we see from a distance! By 1:52–53, where Solomon finally speaks and acts, the main tension in the chapter has already been resolved: Solomon has become king—but we have no idea what he is like. Moreover, even in 1:52–53 his words and deeds are entirely ambiguous. Merciful and lenient as they appear, their slipperiness is glimpsed just below the surface: Who shall decide whether Adonijah "proves to be a worthy man"? Who will judge whether "wickedness is found in him"? And is "Go home" a polite dismissal or a decree of house arrest?

Conversely, an overdeveloped secondary character is a paradox. Biblical narrators typically do not indulge in much description of their characters, and when they do it is to point out traits that are or will become significant as that character develops. The less important the character, the less likely the narrator will bother with extra details. So when the narrator embellishes an apparently secondary character with description, the reader should be on the alert. Either this character is destined for a larger role in the future, or the description itself has a role to play in the story. There are only a couple of very mild examples of this narrative technique in 1 Kings 1. One is how the narrator's insistence on Abishag's beauty (1:3–4) heightens the opposing roles of the young woman who now stands at David's side and of Bathsheba, who no longer does. Another is Benaiah's emergence as a sycophant (1:36–37), which points forward to his function as Solomon's hatchet man in 2:25, 34–35, and 46a.

Elsewhere in the Solomon story, however, we have a fine example of an overdeveloped secondary character in the person of Hadad the Edomite in 11:14–22. Hadad is mentioned nowhere else in the Old Testament, and the reader has no need to know this much about him. The unexpected wealth of detail calls attention to itself, and close attention reveals the narrator's subtle intent. Like Solomon's later and more significant adversary, Jeroboam (11:40), Hadad takes refuge in Egypt from Jerusalem's threat to his life. Like Solomon himself (3:1), Hadad marries into the Egyptian royal family—in fact, his relationship to the pharaoh seems far more intimate and familial than Solomon's (see 11:19–20), whose marriage is described in purely political terms.[11] The whole passage invites the attentive reader to reevaluate several elements in Solomon's story, to Solomon's distinct disadvantage. The apparent glory of his marriage alliance with the great power to the south dims when one realizes that two of Solomon's chief enemies have even closer ties to Egypt. And the narrator contradicts Solomon's boast to Hiram of Tyre that he had no "adversary" (5:4 [= Hebrew 5:18[12]]) by using the same term to identify both Hadad the Edomite and Rezon of Damascus as Solomon's "adversaries" (11:14, 23).[13]

EXPLORING THE STORIES

The Jeroboam Story

1. The main character in the Jeroboam story as a whole (11:26–14:20) is, of course, Jeroboam himself. He appears first, last, and most often in the narrative unit, and figures as the main character in most of the subunits in which he appears. (He is absent only from 11:41–43; 12:21–24; and 13:11–32.) On the

other hand, a few subunits feature prominent characters who may arguably be more central to the subunit than Jeroboam himself. Who, for instance, do you deem the main character in 11:26–40? Is this scene a story primarily of Ahijah the prophet or of Jeroboam? And what about 13:1–10? Is Jeroboam or the man of God from Judah the more important figure? Does frequent naming point to any other dominant presence in the passage?

2. Jeroboam's son Abijah, though tragic, is certainly one-dimensional. His only function in the story is to die. Yet that is not the only thing we are told about him. Why does Ahijah, speaking for Yhwh, tell us that Abijah alone shall be buried in his family's grave? (Hint: Think about how the narrator's insistence on Abishag's beauty functions in 1 Kings 1.)

3. Identify three "group" characters in 12:1–20.[14] Do any of these groups have an identifiable individual who speaks for them? Why is this surprising for at least one of the groups? Would the story affect a reader differently if the opinions expressed by the groups were presented as the opinions of individuals?

4. The most complicated set of interactions takes place in 12:1–16. Trace the action carefully to see whether the conventional maximum of three principal characters is ever violated.

5. There are two main characters in 13:11–32, the man of God from Judah and the prophet from Bethel. Would you consider either (or both) of these characters an overdeveloped secondary character in terms of the whole Jeroboam story? If so, can you see any ways in which apparently unnecessary details about them might function on narrative levels larger than the single story in 13:11–32?

6. One of the principal characters in 14:1–18 is the wife of Jeroboam. What do you think about her? Perhaps more significantly, what do you *feel* about her? Does your response change the longer you reflect on her role in the text? What do you think about the way the narrator treats her?

The Elijah Story

1. In most of the narrative units and subunits of the Elijah story, main characters are easily distinguished from secondary ones. In two scenes, however, the narrator sends us mixed signals. In 18:3–6 would you consider Ahab the main character in the scene and Obadiah secondary, or vice versa? In other words, which of the two is the focus of the scene? What is there in the scene that leads you to that reading? Similar questions can be posed about 18:7–16: Is Elijah the main character in the scene or is Obadiah? What signals does the narrator give that point to your conclusion?

2. Several very flat characters appear in 19:1–18.[15] How many can you find and identify? How does each of them contribute to the atmosphere of the story?

3. Find two group characters in 18:21–40. What are some of the characteristics each group displays? Would you call them flat or round characters—in other words, do they fill simple, stereotyped roles or do they display complexity and development? Notice that neither of the groups is represented by an

individual spokesperson. What effect does that have on each group's function in the narrative?

4. Trace the character interactions in 18:21–40. Is the conventional maximum of three principal characters preserved intact through the passage? When there are three principal characters active, does it ever occur that each one interacts with both of the others?

5. There is no strong example of an underdeveloped main character in the Elijah story.[16] There is, however, one prime example of an overdeveloped secondary character. Obadiah appears in 18:3–16, and nowhere else in the Hebrew Bible.[17] Yet he is rather oddly prominent in the two scenes in which he appears, and we are given a whole backstory for him not just once but twice (18:3–4, 12–13). What characteristic of Obadiah emerges most saliently from these two scenes? How does that characteristic link him to one of the group characters in 18:21–40?

The Ahab Story

1. Whom would you identify as the main character in 21:1–16? What narrative signals lead you to this reading? (Remember what I said earlier about how 21:1–16 can be read as a self-contained story. It is also possible, of course, to read the entire chapter as a single story; but the main character might be different, since in 21:17–29 Ahab figures prominently, while Jezebel and Naboth are mentioned only in passing. For purposes of this exercise, limit the narrative unit under consideration to 21:1–16.)

2. The unfortunate prophet whose career lasts only two verses (20:35–36) is surely among the most ephemeral figures in the Hebrew Bible, yet even he has a couple of characteristics that serve to identify him. What do you discern about him from the story? How does his story contribute to the larger narrative? (Or, to put it another way, how would the larger narrative be different if 20:35–36 were not there?) Finally, in a larger context (outside the limits of the Ahab story), do you detect an echo with another passage in 1 Kings? What might that echo portend?

3. There are several "group" characters in the Ahab narratives. Particularly prominent is the group of prophets in 22:5–28. Unlike many group characters, this one has a representative spokesperson. What effect does that have on the way one reads the story? (Hint: Contrast this with the group character "prophets of Baal" in 18:21–40, who do not have a representative spokesperson.)

4. The most complicated scene in the Ahab narrative is 22:15–28. Trace the interactions carefully to determine whether they conform to the conventional maximum of three principal characters. How do the interactions of the characters shift the focus slightly from the character relationships in 22:1–12?

5. There are no important characters in the Ahab narrative that are underdeveloped relative to their importance, as Solomon is in 1 Kings 1. Jehoshaphat, who appears at Ahab's side throughout chapter 22, is sufficiently developed for

his role in this chapter, although his status as king of Judah could invite more. Earlier Jehoshaphat appeared only in 15:24, where he was named as succeeding his father Asa on the throne of Judah. What do we learn of him in chapter 22? Perhaps more to the point, what do we *not* learn of him that aspects of his appearance in chapter 22 might make us curious about?

6. Chapter 22 presents a very prominent figure, whom it displays from several sides. This is Micaiah, son of Imlah, who appears nowhere else in the Hebrew Bible. How do Micaiah's words contribute to the development of the story line? List some of the things we learn about Micaiah that do not seem relevant to the immediate story line.

Chapter 4

Characterization

Have you ever wept while reading a story? Perhaps your tears were because the hero, righteous and admirable, tragically lost everything despite his or her innate goodness; or perhaps they were tears of joy when, at the last minute, the hero you were rooting for was rescued from almost certain disaster. Or perhaps you have felt an adrenaline rush when your favorite character was in the midst of exciting and harrowing adventures. What is going on here? After all, you were *reading a story*! The characters were not real people; they were nothing but *words*. How does a narrator move us to such an intense, even visceral, response? How does he get us to admire one set of words and to despise another set? How does he invite us to step into the secondary world and to treat its inhabitants as real people who matter to us?

One way in which the narrator does this lies in the methods used to construct characters—in other words, in techniques of *characterization*. In this chapter, we will explore this facet of the narrator's activity. Note the difference between this chapter and the last. There, we looked at the characters themselves, their relative importance and comparative complexity. Here we are looking at the *processes* by which the narrator endows those characters with importance and complexity. To put it another way, we are more interested here in the world of the *narrative*, and the narrator's activity, than in the world of the *story*, and the characters that inhabit it.

TECHNIQUES OF CHARACTERIZATION

Basically, a narrator can present us with a character in three different ways. These are not always neatly distinct (in some character presentations these techniques can overlap and blend); but for analytical purposes the distinction is useful. A narrator can *tell* us about a character (telling), or *show* us the character speaking or acting (direct showing), or show us *other* characters speaking or acting with reference to the character we are interested in (indirect showing). Each of these techniques contributes to the construction of a character in the reader's imagination, but their effects on the intensity of the reader's engagement with that character differ considerably.

Telling

Telling is the simplest technique of characterization. In it the narrator explicitly *tells* us that the character has such-and-such a quality. The quality may be an enduring one ("King David was old and advanced in years," 1 Kgs. 1:1; Adonijah was "a very handsome man, and he was born next after Absalom," 1:6; Hiram of Tyre was "full of skill, intelligence, and knowledge in working bronze," 7:14); or it may be a transitory one (the mother of the living baby was willing to give it up "because compassion for her son burned within her," 3:26; all Israel "stood in awe of the king," 3:28;[1] when the Queen of Sheba saw Solomon's glory, "there was no more spirit in her," 10:5[2]).

The examples above are all technically "predications," that is, clauses in which the narrator tells us that "X is like this." Another, subtler form of telling is the use of descriptive terms (technically, nouns in apposition and, less commonly, attributive adjectives). For instance, to speak of "King David" *tells* us that David is a "king." To speak of "Bathsheba, Solomon's mother" (1:11), *tells* us something about her (and about him!). To speak of "the prophet Nathan" (1:8) *tells* us something about Nathan.

It is important to remember that God, too, is a character in the story and that the narrator can use the same techniques to construct God's character out of words. The narrator *tells* us, for instance, that Yhwh was "pleased" (3:10), and later that he was "angry" (11:9). There is another implication to the statement that God is a character in the story world. Just as the story world (the secondary world) is separate from the world of the reader (the primary world), so too the characters (human or divine) in the story world need not be mirror images of beings in the real world that bear the same names. Adonijah, for instance, is "handsome" in the story world (1:6). This description enables the narrator to draw strong connections between Adonijah and his late older brother, Absalom (compare 2 Sam. 14:25). It does not necessarily mean that the historical Adonijah was handsome. Literary license is not a modern invention! This warning is equally true of the character "God." Nothing would prevent an author from creating a narrative world in which the character "God" has traits different from those of the God the author worships.[3]

"Telling" is the least common of the three techniques of characterization. It is also the least powerful in terms of its effect on the reader. It supplies the reader with information useful for understanding the story, but does not engage him or her in the process of actively drawing implications out of what is said. If the narrator tells us that "King David is old," we simply accept that statement as factual—David is a king, and David is old—and we move on. As we shall see, direct showing and indirect showing demand much more collaboration on the part of the reader.

Direct Showing

Instead of telling us that the character possesses a particular quality, the narrator can *show* us the character speaking or acting. It is up to us, then, to infer from the character's behavior what that behavior reveals about the character. This is *direct showing*. Occasionally the distinction between telling and direct showing can be immaterial. For example, in 1:49 the narrator tells us that Adonijah's guests "got up *trembling*." Is the narrator *telling* us that the guests were afraid, or is he *showing* us the guests "trembling" and leaving us to draw the conclusion that they were afraid? It hardly matters. The conclusion is inevitable, and the characterization is effectively the same no matter which label we put on it. More often, however, the speech or action portrayed requires interpretation on the part of the reader, and what that interpretation will be may vary from reader to reader. When Adonijah says, "I will be king" (1:5), is he gleefully (and tastelessly) anticipating that he will ascend to the throne as soon as his father dies? Or is he voicing his intention, in view of David's helplessness, to seize the throne immediately? When Bathsheba "bowed and did obeisance to the king" (1:16), does it betoken her continuing respect for him, or is it a calculated act of flattery she hopes will win his sympathy for her cause?

In interpreting such speech or action, the reader must take into account the context. To whom is the character speaking? Who knows about the character's actions? A king speaking to a trusted adviser may say what he really thinks, while speaking to a political ally of uncertain loyalties he may dissemble. Or he may act one way in public and entirely differently in private. Nathan's words to Bathsheba in 1:11–14 imply his partisanship for Solomon; his words to David in 1:24–27 do not (except to the reader: because we already know of this partisanship, we can discern its subtle presence in the words "your servant Solomon" at 1:26).

One particular case of showing is when the narrator shows us what a character is *thinking*.[4] When I talk to myself, I usually say what I really think, without any pretense or dissembling. Likewise, when the narrator shows us a character engaged in internal monologue, we can usually take for granted that the character is speaking straightforwardly, and that what the character's words reveal about him or her is reliable. There is an interesting example of this in 3:23. Once Solomon has heard the case presented by the two women, he realizes that the evidence is insufficient to reach a decision. It is simply a matter of one woman's word against the other's. He expresses his dilemma by repeating the women's words (compare 3:22 with 3:23—in Hebrew the repetition is even closer to verbatim than it is in the NRSV). The narrator tells us that Solomon "said" this—but it seems likely that he said this only internally, to himself. Judges do not usually expose their uncertainty to plaintiff and defendant. In another example, Hiram expresses joy that Yhwh "has given to David a wise son to be over this great people" (5:7 [= Hebrew 5:21]). Since this is his reaction to the letter he received from Solomon, he probably says this to himself, rather than to some unmentioned audience. We can assume, therefore, that these words reflect his true opinion.[5]

Prayer is often like internal monologue. Usually, when a character prays (that is, speaks to God), he or she speaks honestly and straightforwardly. This is not always the case, however; a character will sometimes use rhetorical techniques to try to persuade God to his or her point of view. The reader must keep a few grains of salt handy when a character—especially a very complex and round character—is praying!

As in the case of telling, the narrator also shows us God speaking and acting. And just as with any other character, it is up to the reader to infer the qualities of the Deity that are revealed in what God says or does. It is inevitably a temptation to the modern reader to interpret the character of God in the story in accord with one's own theological understandings of the Deity. But this is clearly inappropriate: we have no guarantee that *our* understanding of God is identical to the one the implied author expects the implied reader to bring to the text. Furthermore, as I mentioned above, it is not impossible for an implied author to create a story world in which the character called "God" speaks or acts in a way different from what the author would expect of the Deity the author worships in the real world.

God's explicit words and deeds are relatively limited in the Solomon story, but they nevertheless supply us with some interesting examples. God speaks to Solomon four times (3:11–14; 6:12–13; 9:3–9; and 11:11–13). One element in those speeches is God's repeated insistence on the conditionality of the divine promises: "*If* you obey my commands . . ." Note, too, how that conditional element expands in each successive speech, and especially how it dominates 9:3–9, where the reader might have expected more emphasis on the glory of the temple Solomon has just built (which Yhwh mentions only in 9:3) and less on its destruction (9:7–9). We learn something about Yhwh from these speeches, and about the much higher value he places on obedience than on religious display. In his last speech, Yhwh says that he will delay the punishment for Solomon's sin and punish Solomon's son instead (11:12). This does not square with our theology or our notions of justice, divine or human; however, it would not bother the ancient Israelite implied reader. Transgenerational reward and punishment was a theological axiom for preexilic Israel (see Exod. 34:6–7).

Actions explicitly attributed to God are likewise rare in the Solomon story. He "appears" to Solomon (3:5 and 9:2); he gives Solomon wisdom, as he had promised (4:29, repeated in 5:12a [= Hebrew 5:26a]); he (in the form of "a cloud" and "his glory") enters the temple (8:11–12); he raises up adversaries to Solomon (11:14 and 23). In all of these instances, Yhwh's behavior is consistent with his behavior elsewhere in the Bible, and in particular with the conditionality of the promises to Solomon that is emphasized in Yhwh's speeches. In other parts of the Scriptures, however, Yhwh's actions can be surprising, even scandalous. The Deity portrayed in 2 Samuel 24, who commands David, then punishes him for obeying the command, is puzzling, to say the least. And the God who is willing to put Job to torture in order to win a bet with the Adversary[6] is certainly not acting the way we would expect of a Deity.

How does direct showing affect a reader? Two aspects of the technique render it very powerful in inviting the reader to engage with the character. First, not telling the reader about the character's qualities makes it necessary for the reader to think about and draw out the implications of the character's speech or action. The reader thus actively collaborates with the narrator in constructing the character. As in telling, some aspects of the character's personality arise from the text itself; but in direct showing other aspects are inferred by the reader, and are therefore shaped by the reader's unique understanding and appropriation of the text. The reader becomes, to some degree, a coauthor and, like the ancient real author, puts something of himself or herself into the text.

Second, the technique of showing is one of our principal ways of knowing people in the primary world. In the primary world, we have no transcendent narrator who *tells* us that person A is admirable and person B is bad. We experience person A or person B as we interact with them in everyday life, or we watch person A or person B as they interact with others, and we make judgments about them based on what we observe. This is closely analogous to what readers must do when the narrator *shows* them characters speaking or acting. Therefore our experience of reading strongly parallels our experience of everyday life. This increases our sense of the "reality" of the secondary world and thus its ability to affect us.

Indirect Showing

Indirect showing is the most complex of the three techniques we are considering, and it demands the greatest involvement by the reader. Picture a scene in which the narrator shows us one character speaking to another. This is direct showing of the speaking character, but it is indirect showing of the one he or she speaks to. Why indirect? Because we do not witness the character who interests us speaking or acting, and therefore cannot infer anything directly from what he or she says or does. Rather, we can only infer things about this character indirectly, by watching the way the speaking character addresses the other character. So, in indirect showing, we must draw our inferences about one character *through the mediation of another character's behavior*.

This puts a double burden on the reader. First, the reader must make judgments about the intermediate character. What is the intermediate character like? Is he or she generally reliable? What motivates the intermediate character to speak or act in such a way? Then the reader must discern and evaluate the intermediate character's apparent view of the other character. What does the intermediate character's behavior suggest about his or her opinion of the character we are interested in? How well does he or she know the character we are interested in? Is the intermediate character's judgment about our character consistent with what we have inferred (or been told) elsewhere? In this way the reader is drawn very strongly into the process of *creating* the characters in the story.

Like direct showing, indirect showing is a *realistic* device. Much if not most of our opinion about others in the primary world is shaped by secondhand knowledge. We form our views, perhaps tentatively but nonetheless really, on what we learn about others from third parties. This is completely analogous to indirect showing, and considerably deepens the reader's sense of the reality of the secondary world and the characters that inhabit it.

Look, for example, at Bathsheba's words about Adonijah in 1:18. She says that Adonijah "has become king." David can only take this at face value, and must assume that Adonijah has attempted a coup d'état similar to that attempted by his older brother Absalom in 2 Samuel 15–18. The reader, however, is privy to information that David does not have. In 1 Kings 1:5 Adonijah said, "I *will be* king," not "I *am* [or *have become*] king." As I said above, there is an ambiguity in Adonijah's claim; it is not clear whether he is seizing sovereignty or merely anticipating his future accession. Bathsheba, however, removes all ambiguity by putting the verb in the past tense. This *indirectly* shows us a view of Adonijah that we are right to question.[7] Or look at 2:19. When Bathsheba comes before her son Solomon, who is now king, he rises to meet her, bows to her, and has a throne for her set up next to his own. Granted, she is his mother; granted further, the queen mother in Judah was a very important and highly influential member of the royal household. So it would come as no surprise to the implied reader (and it comes as no surprise to us) that Solomon would evince respect for Bathsheba and recognize her dignity. But the king "bows down" to her? This is what petitioners do when they come before the king—see 1:16, 23—not vice versa! And he seats her on a "throne"? These go beyond what one would expect and suggest that Solomon's deference to his mother is unusual. Perhaps he is aware of the role she played in his succession by court intrigue and he is demonstrating his gratitude (or does not want to risk offending her!). Whatever it reveals about Solomon, it shows us clearly (and indirectly) that Bathsheba remains a formidable power in the royal court.

Further examples of indirect showing appear in 1:1–4. "They" (unnamed and unspecified) cover the decrepit David with clothes (1:1b), and his "servants" (that is, his courtiers) propose and implement a more ambitious plan to relieve the king's maladies. This is direct showing of the courtiers, though it leaves the courtiers' motivations unclear. They may be very devoted to David and intend nothing but the best for him. Or they may be thinking that their loyal service to David will stand them in good stead with the successor once the dying king is gone. In either case, though, their attempts to ameliorate David's condition are *indirect showing* of David, and they confirm (and go beyond) the narrator's simply telling us that David was "old and advanced in years."

EXPLORING THE STORIES

The questions below are more general than my questions have been in the preceding chapters. My suggestions in the appendixes, therefore, are (even more than usual) not to be taken as the answers you should have gotten but as examples of the *sort* of answers you should have gotten.

The Jeroboam Story

1. Find examples where the narrator *tells* us about Jeroboam. Find other examples of the narrator creating a character by *telling* us about him, especially in 1 Kings 13. Can you find examples of *telling* that describe lasting traits and others that describe more transitory qualities?

2. Find an instance where a character's inner thoughts are revealed (internal monologue). What can you infer about the character from those thoughts?

3. Identify three places where, in your opinion, a character reveals something significant about himself or herself through *speech* (direct showing). The speech does not need to be *about* the character, nor does it even need to be *true*. Sometimes one reveals much about oneself by talking about others, or by lying. What do you infer about the speaker from what she or he says? Why? Do you think a different reader might understand the character's speech in a significantly different way?

4. Identify three places where, in your opinion, a character reveals something significant about him- or herself through *actions* (again, direct showing). What do you infer about the character from what she or he does? Why? Do you think a different reader might interpret the character's behavior in a significantly different way?

5. Identify two places where, in your opinion, one character's words or deeds enable the reader to infer things about *another* character (indirect showing). Is the first character reliable? What basis do you have for that decision? What do you infer about the second character from the first character's words or deeds?

The Elijah Story

1. Find at least three examples of the narrator creating a character by *telling* us about him or her. Can you find examples that describe lasting traits and others that describe more transitory ones?

2. There is no real example of internal monologue (that is, a character talking to him- or herself) in the Elijah story. On the other hand, *prayer* can sometimes (but only sometimes) enjoy the same sort of reliability, since we (usually!) speak our mind honestly when we talk to God. Look carefully at the prayers Elijah prays in the course of these three chapters. Which of them, in your opinion, most fully reveals something about Elijah himself?

3. Identify three places where, in your opinion, a character reveals something significant about him- or herself through *speech* (direct showing). The speech does not need to be *about* the character, nor does it even need to be *true*. Sometimes one reveals much about oneself by talking about others, or by lying. What do you infer about the speaker from what she or he says? Why? Do you think a different reader might understand the character's speech in a significantly different way?

4. Identify three places where, in your opinion, a character reveals something significant about her- or himself through *actions* (again, direct showing). What do you infer about the character from what he or she does? Why? Do you think a different reader might understand the character's behavior in a significantly different way?

5. Identify two places where, in your opinion, one character's words or deeds enable the reader to infer things about *another* character (indirect showing). Is the first character reliable? What basis do you have for that decision? What do you infer about the second character from the first character's words or deeds?

The Ahab Story

1. Find at least three examples of the narrator creating a character by *telling* us about him or her. Can you find examples that describe lasting traits and others that describe more transitory ones?

2. There are no clear examples of internal monologue in the Ahab story, nor are there any explicit prayers. There is one case in 22:32 where the words *may* be internal monologue, though it is not certain.[8] The Aramean captains say, "It is surely the king of Israel." Does it make a difference in interpretation whether they say this to one another or internally to themselves? What contribution does this verse make to the effect of the larger narrative?

3. Identify three places where, in your opinion, a character reveals something significant about himself or herself through *speech* (direct showing). The speech does not need to be *about* the character, nor does it even need to be *true*. Sometimes one reveals much about oneself by talking about others, or by lying. What do you infer about the speaker from what he or she says? Why? Do you think a different reader might understand the character's speech in a significantly different way?

4. Identify three places where, in your opinion, a character reveals something significant about herself or himself through *actions* (again, direct showing). What do you infer about the character from what he or she does? Why? Do you

think a different reader might understand the character's behavior in a significantly different way?

5. Identify two places where, in your opinion, one character's words or deeds enable the reader to infer things about *another* character (indirect showing). Is the first character reliable? What basis do you have for that decision? What do you infer about the second character from the first character's words or deeds?

Chapter 5

Point of View

In the preceding chapters we considered elements that belong to the story—dynamics of the plot, characters, and techniques of characterization. In this last case, however, we began to step back a bit and look not just at components of the story but at how the narrator *tells* the story. Characterization is more than a story component; it is also a strategy of narrating. In the next few chapters we will explore several more strategies of narrating: how the narrator manipulates our sense of space and time in the story, how the narrator uses the complex possibilities of language and silence to layer meanings in the story, and, finally, ways in which the narrator's own presence and voice can influence the reader's experience of the narrative. Since, as I mentioned in chapter 1, my working assumption is that reader response is a constitutive element of the meaning a narrative critic seeks, all the strategies that elicit responses from readers—that is, all the devices narrators use to evoke the reader's experience of the story—contribute to the meaning of the story. We begin by examining how the narrator manages the narratee's (and therefore the reader's) sense of space by creating a feeling of *presence* and a vantage point within the scene of the action. This vantage point, or in technical terms "point of view," is a constitutive element of meaning, since it gives the narratee (and reader) the experience of being *here* rather than *there* and of looking in *this* direction rather than *that*.

For several decades, point of view has been a topic of intense interest for theoreticians of narrative. Its nature and varieties have been explored in several different ways. For our purposes, however, this scholarly discussion is far too abstruse and technical; we are interested in a practical exploration of how point of view, in a simple and basic sense, works in narrative. Those who are interested in learning more about the theoretical complexities of point of view (or "focalization," as it is called in some recent writing) will profit from the treatments of Adele Berlin and Jean Louis Ska.[1]

THE CAMERA'S EYE

Consider the difference between attending a stage play and watching a movie. When you watch a live production on stage, the world of the story is always separate from your vantage point. You observe the action, but you do so from a distance and, more importantly, *across a boundary*. You perceive the limits of the stage (the world of the story), and you are always aware that you are outside them. Obviously, this is because your location is in a fixed seat in the audience, and not on stage with the actors. In cinema, by contrast, your perspective on the action is from *within* the story world. Even when your view is a long-distance one, you never see the *set* of the movie, which would be analogous to the wings and proscenium of the stage and would establish a tangible boundary between you and the action. This is because your perspective is not determined by where you are sitting in the movie theater, but by the camera's position. The movie camera supplies the traditional analogy for point of view in narrative. The director (read "narrator") positions the camera (read "establishes the point of view") from which you view the action. There are two aspects to this positioning, both of which can have a profound impact on the narratee's (and the reader's) response to the story: angle and distance.

Angle

When we look at something, we stand in a particular place relative to what we are observing. In other words, we have a particular *angle* to our view. The angle of our view determines what appears central and what appears peripheral to us; perhaps more importantly, it decides what we can see and what we cannot. Some characters and some events may be outside our field of vision. In cinema the director controls the angle of our view by where he or she positions the camera. In narrative the narrator controls it. Let's consider the possibilities and how the narrator maneuvers us into the position he wishes.

In much biblical narrative, the narrator is "omniscient," that is, the narrator is aware of everything that takes place in the story world—all events, all words, even all thoughts. An omniscient narrator need not share all of that information with the narratee (and the reader), but he certainly possesses it. If the narrator shares with us information that no character could have (such as the inner thoughts of more than one character, or events that happen simultaneously at different places, for instance), then he endows us too with an omniscient point of view. One might imagine this as a point of view "from above," where everything in the story world is visible and nothing is hidden.[2] One of the common features of an omniscient point of view is a sense of *distance* from the characters,[3] because we know more than any of them and, therefore, cannot share their limited perspectives. Sometimes, particularly if the narrator informs us in advance of the way the current arc of tension will be resolved,[4] an omniscient point of view puts distance also between the reader and the *action* of the scene. Instead of being gripped by the question, What happens next? the reader can turn his or her attention to other aspects of the story, such as moral evaluation of characters and their behavior. A classic example of this is the story of Abraham and Isaac in Genesis 22. The narrator tells us right from the start that "God tested Abraham" (22:1). Given that information, which only God, the narrator, and the reader are aware of, we read the story relatively certain that this will not be a story of human sacrifice, but a story of measuring Abraham's obedience. This gives us a perspective somewhat removed from the arc of tension that marks the plot (will Abraham kill Isaac?) and enables us to focus on the many facets of Abraham's moral dilemma and his response to it—his complete silence in the face of God's command; his ambiguous and ironic words to Isaac (22:8), the truth of which even Abraham himself realizes only in 22:14; and his continued silence in the face of the divine promises given him in 22:15–18. Examples of an omniscient point of view in the Solomon story would include 1 Kings 3:3–15, where we learn not only the contents of a dream Solomon has, but also the inner emotions of God ("It pleased the Lord . . . ," 3:10). The effect of this scene (at least on me as a reader) is a rather cool detachment. I understand what Solomon is asking, and I approve it; but I do not find myself drawn to identify strongly and positively with him. (This is no doubt in part because his protests about his own naiveté [3:7] ring a bit hollow in my ears after his machinations in chap. 2!) And I understand why the Lord is pleased with Solomon, but I do not find myself sharing the sentiment to any great extent.

A second perspective might be called "neutral external." This is when the narrator positions the reader's point of view *among* the characters, but not in association with any of them. The reader sees and hears only what any neutral observer would see and hear; this is what distinguishes the neutral external point of view from the omniscient one. Unless we learn things that cannot be known by a neutral observer (such as one or more characters' inner thoughts or feelings, or distant events that are taking place simultaneously), then it is better to treat the point of view as neutral external. By sharing with the reader nothing of the characters' inner life or motivations, the narrator tends to focus our attention on the *action* that is unfolding before our eyes. But since that focus involves direct showing as the primary mode of narrating, it also invites us to ask questions about the unspecified motives of characters and the future consequences of their actions and to read the text more closely to find any clues that might point to answers. This is an extremely common manipulation of the reader's point of view in biblical narrative. We will look at only one example here: the conversation between Bathsheba and Adonijah in 1 Kings 2:13–18. Adonijah's request to have Abishag as his wife is puzzling, but the narrator gives us no indication of why he makes it.[5] Bathsheba's thoughts and motives are even more obscure. She gives no indication of how she feels about Adonijah's request.[6] Is it, as one (male) commentator puts it, a matter of "Bathsheba's womanly interest in his love-affair, to which she finds no objection"?[7] Or does she see this as an opportunity to effect political reconciliation between the rival brothers? Or is she fully aware of how Solomon will react to this request, and gleefully anticipates bringing him precisely the excuse he needs to get rid of Adonijah?

Finally, the narrator can position the reader's point of view close to, or identical with, that of one of the characters. We might call this an "involved" point of view. In this case, the reader sees and hears things as that character does and may have some insight into that character's inner life (though not that of other characters). The effect of this is to increase a sense of identification with that character[8] and to focus the reader's attention on whatever that character is attending to at the moment.

A very powerful example of this last technique is in 3:16–28. This story also demonstrates how the narrator can *shift* the reader's point of view almost instantaneously. The story begins with a neutral external point of view in 3:16. We watch two women enter the royal audience hall and approach the king.[9] But that changes immediately, as "first woman" tells her tale to Solomon and then becomes embroiled in an argument with "other woman." The lengthy speech and subsequent altercation focus our attention directly on the women and the case they are presenting. In other words, we stand with Solomon, and our point of view approximates his. We see what he sees; we hear what he hears; and we, like him, are stymied by the problem. When he voices (internally?) the insolubility of the dilemma in 3:23, he voices our bafflement as well, and our point of view is almost completely identified with his. However, his next words turn us around 180 degrees: "Bring me a sword!" We hear this bewildering and ominous command *as the women do*; and we find ourselves from that point on standing with them, attending to and focused on the king. Since we now share *their* point of view, and no longer share the king's, the narrator can give us knowledge that the two women have, but that the king does not: the narrator can tell us which is truly the mother of the living child (3:26). And the narrator can withhold from us information that only the king has, namely, how Solomon manages to discover the truth.[10] Finally, in 3:28 the narrator shifts the point of view once more and gives us a distant view of popular reaction to the king's judgment. This is neither the women's point of view nor the king's; it is a neutral, external point of view.[11]

Distance

If the angle of our point of view affects what we see or do not see, the distance between us and what we see affects the intensity with which we respond to it. Let's return for a moment to the analogy of cinema. If the camera shows us two people across the room shouting at one another and gesturing angrily, we say, "Wow! Those two are really upset!" But if the camera zooms in on them, so that we hear their angry exchange and see their enraged expressions in close-up, we are likely to react viscerally: our own adrenaline level will begin to rise, our muscles will tighten, we may feel ourselves shrink back from a threat of violence. The intensity of our reaction is, at least in part, a function of how close we are to the action.

Compare, for instance, the two scenes that depict Adonijah's gathering at En-rogel. The first scene (1:9–10) is told from a neutral, external point of view, and from a distance. We can see the animals Adonijah sacrifices, and who is present and who is not; but we hear nothing and see no particular details. Our response to this scene is almost entirely intellectual: it gives us *information*, but it does not *move* us. In contrast, the second scene (1:41–49) is presented from a much closer perspective. We hear Joab's question, Adonijah's greeting of Jonathan, and Jonathan's account of Solomon's accession and enthronement. We have some limited insight into the characters' feelings, though the scene probably still qualifies as an external presentation: we know what they hear (1:41) and we see them tremble (1:48). Our point of view is less neutral and closer to that of Adonijah's guests, particularly as we listen to Jonathan's recital along with them. As a result, we *feel* their apprehension. We are not simply observers, but in some measure we *share* their experience.

One other example may clarify this even more. In the scene of Solomon's anointing (1:38–40), although we are close enough to see Zadok anoint Solomon, we are too far away to hear anything except the trumpet and the people's acclamation—and those were so loud that "the earth quaked" (1:40) and people a half-mile away at En-rogel also heard them (1:41). The distance diminishes our emotional response, and we recognize and appreciate—but hardly join in—the popular enthusiasm.

ESTABLISHING POINT OF VIEW

How does the narrator manipulate our point of view? There are several techniques, though not all readers will respond to them in identical fashion. Our individual personalities and proclivities as real readers will also have a bearing on the point of view we assume. We will find it easier to see things from the perspective of characters we admire or characters with whom we share certain traits.[12]

The simplest technique is by showing us what we can see and hear. If we are not shown details, but we do have a wide overview of the setting and the characters within it, we must be at some distance from the scene in order to take in a broader view. For instance, in 1:38–40 we not only see the anointing of Solomon but we also watch his ride from the city down to Gihon and, afterward, the parade that follows the new king back up the hill to the city.[13] Notice that we do not seem to *join* the parade; we watch it from a distance. We must be close enough to discern what is happening at Gihon, though without hearing what anybody says there, yet distant enough to have a clear view of the road that leads from the city gates to the spring at Gihon.[14] On the other hand, when we see relatively small details (like the people "trembling" in 1:49[15]), or hear people speaking, we are not far from the scene.

The use of direct speech is a complex technique in close-up scenes. Think again of cinema, and the many ways the director can show us a conversation. Sometimes we will see it from a neutral perspective that encompasses both speakers. Sometimes we will see the entire dialogue from one participant's point of view. Sometimes the camera will shift back and forth, watching each character in turn as he or she speaks. And sometimes the camera will shift back and forth, watching each character in turn as he or she listens. Each choice will evoke a different response from the viewer. In narrative, too, dialogue can evoke a variety of responses. If, for instance, the speaker is saying things that we are already aware of, our point of view is likely to be close to the speaker's, with our attention focused on the hearer's reactions (for instance, Solomon's comment about the inconclusiveness of evidence in 3:23). If, on the other hand, the speaker is saying things that are unknown to us, we will usually find ourselves in the same position as the listeners, and we will focus on the speaker and his or her words (for instance, Solomon's words in the very next verse, 3:24, shift our point of view to that of the two women; similarly, we listen to David's speech in 2:2–9 along with Solomon). In a conversation where neither party is saying things that are familiar to us, we may find ourselves in a neutral position between them. (For instance, in the conversation between Adonijah and Bathsheba in 2:13–18, we are equally interested in Adonijah's tongue-tied[16] attempts to articulate what he wants and in Bathsheba's cool, noncommittal replies.)

None of these are hard-and-fast rules, however. Exceptions are not unknown, especially when the speech is a repetition of something we have already heard. For instance, when Bathsheba confronts David in 1:15–21, we already know what she is going to say, since Nathan wrote the script for her in 1:13. Nevertheless, even though our attention is on David to see how he will react to Bathsheba's claims, we will notice (if we are attentive) that Bathsheba does not follow Nathan's script exactly; and, along with our curiosity about David's reaction, we will also consider Bathsheba's speech to try to determine whether her deviations are accidental or deliberate.[17] In other words, our point of view will be a neutral one, watching both participants in the dialogue. Similarly, when Jonathan speaks in 1:43–45, we realize that he is simply recounting what we have already witnessed in 1:38–40; as a result, our attention is drawn first to Adonijah's guests and the horror that must be dawning on their faces as they realize that their patron has lost the struggle for the succession. However, Jonathan continues past what we have already witnessed (1:45b–48) with information that is entirely new to us; thus our attention is suddenly drawn back to him and the additional news (let's be honest: the additional *gossip*) he brings.[18] In other words, we begin the scene somewhat neutral (Joab's question in 1:41 is not our own; we already know what the "uproar" is all about). It shifts to share Jonathan's perspective as he recounts the bad news (note the irony: Adonijah has just welcomed him as a bearer of good news; *Jonathan* knows better, and *we* know better; thus the narrator puts us in Jonathan's point of view, where we will stay at least until 1:45). Finally, as Jonathan starts to give us new information, the narrator switches our perspective to that of Adonijah's guests, thereby preparing us to consider their "trembling" (1:48) and what it might mean about their inner emotional state.

There is a technique in Hebrew that rarely, if ever, survives translation in modern versions of the Scriptures. It is a grammatical construction that almost forcibly imposes a character's point of view on the narratee/reader. The key word in Hebrew is *wĕhinnēh*, translated in older English versions (like the KJV) as "and lo!" or "and behold!"; more modern translations regularly paraphrase to avoid such archaic language. The construction works this way. After an initial clause that often, but not always, includes a verb of perceiving, the narrator uses *wĕhinnēh* to indicate precisely what the character perceives. The effect is usually an intense sense of *present* action, as though the narratee/reader were perceiving the object through the character's eyes in the same moment that the character does. Although the construction is fairly common in Hebrew, if it is translated literally it appears contrived and artificial in English. A couple of literal examples will illustrate what I mean. In 1:15–21 Bathsheba has an audience with David, and in 1:22 Nathan enters the scene. The transitional verse, translated literally, reads: "And look! While she was still speaking with the king, Nathan the prophet comes in!" Or 3:21, where one woman testifies to Solomon, "Then I got up in the morning to nurse my son, and look! He's dead!" This is obviously a powerful device for fixing the reader's point of view, but it is, sadly, virtually impossible to detect in modern English translations of the Hebrew Bible.

There is another subtle technique that is easy to miss, though it can be discerned in translation by a very careful reader. This occurs when the narrator shows us something through a character's eyes but *does not tell us that he is doing so*. Just about the only clues we have to such situations are (1) that the information is already known to us and (2) that another character is mentioned in the immediate context as a potential anchor for the point of view. The first chapter of the Solomon story provides two excellent examples of this technique. By the end of 1:3, we know that Abishag is beautiful. The courtiers had set out to find a beautiful virgin, and they found Abishag. Why, then, does the narrator tell us in 1:4 that "the girl was very beautiful"? Notice that the last words of 1:3 are that the courtiers "brought her to the king." The first words of 1:4 are not the narrator's telling us about Abishag's beauty, but *David's perception of her beauty*.[19]

The courtiers "brought her to the king and [the king saw that] the girl was very beautiful."[20] Now look at 1:15. When Bathsheba enters David's chambers, the narrator tells us, "The king was very old; Abishag the Shunammite was attending the king." We already know both of these facts from 1:1 and 1:4. Here too the narrator, without saying so explicitly, gives us a character's view: this is what Bathsheba sees as she enters the king's chambers. Her first perception is of how David has aged (this suggests that she has not been called to his bed for quite some time). Her second perception is of the beautiful young woman who now stands at David's side, where Bathsheba herself once stood. (One can just imagine what goes through Bathsheba's mind at that sight; but perhaps one ought not to put it in print!)

EXPLORING THE STORIES

As you undertake the following exercises, here are a couple of suggestions about how to proceed profitably. First, do not consciously seek to identify the techniques the narrator uses to establish point of view and then try to figure out from those techniques what your point of view should be. (In other words, do not approach the issue this way: "Hmmm. This character is saying things I already know, so my point of view should be focused on whoever is listening to him.") Rather, *read the story*, and let the words paint the scene as vividly as possible in your imagination. Then ask yourself, "Where am I visualizing this *from*? What am I focusing my gaze on? How close am I to what I am looking at?" Then, and only then, ask yourself what it is in the narrator's presentation that has maneuvered you into that position. Second (and this technique is good for many analytical questions besides understanding point of view), ask yourself, "If the story were different—or were told differently—would my response be the same or different?"

For instance, if, in 3:16–22, the narrator had Solomon ask the two women a series of probing questions, would our response to this part of the story be the same? I do not think it would, because it would change our mode of involvement with the characters. In the present story, Solomon's apparent bewilderment (which comes to such clear expression in 3:23) parallels our own, and this establishes our point of view as virtually identical with his. Like him, we ask, "Which woman is the mother of the living child?" Were Solomon to ask probing questions in 3:16–22, we would wonder what he was after and we would not be able to identify our perspective so completely with his. At least part of our attention would be focused on Solomon and on figuring out his agenda: What sort of clues is Solomon looking for? How is he intending to find the truth? (This is what happens when Solomon speaks in 3:24: our anxious uncertainty about what he plans to do with the sword suddenly focuses our attention on him, rather than on the women.) So Solomon's silence, up to the point where he articulates our own bafflement in 3:23, strengthens our focus on the women and on solving the challenge posed by the case rather than on Solomon and the opportunity the case gives him to display his extraordinary wisdom.

Point of view is often not strongly marked in a scene. As a result, the reader's subjectivity can come into play decisively. As usual I have commented on each of the following questions in the appendixes, but my comments should not be taken as indicating the only point of view from which any given scene can be viewed. They explain the points of view I find myself taking, and what in the text seems to put me in that position. Your results, as they say, may vary. The important thing is to become *aware* of the point of view you find yourself taking, and to try to determine how the text has moved you to take it.

The Jeroboam Story

1. There are numerous parallels between the episode in 11:26–40 and that in 14:1–18. Obviously, each episode is dominated by a speech by Ahijah to a silent listener, Jeroboam in chapter 11 and Jeroboam's wife in chapter 14. Each episode, too, gives some introductory information about the listener (11:26–28 and 14:1–5[21]) and a brief narrative epilogue, also about the listener (11:40 and 14:17–18). As you read each episode, how do you visualize Ahijah's speech? In other words, what is your point of view? Do you visualize the scene from a neutral perspective, standing midway between speaker and listener? Or do you find yourself standing close to the listener, focused on Ahijah? Is there a difference in your response to the two scenes? If so, what could account for the difference?

2. The reader's point of view changes frequently in 12:3–16. As you read the passage, visualize it at each step of the way, and try to identify how your point of view changes and what in the text positions you there.

3. What points of view do you find in 13:11–32? What in the text invites you to one point of view or another? (Do not get too detailed here. Take the story in three main blocks of text, 13:11–19, 20–25, and 26–32. Try to identify the dominant point of view in each of the three movements.)

The Elijah Story

1. How would you describe the point of view in 17:17–24? What are the indicators that lead you to that decision?

2. The contest on Mount Carmel (18:21–40) involves a series of scenes. Elijah speaks to the people, then to the prophets, then to the people, then to Yhwh, and finally in 18:40 again to the people. Examine your point of view as you go through this section. Is there anything that you know that none of the characters knows and that therefore gives you an omniscient (or at least superior) perspective? Are you a neutral, external observer of the action? Do you find yourself sharing (or at least close to) the perspective of one of the characters (including the group characters)? You may find, too, that your point of view changes as you

go through the passage. Try to identify the elements in the text that situate you at one point of view rather than another.

3. We end chapter 18 with a rather distant point of view, watching Elijah race ahead of Ahab's chariot to the city of Jezreel. Much happens in the next verses, 19:1–8: Ahab speaks to Jezebel, Jezebel threatens Elijah, Elijah flees into the Negev Desert, where he encounters a "messenger" (NRSV "angel") twice. As you read through these verses, do you maintain a distant observer's point of view, or does your point of view move closer to the action at some point? If you find yourself coming closer, what is it in the text that evokes that reaction? Is your point of view still neutral or does it ever become identified with Elijah's?

4. This question is perhaps a bit unfair, but it is intended to demonstrate how translation-dependent we are. In the same passage we just considered, 19:1–8, *wĕhinnēh* occurs twice in 19:5–6. A more literal translation of those two verses would be: "Then he lay down under the broom tree and fell asleep. And see here! There is a messenger touching him! And he said to him, 'Get up; eat.' And he looked round, and see! At his head there is a cake of flatbread and a jar of water! He ate, drank, and lay down again."[22] Does this translation have a different effect on your point of view than the translation you used for question 3? Note that *wĕhinnēh* does *not* appear in verse 7; does this contrast between the messenger's first appearance and his second change the way you visualize the two encounters?

The Ahab Story

1. Trace the point(s) of view in 20:1–12. How does the narrator establish the point of view?

2. What point(s) of view do you find operative in 20:35–43?

3. This final question may be a bit tricky, but it will introduce an issue we will consider at greater length in chapter 9. Whose point of view is operative in 21:25–26?

Chapter 6

Manipulation of Time

In the preceding chapter on "Point of View" we explored ways in which the narrator can manipulate the narratee's (and the reader's) experience of *space* within the narrative world by fixing the reader's position and angle of vision. In this chapter we will explore how the narrator can affect the narratee's (and the reader's) experience of the dimension of *time*. The narrator does this by taking advantage of the fact that there are two different time lines involved in the narrative world: the *story* time, in which the events of the plot unfold, and the *narration* time, in which the narrator recounts those events to the narratee. The way the narrator tells the story in narration time effects and affects the way the narratee experiences story time. The narrator's manipulation of time can occur in two different arenas: the *tempo* of the narration, and the *order* of its events.

TEMPO

By "tempo" I mean the speed or pace at which the story unfolds. We have all had experience of novels whose rapid action gets our heart beating faster. Often this is reflected in an unconscious urge to *read* faster. (Reviewers regularly describe such books as "real page-turners.") Conversely, we have also had experience of stories that seemed to drag; some of us find ourselves looking ahead to find out how many more pages we have to go. How do authors (and their narrators) produce such responses in readers (and narratees)? We begin exploring this by making a triple distinction: Events can take more time to happen than to read about (this is the usual situation); or they can take approximately the same length of time; or they can take less time to transpire than to recount.

Events Take Longer to Happen than to Read About

First, the ordinary case: It takes events longer to happen than it does to read about them. It takes only a second to read "John walked all afternoon," though it took John several hours to do so. Most stories take less time to read than it took their reported plot to occur.[1] So when the story unfolds more quickly than the events it depicts, that fact in itself has no particularly noteworthy effect on the reader. However, even in this case, a story can move relatively more rapidly or more slowly. When a story moves relatively quickly, it tends to rivet our attention on the action (it is a "page-turner"). The more slowly it moves, the more leisure we have to reflect on what is happening, to imagine scenes in detail, to evaluate characters, to wonder about unspoken motivations, to make moral judgments, and so on. (And if in a slow-moving story we find no incentive to undertake such reflection, we will first experience increased interior tension—"Get *on* with it!"—and then, if the story continues to drag, we will usually deem the book boring and stop reading.)

How does the narrator evoke our sense that a story is moving rapidly or slowly? High on the list of techniques is the ratio of verbs of action[2] to other words. Verbs of action make a story *move*, and the greater their frequency in the text the faster the pace of the story. Conversely, a high ratio of nominal clauses (that is, clauses without verbs[3]), of subordinate clauses, or of circumstantial clauses will slow the tempo of the story considerably.

This technique can be extraordinarily evocative. (Unfortunately, the disparities between Hebrew and English syntax usually make it difficult for a translator to achieve the same effects as the original.) I have gone outside 1 Kings for two striking examples. In Genesis 3:6a the woman stands contemplating the tree, weighing the advantages of eating the fruit. She does this in a series of three verbless clauses (in Hebrew, twelve words) following the initial verb, literally, "and-saw the-woman that good [was] the-tree for-food, and-that pleasant [was] it to-the-eyes, and-desirable [was] the-tree to-succeed . . ." The slow pace (virtually no action at all) mirrors the woman's stillness as she stares at the tree, trying to come to a decision. In Genesis 3:6b, however, she has made up her mind, and the action explodes in a series of three verbs in four words: "and-she-took from-its-fruit and-she-ate and-she-gave . . ." Once she has decided, she acts hurriedly (lest she lose her nerve? lest God stop her?) to pick, to eat, and to invite her husband to implicate himself in her actions.

A second example comes from 2 Kings 7:8. The situation is this. Israel is at war with Aram, which has besieged Samaria. The capital city is in dire straits—famine has reduced the citizens to infanticide and cannibalism (6:26–29). In response to a royal threat, Elisha has promised relief from the famine within twenty-four hours. Meanwhile, outside the city, a group of lepers (who, because of their skin disease, cannot enter the city and would not know of Elisha's oracle) realize that they are starving to death. They decide that surrender to the Arameans is their only chance for survival or at the least for a less lingering death. So they make their way to the Aramean camp. When they find it abandoned, they are astounded, but take immediate advantage of their luck. Literally, "these lepers entered the-edge of-the-camp and-they-entered into-one tent and-they-ate and-they-drank and-they-took from-there silver and-gold and-clothing and-they-went and-they-hid [it] and-they-returned and-they-entered into-one tent and-they-took [what?] from-there and-they-went and-they-hid [it]." Twelve independent action verbs in twenty-five words! (Notice how the narrator even omits some necessary direct objects in order to intensify the rapid-fire activity.) The point here is not simply to portray gripping action. It is to show the headlong haste of the lepers, who—not knowing that Yhwh has made the Arameans flee (7:6)—cannot help but fear their return while the lepers are plundering the camp. The narratee—and the reader—*experience* the lepers' haste in the piling up of verbs of action.

Tempo, however, is not a simple matter of counting verbs. If a passage recounts only main actions over a span of time, it will seem to move faster than one that gives a step-by-step recital filled with details. Of course, the circumstantial details will usually lower the ratio of active verbs in the second case, but what strengthens the impact of the textual tempo is the ratio of text length to event length. For instance, compare the brief account of Solomon's inauguration ritual in 1 Kings 1:38–40 with the longer account of the installation of the ark of Yhwh in Solomon's new temple in 8:1–11. The ceremonies were probably similar in their duration; however, the description of the second, filled with details and asides to the reader, moves much more slowly than the first.

Finally, the narrator can simply skip over a period of time with a summary word or phrase. In 2:36–37 Solomon commands Shimei to remain within the city limits of Jerusalem. In 2:38b we are told simply that Shimei obeyed "for many days"; this becomes more specific in the next verse, which begins, "Then, at the end of three years . . ." The narrator simply passes over the intervening years in silence. In cases like this, though time moves very quickly, it has no overt effect on our sense of tempo since the elapsed period is narratively empty.[4]

Event and Recital Take Approximately Equal Lengths of Time

When the narrator recounts events by portraying a scene with characters speaking and acting, the duration of the events approaches the time it takes to read about them. Dialogue in particular takes approximately as long to read as it does to speak; and biblical narrative is often little more than extensive dialogue connected by a minimum of narrative transitions. Look again, for instance, at the story of Solomon and the two harlots (3:16–28). Dialogue dominates the scene. (In Hebrew over two-thirds of the story is direct discourse. There are 138 words of direct speech, and only 67 words of narrative.)

The effect of constructing a scene this way is to enhance verisimilitude (that is, our experience of the scene as *real*). We encounter figures speaking and acting, just as we do in real life. Dialogue brings us close to the characters (close enough to hear them, at least), and the correlation of the time it takes to read the scene with the time it would take to experience the scene in reality strengthens this sense of verisimilitude. Scenic presentation focuses our attention on the characters and their doings, and makes any sort of reflection and evaluation more difficult. In 3:16–28, for instance, it is not until we reach the relatively distant point of view in 3:28 that we can easily take stock of what has happened and compare our reaction to Solomon's achievement with that of "all Israel."[5]

To see the difference in effect between a purely narrative presentation and a scenic presentation with dialogue, compare 10:4–5 with 10:6–9. In both passages we learn how deeply the luxury of Solomon's court has impressed the Queen of Sheba. But in the second passage, because we learn it from her own mouth, we *feel* her wonderment rather more intensely than we do in the first passage.

Events Take Less Time to Transpire than to Recount

The third possibility is found when it takes longer to read the story than it would for the recounted events to transpire. How can a narrator achieve this? By supplying material that gives the narratee/reader information without advancing the action. That information can be of several sorts and can have differing effects on the reader. The piling up of examples, perhaps with comments,[6] can slow the movement of a text considerably; see, for instance, 4:29–33 (= Hebrew 5:9–13). Sometimes this piling up of details takes the form of an extensive list, as in 4:1–19. In all such cases the pause in the action distances us from it; but that can have a variety of results. If we have been strongly focused on the action itself—that is, if "What happens next?" has been in the forefront of our attention—then we are likely to become a bit frustrated by the delay. This will increase our tension, build up a bit of suspense, and push us to read faster to get to "what happens next." For many modern readers, this is the excruciating effect of the long description of the temple in chapters 6 and 7. The plot line has, to all intents and purposes, stalled. Even though it takes Solomon seven years to build the temple (6:38b), we do not experience time passing. We feel rather that we have gotten lost in a maze of walls and decoration.[7]

On the other hand, if the narrator has given us reason to be more reflective about the text—for example, by portraying surprising behavior without revealing a character's motivation, or intensifying our emotional involvement with a particular character, or posing a moral dilemma that impels us to evaluate and judge the action—then this pause gives us a chance to pursue and deepen our reflection. In 4:29–34 (= Hebrew 5:9–14), for instance, we gain evidence of just how widely Solomon's wisdom was admired (international superiority and recognition) and how broadly its purview reached (proverbs, songs, scientific knowledge). And we learn this under the heading of "divine gift" ("God *gave* Solomon . . . ," 4:29). The details become a testimony to Yhwh's loyalty to the Davidic line and his fidelity to his promise to Solomon (3:12). In other words, we are offered a deeper insight into the character of both Yhwh and Solomon, and the pause in the text's action gives us a chance to appreciate that insight and its implications. In 4:1–19 we learn (in almost too much detail) how Solomon's wisdom led to efficient organization of his kingdom, both at the central court and in territorial administration. The piling up of names of officials and territories almost overwhelms us; I suspect that we, like the Queen of Sheba later, can be left "breathless" (10:5[8]). What results is a richer sense of the immensity and complexity of Solomon's kingdom, and this sense redounds in our imaginations to a greater glory for Solomon.

Another means the narrator has to delay the plot line is by inserting descriptions, whether of characters or of settings. Contemporary literature makes extensive use of description. Characters' personalities are regularly suggested by describing their physical features ("sparkling eyes," "sensual lips," "unconvincing smile," "gentle bearing," and the like); atmosphere is created by describing the setting ("oppressive rain," "glorious sunshine," "sullen clouds," and so on). This is not at all the case in Biblical Hebrew narrative. I have already mentioned that biblical narrators are exceedingly sparing in their descriptions of characters. They are not much more generous with their descriptions of settings. But when such descriptions appear, they slow the action noticeably, giving the narratee (and reader) an opportunity both to visualize the description in imagination and to register it in memory. This is because such a description will usually have another significant function somewhere in the story. For example, the description of Adonijah in 1:6b ("he was a very handsome man, and he was born next after Absalom") is part of a strategy on the narrator's part to draw suggestive parallels between Adonijah and his late older brother (who rebelled against their father David and died in the course of the resulting civil war, leaving Adonijah the heir apparent). Compare 1:5–6 with 2 Samuel 14:25 and 15:1.[9] An example of a description of setting is the extravagant language used to describe Solomon's wealth and commerce in 1 Kings 10:21 ("all King Solomon's drinking vessels were gold . . . ; none were of silver—it was not considered as anything in the days of Solomon"), 10:26 (Solomon had "fourteen hundred chariots and twelve thousand horses"), 10:27 ("the king made silver as common as stones in Jerusalem"), and 10:29 ("a chariot could be imported from Egypt for six hundred shekels of silver, and a horse for one hundred fifty"). And we should not stop there. According to 11:3, Solomon had in his harem "seven hundred princesses and three hundred concubines"—wives too were a sign of wealth and peaceful diplomatic relations. These lavish depictions are not innocent. The ancient Israelite implied reader could not possibly read them without thinking of the warnings in Deuteronomy 17:16–17, which forbade the king to "acquire many horses for himself, or return the people to Egypt in order to acquire more horses," or to "acquire many wives for himself... also silver and gold he must not acquire in great quantity for himself." The description of Solomon's wealth, then, serves characterization but, to our surprise, it serves *negative* characterization. Solomon is in direct violation of the Deuteronomic law that David enjoined him to obey (1 Kgs. 2:1–4).

ORDER

Although it sounds odd to say it this way, the events of a story always take place twice. They take place first when they happen; then later they take place again narratively, when the narrator recounts them to the narratee. This duality offers the narrator an additional tool for manipulating time and evoking responses from the narratee. That is because the narrator is under no obligation to recount the events in the same order in which they actually occurred.[10] The narrator can leave things out, only to mention them later; or he can anticipate later developments by hinting at them in advance. The first is commonly called "flashback" (the technical term is "analepsis"); the second is "foreshadowing" (or "prolepsis").

Flashback

A flashback occurs when the narrator informs us about some event that transpired prior to the story he is currently telling. (Alternatively, the information might come from a character, but then we have to weigh that character's reliability, much as we did in the case of characterization by indirect showing.) We may or may not have been told about the event when it actually took place. If we were, then the flashback functions as a reminder; but it also urges the narratee (and reader) to consider the earlier account along with the present one as parts of a single story. In this way it broadens the reader's horizon and points to the possibility of a wider context of understanding.[11] If we were not informed earlier, then the first question is why we did not learn about the event at the time that it happened. There could be a trivial explanation; for example, the event may not have occurred at a time or place that is otherwise part of the story. Or perhaps the event took place so long in the past that the reader needs to be reminded of it.[12] Very often, the flashback will serve to characterize a figure who has just been mentioned for the first time, as in 1:6. In such cases, the flashback is simply supplying us with background information necessary for us to understand what is going on now. An example of this is the remark that "Hiram had always been a friend to David" (5:1 [= Hebrew 5:15]). The language is diplomatic: "to be a friend" here means to be a treaty partner. This is useful background information, because it explains why Solomon's overtures to Hiram are reasonable.[13]

However, flashback can have much greater impact on a reader than simply supplying useful background information. When the narrator, or a reliable character, tells us something new about a past event, it can force us to reconstrue that past event and, perhaps, everything that has subsequently occurred as a result of it. Our impression from 4:7–21 (reinforced by Solomon's remark to Hiram in 5:4 [= Hebrew 5:18]) is that Solomon had complete control over his own kingdom and peaceful relations with all surrounding realms, most of which were subject to him as tributary vassals. In 9:16, however, we suddenly learn that Gezer, a strategically important city located only about twenty miles from Jerusalem, was not under Solomon's control, was conquered by the pharaoh who was Solomon's father-in-law (what was an *Egyptian* army doing in Solomon's land?!), and was given to Pharaoh's daughter as a wedding present![14] We are compelled to reconsider our earlier impressions about the completeness of Solomon's authority. Perhaps without Egyptian support his sovereignty would have been much narrower; perhaps the picture implied in 4:7–21 owes some of its luster to the rhetoric of Solomonic Realpolitik, rather than to the political realities of Solomon's day.

When a character of uncertain reliability supplies us with a flashback, the situation gets even more dubious. Nathan tells Bathsheba to remind David of a promise he is alleged to have once made (1:13), and Bathsheba does so (1:17). Is the allegation true? Did David ever make such a promise? It would have been the easiest thing in the world for the narrator to confirm—or to deny—the claim. Insert, "Now David had said that Solomon would sit on the throne after him," before 1:11; alternatively, insert, "But David had not said so" after 1:14. Then all would be clear. But the narrator does not do so.[15] And so the flashback remains an irreducible riddle. Without it, Nathan and Bathsheba's plot is a clear instance of a palace coup. With it, we must consider the possibility that it is an attempt to carry through wise provisions David made for his kingdom before he entered his dotage; but we must also consider the possibility that it is a desperate falsehood intended to take advantage of the old man's confusion.

Foreshadowing

"Foreshadowing" refers to remarks, usually by the narrator, that reveal in advance to the narratee and the reader something about what will happen later in the story. In most cases, foreshadowing gives the narratee and the reader information that characters do not have. (In a moment we shall look at a class of foreshadowings that constitutes an exception to this general rule.) This inevitably distances us from the characters, since we know more than they; it also distances us somewhat from the *action*, since we already know to some degree what happens next. The effects of this distance can vary. Paradoxically, it can either reduce or increase tension. By anticipating the course of the arc of tension, it can reduce our focus on what happens next and, like other techniques that distance us from the action, give us room to reflect on motivations and characters, or to make moral judgments. On the other hand, particularly if the foreshadowed development seems unlikely, it can shift the tension from "what happens next" to "how can *that* happen?" This tends to focus us on action rather than on reflection; we look for the course events must follow to get to such an unexpected outcome.

In 3:1 we have a combination of background information (Solomon's political alliance-by-marriage with Pharaoh[16] and the arrival of Pharaoh's daughter in Jerusalem, the "city of David") and foreshadowing (in the future, Solomon will build a "house" for himself, a "house"—that is, a temple—for Yhwh, and a wall around the city). The word "until" in the middle of the verse further implies that after, and only after, these three building projects are completed will Solomon turn his attention to his Egyptian wife. The foreshadowed elements set an agenda of expectation for the reader. We anticipate learning more about all three building projects, and we wonder what specific form Solomon's attention to his wife will take once they are finished. The construction of Solomon's "house" (actually, a whole complex of governmental buildings, of which Solomon's residence was a small part) is covered in 7:1–12; and the account of the building of the temple begins in 6:1 and ends in 9:25b. There is no account of the building of the city wall, though it will be mentioned again in the summary remark in 9:15. Solomon's effort on behalf of Pharaoh's daughter turns out to be the construction of a house for her (7:8b; 9:24).

These scattered remarks, however, are only the tip of an iceberg. The order of the narrator's presentation is very different from the implied chronology of construction. Solomon spent twenty years on the temple and the administrative buildings, of which he spent the first seven on the temple and then thirteen more on "his own house."[17] Yet the account of the construction of the administrative buildings (7:1–12) is brought forward to interrupt that of the construction and furnishing of the temple (6:1–38; 7:13–51). To what effect? It enables the narrator to juxtapose the seven years Solomon spent on Yhwh's "house" to the thirteen years he spent on his own (6:38b and 7:1). While this is not an overt criticism of Solomon, the disparity is difficult to overlook; and the narratee (and the reader) may well wonder whether it says something about the relative value Solomon placed on the two "houses." There is more. Solomon did not build the "house for Pharaoh's daughter" until both Yhwh's "house" and Solomon's own "house" were completed (compare 3:1 and 9:24; the latter verse is in its proper chronological place in the story). Yet in 7:8b—before either Yhwh's house or Solomon's has been completed—we are reminded that "Solomon also made a house ... for Pharaoh's daughter."[18] For the narrator, Solomon's marriage to the Egyptian princess was only the first and most striking instance of the infidelity for which Solomon will finally be condemned—marrying foreign women (11:1–4). And so he scatters reminders of it throughout the story.

As we shall see in chapter 9, narrators in the Hebrew Bible tend to remain in the background. Consequently, straightforward foreshadowing like 3:1b is relatively uncommon. More frequently we will find subtler forms, like setting out a pattern that will find repeated instantiations as time goes on. In the book of Judges, for instance, a pattern of infidelity, punishment, cry for help, and salvation is set out at the beginning in generalized terms (2:11–19); that pattern supplies the paradigm for the following stories of each judge's career.[19] An even more subtle use of foreshadowing is found when an event, recounted in the ordinary way and in proper chronological order, resonates with a later event in ways that can only be appreciated post factum. These are, in one sense, like literary winks from the narrator to the narratee, inviting the narratee to appreciate the narrator's cleverness at double entendre. In 1 Kings 3:4 Solomon offers a lavish sacrifice to Yhwh at Gibeon, "the principal high place," because there was as yet no temple in Jerusalem. After his sacrifice, still at Gibeon, Solomon encounters Yhwh in a dream. Upon waking, he returns to Jerusalem, where he offers another sacrifice to Yhwh "before the ark of the covenant." In themselves, the two sacrifices simply attest to Solomon's devotion. But in light of Solomon's whole career, they portend his centralization of worship in the Jerusalem temple at the expense of the Yahwistic high places outside the city.

By far, foreshadowing in the Hebrew Bible occurs most commonly in the form of a divine word, whether delivered by God himself or, more often, through a prophet. In such cases, the foreshadowing is known to characters (God, the prophet, the prophet's audience) as well as to the narratee. Since God's power is unquestioned, a divine announcement about the future is assumed to be reliable; the reader's attention then will focus not on what happens next, but on how it will come about.[20] After Yhwh's promises to Solomon in 3:12–13, we do not wonder about Solomon's displays of wisdom and wealth in subsequent chapters; we simply enjoy them. Conversely, after Yhwh's warning to Solomon in 9:6–9, we are not surprised at the eventual destruction of Jerusalem and exile of Israel, though the story takes a long and tragic time to reach that point.

Once in a rare while the narrator will throw us a curve, and a prophecy will not be fulfilled, or will be fulfilled in unorthodox fashion, or will even be rescinded by Yhwh. In such cases the problematic issue is not specifically a foreshadowing, but a matter of characterization: Yhwh said one thing and did another. The foreshadowing, however, was a necessary component in the construction of the problem. There are no instances of this in the Solomon story, but a crucial one for the entire Deuteronomistic History is the unconditional promise to David in 2 Samuel 7, which guarantees him a dynasty that will rule "forever." Reconciling that promise with the destruction of Jerusalem and the eventual disappearance of the Davidic line has stimulated Jewish and Christian theological reflection since the time of the Babylonian exile.

Foreshadowing by prophecy has another function in the biblical text as well. Very often prophetic predictions are matched by fulfillment notices later in the text. Such correlated passages may be close together (see, for example, 2 Sam. 10:5–6, fulfilled in 10:9–10), or they may be separated by long spans of time and text (see, for example, Josh. 6:26, fulfilled in 1 Kgs. 16:34). On a literary level, this is a technique for forging unity in the story: the prophecy functions as a foreshadowing, and the fulfillment often includes an explicit flashback to the prophecy, thus implying that they form parts of a single story. On a theological level, prophecy and fulfillment notices establish the claim that behind the apparent vicissitudes of history lie the knowledge and will of a Deity who remains in control of events.

A Note on Simultaneity

I spoke in chapter 2 about the *linear* character of narrative. One consequence of this linearity is the impossibility of depicting true simultaneity. In visual art, a painter can paint a diptych, or put two different scenes on the same canvas (in two different rooms of a house, for example). Or a cinematographer can split his screen to show different events at the same time. Not so the storyteller, who must deliver his story one word at a time. Narrators make do with "meanwhile" and "at that time" and the like; and the reader obligingly treats the reported events as simultaneous. But the reader still *encounters* them serially. It is virtually impossible to convey the experience of simultaneity in a linear medium.

Authors, however, are not always willing to abandon the effort. And occasionally (though rarely) they almost achieve it. Look at 1 Samuel 1:12–13.[21] Hannah, distraught because of her barrenness and the disdain with which Peninnah, Elkanah's other wife, treats her, is praying to Yhwh at the sanctuary in Shiloh. Eli, the priest of the sanctuary, stands watching her. Because she is not speaking aloud, he does not realize she is praying. But he can see her emotional state, which he attributes to drink. There are, accordingly, two simultaneous but very different points of view involved, Hannah's and Eli's; and the narrator attempts to situate us in both at the same time. He switches back and forth between Hannah's point of view, with its focus on prayer and speaking, and Eli's point of view, with its focus on what the priest is seeing and thinking:

> (Hannah's viewpoint:) As she continued praying before the LORD
>
> (Eli's viewpoint:) Eli observed her mouth
>
> (Hannah's viewpoint:) Hannah was praying silently
>
> (Eli's viewpoint:) only her lips moved
>
> (Hannah's viewpoint:) but her voice was not heard
>
> (Eli's viewpoint:) therefore Eli thought she was drunk.

If we do not perceive an attempt to depict simultaneity, a passage like this can look terribly disorganized. Such passages are relatively rare in the Hebrew Bible. I have made a point of exemplifying it here because there is another example in the Ahab story, which I will indicate below.

EXPLORING THE STORIES

The Jeroboam Story

1. In 1 Kings 13:11–19 there is an alternation of narrative and dialogue. Look carefully at the narrative sections. Do some seem to move more slowly than others? (For example, compare 13:11–13 with 13:14. Do not try to *measure* the time—for instance, by asking, "I wonder how long it takes to saddle a donkey." Rather, monitor your own responses: "This seems to be dragging a bit . . ." or "This seems to jump rather quickly.") What has the narrator put into the text that evokes these feelings of delay or of speed for you? How do those feelings affect your experience of the story? Narrative usually takes less time to tell than to happen; dialogue takes approximately the same amount of time. How do the dialogues, which are the slowest parts of the passage, fit into the narrator's manipulation of time?

2. Find an example of description (that is, the action does not progress at all) in 13:27–30.

3. There is a flashback in Jeroboam's speech in 14:1–3 to something the reader already knows. What is the effect of reminding the reader of this here? (To put it another way, would the story be any different if the flashback were not there?)

4. Can you find any examples of foreshadowing in 12:16–19? What effect would they have on an ancient implied reader? Do you think that effect would be different if the ancient implied reader were Israelite or Judahite?

The Elijah Story

1. In 17:17–24 there is an alternation of narrative and dialogue. Look carefully at the narrative sections. Do some seem to move more slowly than others? (Do not try to *measure* the time—for instance, by asking, "I wonder how long it took Elijah to climb the stairs." Rather, monitor your own responses: "This seems to be dragging a bit . . ." or "This seems to jump rather quickly.") What has the narrator put into the text that evokes these feelings of delay or of speed for you? How do those feelings affect your experience of the story? Narrative usually takes less time to tell than to happen; dialogue takes approximately the same amount of time. How do the dialogues, which are the slowest parts of the passage, fit into the narrator's manipulation of time?

2. At one point in 17:5–7 the tempo of the narrative seems to stop almost completely for a few words. What effect does this have on you as a reader?

3. In 19:18 Yhwh's words contain a flashback to past information that the reader did not have. Does that information force you to revise your understanding of any of the previous story?

4. There are two narrative sections in 18:26–35: the actions of the prophets of Baal, interrupted by two speeches of Elijah (18:26–29); and the actions of

Elijah and the people, again interrupted by a few brief speeches (18:30–35). Which passage seems to move faster? How does the tempo of each passage shape the effect it has on the reader?

The Ahab Story

1. Trace the tempo of the narrative in 22:29–36. Where does it seem to move faster and where does it seem to move more slowly? (There is one example of flashback in the passage as well.) What effects do these manipulations of time and tempo have on you as a reader?

2. Find an example of pure description in 22:9–12. Is this simply background information or does it, perhaps, set a mood? Or can you perceive a deeper effect? (Hint: take a look at 22:19 before you answer.)

3. In 22:38 there is a flashback to an earlier prophetic prediction. Can you find the foreshadowing it may point to in chapter 21? Compare the foreshadowing to the fulfillment. Do they correspond accurately? What effect does this correspondence (or lack thereof) have on you as a reader?

4. Analyze 20:15–21 as an attempt to portray simultaneity in a linear, literary medium. (See the analysis of 1 Sam. 12:12–13 above for an idea of how to do this.) Do you see any difference between the two attempts to portray simultaneity? Do you respond to the two attempts differently?

Chapter 7

Gaps and Ambiguities

The preceding chapters have focused on the world of the story. (Refer back to p. 6, figure 1, to see the relationships among the worlds of the story, the narrative, and the text.) That is, they have described aspects of characters, events, and settings. In each chapter, although we have also examined the means the narrator uses to construct characters, connect events and pace their unfolding, and position readers within the world of the story, our attention has centered more on the story elements that the narrator creates by these means than on the means themselves. In the next few chapters we will step back a bit and focus more directly on some of the devices the narrator uses in *telling* the story. In other words, we will be more interested in the "world of the narrative," and in the dynamic that relates the narrator to the narratee. It is this dynamic, of course, that produces the story; and so our considerations will ultimately illuminate our experience of the story itself. But our attention will center more on aspects of *how* the narrator communicates than on *what* he communicates.

In this chapter we will examine two devices narrators use to layer multiple meanings within a single text. Perhaps more than any other narrative techniques, gaps and ambiguities offer the reader room to collaborate with the narrator in the creation of the story. But that means, as we shall see, that they also permit different readers to realize a story in different ways. In other words, the narrator supplies the reader with the *potential* for many variant stories; it is ultimately the reader who determines which of those variants to actualize.

GAPS

Every story has gaps. That is, every story leaves out an enormous amount of material that could have been included. Most of it is utterly irrelevant to the story; its absence has no effect. (What did Hamlet study when he was away at school in Wittenburg? It does not matter in the slightest; our appreciation of Shakespeare's play does not require this information.) Different cultures have different conventions about what gaps are important. Modern English-language literature makes extensive use of descriptions of characters and settings to imply characterization and to establish mood. As I mentioned in earlier chapters, physical description, particularly of characters, is rare in Biblical Hebrew narrative. We are told nothing of Solomon's looks, his height, or his mannerisms, all of which a modern author would probably use to suggest something of his character. The absence of this information from the biblical narrative is inconsequential.[1]

On the other hand, some gaps are indeed important. For convenience, we will consider such gaps under three headings: gaps of fact, gaps of motivation, and gaps of continuity. (There would certainly be other ways to categorize them. This is simply a rough-and-ready approach to the issue; but it will give us a chance to explore several aspects of the device.)

Gaps of Fact

Gaps of fact occur when the narrator withholds from us some datum that is crucial to our understanding of the plot. If the missing information is true, we should understand things one way; if it is false, we should understand them differently.[2] What are our options? Assuming we recognize the gap, we test both possibilities and extrapolate what each would mean for our understanding of the story. Sometimes we will opt tentatively for one reading, sometimes for another;[3] and sometimes we will try to keep our options open for the time being (though ultimately, if we hope to make sense of the story, we will have to choose). The narrator may or may not supply us with the information we lack at some later point in the narrative. If the narrator does, it will either confirm our tentative understanding or force us to reconstrue what we thought we had understood. If the narrator does not, then we might retain our understanding, but we can never forget its tentative nature.

A striking example of this sort of gap is found in 1 Kings 1:13. Nathan advises Bathsheba to tell David that he had at some past moment sworn an oath to put Solomon on the throne. Is that claim true? There is a strong argument that it is, since David will later seem to confirm having sworn such an oath (1:30). But of course this is not conclusive. David, feeble as he is, may not remember; he may simply have been swayed by Bathsheba's impassioned speech. Or, if we suspect that David is sharper than either Nathan or Bathsheba seems to realize, he may still have gone along with Bathsheba's ploy for his own private reasons. There are also arguments against the claim. The narrator says nothing anywhere in the David story, before or after this chapter, to tell us whether David ever uttered such an oath. Nathan's words are the first mention we have of it. And Nathan does not *remind* Bathsheba of the oath; rather he instructs her to remind David of it.

The crucial issue is that the narrator could easily have resolved the problem (for instance, by including an oath-swearing scene earlier in the story or by an aside to the reader),[4] but does not do so. The narrator therefore leaves a gap that we feel compelled to fill. If we accept as true the claim that David had once made such an oath, then we will understand David as having lost almost complete control of the kingdom. Adonijah is using his position as eldest surviving son to lay claim to the throne behind his father's back. Nathan and Bathsheba, then, are not only safeguarding their own interests; they are also acting to assure the moribund David's right to choose his successor. David's eventual reiteration of the oath both reclaims his authority and vindicates Nathan and Bathsheba. If we do not accept the claim as true, then our views of all three are considerably different. David has procrastinated seriously in not clarifying the succession[5] (a trait already characteristic of the David of 2 Samuel, and recalled by the narrator in 1 Kgs. 1:6 as well). Nathan and Bathsheba are engaged in a last-ditch palace intrigue to do an end-run around the heir presumptive. They believe that they can befuddle the old man (they probably imagine he is a bit senile), and so they elaborate a scheme to assure that power remains with their candidate. David's eventual concurrence with the alleged oath accomplishes their goal, but it opens a further gap. If David has never made such an oath, why does he say that he has? Have Nathan and Bathsheba succeeded in bamboozling a dotard, or does David have his own reasons for playing along? This is a gap of motivation.

Gaps of Motivation

Gaps of motivation are quite common in literature, since most people rarely express their motivations openly. Unless the narrator gives us a glimpse of a character's inner thoughts, we must infer a character's motivations from the context. Yet those motivations are often crucial for our understanding of the character and of the story. We have just raised one such example: If we assume that David never made the oath alleged by Nathan and Bathsheba, then why does he agree in 1:30 that he made it? The simplest explanation is that his mental faculties are at an ebb, just as Nathan and Bathsheba seem to believe. However, immediately thereafter, he shows himself alert to the situation, makes a firm decision, and demonstrates (as we shall see in chapter 10) a gift for elaborate rhetorical flair (1:33–34). Still later his final advice to Solomon (2:5–9) manifests a shrewd unscrupulosity that reminds us shockingly of the David who, at the height of his powers, engineered the secret murder of Bathsheba's husband, Uriah (2 Sam. 11:14–27). Such passages make it difficult to maintain that David is a dotard, and may require us to revise our thinking about David's motivation in 1 Kings 1:30.

We have already discussed at some length another example of a gap in motivation: When Adonijah seeks Bathsheba's support in his request for Abishag (2:13–18), why does Bathsheba agree to speak to Solomon about the matter? (See the fuller discussion in chap. 5.)

Gaps of Continuity

Finally, there are gaps of continuity. By this term I refer to places where there seems to be no logical connection between one passage (such as a speech or even a whole scene) and the next. From a historical-critical point of view, this often indicates a point at which two originally independent sources have been conflated. From a *literary* point of view, however, such an explanation—true as it may be in terms of the history of composition of the text—is unsatisfactory, because it denies the coherence of the text as a meaningful literary unity; and that coherence is axiomatic for literary criticism.

Gaps of continuity strike the reader at first as points of disorganization. The story does not seem to flow smoothly. At times the disruption is slight, and the reader can perceive the deeper continuity with a bit of reflection. This is particularly true of flashbacks and asides. In 1:6, for instance, the flashback to the way David had always treated Adonijah and the descriptive aside about Adonijah's looks and birth-order interrupt the story of how he anticipates an imminent succession to the throne (1:5 + 1:7). It is not difficult, however, to see the interruption's function in the text. It characterizes Adonijah as having long been overly indulged, and it draws parallels between him and his late older brother Absalom (see 2 Sam. 14:25 and 15:1), who rebelled against his father, David, in an attempt to usurp the throne and died in the battle that ensued.

At other times discerning continuity across the gap is more challenging. It is possible (and often tempting) simply to dismiss the matter as an example of inferior writing. This cannot be excluded as a possibility, of course; but to decide too quickly is to foreclose the possibility of discovering a more subtle meaning the narrator wishes us to ferret out from between the lines. Gaps of continuity can occur in the narrator's own words or in the speech of one of the characters. Let us look at an example of each.

In 1 Kings 10:1–13 we have the justly famous scene of the visit of the Queen of Sheba to Solomon's court. The story flows smoothly, climaxing in a royal exchange of gifts in 10:10 (the queen's gifts to Solomon) and 10:13 (Solomon's gifts to the queen). But this exchange is unexpectedly interrupted by two verses about the great wealth Hiram's fleet brought Solomon (10:11–12). Why are these two verses present at this point? Any explanation we may propose is completely conjectural since neither the narrator nor the author has left us a commentary on the story. On the other hand, to say that the narrator had *no* reason for what he did is equally conjectural. In other words, the reader must take responsibility here for actualizing one or another possible reading of the story. The first observation I, as a reader, would make is to note the parallels between 10:10 and 10:11–12.

10:10	10:11–12
120 talents of gold	gold from Ophir
a great quantity of spices	a great quantity of almug wood[6]
precious stones	precious stones
never again such spices	never again such almug wood

These parallels link the interruption about Hiram's fleet closely to its context in the Queen of Sheba story and highlight the importance of the queen's gifts to Solomon as a climactic moment in that story, especially since they echo the beginning of the story as well ("spices, gold, precious stones," 10:2). The story itself has two dominant motifs; Solomon's wisdom and ability to answer the queen's challenging questions (10:1, 3, 7, 8), and the opulence of Solomon's court (10:4–5, 7, 13). The theme of wealth and opulence dominates the larger context, and the parallels between 10:10 and 10:11–12 underscore that theme and give it the edge in the immediate story as well.

I would propose a further, somewhat whimsical effect that this interruption has on me as a reader. The remark about Hiram's fleet echoes 9:26–28, where Solomon has a fleet manned by sailors lent to him by Hiram; this fleet also collects gold from Ophir. And again in 10:22 there is mention of a fleet belonging to Solomon that sailed triennially, accompanied by a fleet belonging to Hiram; it too brought Solomon gold, as well as all sorts of exotic fauna. It is not clear whether these three passages all refer to the same fleet,[7] but is it too far-fetched to see in the isolated placements of these three passages in their context a playful allusion to the maritime wandering and sporadic appearances of the fleets in their home port?

Characters' speeches are usually relatively coherent. However, David's speech in 2:2–9 has long plagued commentators because it falls clearly into two parts distinguished by a startling difference in tone. In 2:2–4 David seems pious in the extreme; in 2:5–9, by contrast, he advocates convenient murder. Historical critics regularly treat the first part as "standard Deuteronomistic theology," and do not attempt to interpret it as part of David's dying advice to Solomon.[8] From a literary perspective, however, the question is whether it is possible to read the whole speech as a coherent statement instead of an editorial splice. It is, but the process reveals that, in David's mouth, the so-called Deuteronomistic piety becomes deeply cynical.

David's advice in 2:2–4 is indeed couched in typical Deuteronomistic language. (Compare, for instance, Yhwh's words to Solomon in 3:14; 6:12; and 9:4–5 for virtually identical vocabulary.[9]) Two points are worth noting, however. First, the purpose of the advice is Solomon's self-interest: "so that you may prosper in all that you do and wherever you turn" (2:3b). Second, *David's advice is all about following the letter of the law* ("statutes, commandments, ordinances, and testimonies, as it is written . . ."; 2:3a). Only when he quotes Yhwh's promise does he mention—without expressly advocating—internal adherence ("faithfulness, heart,[10] soul"; 2:4). It is not inconceivable that David is putting a pragmatic spin on his piety: "To prosper, you need to obey the [letter of the] law; beyond that, the prosperity of your successors will depend upon your inner devotion." In that light, 2:5–9 spell out challenges Solomon will face immediately and what he has to do to surmount them within the strictures of the law. He must rid himself of two enemies who pose threats to his rule, Joab and Shimei, both of whom David himself has reason to hate. But he cannot simply execute them arbitrarily; such a violation of the law could bring down Yhwh's wrath. So David's instructions are oblique: "Don't let him [Joab] reach a happy old age." In Shimei's case, the advice is only slightly more direct: "bring his gray head to Sheol with bloodshed." In both cases Solomon is urged to act with "wisdom" ("according to your wisdom," 2:6; "you are a wise man; you will know what you ought to do to him," 2:9). In the light of 2:2–4 this sounds like a reminder to act *within the law*, so that Solomon's own prosperity is not jeopardized. And in both cases David supplies Solomon with a basis on which to act without violating the letter of the law: Joab had committed unprovoked murder, and Shimei was guilty of lèse-majesté against David.[11]

AMBIGUITIES

Ambiguity occurs when a text can be understood and interpreted in more than one way. Ambiguity—at least as we are concerned with it here[12]—is essentially rooted in the language of the text. For instance, a word may have more than one applicable meaning or a phrase may be construed in more than one way grammatically.

Since ambiguity is basically a *linguistic* phenomenon, we must pause for a moment to consider some aspects of a linguistic procedure that lies between the (original) text and most readers of the Bible, namely, translation. Few readers of this book will regularly read the Hebrew Bible in Hebrew (and Aramaic); they are therefore dependent upon a translator to convey to them what the text means. But there is a deeper problem than that. *No one* today—no commentator, no translator—is a native speaker of ancient Hebrew. As a result, there are in our texts nuances of meaning, shades of emphasis, subtleties of grammatical construction, idioms, and elisions—all the fascinating paraphernalia of a living language—that are, we must assume, forever lost to us. So, when a translator encounters a passage whose meaning is not entirely clear to him or her, the first task is to make a prudential judgment. Is the lack of clarity due to the translator's own limited knowledge of ancient Hebrew, or would it have been perceptible to a native speaker of the ancient language?[13] In the first case, the translator will simply render what he or she considers the most likely meaning, and will footnote the problem for the reader. (See, for example, note *f* on 1 Kgs. 6:4 in the NRSV.) This is not a true case of ambiguity, since there is no reason to think that the ancient reader would have found the text unclear.

In the second case, however, things get more complicated, and the translator faces a second judgment call. When inherent ambiguity makes the text susceptible of different interpretations, what is the translator's responsibility—to disambiguate the text and deliver a single, clear meaning to the reader or to preserve the ambiguity and transmit it to the reader intact? Perhaps it is unfair to pose the dilemma so baldly. A translator translates for a particular public and must take the nature of that public into account in any such decision. Translations of the Bible are commonly made for liturgical or devotional purposes, usually in denominational contexts. In such settings, ambiguity is most often perceived as a flaw; readers desire clarity about "what the text means." And so translators typically choose what they judge to be the single meaning "most likely intended by the original author,"[14] and they render that meaning unambiguously in the target language.[15] In scholarly circles, however, an accurate rendering of the text would preserve, as far as possible, the same ambiguities in the target language as the text had in the original. In theory, this is desirable; in practice, at least in the past, even scholarly translators have felt duty-bound to "clarify" by disambiguating the original.[16]

The reader of a translation, therefore, is at the mercy of the translator in such situations. In at least some of the examples I cite below, most modern translations will have eliminated the ambiguity I am discussing. In those cases, I will try to explain as clearly as I can what the problem is in the Hebrew text and what its possible readings are; because of the translator's "clarifications," however, one or another of those readings may not appear reasonable in terms of the English text you have at hand.

Ambiguity is a complex and multifarious device. I will treat my examples under two headings: semantic ambiguities (where the words or phrases are capable of being understood more than one way) and syntactic ambiguities (where the grammar is capable of being construed more than one way). Even more than in the case of gaps, my categorization is one of convenience only. As we will see, there are quite different types of ambiguities in each category, and there are some cases that could be classified either way.

Semantic Ambiguities

Semantic ambiguity means that a word or phrase in the text can have more than one meaning. A clear example of this is when a single word has two entirely different meanings, but either of them could be appropriate in the context. In English, "the acolyte incensed the priest" could mean that the acolyte wafted scented smoke toward the celebrant, or it could mean that the acolyte seriously angered the priest. Double meanings like this are almost inevitably impossible to preserve in translation, since the target language will rarely contain a word that carries the same two meanings. Fortunately, such puns are relatively rare in Hebrew. When they do occur, however, they are most definitely *not* an exercise in humor; rather, they can be an attempt to imply a deep but hidden connection between two things that appear otherwise unrelated.

The closest example I can find to this in the Solomon story does not hinge on two independent meanings of a single word but on unrelated terms that *sound* almost identical. In Hebrew, the noun "king" (*melek*) and the verb "to reign" (*mālak*) come from the same root. (The verb would be best translated "to king" if we had such a word in English; the NRSV often renders it "to be king" or "to become king.") The noun *melek* appears frequently in 1 Kings 1, almost always in reference to King David. The verb *mālak* is a thematic word that occurs repeatedly in the central leitmotiv, "Who shall become king [that is, who shall *mālak*] after David?" (see 1:5, 11, 13, 17–18, 24–25, 30, etc.). Now look at 1:16. Bathsheba has entered David's presence to initiate the campaign to persuade him to name Solomon as his successor. David greets her with a standard, idiomatic Hebrew question that the NRSV renders, quite correctly, "What do you wish?" But the Hebrew idiom is, literally, "what is your [concern]?"; and the Hebrew phrase is *mah-lāk*! Aurally, it is probably[17] indistinguishable from *mālak*. With royal succession on her mind, Bathsheba is as likely to hear David say, "He has become king" (and wonder, "Who?"), as to hear, "What do you wish?" Note that this is not an ambiguity *for the reader*; it is an ambiguity *within the story world*, since it is Bathsheba, not the reader, who has to cope with two possible meanings.[18] But the Israelite implied reader would surely have appreciated the ironic possibilities of the wordplay.

Another sort of ambiguity surfaces when a word has a wide range of meanings and the narratee or reader is unsure which nuance to infer in a particular context. The Hebrew word *ḥokmāh* is usually translated "wisdom"; but that English word is much narrower than the Hebrew. In English "wisdom" is essentially a positive, admirable quality. In Hebrew the positive meaning is common; but *ḥokmāh* can also refer to a morally neutral idea like "artisanship" (see 7:14, where the NRSV renders *ḥokmāh* as "skill") and even to a morally shady quality like "cunning" (see 2 Sam. 13:3, where Jonadab, who devises the plan whereby Amnon is able to rape his half-sister Tamar, is called *ḥākām mĕ'ōd*, "very wise" [NRSV "very crafty"]). Since the story of Solomon presents "wisdom" as one of his key characteristics, it is revealing to examine how the term is used in his regard. Surprisingly, its first appearance with reference to Solomon is in the sense of morally dubious shrewdness (see 1 Kgs. 2:6 and 9). Later it appears as a very positive quality, the ability to govern well (3:12).[19] These disparate usages set the context for its appearance in 3:28, where "all Israel" reacts to Solomon's judgment of the case of the two harlots. Is the "wisdom of God" that is here attributed to him to be understood as a divine gift for insightful governance and decision making—therefore a positive quality—or as his use (misuse?) of the divine gift in a ruthless exercise of terror?[20]

Another example of this sort of ambiguity is found not only in the Solomon story but also frequently throughout the Hebrew Bible. The Hebrew verb *yāšab* (pronounced "yahSHAHV") has two different meanings.[21] It can mean "to sit," as on a chair or throne; and it can also mean "to dwell" in a place as in a residence. The meanings seem clearly distinct enough that the ancient Israelite would probably not have felt them to be identical and would have recognized the potential for ambiguity. So when Solomon celebrates that Yhwh has chosen to *yšb* in the temple Solomon built (e.g., 8:13, 27), even though the place he *yšb* is in heaven (8:30, 39, 43, 49), is he *equating* God's presence in the temple with his presence in heaven, or is he *distinguishing* the two? There is a serious theological issue here, since a God who *dwells* in the temple is at the beck and call of king and people; they always know where to find him. But a God who *sits* "enthroned upon the cherubim,"[22] as the common phrase goes, but whose throne is in heaven while the earth is his footstool, is in no way *contained* in a temple (compare Isa. 6:1). It is his pedestal on earth, but he remains sovereignly free.

It is also possible for the different senses of the term to be both appropriate and compatible. In such a case the reader may feel no need to choose between them, and can accept both meanings. (This device is a form of double entendre, and is more typical of the Bible's poetry than of its prose, but it occurs occasionally in prose as well. I find only one example in the Solomon story, but there are a few others in some of your exercises. I will use some New Testament passages as additional examples.) David's inability to "get warm" (1:1) is one example; as I suggested earlier,[23] it probably refers both to circulatory problems due to the king's old age and to the loss of sexual potency that renders him incapable of "knowing" Abishag (1:4).

Clearer examples, from other parts of the Bible, can be found in the Gospel of John, which delights in this sort of double-meaning language. For instance, look at John 11:50–52, where the narrator points out to us that Caiaphas's counsel of political expediency has a second meaning intended by God of which Caiaphas himself is completely unaware. Or consider the two meanings layered in Jesus' words in John 12:32, referring both to his crucifixion (as 12:33 makes explicit) and to the expansion of Christianity in the postresurrection period (a meaning that Jesus' hearers would have missed, but John's readers would have celebrated).

Sometimes the ambiguity lies not in the meaning of the word itself, but in a nuance of its usage. I mentioned above, in chapter 4, the ambiguity of Adonijah's statement, "I will be king" (1:5). Formally, the form Adonijah uses expresses a simple future ("I will be king [in the future, as soon as my father dies]"). But, just as in American English, that same form can also be used to express determination ("I *will* be king [come hell or high water]!"). There is no doubt that Adonijah is anticipating his imminent rise to the throne. What is unclear is whether he is simply awaiting it as a future development or deciding to take the throne immediately in the face of David's presumed incompetence. How the reader decides to read Adonijah's words will determine how he or she understands much of what follows: Is Adonijah's gathering at En-rogel simply a way to solidify his support among the influential, or is it a clandestine inauguration ceremony? Are Nathan and Bathsheba representing the situation accurately when they transform Adonijah's anticipation ("I will become king") into an unambiguous fait accompli (". . . *has become* king," 1:18, 25)?

Syntactic Ambiguities

In many cases the meanings of the words are clear, but the relationship between them (that is, the syntax of the sentence where they appear) is susceptible of alternative readings. Sometimes the ambivalent grammar is clarified by the time the sentence ends. In such a case, the ambiguity, though real, is only temporary; the grammar of a sentence will appear to make sense one way, but then will resolve itself in an unexpected direction. Often, though, the ambivalence remains, and the reader is left to choose between the possible ways of understanding the grammar.

A first example achieves ambiguity through its word order. Hebrew word order is quite unlike that of English. Hebrew can be much more flexible, and that flexibility offers opportunities for nuance and emphasis, as well as for (intentional?) ambiguity. Take 1:9b–10, for instance. A literal rendering of the Hebrew would be: "He invited all his brothers, the king's sons, and all the men of Judah, the king's servants, and Nathan, the prophet, and Benaiah, and the warriors, and Solomon, his brother, he did not invite." It is clear that the lengthy list of people between the two verbs includes both those invited and those not invited; but there is no indication in the Hebrew sentence where to draw the line between the two groups.[24] The reader is required to draw that line based on knowledge given in 1:7–8, where those who supported Adonijah are distinguished from those who did not.

Another example where the reader is required to reconstrue the grammar of the text retroactively is found in the Ahab story. (I hope those who are working through the exercises on the Ahab story will forgive me for stealing this example from their passage.) As you will have realized by now, Hebrew narrative is very strong on dialogue; often a scene is dominated by characters' speeches to the point where the narrator has very little to say at all. However, ancient Hebrew has no punctuation corresponding to quotation marks. And so, even when dialogue dominates, the narrator must signal the changes of speaker verbally. This is why each new speech is usually introduced with "and he said" or the like, where an English text can get by simply with closing quotation marks followed by opening quotation marks to indicate a change of speaker.

Now look at 20:33b–34; if you are using the NRSV, look especially at the translator's two notes on verse 34. A literal translation of the Hebrew would read: "So Ben-hadad came out to him and he made him go up into the chariot and he said to him the cities that my father took from your father I will return and markets you will establish for yourself in Damascus as my father established in Samaria and as for me I will dismiss you with a treaty and he made with him a treaty and dismissed him."[25] After the naming of Ben-hadad, all references to either king are pronouns. Who "said to" whom? Did the king of Israel speak first (as we would expect, since he as victor would claim the right to impose terms on the conquered Ben-hadad)?[26] It does not become clear until the word "Damascus" that in fact Ben-hadad has spoken first, and is offering his own terms. But then who offers to "dismiss" the other "with a treaty"? There is no indication in Hebrew that the speaker has changed, but it can only be Ahab speaking here.[27] (This absence of anything to indicate the change of speaker is a truly striking departure from standard Hebrew narrative grammar.)

It would be possible to dismiss all this simply as sloppy composition. But, as in the case of gaps, to do so without exploring the possibility that the fog of vague pronouns may have a purpose would be to foreclose in advance the chance of deeper meaning. As a reader, I am struck by the fact that Ahab, who was in vassalage to Ben-hadad at the beginning of the story (20:2–4), does not use his crushing defeats of Ben-hadad (20:21, 29–30) to subject his former master to the same sort of vassalage. On the contrary, when Ben-hadad's emissaries speak of him as Ahab's "servant" (20:32a), Ahab immediately counters that Ben-hadad is his "brother" (20:32b), an offer of equal status that Ben-hadad's representatives are quick to capitalize on (20:33). The story goes on to level other distinctions between the kings as well. Ahab brings Ben-hadad up into his chariot, that is, to a position on his own level, not one of subservience. Ben-hadad offers Ahab commercial rights in Damascus comparable to those Ben-hadad was already enjoying in Samaria—and there is no indication that Ben-hadad's presence in Samaria will be in any way diminished. All in all, the relationship between the two kings is growing so even that it is difficult to tell one from the other. The fog of pronouns enhances this effect: it does not much matter who says what to whom, or who does what to whom; Ahab and Ben-hadad, Ben-hadad and Ahab, it is tough to tell them apart. This, of course, implies a severe, though tacit, disapproval of Ahab, who, as king of the northern realm of Yhwh's people, ought to be preserving the *uniqueness* of Israel, not promoting its assimilation to the ways of pagan nations.

A pronoun is the key to another, much more unsettling example as well. The story of King Solomon's judgment between the two harlots (3:16–28) reaches a peak of tension when Solomon gives the order to divide the living child in two. The narrator tells us that the living child's mother was "moved with compassion" and offered to surrender her child to her rival in order to save its life (3:26). Her words are: "Please, my lord, give her the live baby; surely don't kill it!"[28] It is clear that Solomon recognizes that this woman is the living child's true mother, for when he renders his verdict he quotes her words almost verbatim: "Give her the live baby; surely do not kill it. She is its mother" (3:27a).[29] On first reading, we unhesitatingly assume that he awards the child to the woman he has discovered to be its true mother. But look at 3:26b. Between the true mother's plea for her baby's life and Solomon's verdict, we read, "But this one [presumably the other woman] said, 'Neither I nor you will have it; divide it!'" The other woman's heartlessness can blind us to the narrator's insidious use of a pronoun. What is the antecedent of "her" in Solomon's verdict? As the nearest preceding feminine noun, "this one" (the other woman) would seem to be the grammatical antecedent. Indeed, that is certainly the person "her" meant in the true mother's original statement, which Solomon is quoting. The pronoun forces an attentive reader to consider the disturbing possibility—even if only to reject it—that Solomon took the true mother's surrender of her child as resolving the dilemma and awarded the child to the other woman. (Notice how virtually all translators are aware of this ambiguity and try to protect the reader from it by replacing "her" in Solomon's speech with "the first woman" or something similar.)

HOW DO THEY WORK?

How do gaps and ambiguities work as narrative devices? What effects do they have that more complete and straightforward writing would fail to achieve? There are at least two. The first is fairly obvious: Gaps and ambiguities require the reader to put much more effort into *making sense* (that is, *creating the meaning*) of the story. This not only increases the investment of the reader in the story; it also makes the story that results in some measure a reflection of each reader's unique, personal approach to people and to life.

The second effect we might sum up in a phrase: "seeing double." Gaps and ambiguities require the reader to consider multiple possibilities for understanding a text. When the multiple ways of filling a gap or resolving an ambiguity are compatible with one another, the effect is a layering of meanings, and we cannot dismiss the possibility that the narrator wants us to accept some or all of them as valid simultaneously. More commonly, however, if the story is to have a coherent meaning for us, we must fill the gaps and resolve the ambiguities by choosing one possibility and rejecting the others. But even in these cases—and this is the crucial point—*we will have thought of the possibilities we reject, and rejecting them does not mean forgetting them.* We will always remain aware of them precisely as *possible* meanings that we have ruled out. Whenever we consider the story, there will be a counterstory in the back of our mind as an alternative. We may be utterly convinced that Solomon gave the living baby to the woman he knew was its true mother. The alternative is simply not believable. But it is not *unthinkable*. And so we can never entirely forget that we have wondered whether, . . . perhaps, . . . No! it *couldn't* be true!

For a less disquieting final example, look at the end of Bathsheba's audience with David in 1:22. Earlier, Nathan had told Bathsheba that he would approach David while she was still present with the king (1:14), and this is exactly what he does ("while she was still speaking . . . ," 1:22). What does Bathsheba do? Does she remain or does she leave? There is a gap in the text, since we are not given that information. Because the narrator does not explicitly say that she leaves, we are likely to see her as stepping into the background but remaining in the room. It is only several verses later, when David has her summoned (1:28), that we realize she must have left during Nathan's audience. The same thing happens at the end of Nathan's audience. The narrator does not mention that he leaves, but in 1:32 he too must be summoned back to David's presence. What is the effect of these gaps on a reader?

On the simplest level, the effect is that David and the reader will have different perceptions of the series of scenes. For David, the carefully choreographed entrances and exits keep Bathsheba's and Nathan's audiences distinct, despite their convergence on the topic of succession. Their agreement means that he sees two independent but concurring witnesses to Adonijah's behavior, which both witnesses portray as treason. However, since the reader learns of the exits only retroactively, the reader first imagines Bathsheba present for Nathan's audience and vice versa. For me as a reader, it is almost as though Bathsheba leaves the scent of a signature perfume in the room when she goes; though absent, she is present in a way that cannot be ignored. This reflects what I already know (but David does not know): that their identical topics and nearly identical words (compare 1:17–19 with 1:24–25, and especially the wording of 1:17 with that of 1:24) are a sign that they are speaking with one voice by prearrangement.

There is a deeper effect too, but we must expand our narrative horizons to appreciate it. In the past, David has acted as if there could be a clear separation between his private family affairs and issues of state policy. The so-called Court Succession story (2 Samuel 9–20) implicitly criticizes David for this attitude by demonstrating how David's failures as a father had serious political repercussions. That story begins with David's "private" acts of adultery with Bathsheba and the murder of her husband Uriah. It goes on to describe how Amnon (David's firstborn, the heir apparent) raped his half-sister Tamar (implicitly a parallel to David's crime of adultery); and it displays David's unwillingness to punish Amnon (a character flaw that appears again in the remark of our narrator in 1 Kgs. 1:6). Then it parallels David's crime of murder by recounting how Absalom (the full brother of Tamar and heir apparent after Amnon) murdered Amnon. Finally, it shows how Absalom based his rebellion and attempt to usurp David's throne on what he perceived as David's practice of injustice (2 Sam. 15:2–6). In our passage in 1 Kings, David's blindness to the political impacts of his negligence as a father is assaulted by the convergence of Bathsheba's and Nathan's apparently independent claims that now *another* son has risen up against him. That focuses David's attention on what he can only perceive as a conspiracy on Adonijah's part—even though he has only Bathsheba's and Nathan's allegations to that effect—and directs it away from what we readers know is a *real* conspiracy involving collusion by the two witnesses.

EXPLORING THE STORIES

The Jeroboam Story

1. There is an odd gap of fact in 11:30–32. Can you spot it? Does it strike you as significant for your understanding of the story?

2. In 14:5 Yhwh is about to tell Ahijah what to say to Jeroboam's wife. But the narrator does not allow us to hear the message; instead, he replaces the message with "thus and so." What effect does this gap have on you as a reader here, and as the story proceeds? (Think of it this way: If the narrator had told you at this point what Yhwh said to Ahijah, would the effect of the rest of the story on you be any different?)

3. Sometimes the two meanings of an ambiguous word or phrase are equally appropriate in the context, and entirely compatible with one another. In such a situation, there is no need to choose between the two meanings of the ambiguity. Allowing both meanings enriches our appreciation of the narrative (and, perhaps, of the author's cleverness). Look at 11:29. Can you find a phrase in that verse that, in addition to its plain narrative meaning in the context, has another, deeper sense that points forward to the story's later development?

4. A similar ambiguity occurs in 13:11–32, with the frequent description of the old prophet of Bethel as "the prophet who had brought him [the man of God] back" (13:20, 23, 26). To explore this question fully, we have to take a bit of a detour into some Hebrew (as we did with the verb *yšb* a few pages back). The common Hebrew verb *šwb* (pronounced "shoov") means, basically, "to come back, go back, return" (see 13:16, 17, 19, 22). It can also be used metaphorically in the sense of changing one's course of action, whether from bad to good ("to repent, be converted") or from good to bad ("to become apostate").[30] There is a form of this verb (technically called the "causative" form) that means "to *cause* [someone or something] to *šwb*"; this is often translated "to bring back," as it is frequently in our passage (13:18, 20, 23, 26, 29). In the light of the frequent use of the verb *šwb* in the story and of its variety of meanings, how many different but appropriate senses can you see for the description "the prophet who brought him back" (literally, "the prophet who caused him to *šwb*")?

The Elijah Story

1. There are two gaps of motivation in 1 Kings 19.[31] The first attends Ahab's report to Jezebel in 19:1. At least two different attitudes may motivate the report (see the discussion of question 3 under "Point of View" in appendix 2). Would these different motivations require you to understand Ahab's character differently? (Granted, Ahab does not appear again in the Elijah story; but since he is the main character in 1 Kings 20–22, the present passage could be pivotal for establishing a starting point for his character development in those three chapters.)

The second gap of motivation has to do with Elijah. Why does he go to Mount Horeb? At least superficially, there seems to be a contradiction between 19:3 (he flees to save his life) and 19:4 (he asks to die). More problematically, his complaints to Yhwh in 19:10 and 14 are identical (we will consider this aspect in the next chapter), and neither of them gives any indication of what Elijah wants from Yhwh. Can you conjecture any plausible motivation(s) for Elijah's journey? It (or they) should, insofar as possible, be able to explain all of Elijah's behavior.

2. Elsewhere (see appendix 2, n. 15) I explain that the words Elijah tells Obadiah to deliver to Ahab ("Elijah is here," 18:8) actually carry two completely different meanings in Hebrew: "Here is Elijah!" (*hinnēh 'ēliyāhû*) and "Look: Yhwh is my God" (*hinnēh 'ēlî yāhû*).[32] What differences in understanding the story does each reading produce? Are the two readings compatible or mutually exclusive? Do you find one reading more likely than the other? Do you see any way in which the second reading points forward to the contest on Mount Carmel?

3. Sometimes the two meanings of an ambiguous word or phrase are equally appropriate in the context, and entirely compatible with one another. In such a situation, there is no need to choose between the two meanings of the ambiguity. Allowing both meanings enriches our appreciation of the narrative (and, perhaps, of the author's cleverness?). Look at 18:6. Besides its plain sense, can you see another way of understanding this verse as alluding to something else about Obadiah and Ahab?

4. At the risk of stretching the definition of "ambiguity" to the breaking point, I would include here an example that is more properly called an "oxymoron," that is, a paradoxical or self-contradictory expression. Such a phrase challenges the reader to find some coherent understanding of terms that are, on the face of it, incompatible. We have a well-known example in 19:12, at the climax of Elijah's theophany on Mount Horeb: a "sound of sheer silence" (in the NRSV's brilliant rendering). The KJV's traditional "still, small voice" is equally good.[33] Using those two versions as a starting point, what images come to your mind for this peculiar manifestation? (In my remarks in appendix 2 I try to enrich the discussion with some input from the Hebrew as well.)

The Ahab Story

1. One gap of fact appears in 20:42. The prophet who confronts Ahab claims that Yhwh "had devoted to destruction" the defeated Aramean king Ben-hadad. But there is no clear evidence in the text that Yhwh has expressed such an intention, or that Ahab has been told of such a demand. (The situation seems comparable to 1 Kgs. 1, where the narrator gives no indication whether Bathsheba's claim that David had sworn an oath to put Solomon on the throne is true or false.) What different ways of filling the gap can you imagine? How does your appreciation of the characters change, depending upon which of these possibilities you accept? Do you see any evidence in the Ahab story that would sway you toward one or another of the possibilities?

2. Two gaps in 22:13–16 may be related to one another. Why does Micaiah, after protesting that he will say only what Yhwh tells him to say (22:14), utter the same untrue prophecy as the four hundred prophets (22:15)? And when Micaiah agrees with all the other prophets, why does Ahab disbelieve him and insist on "the truth" (22:16)? These might be considered gaps of motivation (Why?) or gaps of continuity, since in each case the speaker's attitude seems to be seriously at odds with his prior behavior. Can you think of any explanations for these two speeches that would preserve the coherence of each character?

3. Although there are several places in the Ahab story where translators differ in their understandings of the text (see appendix 3, n. 40, for two examples), these are not true ambiguities in the Hebrew text. The translators' uncertainty is due to the limitations of our knowledge of ancient Hebrew. The Hebrew would no doubt have been quite clear to the ancient reader. One verbal ambiguity—though of relatively small significance—is found in 22:24. Zedekiah ben Chenaanah, spokesman for Ahab's four hundred prophets, reacts with great hostility to Micaiah's claim that Yhwh intends to trick Ahab. He strikes Micaiah and asks him an insulting question. Precisely what does his question mean? Can you think of two slightly different ways of understanding it? (Hint: what exactly is the "spirit" Zedekiah refers to?)

4. There is one other noticeable verbal ambiguity in the text, though it generally disappears in translation. In 22:34 the narrator describes the archer who kills Ahab as drawing his bow *lĕtummô*. The word is problematic. It comes from the noun *tōm*, which has the basic idea of "completeness" or "wholeness." But *tōm* can be used in a more physical sense ("fullness"; see Isa. 47:9 [NRSV "in full measure"]) or in a moral sense ("integrity, innocence"; see 2 Sam. 15:11 [NRSV "in their innocence"]). Do you see different meanings for the passage, depending upon which sense of the term you apply? Do you prefer one over the other? Why?

Chapter 8

Repetition and Variation

This chapter, like the last, will consider a technique the narrator uses in telling the story. Like gaps and ambiguities, *repetition* enables the words of the text to convey layered meanings.[1] By itself, repetition establishes a link between two passages, potentially endowing each with new significance from its connection to the other. Then, once a context of repetition is clearly established, *variation* within that repetition can add still more facets to the meaning of a passage. As has been the case so often in earlier chapters, so also in this chapter, repetition requires a judgment call on the part of the reader: Does this particular instance of repetition enrich the passage? Repetition is not always surcharged with meaning; sometimes it is simply the most convenient or economical way to tell the story. But just as in cases of gaps and ambiguities, we should not prematurely foreclose the possibility that a repetition is offering us more meaning than first appears.

In what follows we will look at many different examples of repetition, with and without variation; and we will see a wide variety of effects it can produce. I do not claim that the following treatment in any way exhausts the possibilities. I simply intend to illustrate to you how to attend to instances of repetition on their own terms and in that way to be open to appreciating the potential of the technique.

For convenience I will consider repetition under two headings. The first I call "strict repetition." This occurs when the same event, speech, or piece of information is recounted more than once in the text, whether by the narrator or by one or more characters. The two (or more) passages are intrinsically linked because they both refer to the same story element. The identicalness of the referent makes the presence of repetition reasonable, though—as we shall see—not usually necessary. Most instances of meaningful variation-within-repetition are found in cases of strict repetition. The second heading will be simply "other repetitions"; in other words, instances where a repeated word, phrase, or idea establishes a link between two otherwise separate and distinct story elements. Here, because the referents are different, it is the repeated word, phrase, or idea itself that creates the link.[2]

STRICT REPETITION

When a specific piece of information or a particular event or a single speech is recounted more than once, we have a case of repetition in the strict sense. On the face of it, this sort of repetition would not seem especially remarkable, since two references to the same story element would naturally tend to use the same language. However, two characteristics of Hebrew prose style underscore the noteworthiness of such repetition. Since both are quite different from English prose style, we need to be aware of them. First, Hebrew narrative prose tends to be *laconic*. Excess verbiage is rare; and, on the face of it, repetition appears to be excess verbiage. When it occurs—at least when it occurs in any obtrusive fashion—it will draw the attention of anyone accustomed to the spareness of Hebrew style. Second (and perhaps paradoxically), Hebrew prose does not consider *verbatim* repetition a stylistic flaw, as English prose does. So, in situations where the Hebrew narrator does consider verbal repetition of earlier material warranted, he has no stylistic need to vary the terms in which that repetition is worded. Thus, to the degree to which the repetition calls attention to itself, it creates a setting wherein *variation* within the repetition can *also* call attention to itself.

In general terms, strict repetition (with or without variations) can happen in four different ways. Least common is for the narrator to give us the same information twice, in more or less the same words. Second, a character may speak, then part or all of the speech may be repeated later by the narrator. Third, conversely, the narrator may tell us something, and later a character will say much the same thing. Finally, one character may repeat part or all of an earlier speech (his or her own, or another character's) in a different context. And any of these forms of repetition, if they are obtrusive enough to be noticed, can incorporate variations.

In a moment, we will consider several examples of strict repetition with and without variations. But first we must examine two fundamental principles that will guide us as we interpret the examples. We start with the dependability of the narrator.[3] Unless there is clear reason to think differently, we take the narrator at his word—at least within the world of the narrative. When the narrator tells us something about a character, or when he tells us how such-and-such an event happened, we assume that the narrator knows what he is talking about and is portraying that character or event accurately.[4] In technical terms, the narrator in the biblical text is "reliable." Therefore, when we have two versions of something in the story, as a rule the narrator's version will set the standard against which any character's version must be measured.

The second principle is that, when a character speaks, his or her words must be evaluated in terms of the situation in which the speech is uttered. To whom is the character speaking? What response does the character seem to expect, or wish to evoke, from his or her listener? Any divergences between the character's version of things and the narrator's ought to be examined in the light of this context. Even when a character repeats the narrator's words exactly, the *accuracy* of the repetition gains meaning from the character's speaking context that it does not have when the narrator utters the words to the narratee.

Examples

Now let us look at some examples. I warn you in advance that some of these examples (and some of my readings of your practice texts, too) involve judgment calls on my part with which you may disagree—particularly in the interpretation of variations within repetition. It may seem, at times, that I am egregiously overreading the text. And I may well be. My rule of thumb is this. Given that Hebrew prose style does not object to verbatim repetition, I presume that the narrator has a purpose in mind when he varies the wording of the repetition. So if I can think of any plausible (to me) reason for a variation *other than* stylistic ornamentation (that is, variation just for the sake of variation, with no impact on the meaning of the passage), I will tend to prefer it. Only when I cannot think of any such alternative will I settle for stylistic ornamentation.

Narrator Repeats Narrator

In chapter 5 on point of view we looked at two examples where the narrator repeats material to signal to the reader that the narrator's words are actually expressing a character's point of view. From 1:3 we infer that Abishag is the beautiful girl the courtiers have sought. So when, in 1:4, the narrator repeats what we already know, namely, that Abishag is very beautiful, the narrator is actually showing us Abishag through David's eyes, to whom she has just been presented. Similarly, in 1:1, we learn that David is old and in 1:4 we learn that the beautiful Abishag is now his body servant (literally, "she served him"). So, when the narrator tells us the same things again in 1:15, we realize that we are actually seeing the scene through Bathsheba's eyes. She has just entered his room and is no doubt stunned to see how severely her king and former lover has aged and to see the nubile young woman standing at the king's side (literally, "was serving the king") where she herself once stood.

There is an intriguing example of the narrator repeating material in 2:12b ("his [that is, Solomon's] kingdom was firmly established") and 2:46b ("the kingdom was established in the hand of Solomon"). Although they are not identical, the two sentences are very similar, and the second seems to say approximately the same as the first. Why does the narrator bother to put both sentences into the story? At first glance, it is the *first* occurrence that is problematic; the *second* instance makes complete sense: Solomon has solidified his position as king by eliminating enemies. So why does the narrator tell us that "his kingdom was firmly established" *before* the king begins his purge?

To understand the effects of this repetition, we must distinguish the repetition itself from the variations the narrator has put into it. The repetition itself functions to structure the narrative. It is an example of "inclusion," a form of repetition that marks the beginning and ending of a literary unit or subunit. (We will look at inclusion in more detail in chapter 10.) Here it instructs the reader to read everything between 2:13 and 2:46a as connected. The intervening stories do not simply recount four events—the execution of Adonijah, the exile of Abiathar, the killing of Joab, and the execution of Shimei. They are to be read as a unified set with a coherent purpose. It is up to the reader to discern the continuity, but "Solomon's elimination of his enemies" is a pretty obvious inference.[5]

Of greater interest for our purposes in this chapter are the variations between the two sentences. There are two main differences, only one of which emerges in the NRSV. The two words translated "kingdom" have different nuances. In 2:12b the word is *malkût*, from the root *mlk*, "to be king"; *malkût* means "kingship" or "royal dominion." In 2:46b the word is *mamlākâ*, from the same root, and means "kingdom" or "realm." The two words are clearly related, but the first connotes "kingdom as a sphere of power" while the second connotes "kingdom as territory." The second difference is the shift from "firmly" (literally, "very") in 2:12b to "in Solomon's hand" in 2:46b.

How do these two variations offer new layers of meaning? We first observe that the intervening episodes all demonstrate Solomon's brutal use of power to eliminate people he perceives as threats. The narrative progression is from "Solomon's power [*malkût*, kingship] is secure" through "Solomon uses his power" to "Solomon's realm [*mamlākâ*, kingdom] is secure." But this does not necessarily mean that Solomon's *mamlākâ* was insecure before the bloodbath. A second progression is from Solomon's power being "very" secure beforehand to the kingdom being secure "in Solomon's hand" at the end. If we read this not as a change in the locus of power—after all, it was Solomon's power both before and after—but as a shift in point of view (2:12b represents a neutral, external point of view, while 2:46b represents *Solomon's* point of view), then the progression is from "Solomon's power is secure" through "Solomon uses power" to "Solomon feels secure." In this light, the narrator may well be suggesting that Solomon's high-handed acts—no matter how justifiable they might have been according to the letter of the law[6]—were motivated not by any real need to consolidate his grasp on the throne but by personal feelings of insecurity and vendetta against those who had not supported him.

Narrator Repeats Character

This is an extremely frequent device. It occurs when a character utters a speech and the narrator later uses the same or similar words to describe a subsequent event that corresponds to the character's speech. Very often the character expresses some sort of desire for action on the part of another character: gives a command, urges a course of action, implores God for a favor, or the like. Another common occurrence is when the character announces a future event, particularly when a prophet makes such an announcement in God's name. The narrator then repeats words from the character's speech to describe the compliance with the command, the carrying out of the action, the answering of the prayer, or the fulfillment of the prophecy.

Note, first of all, that such a repetition is completely unnecessary. The narrator has several ways to avoid it. He can, for instance, elide the fulfillment entirely. In 1:28 David commands, "Summon Bathsheba to me." The narrator does not tell us that anyone actually "summoned Bathsheba" but simply that "she came into the king's presence." Or the narrator can even elide the character's speech. In 2:46 the king commands Benaiah, but what the command is we are not told; we infer it from Benaiah's actions: "he went out and struck him down." Either way, we understand that the command is both given and carried out, though we hear its content articulated only once.

Sometimes, however, the narrator will repeat part or all of the character's words in recounting their fulfillment. Here, as so often, the reader is faced with a judgment call. Is the repetition obtrusive enough that it would have drawn the attention of an ancient Israelite implied reader? If both command and narrative fulfillment are very simple and brief, or the extent of the repetition is very limited, it probably would not.[7] Likewise, even if the speech is lengthy and complex but the narrative fulfillment is selective and abbreviated, it may be nothing more than the narrator's way of implying that the fulfillment corresponded to the speech. See, for example, 2:36, where Solomon gives Shimei a triple command: (1) build yourself a house in Jerusalem; (2) live there; (3) do not go out from there. Shimei's obedience is captured in a single clause: he "lived in Jerusalem many days" (2:38). By drawing on each element of Solomon's order ("lived" corresponds to Solomon's second command, "in Jerusalem" to the first, and "many days" implies a lengthy period of conformity to the third), the narrator manages to suggest Shimei's obedience to all three commands without undue repetition.

On the other hand, when the speech is lengthy and the narrative fulfillment repeats it beyond due measure, the repetition should draw the reader's attention, since such repetition is not necessary simply to recount action. It falls to the reader, then, to decide what additional significance the repetition might imply. For instance, in the case of a command, a prayer, a prophecy, or the like, repeating the speech verbatim to describe the fulfillment can imply the letter-perfect conformity of fulfillment to speech.[8] In the case of a command, this contributes to characterization by emphasizing the meticulous obedience with which the command is carried out. In the case of a prayer, it demonstrates the full providence of divine favor (which is both a direct characterization of the Deity and an indirect characterization of the one who uttered the prayer). In the case of a prophecy, it demonstrates both the precision with which God fulfills his word and the validity of the prophet's credentials.[9]

I find only one clear example of this sort of exact repetition in the Solomon story, though there are a number of others in the Jeroboam, Elijah, and Ahab stories. In 2:18 Bathsheba tells Adonijah, "I will speak to the king about you"; in 2:19 the narrator tells us that "Bathsheba went to King Solomon, *to speak to him about Adonijah.*" Bathsheba's promise is carefully noncommittal.[10] This continues the attitude she has displayed throughout Adonijah's audience with her. Notice her guarded "Go on" in 2:14, 16; she is no more revealing of her thoughts and feelings in 2:18. The narrator too withholds any indication of her intent. By repeating her words without variation, the repetition focuses attention on the noncommittal character of Bathsheba's words and thereby builds some narrative tension: What is Bathsheba planning?[11]

Another instance occurs in the first chapter of 2 Kings. In 1:10 Elijah utters a sort of prophetic warning: "If I am a man of God, let fire come down from heaven and consume you and your fifty." The narrator does not simply tell us something like, "And so it happened." He says, "Then fire came down from heaven and consumed him and his fifty." The lengthy verbatim repetition is unmistakable. It implies that the relationship between Elijah the prophet and the God for whom he speaks is so intimate that when Elijah urges God to a particular course of action, the Deity responds with unwavering precision.

When the narrator repeats a character's speech, variation within the repetition is not uncommon. Here the possible meanings are manifold. For instance, the narrator may simply wish to highlight some aspect of the situation that it would not have been appropriate for the character to mention. Or the narrator may be suggesting that the fulfillment itself was less than (or more than) what was specified in the terms of the original speech.

For a first example, look at Nathan's words to Bathsheba in 1:13: "Come, go in to King David."[12] When Bathsheba follows Nathan's advice, the narrator tells us that she "went to the king *in his room*" (1:15). What does the phrase "in his room" add to our (or at least to *my*) understanding of the scene? First, it reminds me of David's physical condition. The description in 1:1–4 is of someone moribund and probably bedridden (this will be confirmed in 1:47)—therefore probably confined to his private chambers. Second, it reminds me of Bathsheba's own backstory. She is the woman for whom David committed adultery and murder (2 Sam. 11), and whom he "consoled" after the child of their adulterous encounter died (a "consolation" that, significantly, produced Solomon: 2 Sam. 12:24). She is no doubt very familiar with the king's private chambers. Yet she is no longer the king's preferred companion and has probably not been to his room for some time. By mentioning the room, the narrator eases me into Bathsheba's point of view, seeing the king's room as Bathsheba sees it, with the beautiful young Abishag standing solicitously behind the old man.[13]

There is a much more ambitious example later in 1 Kings 1. In 1:33–35 David addresses a lengthy series of directives for Solomon's anointing to "the priest Zadok, the prophet Nathan, and Benaiah, son of Jehoiada." In 1:38–40 those worthies carry out the commands. There is a complex weave of repetitions and variations in the passage, of which we will consider only one. David tells the three officials to "take with you the servants of your lord"; when the three officials comply, they are accompanied by "the Cherethites and the Pelethites." (The "Cherethites and Pelethites" were mercenary troops of non-Israelite blood that served as David's private guards; they were under Benaiah's captainship.) Benaiah interprets "the servants of your lord" to mean the king's private, non-Israelite armed guard. His precautions suggest that he anticipates danger in the endeavor to anoint Solomon. He may well be aware that a large number of Adonijah's supporters are gathered at En-rogel, less than half a mile south of the Gihon spring. The question the narrator's variation leaves open is, "Are these the 'servants' David has in mind?" If so, then David too is aware of the danger. But he may simply mean "courtiers" in general (compare "servants" in 1:2) as witnesses to the legal transfer of power. In this way, the narrator underscores Benaiah's familiarity with the tense political situation without revealing David's level of awareness.

Character Repeats Narrator

Once we learn something from the presumably reliable narrator, any repetition of the same information by a character is inevitably compared to the narrator's version. If the character repeats the narrator's words accurately, then the reliability of the character—at least in that situation—is confirmed. (The reliability of a character in one speaking context is, of course, no guarantee that he or she will be equally conscientious in another.) Variations in the character's speech, however, do not necessarily *disconfirm* reliability. They simply invite the reader to speculate on the character's motives for using different terms. The character, of course, does not know what the narrator said; the narrator's words are spoken only later, when the narrator tells the story to the narratee. So the precise question should not be, Why did the character change the narrator's words? but, Why did the narrator not coordinate his words with the speech he gave the character? Often the differences will contribute to characterization. The contribution may be positive; for instance, the character may diverge from the narrator's words out of modesty. Or it may be neutral: the character may simply be unaware of parts of the information the narrator has revealed to us or may know the information from a different point of view. Or, indeed, it may be negative: for the sake of deception, the character may intentionally misrepresent facts that the narrator has revealed to us more accurately.

I find no examples of repetition of this sort *without* variation in the Solomon story. But there is a complex example of repetition *with* variation that involves two characters' speeches repeating information the narrator has already given us. Compare the narrator's words in 1:9–10 with Bathsheba's words to David in 1:19 and Nathan's in 1:25–26. All three describe Adonijah's gathering at En-rogel, but each character puts a different spin on the description.

1. Both Bathsheba and Nathan describe the animals Adonijah has sacrificed as "abundant"; the narrator does not describe them that way. This would give David a stronger impression of the significance of Adonijah's gathering than the narrator's words gave us.[14]

2. Both Nathan and Bathsheba omit the location of Adonijah's gathering, which the narrator specified in 1:9. I have no convincing explanation for their omission, and can only guess about motivation here. Perhaps they did not wish to supply extraneous details that might distract David—who, after all, they already think is a bit dotty—from their main point: they want him to name Solomon as his successor.

3. Both Bathsheba and Nathan supply David with lists of people Adonijah has and has not invited to his gathering. In agreement with the narrator, both list "all the king's sons"[15] among the invited. However, where the narrator simply generalizes that Adonijah invited "all the royal officials of Judah" (literally, "all the men of Judah, servants of the king"), Bathsheba specifies that he invited "the priest Abiathar" and "Joab, the commander of the army." The participation of such prominent people adds weight to what she has just insinuated, namely, that Adonijah's gathering is actually a premature inauguration ceremony intended to usurp David's throne. At the same time, it avoids any suggestion that Adonijah has widespread support among "all the royal officials." Hearing Bathsheba's version, David can easily envisage a rash act on the part of his spoiled son (don't forget 1:6!), urged on by two highly placed courtiers who have the power of religion and army behind them, and who hope to become Adonijah's éminences grises. Nathan's version also names "the priest Abiathar"; but instead of naming "Joab, the commander of the army," Nathan simply says "the commanders [sic] of the army."[16] In this way, Nathan subtly confirms the accuracy of Bathsheba's information (and thus supports the "conspiracy theory" she has already intimated); but he does not echo her words quite closely enough to alert David to the fact that the convergence of Nathan's information with Bathsheba's is the result of collusion.

4. The list of the uninvited is much more specific in the narrator's version, enumerating one group ("the warriors") and three individuals by name. Bathsheba, as the distraught mother, appropriately mentions only one uninvited person, her son Solomon—to whose name she adds the description "your servant," asserting his loyalty. Nathan, the court official, lists all three uninvited individuals named by the narrator (though he leaves out "the warriors"[17]), and adds a new name, Zadok the priest, thereby countering the presence of Abiathar among the invited. And he surrounds the whole list of the uninvited with an aura of loyalty by beginning and ending it with "me, *your servant*," and "Solo-

mon, *your servant.*" Thus he suggests that the uninvited are David's *true* servants and implies by contrast that Adonijah and his followers are not. Since the goal of the two conspirators is to get Solomon installed as king, Nathan's mention of "the priest Zadok" can also lead David's thinking in the direction of a ceremony of royal anointing, which would, in effect, mean Solomon's *immediate* accession to the throne as coregent.

Character Repeats Character

In cases where one character speaks and the words are repeated in a later speech by the same[18] or another character, the context of both speeches is crucial to understanding the significance of both the repetition and any variations within it. As when a character repeats the narrator, the repetition is often a means of characterization and a basis for inferences about motivation.

Let us look once more at a scene we have considered several times: Bathsheba's speech to David in his private chambers. Nathan has already scripted her speech for her (1:13). But when she delivers it (1:17–18), she makes some notable changes in Nathan's script. First, Nathan advised her to ask a question of David ("Did you not, my lord the king, swear . . ."); Bathsheba takes a more direct and confrontational tone: "My lord, you swore. . . ." And she increases the weight of her charge by adding that David's purported oath was "by Yhwh your God"—her claim is that David took his oath *in Yhwh's name*, but has not fulfilled it. Given the likelihood that the implied reader is familiar with the Decalogue, this is tantamount to accusing David of "making wrongful use of the name of Yhwh your God" (Exod. 20:7)—a charge Nathan did not (or did not dare?) suggest. A few words later, she again changes Nathan's more reticent question ("Why has Adonijah become king?"[19]) into an assertion: "Adonijah has become king." And both Nathan's question and Bathsheba's assertion are repetitions of a still earlier character speech, Adonijah's "I will be king" in 1:5, with one significant variation. Adonijah used the Hebrew imperfect tense, roughly equivalent to an English future; both Nathan and Bathsheba use the Hebrew perfect tense, roughly equivalent to an English past tense. So what Adonijah uttered in anticipation, the two conspirators claim is already a fait accompli.[20]

While it is not impossible that all of these changes could be dismissed simply as due to Bathsheba's inability to get Nathan's instructions right, it is more satisfying to note, first, that each and every one of her modifications of Nathan's script puts greater pressure on David than Nathan's more roundabout approach would have. This is a woman who knows David well. She knows just how and when to push his buttons. So we infer that Bathsheba may not be the passive, flat character who had only a cameo role in 2 Samuel. Here she shows signs of becoming a strong, complex character who knows how to get what she wants and is willing to take risks to get it.

A second, more subtle example of character repeating character also stars Bathsheba. We have already commented on how noncommittal she is when

Adonijah comes to her with his request for the late king's concubine, Abishag. Adonijah dithers incoherently for a long time, but in essence his request is, "I have one request to make of you; do not refuse me.... Please ask King Solomon—he will not refuse you—to give me Abishag the Shunammite as my wife" (2:16–17). When Bathsheba conveys Adonijah's wishes to Solomon, she begins, "I have one small request to make of you; do not refuse me.... Let Abishag the Shunammite be given to your brother Adonijah as his wife." There are four changes. Bathsheba describes the request as "small"; she omits Adonijah's flattering "he will not refuse you"; she uses the passive to describe Abishag's "being given," rather than specify that *Solomon* would give Abishag; and she describes Adonijah as "your brother." Are these changes innocent?

At first glance, it can seem so. None of the changes modifies Adonijah's request in any substantial way. They are precisely the sorts of changes one might expect when one person repeats another without any serious attempt to do so word for word. However, as readers we must not forget that the text in our hands is an artifact and that every word of it is the (presumably deliberate) choice of an author. The author created a narrator, and the narrator relates to the narratee that the second character did not speak in the same words as the first. It behooves us—especially in view of the verbal deftness Bathsheba manifested in our last example—to explore the possibility that here too she has a hidden agenda.

Before we look at the changes, there are two cultural facts that the implied reader would have been aware of, but that most modern readers are not. First, in the royal court of Jerusalem the queen mother held a particularly important official role. She was called *haggĕbîrâ*, or "The Lady," and certainly acted as one of the king's counselors; it is likely that her influence was particularly strong in palace affairs, such as governance of the harem. Thus Adonijah approaches her not simply because she, as Solomon's mother, would be an effective intermediary, but also because, as *haggĕbîrâ*, she may wield some degree of authority over Abishag's destiny. Second, it was customary for the new king to inherit the harem of his predecessor, just as he inherited everything else pertaining to the throne. (See, for instance, a prophetic rebuke to David that is explicit about his inheritance of Saul's harem: 2 Sam. 12:8.) Adonijah's request for Abishag, therefore, is ambiguous and potentially loaded. Is he simply asking for some sort of consolation prize, now that he has formally surrendered his claim on the throne; or, on the contrary, does he seek a former member of the king's harem as a way of surreptitiously maintaining that claim alive? (This is how Solomon will take the request: see 1 Kgs. 2:22.)

Given that background, Adonijah's request is anything but "small." And if Bathsheba is as astute as she seemed to be in her audience with David, isn't it likely that she knows this request brings Solomon precisely the ammunition he needs to eliminate his rival—and that she is confident Solomon will react exactly as he does? When I read Bathsheba's words in 2:20, I hear "small" in an ironic tone of voice, and I see a look of utterly false innocence pass between mother and son. Behind it all I perceive a gleeful subtext, "We've got him now!"

Her omission of Adonijah's flattery ("he will not refuse you") is proper behavior for a courtier addressing the king. (But note how the narrator cleverly transfers the words to Solomon's mouth: at precisely the correct moment, he interrupts her to say, "I will not refuse you"!) Bathsheba's other changes to Adonijah's request simply ice the cake. She does not ask Solomon to "give" Abishag (since, presumably, the king could have done so on his own authority, but then there would have been no basis for imputing disloyalty to Adonijah); instead, she asks that Abishag "be given," focusing attention on Adonijah's desire, rather than on Solomon's power to grant it. And she deftly reminds Solomon that Adonijah is his "brother"—in fact, his *older* brother—and therefore has an equal, if not better, claim to Solomon's throne.

OTHER REPETITIONS

"Other repetitions" is rather a miscellaneous category. I mean by it simply those instances of repeated words, phrases, or ideas where the appearances of the repeated terms do not point to a single narrative element (the same speech, event, character, or the like) but to different narrative elements. This sort of repetition seeks to forge in the mind of the hearer or reader a link between two otherwise independent referents and to invite the hearer or reader to discern some additional meaning in their juxtaposition. The examples that follow are intended only to sample some of the effects this technique can produce.

Examples

Leitwort and Leitmotiv

A repeated word or phrase can become thematic for a passage (the technical term is "leitwort" for a single word or "leitmotiv" for a phrase or concept). This is not difficult for us to grasp, since the same technique (sometimes called "key word") occurs in English literature as well. Nor is it particularly demanding on the reader or hearer. The recurrence of the term drives home the centrality of the idea it expresses. For example, the word "gold" runs through 1 Kings 9:26–10:25 (fifteen times in twenty-eight verses) to emphasize that Solomon's *wealth* is a central issue in this passage. Similarly, the word "wisdom" (in a wide range of senses) appears frequently throughout the Solomon narrative, and identifies one of the overarching motifs of the whole story. The phrase "shall succeed me as king and shall sit on my throne" sums up the crucial dramatic tension of 1:1–53 (see its many and varied repetitions in 1:13, 17, 20, 24, 27, 30, 35, 46, 48).

Analogy and Allusion

Another type of repetition appears when two independent scenes, events, or characters are linked allusively, so that the reader is led to see similarities between them and to interpret one in the light of the other. In earlier chapters

I have already mentioned some examples from 1 Kings 1. The description of David's view of Abishag ("the girl was very beautiful," 1:4) recalls David's similar reaction to seeing Bathsheba bathing ("the woman was very good-looking," 2 Sam. 11:2[21]). The allusion contributes to David's characterization—as decrepit as he is, he still has an eye for feminine beauty. And it may hint (though I am going out on a limb here) that, in the court intrigue, Abishag is Bathsheba's counterpart (as Benaiah balances Joab and Zadok balances Abiathar). Could Abishag have been a partisan of Adonijah, insinuated into David's intimacies to whisper her patron's name in the king's ear?

A second example appears in the next few verses. Adonijah is described in terms that allude to (and even explicitly invoke) his late older brother Absalom (see 1:5 [compare 2 Sam. 15:1] and 1:7 [compare 2 Sam. 14:25]). These allusions inevitably raise in a reader who is aware of them questions like, Is Adonijah attempting to usurp the throne as Absalom did? and Will Adonijah be killed for appearing to oppose the king as Absalom was?

Echo

A more subtle and easily overlooked link by repetition occurs when a single word or phrase—one that is particularly noticeable, usually because of its rarity—appears in two different contexts. If the two passages are close together, the repetition may be relatively unobtrusive. However, if the two passages are at some distance from one another, it will take a fairly attentive reader or hearer to perceive the echo between them; in that case, the word or phrase will likely stand out as memorable. There is one complex example in the Solomon story that combines both of these possibilities. In 5:4 (= Hebrew 5:18), Solomon writes to Hiram, "Now Yhwh my God has given me rest on every side; there is neither adversary nor misfortune." Solomon's claim seems reasonable; after all, the narrator has just told us that, under Solomon's leadership, "Judah and Israel lived in safety, from Dan [the northern border] even to Beer-sheba [the southern border], all of them under their vines and fig trees" (4:25 [= Hebrew 5:5]). The word "adversary" (*śāṭān*[22]) is quite uncommon in the Hebrew Bible. But it occurs three more times in the Solomon story (and never again in 1–2 Kings): in 11:14 we learn that "Yhwh raised up a *śāṭān* against Solomon," Hadad the Edomite; in 11:23 we learn that "God raised up another *śāṭān* against Solomon," Rezon of Damascus; and in 11:25 we learn that Rezon "was a *śāṭān* of Israel all the days of Solomon." The repeated echo of that rare word in the narrator's remarks in chapter 11 invites us to compare the two passages. When we do, we realize that Solomon's letter to Hiram was painting a false picture. Solomon is either trying to deceive Hiram or is perhaps deceived himself. In either case, it reflects badly on a king supposedly outstanding for his "wisdom." A similar, though perhaps less severe, criticism of the king is hidden in Solomon's use of the term "misfortune" (*pegaʿ rāʿ*, literally, "evil stroke") in the same sentence. In its verbal form, the root *pgʿ* ("to strike, smite") is fairly common in Hebrew; but in 1–2 Kings all of its occurrences are in 1 Kings 2. It appears five times to describe Benaiah's executions of Adonijah (2:25), Joab (2:29, 31, 34), and Shimei (2:46).[23] The effect of the echo on the alert reader is to invite an ironic comparison of what happened to those who opposed Solomon's accession with Solomon's blithe claim that his reign is free of any "evil stroke." Given the brutality of Solomon's proceedings in chapter 2, such a claim is disingenuous of him, to say the least.

EXPLORING THE STORIES

The Jeroboam Story

1. In the scene of Rehoboam's negotiations at Shechem (12:1–20), the most prominent (and most interesting) repetition occurs when Rehoboam repeats the speech the youngsters supplied, but leaves out the first sentence (12:10–11, 14). I discuss this as an example of characterization (see appendix 1, p. 140). However, there are other examples of repetition in the same passage. Some of them may carry what I have called "layered" meanings. How many examples of repetition can you find? In each, determine who is repeating whom, and whether there are any variations in the repetition. Do you think there is any hidden meaning to be wrung from any of them?

2. In the discussion of plot in appendix 1, I show how the narrator's repetition of 12:30–31 in 13:33–34 functions to create an inclusion around the two intervening stories so that they can be read as having a coherent sense: despite both of those intervening events, Jeroboam did not change his ways (see pp. 135–36). Now look more closely at 12:30–31 and 13:33–34 and notice the variations between the two. Do any of those variations seem to convey additional important meanings?

3. The prophetic credentials of the man of God from Judah are confirmed twice in the first story about him. The narrator tells us of a sign he gave (13:3) and tells us, in exactly the same words, that the sign was fulfilled (13:5); the narrator also tells us that, through the man of God's intercession, Jeroboam's request for healing (13:6a) was granted fully (13:6b).[24] However, narrative fulfillment of the man of God's principal prophecy (13:2) does not occur until much, much later, in 2 Kings 23:20, where it is recounted with only minimal variations.[25] On the other hand, that narrative fulfillment now includes 2 Kings 23:19, "Josiah removed all the shrines of the high places that were in the towns of Samaria." There is a corresponding prophetic announcement for this verse, too, to be found in the Jeroboam story. Can you locate it? How does it affect your reading of the passage where it is found in 1 Kings? (Do not worry about apparent variations in this case; they are due to the translator and not found in the Hebrew.)

The Elijah Story

1. There are numerous places in the Elijah story (especially in chap. 17) where a character expresses a command, wish, or prayer, and the narrator recounts the fulfillment in very similar terms. See how many of these pairs you can find in chapter 17. Are there any variations in the fulfillment accounts? Do any of those variations strike you as particularly significant? In the light of that frequent pattern of repetition, consider the variations in the pattern in 18:19–20 and in 18:41–42. What do those variations suggest to you?[26]

2. One of the most striking repetitions in the Elijah story is the narrator's description of Obadiah in 1 Kings 18:3b–4 and Obadiah's own repetition of that information in 18:12b–13. I discuss how the narrator's words effect characterization in appendix 2 (p. 168). How does having Obadiah repeat the same thing add to our appreciation of his character? There are also minor variations in Obadiah's repetition. How would you interpret those variations?

3. In the section on characterization I also speak of Elijah's two complaints in 19:10 and 14 (see appendix 2, p. 166). But since the second complaint repeats the first verbatim, it adds nothing to the content of the complaint. What significance do you find in the *fact* of the repetition, rather than in its content? (Hint: What happens in between the two complaints?) Furthermore, each complaint is in response to an identical question, the first uttered by Yhwh, the second by "a voice." Do you think the two questions mean the same thing?

The Ahab Story

1. In 20:3 Ben-hadad's messenger delivers a message to Ahab, and in 20:5 the messenger claims to repeat the same message, but there are significant differences. What are they, and what meaning do you find in them? The same message is quoted a third time a couple of verses later. Are there any significant variations in this further repetition of the message? How do you understand them?

2. A similar situation exists in chapter 21, where the original conversation between Ahab and Naboth (Ahab's words are in 21:2, Naboth's in 21:3) is replayed in several different contexts. First, try to locate all of the places where elements of that conversation reappear and whose voice is uttering the repetition. Then identify the differences in each case, and determine which of those differences reveal something about the context in which it occurs. (Use the NRSV as your basis. I do the same in my comments in appendix 3. But in my comments I also explain why I disagree with one element in the NRSV translation and what difference my disagreement makes to understanding the repetitions and variations.)

3. The most striking and obtrusive instance of repetition in the Ahab story is surely the account of Jezebel's letter and of how the elders of Jezreel carried out its scheme (21:8–13). There are several variations in the repetition; do any of them strike you as adding extra meaning to the passage? There is also one

repeated word that, once one notices it, seems odd indeed in one of its contexts. Can you spot it and suggest why it might be there? (Hint: think of the appearances of the uncommon word "adversary" [śāṭān] in the Solomon story and how its occurrence in chap. 11 enriches the meaning we find in 5:4 [= Hebrew 5:18]. The word here in chapter 21 is equally uncommon, and its immediate repetition calls attention to it.)

Chapter 9

Voice(s) of the Narrator

Everything we have discussed in the last several chapters has involved the activity of the narrator. It is the narrator who tells the story to the narratee and, via the narratee, to us. The narrator presents characters in their various roles and varying depths, shapes the narratee's spatial and temporal relationships to the events of the story, and leaves gaps to be filled and ambiguities to be resolved. These things are what the narrator *does*, but who exactly is this figure that does them? How are we to understand the narrator and his role in the complex communication act we diagrammed in chapter 1 (see p. 6, figure 1)?

THE VOICE THAT TELLS THE STORY

In a word, the narrator is *the voice that tells the story*. The simplest way to explain that statement is to begin with an example from a modern novel. Herman Melville's *Moby-Dick; or, The Whale* opens with one of the most famous lines in American literature: "Call me Ishmael." With those words, the narrator of the story of Captain Ahab and the white whale identifies himself as one of the crew who sailed on Ahab's ship, the *Pequod*. At some unspecified time after the events he narrates took place, he tells the story of those events to an unspecified audience (the "narratee"). In technical terms, Ishmael is a "first-person" narrator, because he narrates a story in which he himself participated, and so he can say things like "*I* said such-and-such," and "*I* did thus-and-so."

The identity of a "first-person" narrator is usually clear,[1] and it significantly shapes the story. It privileges the point of view (both physical and moral) of one particular character; and it limits what the narrator can recount to information available to that character. However, many narratives, ancient and modern—and, indeed, almost all biblical narratives—are not first-person narratives. The voice that narrates them does not belong to one of the characters and, in fact, is often not identified at all. The opening words of 1 Kings are: "King David was old and advanced in years." Whose voice are we hearing? Who tells the narratee (and us) this? The narrator is anonymous; in essence, he is nothing *but* the voice that tells the story. Some commentators call this an "impersonal narrator," because the voice is not identified with any specific individual. However, this can be misleading. It could suggest that the narrator is something inanimate, almost like a mechanical device designed to play back a talking book. But someone who reports events in which he or she is uninvolved is no less personal than a participant in them is. It is better, then, to speak of this sort of anonymous voice not as "impersonal" but as a "third-person" narrator. Such a narrator tells a story about others, a story in which he himself does not appear; and thus he talks only of "*he* said such-and-such" and "*she* did thus-and-so."[2]

Qualities of the Narrator

In the last chapter I spoke of the biblical narrator as "reliable." With some qualifications that we will discuss in a moment, this means that when the narrator gives the narratee information about characters or events, we can assume that the information is true.[3] When the narrator tells us that Adonijah is handsome (1 Kgs. 1:6), we accept that Adonijah really is handsome (in the story world, of course). When the narrator recounts the conspiratorial dialogue between Nathan and Bathsheba (1:11–14), we assume that the narrator's account is correct and the speeches he records are accurate—and, therefore, that the narrator's point of view is omniscient; after all, the conspirators' conversation was surely private!

One qualification on the narrator's reliability is that he is not obliged to tell all he knows. What he says is reliable; but, as we saw in discussing flashbacks and gaps, he can withhold relevant information from the narratee and thereby, perhaps, mislead by omission. However, unless there is some reason to suspect such misdirection, our working assumption should be that the biblical narrator's information is both reliable and adequate to understand the story.

A second qualification concerns not the *information* the narrator gives us, but the *attitude* with which he presents it. The narrator is not neutral. Even when he is not himself a character in the story, he has a vested interest in telling it. (People do not tell stories for no reason at all!) It is important to him. He has a perspective on the characters and events that he desires the narratee to share. And, as the preceding chapters have shown us, he employs a whole arsenal of strategies to persuade the narratee to the response he desires. His purpose—whether it be moral exhortation, ideological propaganda, or even simple entertainment—shapes the way he tells the story. Even when the narrator presents his story as a straightforward telling of history,[4] it will be (as is all recounting of history) colored by the subjectivity of the historian, who makes moral judgments about the characters and their deeds, understands the cause-and-effect connections between events in a particular way, and deems certain people and events more significant than others. In other words, even as historian the narrator is engaged in the business of convincing the narratee (and us) that the values and opinions he espouses reflect reality better than others do. The presumed reliability of the narrator's *information* does not guarantee that his *opinions* are infallible. We may well accept the former and still have reservations about the latter.

A third qualification on the narrator's knowledge and reliability we will discuss at greater length below. Essentially it is this. The author, of course, knows the entire story he or she intends to write; when the author creates a third-person narrative voice, he or she can endow that narrator with omniscience.[5] But the author can also choose to limit the knowledge even of a third-person narrator. In that case, the story as the narrator tells it may be skewed or incomplete. Generally speaking, the clearest sign in the biblical text of the presence of a limited narrator is seen when the narratorial voice imparts conflicting information in different places.[6] (See the section below on "Multiple Narrative Voices.")

The Narrator and the Narratee

The biblical narrator's primary function is to tell the story to the narratee. As I suggested in the first chapter, this activity is best thought of as oral storytelling; a useful analogy would be a parent telling his or her adult child about events early in the parents' marriage (though the parent, naturally, would be a *first-person* narrator of those events). In telling the story, the narrator makes use of all the evocative techniques we have already explored to shape the narratee's response to the story as it unfolds. One might say without exaggeration that the narrator's job description is to *manipulate* the narratee.[7]

But storytelling is not the whole of the narrator's business. Imagine a father reminiscing to his daughter about his first date with her mother: "Oh, she was lovely that night. She wore her mother's pearl earrings—I think she still has them somewhere...." Notice the last words. They do not refer to the *story world*, in which the parents' first date was taking place, but to the *present* of the narrator and narratee. The narrator (the father) has stepped out of his storytelling role to say something directly to the narratee, something that is related to the story but not precisely part of it. The technical term for this is "breaking frame"; in other words, the narrator's words "break out" of the box called "story" in our earlier diagram (see p. 6, figure 1) and address the narratee directly.

Breaking frame can serve a number of purposes and have a number of effects on the narratee (and on us). In the example above, the father's words establish a link between this past event and the narratee's present, a link that takes the form of an existing pair of earrings that the narratee may have seen her mother wearing. The story suddenly gains new dimensions of concrete realism and of present and personal relevance to the narratee (it may even encourage her to hope to inherit the earrings in her turn). Biblical narrators often do the same thing. For example, in 1 Kings 8:8, after the priests have carried the ark of the covenant into the new temple's innermost sanctuary, the narrator says that the ark's carrying poles "could not be seen from outside," but "they are there to this day."[8] In other words, he assures the narratee that, even though the dedication of the temple and installation of the ark happened long in the past, and even though the narratee can no longer see the evidence of the ark's presence in the temple, it is still there "today."[9]

In other cases, the narrator will break frame to *comment* on something in the story, often with an implied or explicit evaluation.[10] In 1 Kings 1:5 the narrator introduces Adonijah and his ambition; then in 1:6 the narrator comments that "his father had never at any time displeased him by asking, 'Why have you done thus and so?'" The implication is that Adonijah's callow attitude toward his imminent succession to the throne is due, at least in large part, to David's failure as a parent to teach him discipline and responsibility. Another example is the narrator's allusion in 2:27b to an earlier story, that of the condemnation of the house of Eli of Shiloh in 1 Samuel 2:33; by recalling the story here, the narrator supplies a theological justification for the exile of Abiathar.[11]

As a narrative device, breaking frame has two main, mutually reinforcing effects on a narratee (and on a reader). First, it interjects material not immediately pertinent to the development of the plot—information for the narratee's consideration, moral evaluations for the narratee's agreement (or disagreement), comments that make the story of the past more immediately relevant to the narratee's present, and so on. All of these effects *distance* the narratee from the narrative action (for the moment, What happens next? becomes a less pressing question) and invite reflection and judgment. Second, breaking frame foregrounds the presence of the narrator much more than is the usual case in biblical narrative. The voice that tells the story has suddenly emerged from the background and spoken out on its own. This reminds the narratee that he is *listening to a story*, not witnessing something that is actually happening at the moment. And that in turn reinforces the first effect by affording the narratee (and the reader) leisure to undertake the reflection and distance to make the judgments the narrator is urging.

The Narrator and the Author

One corollary of what we have said so far is that *the narrator is not the author*. This is easily seen in the case of a first-person narrator such as Ishmael in *Moby-Dick*: Ishmael is not Herman Melville.[12] It is less easily seen, but no less true, in the case of a third-person narrator. Our almost automatic inclination to identify a third-person narrator with the author is a consequence of the narrator's anonymity. Without any obtrusive character traits, the narrator becomes virtually transparent. We tend to see through the narrator to the author and to attribute to the latter the works of the former. But this is a confusion. If you look back to the diagram in chapter 1 (see p. 6, figure 1), you will see that the narrator resides *inside* the narrative, where he *tells* the story to the narratee; the author (whether the "implied author" or the real author) is outside it, and *writes* the narrative text for the reader. To recall the distinction we made in chapter 1, the narrator inhabits the secondary world, the world of the narrative, in which the story happened; the author inhabits the primary world, the world in which we read the text. What this means, simply, is that the narrator, even when anonymous and transparent, is a figure within the narrative the author writes and is, therefore, just as much a creation of the author as any character in the story.

The distinction between narrator and author implies that the author can create any sort of narrator he or she chooses to create. It is certainly possible—even common—that an author will create a narrator more or less in the author's own image; but it is not inevitable. A male author might well create a female narrator, or vice versa; or a human author could in principle create a nonhuman narrator.[13] Differences like those, of course, are evident only when the narrator is not anonymous and transparent. But even an anonymous, third-person narrator can differ from the author in one significant way: the author can create a narrator whose opinions and values the author does not share. This is the structure of various sorts of subversive writing, the most common of which is irony. The author creates a narrator who mouths one political or ideological viewpoint or speaks from within one value system; but the author simultaneously subverts the narrator's point of view in subtle ways.[14] Needless to say, identifying such subversions calls for equal subtlety on the part of a reader (and not all readers will agree to the identification).[15]

For an example, look at 1 Kings 5:12a (= Hebrew 5:26a). The narrator tells us that "Yhwh gave Solomon wisdom, as he promised him." But this is an unnecessary repetition of information given us several times already (3:12, 28; 4:29–31 [= Hebrew 5:9–11]; etc.). What is the point of repeating it here? Note first that this sentence immediately follows three others where the main verb is "to give": "Hiram *gave*[16] Solomon . . ." (5:10 [= Hebrew 5:24]); "Solomon *gave* Hiram . . ." (5:11a [= Hebrew 5:25a]); "Solomon *gave* Hiram . . ." (5:11b [= Hebrew 5:25b]); "Yhwh *gave* Solomon . . ." (5:12a [= Hebrew 5:26a]). The four sentences belong together; they form a set. Now look at what was given in each case. Hiram "gave" (that is, "sold") Solomon all the cedar and cypress wood he needed for his temple and palace complex. This was, no doubt, a considerable quantity of a natural resource for which Hiram's kingdom was justly famous; but it would certainly not put any severe pressure on Hiram's timber reserves. Solomon, on the other hand, "gave" (that is, "paid") Hiram roughly half of the amount of wheat he received in tribute from his whole empire,[17] plus a substantial quantity[18] of the purest and most expensive olive oil.[19] The narrator adds, almost like an afterthought, "Solomon gave this to Hiram year after year," then reminds us that "Yhwh gave Solomon wisdom." At first, this seems like a compliment to Solomon's shrewd business sense, implying that he got the better of the bargain with Hiram. But when we take seriously the steep price Solomon pays "year after year," and we come to learn later that Solomon's building projects took twenty years (9:10) and that eventually Solomon was actually constrained to cede territory to Hiram (9:10–11), we may find ourselves asking, Was Solomon's contract with Hiram really so wise after all? Then, recalling the narrator's words that "Yhwh gave Solomon wisdom," we might wonder whether the author was whispering at the same time, "but Solomon sure didn't use it!"

Multiple Narrative Voices

Once we recognize that the narrator's voice need not be identical to the author's, a further possibility opens up for the author's ingenuity. Let us return to the analogy I spoke of before, where the narrator-narratee relationship takes the form of a father telling his daughter about her parents' first date. Put the mother in the picture as well. We now have *two* narrators telling the story. They will almost certainly agree on the main lines of the event, but their points of view will not be identical, nor will their memories of the details. Their voices will usually be in unison, sometimes in harmony ("Oh, and I remember *you* wore that horrid green tie!"), and sometimes they will clash ("No, my mother's earrings were garnet, not pearl"). The narratee will have to navigate the differences between the voices and try to bring concord where there is discord; ultimately, however, some differences may be unresolvable.[20]

There is nothing to hinder an author from writing a narrative in this mode, with multiple narrative voices.[21] Some modern works use the device very effectively. A few biblical literary critics have proposed such readings for some biblical narratives as well.[22] Their results reveal much greater complexity in our biblical texts on at least two levels. First, the narratee (and the reader) must negotiate the variances between narratorial points of view without recourse to a single, normative, "reliable" narrator. So details of the story itself may become uncertain, and the narratee (and the reader) is again faced with ambiguity. In this case, however, the ambiguity is not merely a function of the slipperiness of language, as it was when we considered it above in chapter 7; rather, it is rooted in the author's decision to present the story through narrators whose reliability is limited. Second, and more importantly, the recognition of conflicting narrative voices definitively thwarts any attempt by the reader to identify the narrator's voice with the author's. In order to discern an *authorial* "meaning,"[23] the reader must take seriously the multiplicity of voices—characters' as well as narrators'—that the author found needful in order to achieve his or her purpose. This means not only listening to each voice but weighing the narratorial witnesses against one another, making judgments about their respective agendas, and—tentatively at least—privileging one narratorial viewpoint over another.[24]

Exploration of biblical narrative in terms of multiple narrative voices is a fairly recent development in biblical studies, and it can be dauntingly abstruse. I will limit myself to one relatively clear example, simply to illustrate how the technique can be used. Since I cannot find any good instances of the device in the Solomon story, I will again borrow from the Ahab story.

In 1 Kings 20:1–34 the narrator presents Ahab quite positively, and there is no suggestion in the text that this positive portrayal is intended to be subversive or ironic.[25] Ahab is threatened by his overlord, Ben-hadad of Aram, for no discernible reason. His first responses are respectful, even when they refuse Ben-hadad's attempts at extortion. Ahab consults representatives of the populace before undertaking a dangerous course of resistance. He is supported by his people and encouraged by prophets of Yhwh, who assure him of victory and even advise him in Yhwh's name about military strategy and tactics. He obeys Yhwh's commands meticulously and wins the promised victories.

In contrast, the narrative voice in 20:35–43 is entirely negative toward Ahab. The prophet who condemns him is a true bearer of the divine word (this is the point of the bizarre little episode in 20:35–36); so we are expected to credit his claim that Ahab's release of Ben-hadad has offended Yhwh. Yet nowhere in 20:1–34 is there the least suggestion either that Yhwh told Ahab to hold Ben-hadad prisoner or that Ahab was ever anything but obedient to Yhwh's wishes. The contradictory attitudes toward Ahab in 20:1–34 and in 20:35–43 invite us to treat the two attitudes as reflecting contrary opinions on the part of discrepant narrators, one favorable toward Ahab, the other critical of him. However, the two narrative voices are not on a par. The story in 20:1–34 could stand alone; the story in 20:35–43 is meaningless without 20:1–34 as its premise. Therefore, the narrative voice that tells us the story in 20:35–43 is aware of the story in 20:1–34 *and speaks to counter it*.[26] In this way the author privileges the negative voice over the positive one.

We must take all of these factors into account in any attempt to infer the *author's* attitude toward Ahab. The authorial judgment on Ahab is carefully nuanced. According to our implied author, Ahab's reign was, in political and military terms, a time of great success, reflecting divine blessings. From a vassal state subordinated to a more powerful neighboring kingdom, Israel emerged, under Ahab's leadership, to a position not only of independence but of noble and generous hegemony over its former overlord.[27] Nevertheless, the author cautions us, there was a tragic failure hidden behind the political and military successes. Even if Yhwh blessed his people with victory during Ahab's day, Ahab's relationship with Yhwh was not without flaws.[28] And those flaws would eventually undo Ahab himself and, ultimately, the people of Israel.

We can even conjecture a bit more than that. Since the negative evaluation of Ahab is presented as a corrective to the positive one and stands as the final word in the chapter, the author seems to be giving it the privileged position of a "Yes, *but*..." rejoinder. We may, then, suspect a bit of polemic in the authorial voice, as if the view of Ahab it expects to find in the implied reader is, on the whole, positive, and the implied author wishes to move the reader to reconsider that position. On the other hand, the author simultaneously weakens the negative evaluation of 20:35–43 by not verifying the prophet's claim of Ahab's disobedience. It would have been the simplest thing in the world for the author to have included in 20:1–34 a scene where a prophet instructs Ahab to imprison or execute Ben-hadad. Compare, for instance, the very similar situation in 1 Samuel 15, where Yhwh's command to Saul is explicit in 15:5. The author chose not to do so, and in this way invites us to wonder about the prophet's claim in 1 Kings 20:42.[29] Even if the prophetic condemnation of Ahab proves true, the prophet may have misrepresented the divine *motive* for that condemnation. In this way the author suggests that even if, in the last analysis, his evaluation of Ahab is more negative than positive, his reasons are not necessarily to be found in a simplistic reading of one of Ahab's political decisions.

EXPLORING THE STORIES

The Jeroboam Story

1. The two passages on death and succession (11:41–43 and 14:19–20) are obviously parallel to one another. (Almost every king's regnal account from here to the conclusion of 2 Kings will end with a passage like this.) Whose voice are you hearing here? Do you think this is a narrator or would you attribute these words to the implied author? The words clearly contain *information*; do they also contain *opinion or evaluation*? What effect does this sort of passage have on you as a reader?

2. There is a particularly odd statement in 13:3, though the oddity does not come through well in the NRSV, which smooths the translation a bit. I would render the first words of the verse: "He had given a sign that same day, saying. . . ."[30] Translated this way, does the verse strike you as part of the story or as an example of breaking frame? Does it fit smoothly into the narrative context?

3. There is an obvious example of breaking frame in 12:15. What effects does this verse have on you? Does it have any effect that you suspect it would *not* have on an ancient Israelite implied reader?

4. Find another frame break in chapter 12, one that relates the events of the Shechem story to the present of the narrator and narratee. What attitude or opinion does this frame break seem to impute to the narrator? Do you sense any tension between that attitude and those the narrator seems to hold earlier in the chapter? If so, is the tension severe enough to speak of conflicting narrative voices? And if there is tension, can you see your way to a coherent, unified authorial meaning that can account for the different views?

The Elijah Story

The narrator is usually in the background in biblical narrative, but this is especially true in the Elijah story. I find only a few places where the narrator comes clearly enough to the fore to be remarked upon. Consequently, there are few questions I can draw out of the Elijah story on this topic.

1. Can you find a place in the last part of the episode in 17:8–16 where the narrator's presence becomes just a bit more noticeable than usual? It is not exactly a frame break, since it fits more or less smoothly into the flow of the narrative, but the words are unnecessary and hardly develop the story at all. Can you suggest any function these apparently unnecessary words may fulfill?

2. In appendix 2 I examine the repetition of 18:3b–4, with variations, in 18:12b–13 (see pp. 177–78). One variation is that, where the narrator says that Obadiah revered Yhwh "greatly," Obadiah says that he revered Yhwh "from my youth." I suggest there that Obadiah's change from the narrator's term of intensity to his own term of duration could be interpreted as modesty. However, there is another way to look at this variation. One can ask why the *narrator* chose to use a different word in his descriptive flashback than the one he attributes to Obadiah. What do you think?

3. There is one other clear example of a frame break in the Elijah story, but we have already discussed it and its interpretation at some length in an earlier chapter. Can you find the frame break I have in mind? (Hint: it is somewhere in the scene atop Mount Carmel, 18:21–40.)

The Ahab Story

1. Almost every king's regnal account from the Solomon story to the conclusion of 2 Kings ends with a concluding formula like that in 22:39–40. Whose voice are you hearing here? Do you think this is a narrator or would you attribute these words to the implied author? The words clearly contain *information*; do they also contain *opinion or evaluation*? What effect does this sort of passage have on you as a reader?

2. One of the clearest frame breaks in the Ahab story is 21:25–26, where the narrator levels explicit negative evaluations against Ahab and Jezebel. Read the two verses carefully. Do they present a single, smooth, coherent opinion? Does their evaluation of the actions of Ahab and Jezebel fit coherently into the literary context of chapter 21?

3. Because Hebrew has no markers of direct discourse like quotation marks, it is sometimes difficult to tell whose voice we are hearing. In 21:20–22 clearly Elijah is speaking, and 21:25–26 are equally clearly the narrator's words. But who is speaking in 21:23–24? Are these the last words of Elijah's speech or the first words of the narrator's intervention? Either reading is possible, and neither is entirely without strain. What clues can you find to support assigning these words to Elijah? What clues support their assignment to the narrator? What effect does this uncertainty have on you as a reader? If one reads 21:23–24 as narratorial, how coherently do they fit into the literary context of chapter 21?

Chapter 10

Structure and Symmetry

Consider the page you are reading. It contains all sorts of communication devices besides the words themselves. There is punctuation—dashes, commas, a semicolon, and a period just in this sentence alone—to indicate several sorts of syntactic relationships between words, phrases, and sentences; there are paragraph indentations to signal the beginning of new units of thought that may contain several sentences each. There is a major heading at the top of the page to mark *this* chapter as treating a significantly different issue from other chapters. And in the course of the chapter you will find multiple levels of subheadings to indicate thematic units of text smaller than chapters but larger than paragraphs.

Now consider ancient Israelite society and its texts. Although some Israelites were literate, they would have made up a very small minority in the population, an educated elite comprising a class of professional scribes, probably a limited number of administrators attached to the temple or royal court, and perhaps an even more limited number of upper-class citizens with the time and interest to learn such esoteric skills as reading and writing. Texts in such a society were not only precious—being handwritten, they were labor intensive—they were also not produced for a popular readership. Most texts—at least most narrative texts—would have been read aloud to hearers by someone literate. But hearers would not be aware of inaudible signals like the typographical ones mentioned above. The reader may well have indicated the ends of sentences by vocal inflection, as we do in English. But how would the reader signal larger thematic units—comparable to paragraphs, sections, and chapters—to hearers? A listener would be able to discern the beginnings and endings of such units only if they were evident from the *wording* of the text.[1]

In recent years some scholars have sought to discern how the verbal fabric of the Bible's narrative texts may have signaled thematic units to their hearers. It is becoming increasingly evident that ancient Hebrew narrative has its own repertory of structural devices, and that they are quite different from the visual devices used in later written literature, and especially in *printed* literature. But there is much still to be done in this area of study; and so we must be aware that, to this point, most results remain more or less tentative. This chapter will look at some of the more plausible conclusions such studies have reached.[2]

Before we begin, consider one more text: your Bible. It is, no doubt, a modern translation, printed with several typographical features—paragraph indentations, headings either at the tops of the pages or inserted into the text, and chapter and verse numbers. From what I have said above, you will readily surmise that none of these visual signals forms part of the original biblical manuscripts. Paragraph indentations and thematic headings in particular are modern creations, inserted by translators and differing (sometimes considerably) from translation to translation.[3] They represent, therefore, the interpretive judgments of modern translators; they are not the work of the ancient biblical authors. Since most Bible translators are scholars who are familiar with the ancient languages and texts, their judgments are worth considering; but they are not inspired or infallible. They possess no more intrinsic authority than the interpretive readings of other competent readers.

REPETITION AND ORGANIZATION

In chapter 8 we considered some of the ways the narrator can use repetition to evoke a response from the reader. In addition to that effect, repetition can also serve a structural function by establishing a link between two separate points in a text. Links between passages can indicate the limits of a unit of text either by marking its beginning and end or by organizing its subunits into a discernible pattern. Since such structural units and subunits are often, if not usually, also *thematic* units, discerning the organization of the text is an important step in understanding and interpreting it.

There is a loose but necessary correlation between the repeated elements that form such links and the size of the units they connect. Since those links function only when they are perceived by the listener, the first instance of the repeated element must be memorable enough to be recalled (at least subconsciously) when the second instance appears.[4] Small units of text—a phrase, a sentence—might be marked by something as simple as a repeated syllable or two. Longer units—a passage several verses long, for instance—will require a repeated phrase or, perhaps, the repetition of a particularly unusual word or grammatical construction. As units become still longer—a whole biblical chapter, or several chapters (like the whole Solomon story in 1 Kgs. 1:1–11:43), even a whole biblical book—the repeated elements that organize them will have to be quite notable; in such cases repetition or contrast of a situation or a topic[5] is often the most effective way of forging a link.

The student must be aware of two practical problems in this regard. The first is that translations often cannot capture such repetitions. Particularly when the link is based on repeated *sounds*, it will almost inevitably be lost. And links based on repeated words or phrases will be lost unless the translator takes pains to reproduce them in the target language.[6] The second problem is that *thematic* links (such as repetition or contrast of situation or topic) that do not also use repeated words or phrases call for caution on the part of the reader. That such links are present in our texts is certain.[7] But without clearly repeated vocabulary the modern reader must take care not to impose echoes on the text that the ancient implied reader would not recognize. For example, in 9:10–14 Solomon is visited by a king with whom he has an exchange of goods—cities for gold—but the relationship seems strained; in 10:1–13 Solomon is visited by a queen with whom he has an exchange of goods—gifts for gifts—and the relationship seems harmonious. Is the similarity between these two situations structurally significant? (Without going into details, let me simply say that my study of the Solomon story does not find any such structural significance.) On the other hand, in 3:4 Solomon offers sacrifice at Gibeon; in 3:15 he makes offerings in Jerusalem. There is only a single word common to both verses, *'ôlôt*, "burnt offerings"; this is an almost negligible echo between verses this far apart. But the theme—extravagant sacrifices—and the detail of a place name in each verse are also elements that link the two verses. (On the function of these two verses as a foreshadowing, see p. 61. Note also how they serve to frame the episode of Solomon's dream at Gibeon.)

SYMMETRY

Links forged by repeated elements can structure a text in different ways. The principal technique in Hebrew prose seems to be that the subunits marked by the repeated elements are arranged symmetrically.[8] More important than the simple fact of a pattern, however, is that the particular type of symmetry involved can indicate a particular *interpretive* thrust for the passage.

Inclusion

The simplest pattern is one where the repetition marks the beginning and end of a literary unit. We can symbolize this by *aXa'* where *a* and *a'* indicate the repetition that marks the beginning and end of the unit, and *X* represents everything in between. This is called an "inclusion."[9] The interpretive payoff here is that, by marking a unit's boundaries, the inclusion directs the hearer or reader to think of everything contained within it as having a unified meaning. Often this is obvious. In the example cited just above, 3:4 and 3:15 form an inclusion around the single episode of Solomon's dream at Gibeon; the narrative unity of the episode is evident. Look, however, at the echo of 2:12b ("his kingdom was firmly established") in 2:46b ("the kingdom was established in the hand of Solomon"). There are several episodes between those two sentences: Adonijah's request for Abishag, which led to his death (2:13–25); the exile of Abiathar (2:26–27); the execution of Joab (2:28–34); the appointments of Benaiah to replace Joab and of Zadok to replace Abiathar (2:35); and Shimei's elimination after he falls foul of Solomon (2:36–46a). The inclusion urges us to see all of those separate events as part of a single, coherent process by which Solomon undertook to eliminate opposition to his rule and to consolidate his grip on David's throne and empire.[10]

Inclusion can take different forms. In 3:4, 15 and in 2:12b, 46b, the inclusive element is more or less independent of the material it surrounds. It forms a frame like that around a picture or, perhaps more accurately, like the paired punctuation—such as dashes, parentheses, or brackets—that simultaneously sets apart and unifies part of a sentence. It is equally possible for the repeated elements to form an integral part of the unit they surround. Take, for instance, Nathan's speech to David in 1:24–27, which begins and (almost)[11] ends with the words "my lord the king." This is precisely the sort of rhetorical flair one would expect from a highly placed royal adviser. Moreover, the words call attention to the very issue Nathan is raising: *Who* is really the king? Is it David, who (Nathan allows, though he knows better) may have acted without informing Nathan; or is it Adonijah, who (Nathan plants the seed in David's mind) may be in the process of usurping David's power? Still more, by this phrase Nathan professes loyalty to David ("*my* lord the king") and to whatever David has decided—a profession that we, who know of Nathan's conspiracy with Bathsheba, will recognize as duplicitous.

Another sort of inclusion can occur when two or more units in a row are in some sense parallel. In that case, the author may signal their parallelism by marking the beginning of each unit with one series of repetitions and the end of each unit with another. This might be symbolized $aXb, a'X'b'$ . . . . (The ellipsis points represent that such a pattern could be reproduced indefinitely.) There is a fine example of this in 4:1–25 (= Hebrew 4:1–5:5). In 4:1 and 4:21 (= Hebrew 5:1) we have two clearly parallel statements: "King Solomon was king over all Israel" and "Solomon was sovereign over all the kingdoms from the Euphrates to the land of the Philistines even to the border of Egypt." The first focuses the reader's attention on Solomon's *domestic* dominion, the latter on his *international* hegemony. The first unit ends with "Judah and Israel were as numerous as the sand by the sea; they ate and drank and were happy" (4:20), portraying a prosperous nation, enjoying life in its own land. The second unit ends with, "Judah and Israel lived in safety, from Dan even to Beer-sheba" (4:25 [= Hebrew 5:5]), portraying a nation secure and peaceful within its international borders (Dan was the conventional referent for the northern border of Israel, Beer-sheba was the conventional referent for the southern border). Thus we have an aXb, $a'X'b'$ structure. The enclosed material (X and X') spells out the internal administrative structure of Solomon's empire (element X, 4:2–19) and the lavish tribute Solomon received, presumably from the vassal states to his imperium, and the international peace that marked his dominion (element X', 4:21b–24 [= Hebrew 5:1b–4]).

On a much larger scale, this sort of inclusion is the fundamental organizational principle for everything from 1 Kings 11:41 to the end of 2 Kings. With very little deviation, that entire expanse of over thirty-five chapters comprises just short of forty accounts of royal reigns, each of which begins and ends with stereotyped formulas (see 1 Kgs. 14:21 and 14:29–31 for a typical example of each formula).

Symmetrical Structures

More ambitious arrangements of repeated elements will mark not only the beginning and end of a literary unit but also organize many or all of its constituent subunits into a symmetrical pattern. There are two basic ways in which such symmetries can be arranged: reverse symmetries, where the repeated elements occur in opposite order on either side of the central point; and forward symmetries, where the repeated elements follow the same order in each sequence. The interpretive dynamics differ for each type.

Reverse Symmetries

Reverse symmetries can be thought of as a series of nested inclusions: the first subunit corresponds to the last, the second subunit to the second last, and so forth. This might be symbolized $ABC / C'B'A'$; alternatively, there may be only one central element: $ABCB'A'$. Scholars use a variety of terms to describe these patterns: "chiastic,"[12] "concentric," "envelope structure." Such patterns focus the reader's attention on the central element(s), especially when that element is singular. Often they also invite the reader to see the two sequences as *contrasting* in some way, with the central element(s) marking the turning point.[13] Some examples will make these generalizations clearer. I have chosen my examples also to demonstrate that reverse symmetry can occur in passages of greatly varying lengths.[14]

When David finally brings himself to act in regard to naming his successor, he details the ritual by which Solomon is to be anointed as king. His directions form a concentric pattern (1:33–35).[15] (I have italicized the elements that I identify as the repetitions[16] that establish symmetry.)

   a. ... have my son Solomon *ride on my own mule*
     b. *bring him down* to Gihon.
        c. There let the priest Zadok and the prophet Nathan anoint him *king* over Israel;
          d. then blow the trumpet
        c'. and say, "Long live *King* Solomon!"
     b'. You *shall go up following* him.
   a'. Let him enter and *sit on my throne*.

Several points are worth noting about this arrangement. First, the contrast between the two halves of the pattern is evident: before the center we have the preparations leading up to Solomon's anointing; after the center we have the subsequent celebration. Yet the center is oddly displaced. Thematically, either *c*, the anointing itself, or *c'*, the popular acclamation, would seem a better candidate for the turning point in the action. However, by placing the trumpet in the center the author foreshadows the important narrative function it will later have as the bridge to the scene where Adonijah learns of Solomon's victory (1:41). Second, the dramatic center of the piece, element *c*, where Solomon will actually become king by virtue of sacred anointing, stands out by being notably longer than any of the other elements. Third, and perhaps surprisingly, this symmetry is not imposed by the actions themselves. In David's mouth, the ritual actions follow one another smoothly and fit neatly into the concentric pattern of his rhetoric. Yet both when the narrator describes the same events (1:38–40) and when Jonathan reports them to Adonijah and his supporters (1:43–46), hardly any vestiges of David's symmetrical pattern remain.

On a larger scale, consider the passage where Solomon eliminates Shimei (2:36–46a).[17] The organization here is more complex. First, there are three scenes in the story, arranged *ABA'*: a scene of dialogue between Solomon and Shimei (2:36–38a), a narrative scene (2:38b–41), and another scene of dialogue between Solomon and Shimei (2:42–46a). We will look at the details of the dialogue scenes in a moment. For now, notice that the narrative scene itself has a concentric structure (my translation here is literal, to reflect the Hebrew word order; again I italicize repeated elements in corresponding subunits):

   a. ... *and remained* [Hebrew *wayyēšeb*]
     b. *Shimei in Jerusalem* many days.
        +. At the end of three years, two slaves of Shimei fled to Achish, son of Maacah, king of Gath.
        c. They *told* Shimei,
          d. "*Your slaves* are *in Gath*."
            e. *Shimei* got up,
              f. saddled *his* donkey
                g. and went to Gath, to Achish,
              f'. to look for *his* slaves.

     e'. *Shimei* went,
    d'. and brought *his slaves from Gath*.
   c'. Solomon was *told*
  b'. that *Shimei* had gone *from Jerusalem* to Gath
 a'. *and returned* [Hebrew *wayyāšob*].

This pattern warrants several comments. First, note that subunits *a* and *a'* are, in the Hebrew text, identical.[18] Second, the subunit marked "+" above disrupts the symmetry. (This is true even if one does not consider it an extra subunit. If one includes it as part of subunit *b* or *c*, then the notable disparity in length between that subunit and its corresponding subunit in the second part is similarly disruptive.) I will comment on this asymmetrical subunit below. Third, "Gath" is literally as well as structurally the turning point of Shimei's journey. He goes from Jerusalem to Gath in elements *a* to *f*, reaches there in the central subunit *g*, and returns from Gath to Jerusalem in elements *f'* to *a'*. Finally, the pattern strongly emphasizes the word "Gath," the goal of Shimei's journey, by using the term five times, including in the central subunit of the narrative. The significance of this emphasis will become clearer below when we examine the two dialogue scenes in greater detail.

On a still larger scale, the whole of 1:1–2:12 forms a double-centered chiasm.[19]

 a. King David is dying (1:1–4)
  b. Adonijah exalts himself (1:5–8)
   c. Adonijah holds a feast (1:9–10)
    d. Nathan and Bathsheba conspire to make Solomon king (1:11–14)
     e. Bathsheba and then Nathan have audiences with David (1:15–27)
     e'. David summons Bathsheba and then Nathan to him (1:28–37)
    d'. Zadok and Nathan anoint Solomon king (1:38–40)
   c'. Adonijah's feast is disrupted (1:41–50)
  b'. Adonijah abases himself (1:51–53)
 a'. King David dies (2:1–11)

This pattern points up the contrast between Adonijah in the first half and in the second (subunits *b* and *b'*: exaltation/abasement; subunits *c* and *c'*: feasting/feasting disrupted). In the cases of Nathan and Bathsheba and of Solomon there is progression rather than contrast (conspiracy/conspiracy succeeds). In all these cases, the turning point occurs at the center of the story, when David takes control of the situation and commands Solomon's installation as king. Perhaps most interesting of all is David himself, whose narrative development undergoes a *double* reversal. He begins moribund (unable to get warm; unable to have intercourse with Abishag; unable to greet Bathsheba with more than two weak syllables). At the center of the story he suddenly becomes alert, decisive, and rhetorically brilliant. Even though he is still bed-ridden (1:47), his political and rhetorical shrewdness endures through his final speech to Solomon (2:2–9). But the renewal cannot last, and in the end he dies.

Forward Symmetries

Forward symmetries pattern the linked subunits in the same order in each sequence: *ABC / A'B'C'*.[20] Such patterns differ in two important ways from reverse symmetries. First, they are open-ended. Nothing limits the pattern to two sequences; *ABC / A'B'C' / A"B"C"* (and so on) is entirely possible. Second, the dynamic of "reversal" or "contrast" is usually absent, and in its place there is often a dynamic of *progression*: the second (and subsequent) sequences will build on, add to, or intensify what is found in the first. Like reverse symmetries, forward symmetry can be found organizing texts of greatly varying length.

A simple example of forward symmetry occurs in 11:1–3.[21]

    a. King *Solomon loved* many foreign women (11:1a).
       b. *details about the "foreignness" of the women* (11:1b–2a).
          c. ". . . they will surely *turn away*[22] *your heart* to follow their gods" (11:2b)
    a'. *Solomon* clung to these in *love* (11:2c).
       b'. *details about the number (cf. the "many" of 11:1a) of the women* (11:3a).
          c'. . . . and his wives *turned away his heart* (11:3b).

The progression here is from warning of danger to danger realized.[23]

A far more ambitious use of forward symmetry organizes much of the description of the temple building in 6:9b–36.[24] Two preliminary comments are necessary. First, the description is interrupted by a brief scene in which Solomon receives a divine word (6:11–13), and a transitional verse (6:14) that returns to the description of the building; I leave those verses out of my analysis. Second, the central part of the description (6:20c–28) uses reverse symmetry, not forward symmetry, for reasons that will become evident in a moment. The remaining material (6:9b–10, 15–20b, and 6:29–36) falls into two forward patterns.

    a. cedar roof of the house (6:9b)
       b. dimensions of the external structure (6:10)
          c. cedar paneling and cypress flooring inside the house (6:15)
    a'. cedar walls inside the house; their purpose: to form an inner sanctuary (6:16)
       b'. dimensions of the nave (6:17)
          c'. cedar decorations of the nave (6:18)
    a". the inner sanctuary inside the house; its purpose: to house the ark (6:19)
       b". dimensions of the inner sanctuary (6:20a)
          c". gold decoration in the inner sanctuary (6:20b)

As I mentioned in chapter 6, this progression begins what amounts to a guided tour of the temple. As we read, we move from the building's exterior, where we can view roof and external dimensions, into the nave and finally to the inner sanctuary. Here, seeing sights that the ordinary ancient Israelite would never see, we turn round and round (the symmetries are reverse, not forward), examining first the appurtenances of the inner sanctuary, then the massive cherubim that overtop the ark.

    d. the altar of cedar (6:20c)
        e. the "house within" (the inner sanctuary) covered with gold (6:21a)
            f. gold chains in front of the sanctuary (6:21b)
        e'. the "whole house" covered with gold (6:22a)
    d'. the "whole altar" covered with gold (6:22b)
    g. the cherubim made of olivewood (6:23a)
        h. the height of the cherubim (6:23b)
           i. the length of the cherubim's wings (6:24–25a)
        h'. the height of the cherubim (6:25b–26)
    g'. the cherubim are placed in the sanctuary (6:27a)
        i'. the spread of the cherubim's wings (6:27b)
    g". the cherubim are plated with gold (6:28)

Satisfied (and probably overwhelmed) with our view of the glories that adorn the Holy of Holies, we follow our tour guide as he leads us back out of the building, using forward symmetry.

    j. walls of the "house" decorated with cherubim, palms, and flowers (6:29)
        k. floor of the house plated with gold (6:30)
            l. doorway from inner sanctuary to nave (6:31)
    j'. doors decorated with cherubim, palms, and flowers (6:32a)
        k'. doors plated with gold (6:32b)
            l'. doorway from nave to courtyard (6:33–34)
    j". doors decorated with cherubim, palms, and flowers (6:35a)
        k". doors plated with gold (6:35b)
            l". the courtyard (6:36)

Alternating Repetition

Alternating repetition is a symmetrical pattern that, in a way, blends reverse and forward symmetries. When there are only two alternating sets of repeated elements, we get a pattern that can be symbolized *ABA'* or *ABA'B'* (and, like forward symmetry, can be extended indefinitely). Sometimes, particularly when the pattern comprises only three subunits (*ABA'*), the reverse pattern will promote an interpretive dynamic of contrast; conversely, the forward pattern of four alternating subunits (*ABA'B'*) seems to favor progression. These generalizations are not fixed, however; and each case of alternating repetition should be considered on its own terms. Longer sequences in particular may not clearly display a dominance of either contrast or progression.

One example of such repetition is in the two central subunits of a passage we have already considered, 1:1–2:12a. Each of those lengthy subunits describes *two* audiences, and the four scenes alternate.

   a. Bathsheba has an audience with David (1:15–21)
      b. Nathan has an audience with David (1:22–27)
   a'. David summons Bathsheba to an audience (1:28–31)
      b'. David summons Nathan (and others) to an audience (1:32–37)

Since these four scenes represent the center of a chiastic pattern, we are not surprised to find contrast between the first two (David is passive, the object of everyone else's manipulations) and the last two (David is active, decisive, and in control). At the same time, they have a dynamic of progression. The first two scenes propose the choice of Solomon as David's successor, and the last two scenes accomplish that choice.

A second example also comes from a passage we looked at above, 2:36–46a. The two dialogue scenes that surround the central narrative both comprise two speeches, and each speech has an introductory line. The introductory lines organize the four speeches in an alternating pattern.[25]

   a. "The king sent and summoned Shimei and said to him" (2:36a)
      b. "And Shimei said to the king" (2:38a)
   a'. "The king sent and summoned Shimei and said unto him" (2:42a)
      b'. "And the king said unto Shimei" (2:44a)

The virtually identical words of *a* and *a'* and of *b* and *b'* (the only difference is "to" versus "unto," and the two words are as similar in Hebrew as they are in English) makes the alternating pattern inescapable. But there is a significant variation. Instead of the expected "and Shimei said unto the king" in *b'*, we have the reverse: the king continues speaking to Shimei. There are two important points to notice here. First, the variation calls attention to itself by violating the expectations the repetitive pattern sets up in our minds. (This is another form of the technique we considered in chapter 8, variation within repetition.) Second, in this reversed form, *the line is unnecessary!* The king has already been speaking in 2:42b–43; there is no reason to interrupt his speech to remind us that the king is saying these words. What is the interpretive effect of this pattern?

First, it invites us to read the second dialogue in terms of the first one. But when we read them both together, we notice that in the second dialogue Solomon seriously misrepresents the first one. He claims (2:42b) that Shimei had sworn an oath; yet there is no such oath in 2:38. Shimei *submits* to Solomon's demands, but takes no *oath* to obey them. Further, Solomon claims (2:42b) that he imposed capital punishment on any departure from Jerusalem. In fact, Solomon forbade Shimei to depart from Jerusalem (2:36), but imposed capital punishment only if Shimei crossed the Wadi Kidron (2:37).[26] As the intervening narrative insists repeatedly, Shimei went only to Gath, which lies in the other direction from Jerusalem; Shimei's journey would not have involved crossing the Wadi Kidron. In other words, in 2:42–43, Solomon makes two false claims, and on that basis executes Shimei.

The second effect of the introductory line in b' is to point up that, where we expect Shimei to speak, Solomon keeps talking. In the light of the false claims Solomon makes in 2:42–43, my impression is that he is not willing to let Shimei get a word in edgewise, since Shimei might call attention to Solomon's dishonesty.

Finally, this analysis of the hidden dynamics of 2:42–44 also explains a gap in continuity between 2:43 and 2:44. If Shimei's execution is really motivated by his alleged disobedience to Solomon, why does Solomon have to appeal to the "evil" Shimei committed against *David* to justify it? The words of 2:44 point back to David's instructions to Solomon in 2:8–9[27] and inform Shimei that his trip to Gath is only a legal pretext; the real reasons for his execution are his offense against David and Solomon's fear that Shimei may continue to be a threat to Solomon's own security.

ASYMMETRY

Once symmetry is established and recognized as a stylistic technique with the potential to guide interpretation, another device becomes available to the author as well. The author can create a symmetrical pattern *with a flaw*. This is what I mean by "asymmetry"—not an absence of symmetry, but a flawed symmetry. In an otherwise clearly symmetrical pattern, a deviation from symmetry will inevitably draw a viewer's eye. Similarly in a text, once a reader perceives the symmetrical pattern, any deviation from the pattern becomes a focus for attention. This is a powerful device for manipulating a reader's response to the text.

Authors can skew symmetry in many ways, and there is no simple correlation between the type of asymmetry and an appropriate interpretive dynamic (unlike the two main types of symmetry, which usually correlate: reverse symmetry suggests contrast, forward symmetry suggests progression). For this reason I will simply describe a few of the commoner types of asymmetry here and make some interpretive suggestions. In the last analysis, each instance of asymmetry is best analyzed and interpreted on its own terms.

There may be a noticeable disparity between two corresponding elements, such as a disparity in length. In discussing 1:33–35 I pointed out that making subunit c rather longer[28] than the corresponding unit c' seems to emphasize it and compensate for its not being, as one would have expected, at the very center of the pattern.

Another type of asymmetry occurs when one of the symmetrical sequences contains a subunit that has no counterpart in the other sequence. This might be symbolized, for instance, as *ABC + D / D'C'B'A'*, where + is a series of words clearly separate from *C* and *D*, but there is nothing between *D'* and *C'* to correspond to them. In discussing 2:38b–41 I marked one subunit "+." Nothing in the second half of the pattern corresponds to it. This type of asymmetry is ambivalent for the careful reader. As the reader proceeds through the text in linear fashion, the asymmetry's effect is first felt in terms of its presence or absence *in the second half*, when the fact of an asymmetry becomes clear. Thus in 2:38b–41 a first reading makes the reader feel the *lack* of a subunit between *c'* and *b'* corresponding to +. Reading that way, one gets the impression that Solomon heard of Shimei's departure while he was away and lost no time confronting him immediately upon his return. On the other hand, more reflective reading can also perceive the + unit as a *surplus in the first half*. Then the reader may notice also how verbose the line is (in English one could drop the words "two" and "Achish, son of Maacah, king of," with no loss of coherence[29]). The effect of the + subunit is a great slowing of the pace of the action, and this enables the sensitive reader to *feel* the length of the "many days" Shimei remained obediently in Jerusalem.

Other types of asymmetry include a lack of correspondence between two subunits that we expect to correspond. We might symbolize this as *ABCXD / D'YC'B'A'*, where *X* and *Y* have nothing in common except their corresponding positions. Or there may be a transposition of subunits: *ABCDE / E'C'D'B'A'*. Each of these variations (as well as others) can have different effects on a reader. Let the examples we have examined suggest the avenues of investigation that remain to be explored.

EXPLORING THE STORIES

The Jeroboam Story

1. In earlier chapters I discussed two passages in the Jeroboam story that present examples of inclusion. One is 12:1–20; the other is 12:30–13:34. Look at those passages again with the category of "inclusion" in mind. In each case, identify the repeated elements that mark the beginning and end of the passage and determine how the inclusion affects your reading of the material it encloses.

2. There is another instance of inclusion in the elders' advice to Rehoboam in 12:7, but it is somewhat obscured in the NRSV translation. Here is a literal translation of the verse: "If today you will be servant to this people, and serve them, and answer them, and speak to them good words, then they will be to you servants all days." Identify the repeated elements and suggest what the inclusive pattern might contribute to interpretation.

My next question (on the same passage) is, I admit, very conjectural. Nevertheless, it is a useful exercise. One of the ways to get insight into a passage is to contrast it with what the author *might* have written, but did not. The material inside the inclusion in 12:7 does not display a clear symmetry, but it could with a very minor adjustment. Can you see the adjustment I have in mind? How would the meaning of that hypothetical text differ from that of the present one?

3. Identify as many repeated words and phrases as you can in Ahijah's speech in 11:31–39. Can you discern a possible pattern in these repetitions? (There will certainly be some repeated elements that will not fit into whatever pattern you come up with. That is not a problem. Do not expect this sort of structuring device to be exhaustive. Just look for an arrangement that accommodates the majority of the repetitions throughout the passage.) Can you see any *thematic* correlation to the structure you have discerned?

The Elijah Story

1. Look for repeated elements in 17:18–24. (I use "repeated" here in the looser sense of elements that plainly correspond to one another. Include not just exact repetitions but clear pairs of opposites as well: "go up/come down," "dead/alive," and the like). Do they point to a symmetrical structure? (Remember that not *all* the repeated elements have to fit into the arrangement, but there should be enough that do to make the pattern noticeable.) Does the pattern have reverse symmetry or forward symmetry? Does it display contrast or progression?

2. Some of the repeated elements in 19:9–18 are obvious. Are they sufficient to arrange the whole of 19:9–18 in a coherent symmetrical pattern? Do you think this pattern supports one interpretation more than another? (See pp. 173–74 and 178 for two possible interpretations of the passage.)

3. Obadiah's speech in 18:9–14 contains repeated elements and some symmetrical patterning, but the speech as a whole is not symmetrical. Identify the repeated elements and the partial symmetries it contains. Can you think of any reason why the author would have crafted such a speech for Obadiah?

The Ahab Story

1. The exchange between Ben-hadad's servants and Ahab in 20:32b is brief but neatly structured. Can you discern the symmetry? Can you see any way in which this symmetrical pattern might support the interpretation of the exchange?

2. In appendix 3 I explain how the apparently disorganized passage 20:15–21 can be read as an attempt to express simultaneity (see p. 197). The attempt uses alternating symmetry to create the split-screen impression: our view alternates between the Israelite troops and Ben-hadad's camp. However, at one point this alternating pattern breaks down: 20:20a, "Each killed his man."[30] What effect does this flaw in the symmetry evoke in you?

3. The first half of the story of Naboth's vineyard (21:1–16) can stand alone as a tragic tale of royal malfeasance and judicial murder. Look for repeated elements in those verses that point to a symmetrical structure. (Hint: In addition to repeated words and phrases, look for settings and characters that link scenes with one another.) Does this pattern of symmetry illumine your understanding of the story?

Chapter 11

Responsibilities of the Reader

In this final chapter, we turn our attention to our own place as readers in the communication act we diagrammed on page 6. Just as the structure of *text* turns out to be much more complex than we might have anticipated, so too our readerly relationships to the text reflect similar complexity. In order to read narrative well, we must take on the roles of narratee (with respect to the *story* the narrator tells us) and implied reader (with respect to the *narrative* the implied author writes). Yet, for all that, we remain real readers—inhabitants of our own place and time, with our own unique backgrounds and personalities—with respect to the text that the real author penned in his or her own place and time and that we hold in our hands today. The implications of these three roles, that is, the several relationships we have with the text, will engage us for the first part of this chapter. In the second part, we will consider more briefly some further roles that are available to readers who choose to pursue them.

READERLY ROLES

To discuss the reader's participation in the roles of narratee, implied reader, and real reader successively is to oversimplify the complex. The reader does not read the text three times, sampling each role in isolation. The text is the narrative is the story, so to speak, and the reader's responses on all of those levels of communication will arise in no neat order. Their impact on the reader will be a multiplex experience that weaves together all three levels. The observations below are intended to help the reader discern, reflectively and after the fact, the various dimensions of that experience.

The Reader and the Story

At the heart of the narrative transaction is the *story*, told by the narrator to the narratee. If I am to read the story successfully, I must before all else be able to put myself in the position of the narratee, and receive the story from the narrator in the way the narrator seeks to impart it. This has two main implications. First, I must be fully open to the narrator's manipulations, since the meaning of his story includes the responses he seeks to evoke from the narratee. This means sensitivity to all the narrative strategies we have studied above—strategies that concatenate events and create characters, that establish our point of view and sense of tempo, that tempt us to fill gaps and resolve ambiguities, and so forth—and a willingness to respond to them appropriately.[1]

Second, I must be able to enter the secondary world, since both narratee and narrator are inhabitants of that world. This means that, at least for the duration of the reading, I accept that world as (secondarily) *real*—no matter how different the rules of that secondary world may seem from those of my own. The characters existed, the events happened, and they existed and happened just as the narrator portrays them.[2] Only if I can accept the secondary world as real and operating on its own terms—including such bizarre portents as lions that do not eat (1 Kgs. 13:28), miraculous lightning bolts that do (18:38), and prostitutes who wash themselves in blood (22:38)—will I be able to experience it as the narrator expects the narratee to do.[3] If, however, I can accept the secondary world as (secondarily) real, then I am in a position to experience the full impact of the emotional and visceral responses the narrator evokes. I can exult at moments of triumph, feel my muscles grow tense at dangerous junctures, and have an adrenaline rush when the action races at a furious pace.[4]

The Reader and the Narrative

In contrast to the story, the *narrative* is best thought of as a written text composed by an implied author who has an ideal or implied reader in mind. What the implied author expects from the implied reader, however, is never stated forthrightly in the text. It must be inferred by the real reader from clues in the text (this is what I meant in chapter 1, where I spoke of the real reader as "constructing" the implied reader). One implication of this is that each real reader is likely to have a slightly different take on the characteristics expected of the implied reader; nevertheless, the implied reader's principal traits (general historical and cultural setting and outlook, for instance) ought to be reasonably clear to all attentive and informed readers. A second implication, at least for readers of biblical narrative, is that our ability to identify with the implied reader will always be limited. Since we are not ancient Israelites, sharing an ancient Near Eastern worldview and fluent in Classical Hebrew, we can assume the role of the implied reader of a biblical story only to the degree that we can put on traits like his.[5]

The narrative received by the implied reader recounts *the telling of a story*. It depicts a narrator communicating with a narratee (no matter how transparent both of those figures are in most biblical texts). The implied reader, so to speak, watches from the wings as the narrator elicits the responses he desires from the narratee. This affords the implied reader a certain distance from the narrator's influence and permits a critical awareness of how the narrator wields that influence. In cases where the implied author's values and views are more or less identical to those of the narrator, the implied reader will be conscious of those values and views (since he perceives the narrator's attempt to persuade the narratee of them), and the implied reader will feel no urge to disagree with them (since the implied author has not sown any subversive or ironic clues in the text). The implied reader, then, will be persuaded that, indeed, these values and views are right and proper. Nevertheless, an important factor differentiates the conversation of the narrator and narratee from that of the implied author and implied reader. The former takes place in the secondary world, the world of the story and of the narrative. The latter takes place in the *primary* world, where author and reader live. The implied reader, then, will affirm those values and views as true and good not just within a particular narrative world, but also absolutely, in the primary world.[6]

In the case of narrative, one of the implied reader's responsibilities is to judge the extent to which the story itself (and not only the views and values it conveys) reflects the primary world. In other words, did the events actually occur? Did they occur as described? Did the characters exist? Did they exist as they are characterized? And so on. In and of itself, of course, narrative may depict people and events anywhere on a continuum from pure fantasy to detailed historical accuracy. Different cultures have different literary conventions to alert readers to the degree of facticity a narrative claims, and readers familiar with those conventions will usually have no difficulty coming to such a judgment. But we modern Western readers are often unaware of the conventions proper to ancient Hebrew literature. Correspondingly it can be difficult for us to recognize the degree of historicity the implied author is claiming for a biblical narrative.[7]

In our culture, for instance, the presence of talking animals immediately brands a story as consciously fictional. Is the same criterion applicable to ancient Hebrew narratives? (There is a talking snake in Gen. 3 and a talking donkey in Num. 22.) Many readers of English literature would hesitate to accept contemporary stories of miraculous healings, raisings from the dead, and the like as straightforward, reliable historical accounts. Is that criterion also to be used for ancient literature? When an implied author describes a miraculous event, are we to infer that the ancient author believed that it happened just as depicted, or was "miracle" a recognized literary device to embellish an essentially historical event, or was it, perhaps, a conventional clue to the ancient reader that *this* event is an imaginative "narrativizing" of a theological claim?[8]

On a more general level, "scenic" style—that is, presenting the narrative as something like a staged drama, with characters conversing and interacting, revealing their inner thoughts and feelings, and so on—preponderates in the narratives of the first half of the Hebrew Bible (from Genesis through 2 Kings). In our culture, scenic style is typical of fiction writing and would be out of place in a history textbook. But in classic histories of Greece and Rome it is not unknown (though it does not dominate the story as it does in the Hebrew Bible[9]). How would the ancient Israelite implied reader react to scenic style? Would he understand it simply as a way of making the objective historical data vital? Or would it alert the ancient reader to a significant degree of fictionalization in the writing?

In the rather infrequent cases in biblical narrative where the implied author does not agree with the values and views the narrator proposes to the narratee, it is the implied reader's responsibility to discern the usually very subtle clues of this disagreement and to infer the unexpressed views of the implied author that they hint at.[10] This, of course, entrusts the implied reader with a considerable share of the responsibility for *making sense* (that is, creating the meaning) of the narrative, since the reader must operate on the slimmest of directions from the implied author. Furthermore, the implied reader must ponder the question of why the implied author found it useful to create a narrator with whose views the author differs. Why not create a narrator whose views coincide with the author's own? Why introduce *disagreement* as an essential component in the reader's experience (that is, in the meaning) of the narrative? Perhaps the implied author is attempting to subvert a regnant orthodoxy that he dare not challenge directly. Or perhaps he is using multiple narrative voices to suggest a complex and nuanced view by balancing several simpler and to some extent incompatible views against one another. Or indeed, the implied author's agenda may simply be to confront the implied reader with the complexities of the situation in order to force him to consider the options and make up his own mind.

The Reader and the Text

At the end of the day, we are all *real* readers. That means that we bring to our reading everything that makes us unique—not only our modern Western culture and history, but also the personalities and experiences that have shaped us as individuals. Clearly, this level of interaction with the text maximizes the extent to which subjectivity shapes our reader response to the text and therefore the meaning the text holds for us personally. Equally clearly, this means that each of us must find his or her own way to draw meaning out of the encounter between the ancient text and our modern selves.

From the unique perspective that each of us has, we can consider, evaluate, and agree or disagree with the implied author's attempts to persuade the implied reader to a particular point of view. The most comfortable situation, of course, is when we find ourselves in harmony with the views and values of the implied author (which is as close to the "real" author as we are able to draw). In that case, reading the text is like conversing with a friend with whom we see eye to eye on almost everything. We confirm one another in the plausibility of our views and emerge from the encounter more confident of them.

The danger here—and it is a danger we all succumb to at times—is that the desire to have our views affirmed may skew our reading of the text in the first place. When this happens, we tend to overvalue those elements of the text that support our views and overlook those that do not, with the result that we attribute to the author views that we are in fact imposing upon the text ourselves. Traditionally this has been called "eisegesis" (reading meaning *into* the text) as opposed to "exegesis" (reading the meaning *out of* the text). In principle, there is nothing wrong with eisegesis as long as we are aware that we are elaborating a meaning that has its principal source in ourselves, and that the author is unlikely to have had it in mind. Since, insofar as it is a potential meaning of the text at all, it is unique to our personal reading, we can share it with other readers; but we cannot pretend to be surprised if they fail to find it as persuasive as we do.

More challenging and consequently more productive are readings of the text that propose values and views that differ from our preconceptions. This is akin to a conversation with a trusted friend with whom we disagree on important issues. Because of the fundamentally positive nature of the relationship, we can be open to the disagreement without feeling threatened, and we can permit ourselves to introspect. We may in the end continue to disagree: for example, the author's apparent approval of Solomon's use of "forced labor" to build his temple (1 Kgs. 5:13 [= Hebrew 5:27]) does not convince me of the moral legitimacy of such a system. However, even then the text can remind me that, in the historical and cultural situation of ancient Israel, attitudes may have been more tolerant toward the involuntary conscription of labor than they would be today—or at least than mine are.[11] On the other hand, the text's challenges to my preconceptions may well lead me to a salutary rethinking of my views and values. My discomfort with the conscripting of forced labor, for instance, may induce me to think about my attitudes toward conscripted military service. Are the two institutions morally comparable? Does (dis)approval of one require (dis)approval of the other? If not, why not? Or, to take another example, the text's insistence on the contingency of Yhwh's presence in the temple (see, for instance, 8:27 and especially 9:6–9)[12] can call into question my proneness to rely unreflectively on religious institutions as avenues of access to the Divine and to disregard that, in relation to God, all human realities are contingent and conditional.

Most valuable of all are the intense emotional and physical reactions I sometimes feel to a story. When I am moved to tears or to laughter, when I feel myself grow tense or I experience a catharsis, then I am put to the question on a deep personal level. This is what literary theorists mean when they say that "the text reads the reader." The text has touched something in my own psyche, my own life experience, and tapped a reservoir of energy and feeling whose wellsprings lie outside the story I am reading. To cite a personal example, when I read of Solomon's perjury against Shimei (1 Kgs. 2:42–43; see above, chap. 10), I feel strong sympathy for Shimei, as I would for any victim of injustice. However I also feel some degree of rage, which is only intensified by what I perceive as Solomon's gloating in 2:44. If I undertake the introspection that this response invites me to and do not merely dismiss it as another face of my (self-?) righteous disapproval of injustice, I discover that this story reawakens in me—and displaces onto Solomon—unresolved feelings of anger and betrayal at injustice that *I* experienced at the hands of (in my opinion) lying superiors. (I hope the reader will forgive me the self-indulgence of this admission. I risk introducing it because it aptly illustrates how one's reading of the text can become a starting point for deeper *self-insight*. Part of the text's effect on me—its meaning for me—is to offer me an opportunity to learn something important about myself and, therefore, to undertake a process of growth and transformation.)

Great literature—and, without question, the narratives of the Hebrew Bible include some of the world's great literature—is potentially transformative. It can inform and instruct and entertain, certainly; but its greatest gift to a reader is the opportunity for self-knowledge. It offers insight into universal human truths (and, sometimes, even into the Ultimate Truth) that call us to become more than we are.

OPTIONAL ROLES

Where does one go from here? We have explored many aspects of the enterprise of reading narrative. It is my hope that these chapters will have deepened and enriched your skills in experiencing not only biblical narrative but also, to some extent, other narratives and narrative genres (cinema, drama) as well. If that has happened, we have both succeeded. But where can one go from here? In what follows I will reflect briefly on three possible directions one can take on the basis of having encountered the biblical text as a reader. None of these directions, strictly speaking, is necessary for successful reading. However, successful reading is a prerequisite for pursuing any of these optional roles with any degree of acuity.

The Reader as Narrative Critic

One avenue for further exploration is to develop a critical awareness of what is involved in the act of reading and of the techniques by which authors affect readers—in other words, to become a *literary critic*. Obviously, this is what we have been about in this book; and anyone who has gotten this far along the road with me, including working through the exercises and reflecting on the material in the appendixes, has made considerable strides in this direction. Congratulations!

However, there is a potential danger in becoming a literary critic. Let me use an analogy. One cannot really appreciate how a clock works unless one takes it apart. But, having done so, one no longer knows what time it is. The literary critic whose whole purpose is to lay bare the workings of authors and texts can become an expert in critical theory; but in the process he or she is liable to forfeit the joyous experience of reading. Critical awareness cannot be the ultimate goal if one is to remain a reader; in other words, taking the clock apart should teach us not only how it works but also how to put it back together. Critical appreciation of how narrative works should enable us to experience the power of narrative more deeply and with greater insight into both the story world and ourselves. This is what philosopher Paul Ricoeur refers to as "second naiveté": a return, after critical analysis, to vulnerability before the full power of the raw text.

Conversely, becoming a literary critic brings with it the potential for great benefit. First, we gain an understanding of the skills a literary artist must master in order to produce a worthy artifact. This cannot but deepen our appreciation of the expertise that undergirds the author's accomplishment and increase our sensitivity to the shades and subtleties with which the skilled author has nuanced the text—shades and subtleties that a less discerning reader will most often miss. The more richly and profoundly a work moves us, the more it testifies to the author's skill. But beyond that, critical awareness of narratorial and authorial manipulations affords us insight into where and how much *we*, as real readers, contribute to the meaning of the text. By learning to identify literary techniques and devices and their typical effects, we learn as well to discern the extent to which our responses grow also out of the historical, cultural, and individual realities that shape each of us. This, in turn, is the starting point for the growth in self-knowledge that great literature can occasion.

The Reader as Believer

Insightful reading of biblical narrative can also enrich the devotional life of the believing reader. It is certainly true that not all readers of the ancient Israelite and early Christian writings belong to Judaism or Christianity. Neither belief system is required in order to read and understand biblical texts, any more than belief in Zeus and the ancient Greek pantheon is required for an intelligent reading of the *Iliad* and the *Odyssey*. However, it is equally certain that the majority of those who read the Hebrew Bible regularly are members of one of the religious traditions that hold that text to be sacred. Such membership adds another layer of context for the believer's attempt to discern meaning in the biblical text.

Insofar as Jewish and Christian communities of belief—each in different ways, of course—hold the biblical texts as foundational for their respective understandings of God, humankind, and the moral life, they are communities of *readers*, drawing from the sacred texts *meanings* to which they ascribe doctrinal and moral authority. But simple observation of the various creeds and congregations that call themselves "Jewish" or "Christian" makes painfully clear that there is little ecumenical agreement on a single meaning acknowledged by all as normative. Our explorations in this book can shed light on this situation, because fundamental to everything we have done is the recognition that a text holds the potential for many meanings and that every individual reading of a given text is likely to actualize a slightly different meaning. Even apart from the subjectivity that we bring to the text as real—and therefore historically (and ecclesially) conditioned—readers, on the level of the story itself we fill gaps, resolve ambiguities, impute motives, respond to characters, and so on, in ways that will differ from reader to reader.

It should be clear by now that I do not consider a text's potential for many meanings a disvalue, as if one were the "right" meaning and all the others were red herrings. I have no doubt that texts can be *misread*, whether intentionally or unintentionally; and they most certainly can be *poorly* read. But the criterion of a particular reading's worth is not its agreement with one normative and authoritative interpretation over against all others. Productive literary criteria—there are two—do not label readings simply "right" or "wrong"; they weigh them as "more or less well-founded": (1) How *adequate* is the reading to account for as much of the text, in all its details, as possible? And (2) how *plausible* is the reading to the broader community of good readers? As one prominent literary critic put it, "the meaning of [a literary text] within the institution of literature is not, one might say, the immediate and spontaneous reaction of individual readers but the meanings which they are willing to accept as both plausible and justifiable when they are explained."[13]

As a community of readers, a religious institution—be it parish or synagogue, synod or denomination—takes its own larger, postbiblical theological tradition as the context within which to situate the readings of its members. That theological tradition continues to develop out of the ongoing conversation among its members about readings of its authoritative texts. The more perspicacious the readers, the more insightful their readings will be, the more profound the theological advances they will engender, and the more solidly grounded the devotional life will be that they support in believers as individuals and in the believing community as a whole.

The Reader as Preacher

Within believing communities, some members are authorized to preach on the biblical texts. What impact can the sorts of critical skills we have explored in this book have on preaching?

Since preaching is a way of opening up for the hearers the meaning of a biblical text, the complexity that we have discovered in trying to define and identify "meaning" is immediately relevant. Among other things, we have seen that the meaning of a text is neither simple nor single. Therefore, no single or simple sermon or homily can ever exhaust its possibilities. As our repeated readings discover new depths and dimensions in the text, our preaching will have new insights to share with our congregants. No one reading, and no one sermon, can pretend to be complete or final.

We have also seen that the meaning we find in a text is not an inert object, like a choice nutmeat lodged in its shell. Rather, meaning is the product of a *dialogue* between ourselves (in the various roles we assume) and the voices of narrator(s) and implied author speaking in and through the text. It emerges from a living encounter in which we readers collaborate actively and to which we contribute creatively. Correspondingly, the goal of preaching is not to speak a definitive word that lays the text out for our hearers like a butterfly splayed and pinned to a specimen book—as if that were even possible! The goal is to help the hearer have his or her own encounter with the living text. For believers, for whom "the word of God is living and active . . . able to judge the thoughts and intentions of the heart" (Heb. 4:12), that encounter is a moment of divine grace. Preaching must facilitate it, not substitute for it; and that means that preaching must bring text and hearers together, not interpose between them.

There are two common missteps by which a preacher interposes something between the text and the hearers. Anyone who has listened to many sermons will have heard both of them; and anyone who, like me, has exercised a preaching ministry very often will probably, like me, have fallen into both of these traps more than once. The first danger arises from the excitement we can feel when a new approach to reading (such as applying literary-critical methods) deepens and enriches our own reading experience. We are tempted to use the preaching opportunity to *share the methods*. In other words, instead of preaching—that is, facilitating our hearers' encounter with the text—we try to teach them *how* to read it in ways that will produce greater insight. In itself, of course, there is nothing wrong with teaching literary criticism; that is what this book is all about. But as a way of *preaching* it aims for the wrong goal: it substitutes skill acquisition for an encounter with the Divine and turns the sermon into a class lecture.

The second danger is also a substitution. When the preacher has had a deep, potentially life-transforming encounter with the text, he or she may be tempted to use the preaching moment to testify to the congregation just how powerful and transformative the encounter with God's word can be. Again, there is nothing wrong with such testimony. In the worship of many faith communities, it is an important way of celebrating the grace of God at work in the community. But it is not a way of opening up the meaning of a biblical text or of facilitating the hearer's encounter with the story. It is a *self*-presentation that focuses on the results reading the text has produced in an individual preacher's life, rather than on the text that produced them.

Expertise in literary-critical approaches to the text does not neutralize the attraction of these dangers, but it can help us navigate between them and steer a course that draws hearer and text together without interference. One of the goals of narrative critical analysis is to become aware of the ways in which the text elicits responses from us and of precisely what it is *in the text* that evokes such a response. A corollary of this awareness is that we also come to realize the ways in which our responses are shaped by influences *outside* the text—such as factors in our personal histories and contexts. This double awareness charts our way between Scylla and Charybdis. To the extent that our reading is shaped by what we ourselves bring to the text, it is not a proper focus for preaching: it is not the text. On the other hand, to the extent that the text uses literary techniques and devices to generate our experience, those techniques and devices are also not the proper focus of *preaching*: they are issues for literary-critical analysis.

A familiarity with literary criticism helps us distinguish between the manipulations that the text operates on us and the influences that we bring to the reading ourselves. This enables us to identify and put aside, for preaching purposes, issues of autobiography and to concentrate on what the *text* has the power to awaken in its audience. Conversely, an awareness of literary dynamics helps us to distinguish between the literary devices the text employs and the evocative effects that result. We can then preach so as to evoke comparable responses rather than lecture on how the responses are achieved. To reprise the analogy I proposed above, preaching should lead the congregation to know what time it is, not how a clock works.

Preaching is a lens. No one uses a magnifying glass to examine the glass itself or the hand that holds it. A lens focuses light and intensifies vision and thereby allows something to impact us with clarity and detail. Preaching—at least in the sense of biblical exposition—ought to focus the power of the text and allow its light to burst into flame within our lives.

APPENDIXES

Appendix 1

The Jeroboam Story

A reminder before you begin. What follows are not answers to the questions in the sense that these are the answers you should have come up with or the analyses you should have produced. They are only examples of the *sort* of answers you might have found. They are examples that, for one reason or another, I find particularly appropriate or interesting; but there are almost always other examples that you could have cited. And my analyses may often go deeper than yours do. (I should hope so! Thirty years of working through 1 Kings ought to give me something of a head start!) When my explanations do go more deeply into the text, ask yourself whether they appear plausible to you (that is, whether they enable richer readings of the text that account for more details than another reading might). If they do, they may help you hone your own analytical skills; and if they do not appear plausible, they may demonstrate ways of *misreading* that you ought to avoid.

PLOT

Simple Arc of Tension

This is a fine example of the dialectic between our perception of a text's structure and our perception of its theme. A first reading of the text suggests that the arc of tension addresses the question, How will Rehoboam respond to the defection of the northern tribes? He begins to respond militarily; but the sudden and unexpected intervention of a prophet (presumably from Rehoboam's own court in Jerusalem) forbids the military solution, and a new situation of stability is reached in 12:24b, when the army disbands and Rehoboam apparently accepts the status quo. On this reading, the next verse introduces a new theme, namely, Jeroboam's undertakings as the new king of the north.

However, what if we ask as our thematic question, How will Rehoboam *and Jeroboam* respond to the dissolution of the realm? On that reading, 12:21–24 detail Rehoboam's aborted attempt at an offensive military solution, and 12:25 describes Jeroboam's defensive counter: he moves his capital out of range of Rehoboam's strike capabilities. The new situation of relative stability, stalemate, is thus reached not in 12:24 but in 12:25.

Which reading is "right"? That is the wrong question. Both readings are quite adequate to the text and display an appreciation of the text's inner dynamism. I have a slight preference for the second, but it is based on what I perceive as a hair's-breadth better reading of the details of the text. There is a clear thematic shift at 12:26 from Jeroboam's political actions to his religious innovation and, grammatically, that change in topic is pointed up by the unnecessary repetition of Jeroboam's name in 12:26 (a simple pronoun "he" would suffice). Those factors lead me to see 12:25 as connected just slightly more strongly with what precedes it than with what follows it.

A More Complex Example

In 13:1 the man of God arrives from Judah, and in 13:10 he departs from Bethel to return to Judah. This establishes the overall arc of tension: Why has the man of God from Judah come?[1] However, 12:33 certainly provides background information for the scene (it explains Jeroboam's presence at the altar in Bethel), and 12:32 is probably background information as well (it explains the date for the ceremony Jeroboam is undertaking).[2] The scene also contains several short arcs of tension. In 13:2 the man of God offers an explicit and detailed prophecy; the tension, as with all prophecies, is, Will it happen? This arc of tension is not resolved.[3] In 13:3 another "sign" is reported by the narrator, and its fulfillment appears in 13:5. Between those two points, another arc of tension starts when the king attempts to seize the man of God, and his hand withers. What will he do now? This partially resolves in 13:6, when at the prophet's prayer the king is healed, but the arc of tension begun by the royal command to seize the man of

God remains open. Surprisingly, it changes into an invitation to share the king's table.[4] In this form the tension is resolved by the man of God's polite refusal of the invitation.

The Whole Jeroboam Story

The following analysis does not go through the story in order. Rather, it reflects my own perception of the arcs of tension and the subunits or scenes they demarcate. I have tried to move from those arcs of tension that seem clearest to me to those whose boundaries seem more obscure. This will make my presentation appear somewhat erratic, as it jumps from one part of the text to another. For clarity's sake, I will recapitulate the discussion in a final paragraph that follows the order of the text.

Some of the major arcs of tension are evident.

1. I have already mentioned 12:21–24 (or 25) and 12:32–13:10 above.

2. The limits of these two blocks of text point to the intervening verses as a separate subunit. In 12:26–27 we see Jeroboam's intention to address the real possibility of his people's religious loyalties remaining with Jerusalem and its magnificent temple. How will he counter that danger? The next verses, 12:28–31, spell out the innovative religious policies and practices Jeroboam institutes for this purpose.

3. The boundaries of the story of Israel's rejection of Rehoboam at Shechem (12:1–20) are clear, at least to me.[5]

4. Clearly the relatively independent story in 13:11–32 constitutes a self-contained development and resolution of tension surrounding the old prophet from Bethel and his behavior. (It also includes several subsidiary arcs of tension as well: Will the man of God from Judah accept the invitation? Will God punish the man of God for his disobedience? Will God punish the Bethel prophet for his deception? And so on.)

5. Ahijah's speech in 14:6–16 is contained within the arc of tension that focuses on Jeroboam's ill son and his fate: 14:1–5 are background information; 14:6–16 develop the tension and begin the resolution; 14:17–18 bring the story to a new, though tragic, point of stability.

6. Similarly, Ahijah's speech in chapter 11 reaches a point of stability in Jeroboam's escape to Egypt from Solomon's attempt on his life (11:40); this suggests that the tension begins with the mention of Jeroboam's attempted rebellion (11:26).[6] In that case, 11:26–28 are background information describing the preceding state of relative stability, and the action proper begins in 11:29, with the appearance of Ahijah of Shiloh.

7. Finally, notice the verbal similarities between 12:30–31 and 13:33–34. We have here a situation similar to that in 2:12b and 2:46. Jeroboam's religious innovations establish a situation of relative stability before and after the two episodes of 12:32–13:10 and 13:11–32. The two episodes, therefore, though each has its own self-contained arc of tension, together describe a larger arc of

tension beginning from Jeroboam's establishment of his religious policies and ending with those policies unchanged. How the first episode fits into that arc is clear: despite the miracles of the man of God and his condemnation of the altar, Jeroboam does not change his ways. How the second episode fits is less clear, but the key is in 13:25: news of the man of God's miraculous death was known "in the town" and, therefore, presumably came to Jeroboam himself. This may have given him some hope that the man of God's prophecy had been nullified, but that impression would immediately have been proven wrong when the local prophet began to proclaim the same message. Nevertheless, Jeroboam did not change his ways.

To summarize: the major arcs of tension I find in the story of Jeroboam are 11:26–40 (Jeroboam's identity, his rebellion incited by Ahijah, and his escape to Egypt);[7] 12:1–20 (Rehoboam's failed attempt to be accepted as king by the northern tribes, and their rejection of the Davidic house); 12:21–25 (the military responses of the two kings to the secession of the northern tribes); 12:26–31 (Jeroboam's religious innovations intended to secure the religious loyalties of his people as well as their political allegiance); 12:30–13:34 (how Jeroboam remained intransigent despite two striking events: 12:32–13:10, the condemnation of Jeroboam's sanctuary at Bethel by a man of God from Judah; and 13:11–32, the betrayal of the man of God from Judah by a prophet of Bethel, and the surprising commandeering of the latter by the divine word); 14:1–18 (the condemnation of Jeroboam's house by his erstwhile prophetic patron, Ahijah). The final verses, 14:19–20, are a stereotyped formula used by the editor of the book of Kings to mark the conclusion of a reign. In terms of arcs of tension, they point to the transition from one king to his successor as (in literary, though often not in political terms) a moment of stability between two reigns ("What happened during Jeroboam's reign?" "What happened during Rehoboam's reign?").[8]

CHARACTERS

1. In the *narrative* unit that stretches from 11:26 through 11:40, Jeroboam is clearly the main character. He is mentioned first, last, and more often than Ahijah. On the other hand, the passage contains an extended introduction (11:26–28) and a brief epilogue (11:40), surrounding a scene that is, essentially, an extended speech by Ahijah (11:31–39), making him the main character in that *scene*, though not in the passage as a whole.

In 13:1–10 the situation is somewhat similar. The roles of king and prophetic figure are well balanced. Jeroboam appears first, the man of God last (13:10); the man of God is mentioned seven times, and Jeroboam seven times (twice by name, five times as "the king"). Each speaks three times, though the man of God's speeches are generally longer than Jeroboam's. Jeroboam appears to change most: The man of God remains loyal and obedient to Yhwh throughout the scene; Jeroboam is hostile, then maimed, then healed, then well-disposed

(13:7, unless the king's invitation is a sham intended to suborn the man of God). In terms just of 13:1–10, either character could be considered the main one. In terms of chapter 13 as a whole, the man of God is clearly more important than Jeroboam, who disappears entirely from 13:11–32. In terms of the whole Jeroboam narrative, however, the opposite is true: Jeroboam is more important than the man of God from Judah, whose appearance is limited to chapter 13.

Perhaps more interesting in 13:1–10, however, is the presence of another "character" (I use the term here rather loosely indeed!) that is named more often than either Jeroboam or the man of God: the altar (named eight times, one of them double: "O altar, altar," says the man of God in 13:2). Besides its frequent naming, the altar is portrayed in a quasi-personal way. The man of God speaks *to* the altar in 13:2 (the literary device of addressing an inanimate object directly—technically called "apostrophe"—is exceptionally rare in the Hebrew Bible). And this "character" too is balanced by another quasi-personal force, the "word of Yhwh" (named four times, plus once "the sign Yhwh has spoken"). Behind the man of God and Jeroboam stand symbols—word and altar—of their respective deities. This encounter marks the beginning of a divine struggle between Yhwh of Jerusalem and the golden calves of Dan and Bethel for the loyalties of the people of the northern kingdom.

2. The prophet Ahijah's condemnation of Jeroboam reaches its climax in the gruesome dynastic curse in 14:11: "Anyone belonging to Jeroboam who dies in the city, the dogs shall eat; and anyone who dies in the open country, the birds of the air shall eat."[9] Death without burial was a sign of Yhwh's ultimate displeasure. Mentioning Abijah's burial in his familial tomb points up Jeroboam's fate by contrast and demonstrates that the child is blameless and that he dies only because of his father's misdeeds.

3. The three "group" characters in 12:1–20 are "the people," who act as a group in 12:3–4, 12, 16, and 18; "the elders," who advise Rehoboam in 12:6–7; and "the youngsters,"[10] who advise him in 12:8–11. All three groups speak as groups, and no single individual acts as the voice of any of the groups. This is rather surprising in the case of the people, because—at least in the Hebrew text[11]—Jeroboam is singled out for special mention in two of "the people's" actions (12:3, 12), and he will later be chosen by "all Israel" as their king (12:20). The emphasis on his presence contrasts with his silence to pique the reader's curiosity.

If either the "elders" or the "youngsters" were represented by a named individual, the reader's attention would likely focus on that individual as a distinct character rather than on the group; compare how the unfortunate Adoram (12:18) draws our notice, but we do not think of him as representative of a class of officials (even though we have already been told that Jeroboam himself exercised a similar office: see 11:28).

4. The convention remains intact in 12:1–16. Rehoboam interacts in turn with a series of "group" characters—the people, the elders, the youngsters, and the people again—but each group leaves the scene before the next group appears.

5. In itself, 13:11–32 does not contribute much to the larger story of Jeroboam. Primarily, it shows that the disobedience of the man of God from Judah will *not* have any effect on the destiny of Jeroboam: the word of Yhwh simply discards the disobedient messenger and commandeers the prophet of Bethel to take his place. As part of a slightly larger context, however, it characterizes Jeroboam as obstinate in his wrongdoing. The echo of 12:30–31 in 13:33–34 implies that the king, despite his encounter with the man of God, and despite widespread knowledge of what transpired in 13:11–32 (see 13:25), remains intransigent.[12]

That small contribution to the characterization of Jeroboam, however, hardly warrants a story this long and detailed, including the introduction of a major player (the prophet) who never appears elsewhere in the Bible. We learn a great deal about both the prophet and the man of God that leads nowhere, at least in the immediate context. In this sense, both the prophet and the man of God are "overdeveloped secondary characters."

Some of the things we learn about them connect with information elsewhere in the narrative; these connections are likely to be noticed, though, only by readers or hearers who are thoroughly familiar with the larger story. For example, the man of God's dire prophecy in 13:2 points forward to its fulfillment in 2 Kings 23:15–20. But elements from the second story in 1 Kings 13 also point in that direction: the prophet's directive that he be buried in the same tomb as the man of God (1 Kgs. 13:31) is picked up in 2 Kings 23:17–18; and the prophet's extension of the man of God's prophecy from Bethel to "the high places that are in the cities of Samaria" (1 Kgs. 13:32) comes to pass in 2 Kings 23:19.

Another example emerges from the narrator's insistence on the origins of the two figures. As far as 1 Kings 13:11–32 is concerned, it is of little consequence that the prophet is from Bethel and the man of God from Judah; all that is needed is that the prophet be at home, and the man of God on a journey. But the specifics of their provenance resonate with the tension between Jeroboam, king of the north, and Rehoboam, king of Judah, that erupted in 12:6–19. There, political unity was ended; but this was Yhwh's will, as the narrator insists (11:31–35; 12:15, 24). Here, once Jeroboam has taken the sacrilegious step of erecting the calf sanctuaries, the political division begins to infect religious life. The north has its own temples, its own priests, its own cultic worship, and, now, its own prophets. This is most definitely *not* Yhwh's will, and he takes strong steps to maintain control of those who bear his prophetic word (13:20).

On a much larger scale, the distinction between north and south points far beyond the reign of Jeroboam. The drama of 1–2 Kings is the drama of one people of Yhwh under two independent political dispensations. The identification of the two prophetic figures with their two kingdoms of origin is facilitated by both being anonymous. (Consider how unusual it is to have characters this prominent that remain unnamed: even poor Shemaiah, with his single, brief speech [12:22–23] is known by name!) The reader is invited to see in them and their relationship something about Israel and Judah and their relationship.[13]

Once the reader reaches the end of the story, things will fall into place. Both Israel and Judah will have sinned against Yhwh; both will have succumbed to the violence of their enemies and been buried in exile far from their homeland. But just as the bones of the man of God preserve the prophet's from desecration (2 Kgs. 23:17–18), so too some hope remains. Even in the tomb of exile, Jehoiachin's release from prison opens the possibility of a future for Yhwh's people (2 Kgs. 25:27–30).

6. Even more of this comment than usual will be based on my admittedly subjective responses to the text. At first reading, I do not think about Jeroboam's wife very much at all. She is almost invisible, except as a presence that allows other people to talk. She has no name; she has no voice; she has, as far as the story goes, no feelings. Yet the more I think about her, the more tragic and poignant she becomes. Everybody uses her. Jeroboam uses her to avoid coming face-to-face with a prophet who despises him. The prophet uses her to condemn the king without confronting him. Even Yhwh uses her to bring about the death of her own child! She is a quintessential victim, and the pain she must feel knowing that "when your feet enter the city, the child shall die" (14:12), is beyond my imagining.

The narrator's depiction of her not only reduces her to the one-dimensional status of "victim," but also prolongs and deepens the victimization. Since the narrator gives her no name, no voice, and no feelings, she is deprived of her personhood, rendered insignificant in the machinations of God and king. Yet, paradoxically, it is precisely that callous narrative treatment of her that arouses my compassion. Could it be that *that* was the narrator's silent agenda?

CHARACTERIZATION

1. Things the narrator *tells* us about Jeroboam include: his parents' names, his tribal affiliation, and that his father was dead (11:26); he was "very able" (11:28); he had a wife (14:2) and at least two sons, one named Abijah (14:1) and one named Nadab (14:20). In chapter 13 examples of telling about other characters include: that the man from Judah is a "man of God" (that is, a prophet) and that he is "from Judah" (13:1); that the person from Bethel is a prophet, that he is old, and that he lives in Bethel (13:11); that he has several "sons" (13:2);[14] that he is the one "who brought him [the man of God] back" (13:20, 26). Examples of more enduring characteristics that the narrator tells us include Jeroboam's tribal affiliation, that the Bethel prophet is "old," and the provenance of both the prophet and the man of God. Examples of more transitory qualities are rare here, but might include Jeroboam's being "very able," and that the old prophet is the one who brought the man of God back (though, I suppose, once he has done so, that quality is permanent).

2. Perhaps the clearest example of internal monologue is Jeroboam's musing in 12:26–27. The narrator tells us explicitly that Jeroboam said this "in his heart" ("to himself," NRSV). Since internal monologue is a generally reliable

guide to the speaker's actual thoughts and feelings, we can infer that Jeroboam is very insecure in his new position, and is concerned about shoring up what he perceives to be fragile popular support for his kingship.

3. Almost any speech is going to reveal something about the speaker. I have chosen three speeches where quite divergent inferences are possible about precisely what the speech reveals of the speaker. The first two are in the scene of Rehoboam's rejection at Shechem. In 12:7 the elders advise Rehoboam to offer conciliation to the people. Two quite different interpretations of this advice are possible. The most obvious is that the elders have a certain degree of sympathy for the way the northerners were treated under Solomon, and they recommend some concessions on Rehoboam's part. (Or, perhaps better put, they recommend concessions on Rehoboam's part whether or not they sympathize with the northerners; being politically experienced, they may realize it is the only way to stave off the schism that threatens.) There is a subtler possibility. The elders only advise *speaking* conciliation to the northerners; they say nothing about following through on the promise. In this reading, they are simply exercising the shrewdness of political doublespeak: "Promise them anything; then, when they have awarded you the crown, do whatever you want with them." Both readings are entirely plausible. I have a very slight preference for the second reading because of the contrast in the elders' words between "today" and "forever."[15] In Hebrew the first word of their speech is "today," and the last words are "all days." The emphatic position of these two modifiers heightens the contrast: "Today, tell them what they want to hear; then they will be yours for all days."

In the same scene, the youngsters advise Rehoboam to speak harshly and threateningly to the northerners. The script they write for Rehoboam (12:10b–11) begins with the odd sentence, "My little finger is thicker than my father's loins" (NRSV). What the NRSV renders "my little finger" is simply "my little" in Hebrew, and the "loins" refers to the part of the body around the waist and hips. Many scholars conjecture that this obscure utterance is an obscene proverb, using a metaphor comparing the size of Rehoboam's *membrum virile* to Solomon's waist as a way of saying that Rehoboam is stronger than Solomon ever was. The remainder of the speech clearly means that Rehoboam intends to treat the northerners more harshly than Solomon did. Note, however, when Rehoboam later delivers his verdict to the northerners (12:14), although he follows the youngsters' advice *he leaves this first sentence out.* Two inferences are possible. One is that Rehoboam simply forgot it. I find this implausible, since in that case the narrator would have no reason to report it in 12:10b in the first place. As a characterization of the youngsters' crudeness, it is unnecessary, since they never appear again in the story. On the other hand, it may indicate that Rehoboam, politically inept as his decision proves to be, at least has the common sense not to insult the northerners with gross obscenity.

In the scene at the altar, after Jeroboam's hand has been withered and healed, he issues an invitation to the man of God to come to the king's home for a meal (13:7). Again, two very different, even incompatible inferences are plausible.

Since the king has just been miraculously healed, it makes perfect sense to read his invitation to the man of God as a gesture of gratitude. On the other hand, Jeroboam may be attempting to establish some relationship of communion with the man of God (table fellowship is a sacred bond in many cultures, including ancient Israel) in hopes of either undermining the man of God's commitment to his message or convincing him to mitigate it. Either reading does full justice to the text of the passage. My slight preference for the second grows out of my conviction that the paraphrase of 12:30–31 in 13:33–34 is intended to indicate that nothing that happened in chapter 13 had any effect on Jeroboam's obduracy (see above, pp. 135–36, 138), and that picturing Jeroboam sympathetically in 13:7 would work at cross-purposes to this agenda.[16]

4. My first example would, I believe, be quite evident to an ancient Israelite implied reader. It is much less likely to be noticed by a modern reader, unless the latter is unusually familiar with the larger narrative of Samuel and Kings. Ahijah is identified as a "Shilonite" (11:29), that is, a native of Shiloh in the northern kingdom. The mention of Shiloh evokes for some readers memories of Eli, who was priest at Shiloh, and Samuel, his servant who later became a full-fledged prophet (see 1 Sam. 1:24–28; 3:1–21). When Ahijah then tears his new cloak into twelve pieces as a sign that Yhwh intends to tear the kingdom out of Solomon's hand, the reader who has Samuel in mind will inevitably be reminded of the scene where Saul accidentally tears Samuel's cloak and Samuel uses that incident to condemn Saul and to prophesy that Yhwh will tear the kingdom away from him (1 Sam. 15:27–28). Ahijah's action reveals his awareness of the Shilonite prophetic tradition that stretches back to Samuel and his implicit claim to embody the continuation of that tradition.

A second interesting example is Rehoboam's willingness to consult advisers before he replies to the demands of the Israelite leaders. In itself, this appears to speak well of him. And that he consults two different groups of advisers could indicate an open-mindedness and a willingness to consider a variety of options before acting. The narrator, however, undermines this impression by his interjection in 12:8. He tells us that, even before consulting the youngsters, Rehoboam "disregarded the advice" of the elders. (Note that the remark is unnecessary at 12:8, since the narrator will say the same thing again, at a more appropriate moment, in 12:13b.) The impression is that Rehoboam already has his mind made up before he consults the youngsters, and the potential impression of open-mindedness that we could have had is transformed into its opposite.

A further example from the same scene is Rehoboam's choice of "Adoram, who was taskmaster over the forced labor" (12:18), as his representative to the leaders of Israel. What could Rehoboam possibly have been thinking? If there was anyone whom the Israelites hated, and with whom they would be unwilling to negotiate, it must have been Adoram! We are hardly surprised when the mob stones him to death. Then the light dawns. Could Rehoboam really have been completely oblivious to this possibility? Or was he perhaps throwing Adoram to the wolves as a way of trying to placate their rage?[17]

A final example is the Bethel prophet's exertions to bring the man of God from Judah back to his home for a meal. What is his motivation?[18] Is it professional courtesy—he recognizes that the man of God is a prophet like himself (13:18a), and offers him hospitality? That possibility is made unlikely by the narrator's aside to the reader that the old prophet was lying about receiving a divine oracle (13:18b).[19] A more probable inference takes its starting point in the information that the prophet's sons "told him all that the man of God had done that day in Bethel; the words also that he had spoken to the king, they told to their father" (13:11). That means that the old prophet knows that the man of God has condemned the altar and sanctuary Jeroboam had built, that he has demonstrated his prophetic credentials by the withering and healing of Jeroboam's hand, *and that he has been forbidden by Yhwh to eat or drink in Bethel.* On this reading, the old prophet's invitation is a conscious attempt to trick the man of God into disobeying Yhwh's command. From that basic inference, one can reason further. If the man of God can be suborned, his prophetic authority may be compromised and the power of his prophetic condemnation nullified. It is likely, then, that the old prophet is "of Bethel" not only in the sense that Bethel is his home, but also in the sense that he belongs to the staff of the new sanctuary there—or at least is positively disposed toward it.

5. When Ahijah addresses Jeroboam with his invitation to sedition (11:31, 35, 37), the implication is that Ahijah considers Jeroboam's loyalty to Solomon to be fragile, despite the fact that Jeroboam is in a position of power and responsibility in Solomon's administration (11:28). Is there any indication in the text that might support Ahijah's suspicions? Yes, there is, though it assumes a certain knowledge of Israelite geopolitics on the reader's part. Jeroboam is from the tribe of Ephraim (11:26), one of the most important tribes of the northern kingdom. Solomon put him in charge of "all the forced labor of the house of Joseph" (11:28). The "house of Joseph" was the most important power bloc of the northern kingdom, comprising the tribes of Manasseh and, yes, Ephraim.[20] In other words, Jeroboam was appointed to be the foreman in charge of oppressing his own people. The likelihood of his being interiorly conflicted is very high, and Ahijah's invitation to sedition would offer Jeroboam a way to escape his divided loyalties. This could well explain why Jeroboam "rebelled against the king" (11:27).

After the northern kingdom has declared its independence of the rule of Jerusalem and chosen Jeroboam to be its first king, Rehoboam organizes a military campaign to regain what he perceives to be a realm that belongs to him (12:21). This is hardly surprising; kings are typically loath to surrender territory over which they claim sovereignty. What *is* surprising is that, once Shemaiah expresses Yhwh's disapproval of the military solution (12:23–24), the army immediately disbands and returns home, apparently without discussion or debate. Note, though, how the narrator attributes this dispersion to an unspecified "they," and tells us nothing explicit about *Rehoboam's* reaction to Shemaiah's oracle and the army's subsequent withdrawal. One may infer that Rehoboam agrees with the decision to disband, since he does not seem to offer any objection; this would imply that Rehoboam is obedient to what he perceives to be Yhwh's will and word. Or one may infer that the sudden disappearance of popular support for Rehoboam's military plans leaves him with no choice but to accept the situation, no matter how he himself might feel about it.

POINT OF VIEW

1. In 1 Kings 11 I find myself fairly strongly sharing Jeroboam's point of view rather than taking a neutral stance between Ahijah and Jeroboam. The length and portentous quality of the speech are the major reasons I attend strongly to Ahijah (as Jeroboam does), rather than to Jeroboam. Jeroboam's complete silence also contributes to this. He never distracts me from Ahijah's words by expressing any feelings about the sedition Ahijah is urging him to. Further, several statements in the chapter have already conspired to strengthen my positive attitude toward Jeroboam (that is, to move me to some level of identification with him). The note that he rebelled against Solomon could cut either way; but from the immediately preceding context, which includes Yhwh's announcement that he will "tear the kingdom away from" Solomon (11:11), I understand Jeroboam's rebellion as part of Yhwh's plan. Further, I have just been told that Jeroboam is "able" and "industrious" (11:28), qualities I can easily admire. For these reasons, I find myself fairly close to Jeroboam, and I listen to Ahijah's speech for what it can tell me about Jeroboam's destiny.

In chapter 14 things are a bit different. I find myself, at least on first reading, in a relatively neutral position.[21] My primary focus is on Ahijah, of course, because of the length and importance of his speech. And the silence of Jeroboam's wife, like Jeroboam's silence in chapter 11, does not distract my attention from Ahijah. However, I know nothing about the woman that would serve to increase my sense of identification with her, and even Ahijah's speech is primarily about Jeroboam and his dynasty, not about his wife. But I find my neutrality changing on subsequent readings. I have already explained how my sympathies for this nameless, voiceless woman increase as I read and reread the passage. As my sympathies increase, I find myself gradually moving closer to her and sharing her point of view. This is why, for me, Ahijah's announcement that her entry into the house will signal the child's death (14:12b) and the fulfillment of that prophecy (14:17b) wring my heart.

2. Beginning in 12:3 I find myself in a relatively neutral position, watching the representatives of the northern kingdom lay their demands before Rehoboam. I am at first primarily focused on them as they present their demands, but I am at the same time curious about Rehoboam and how he will respond. So I stand in a place where I can watch both parties in the dialogue.

In 12:6–11 Rehoboam takes counsel first with the elders, then with the youngsters. Ordinarily, my attention would continue to be split between the dialogue partners, since I am interested both in what advice the elders and youngsters give, and in Rehoboam's reaction to that advice. However, the narrator adds a note that undermines my attention to Rehoboam: he tells me as early as 12:8, even before the youngsters have come on stage, that Rehoboam dismisses the elders' advice. Knowing what will happen distances me from the dialogue. I no longer have to ponder the question, What will Rehoboam decide? That allows me to turn my attention to other dimensions of the scene, such as the caginess of the elders' advice, the overbearing (and possibly obscene) tone of the youngsters' advice, and the character of a king who simultaneously consults advisers and dismisses their advice apparently without weighing it.

In 12:12–16, although I know what Rehoboam is going to say, my sympathies are with the northerners, and their approach to Rehoboam sets my point of view. I stand with them while Rehoboam delivers his decree. I may (if I am attentive) have enough distance from them to notice what they cannot know, namely, that Rehoboam has left out the most insulting part of the youngsters' script. This moves me closer to an omniscient point of view, which is then strongly established in 12:15. The narrator reminds me that the divine will is working itself out behind everything I have witnessed—something that neither Rehoboam nor the representatives of Israel (except Jeroboam) could know. From that omniscient point of view, too, I see the rupture between north and south, that is, the political disintegration decreed by Yhwh, become final (12:16).

3. In 13:11–19 I find myself in a neutral point of view. I cannot share that of the old prophet, because I have no idea what his plans are when he sets out to encounter the man of God; nor, even when I know that "he lied" (13:18), do I know *why* he lied. But the narrator's aside that "he lied" gives me information that is not available to an ordinary observer; and therefore my point of view, though not omniscient (because of all those things I do not know), is nevertheless more informed than that of an external observer. The distance afforded by this point of view means that I am less focused on the action of the scene and can spare more attention to ponder the old prophet's mysterious motivations.

In 13:20–25 I could share somewhat the man of God's point of view while he listens to the old prophet's oracle of condemnation; and that point of view could perdure through 13:23. However, once the man of God is dead (13:24), he no longer has a point of view. By that time I am at a considerable distance from the old prophet's home, watching things happen after the man of God's death. It is probably better, then, to consider this whole section as maintaining the same neutral, partially omniscient point of view that marked 13:11–19.

In 13:26–32 the same somewhat neutral point of view seems present at first, but once we reach 13:28 that changes. We already know about the lion and the donkey from 13:24; so the point of view here is that of the old prophet. Though the narrator does not say so explicitly, it is the old prophet who sees the lion and donkey in 13:28, and goes on to notice something we did not know, namely, that the lion was acting very un-lionlike (13:28b). I am prepared, then, to develop a certain degree of empathy with the old prophet when, upon his return, he mourns and honors the man he had earlier betrayed.

MANIPULATION OF TIME

1. Some parts of the narrative move relatively slowly (13:11–13); other parts move much more quickly (13:14, 19). The narrator accomplishes this by filling 13:11–13 with incremental details (they came and told him; they saddled a donkey and he mounted it) and by including unnecessary words. Look at 13:11b; this is very verbose: "told him all that the man of God had done that day in Bethel; the words also that he had spoken to the king, they told to their father." The narrator could have said the same thing much more simply: "told him all that the man of God had done and said." The reader, after all, knows that it was that day, knows that it was in Bethel, and knows that the king was there. By contrast, there are no wasted words in the faster parts: "he went after the man of God and found him"; "the man of God went back with him and ate and drank. . . ." Whole journeys are summarized in single verbs. The effect (at least for me) is a sense that the slower parts contain the more important elements; the narrator slows the scene down so that I can concentrate on it. I realize that the old prophet knows *all* the details of the man of God's deeds and words (therefore including the command not to eat and drink in Bethel). The donkey gets highlighted because of the role it will play later in the story (13:23, 24, 28). The journeys are of lesser importance,[22] but the fact that the man of God *ate and drank* is significant; so these actions are slowed down with direct objects ("ate food and drank water"—objects that underscore that the man of God is violating the very words of the command he received from Yhwh) and with a superfluous prepositional phrase, "in his house."

Dialogue points up that the old prophet is more important than his sons: his words are given in dialogue form; theirs are not. Dialogue also slows the scene where the prophet encounters the man of God; this allows some suspense to develop, especially when the man of God (unnecessarily, at least from the reader's point of view) repeats the whole command he was given. We have plenty of time to wonder, What is the old prophet up to? Will the man of God fall prey to his lie?

2. This may be a bit strained, but I think the last part of 13:28 is pure description, in the sense that the lion and the donkey are not *acting*. "The lion had not eaten the body or attacked the donkey" implies that they are both standing there unmoving, and the donkey is intact.

On the other hand, look at the words immediately preceding this. The words "with the donkey and the lion standing beside the body" are also descriptive, but there is a trick here. This is information we already know from 13:24. In fact, this is an issue of *point of view*. The old prophet has just arrived, and it is *he* who sees "the donkey and the lion standing beside the body." So, even though the words are descriptive, they are better treated as part of the action because they name what the old prophet sees.

3. Jeroboam recalls that Ahijah "said of me that I should be king over this people." Jeroboam remembers when Ahijah favored him, but presumably (since he sends his wife as his intermediary) he realizes that this is no longer the case. That he recalls the good old days at this moment, when his son is ill, strikes me as showing a wistful nostalgia, and perhaps a desperate hope that Ahijah may retain enough goodwill to intercede for Jeroboam's son. Without that line, Jeroboam would simply seem to be sending his wife for an oracle about the boy; I would have no glimpse of the glimmer of hope he seems to hold in his heart.

There is another flashback in the immediate context, though the NRSV obscures it. In 14:5 it would be more accurate to translate, "the LORD *had said* to Ahijah . . ." instead of "the LORD said to Ahijah." Yhwh's speech, which includes the last words of the verse as well (see chapter 5, n. 21), precedes the moment when Jeroboam's wife "came to the house" (14:4a). It forms part of the background information that includes the purely descriptive note that Ahijah was nearly blind (14:4b); this background information is what enables the reader to understand how Ahijah was able to recognize the woman. (Notice, though, that the narrator does not tell us what Yhwh instructed Ahijah to say to Jeroboam's wife. We will consider this lacuna in the next section.)

4. I see two examples of foreshadowing in these verses. The first is the remark that "Rehoboam reigned over the Israelites who were living in the towns of Judah" (12:17). I would call this a foreshadowing because it really describes a continuing situation subsequent to the immediate debacle at Shechem. Israelite and Judahite implied readers would, I believe, respond very differently to the statement. The Israelite (who, presumably, is now a citizen of the northern kingdom) would feel sympathy for his compatriots living in another realm. The Judahite would feel a degree of self-satisfaction that, even though much of the territory of the Davidic kingdom had been lost, at least the presence of Israelites in Judahite territory had not compromised its integrity. (I would guess too that their respective reactions would also be shaped by which kingdom had the upper hand at the moment, and by whether Israel and Judah were currently at peace or hostile to one another.)

The second example of foreshadowing is the remark in 12:19 that the division has continued right up to the day of the narrator's recital of the story to the narratee.[23] This aside to the narratee[24] makes the story immediately and powerfully relevant to the narratee's own life situation. For a reader, that effect is only as strong as the reader's ability to enter the narrative world and share the narratee's role. Here too an implied Israelite reader and an implied Judahite reader will no doubt respond differently to the remark. But even more, the implied reader will respond differently when the two kingdoms still exist and when one or both of them have been destroyed. An implied reader for whom both Israel and Judah are continuing realities (that is, the Assyrian destruction of the northern kingdom in 722/721 BCE has not yet taken place) will feel the same sense of immediate relevance as the narratee. An implied reader in whose past Israel has fallen, and perhaps Judah as well (587 BCE), will have a more profound sense of tragedy, since he or she sees that the *division* of the two kingdoms was not the worst that could happen.

There is also, in these verses, an attempt at simultaneity, although the NRSV misses the nuance. (See n. 17 this appendix.)

GAPS AND AMBIGUITIES

1. Ahijah tears his cloak into twelve pieces, gives ten to Jeroboam, and pledges to reserve one for the house of David. What happened to the twelfth piece? While the apparent triviality of the gap could suggest that it is a simple oversight on the part of the narrator, it is so blatant (once one notices it) that we have to wonder whether it might not have some deeper meaning. Indeed, when we pursue the story further, there is one tribe whose loyalties are divided. Benjamin, originally a northern tribe, is so immediately adjacent to Jerusalem that Rehoboam dare not leave its territory under northern control. He incorporates Benjamin—or at least as much of its territory as he can manage to seize—under Judahite sovereignty (see 12:21).

2. For me as a reader the effect would be quite different. If I knew in advance what Ahijah was going to say to Jeroboam's wife, it would maneuver me into a more neutral point of view, watching the woman as she receives the bad news. By depriving me of this information in advance, the narrator increases my sense of identification with the tragic woman—I wait for the news just as she does, and receive it at the same moment.

3. In an earlier section I explained why Jeroboam may have experienced a severe conflict in his respective loyalties to his own tribe and to his king, and how this may explain why he "rebelled against the king." In that light, we may well hear layered meanings when the narrator tells us that Ahijah approached Jeroboam "when Jeroboam was leaving Jerusalem" (11:29). On the surface of it, this refers to geographical movement; Jeroboam has presumably been in the capital, perhaps on official business, and he is now on his way somewhere else, perhaps back to supervise the labor gangs. But in view of the disaffection that the mention of his rebellion reveals, and in view of the seditious nature of the oracle that Ahijah is about to pronounce, Jeroboam's "leaving Jerusalem" can also imply an intention (or at least a destiny) to break away from Solomon's service. There is no reason to exclude either of these meanings from our reading.

4. There are several ways, all compatible, to understand the phrase. The simplest and most straightforward is to read it as a reference back to the action of 13:18–19, where, in response to the prophet's invitation, the man of God "went back" (*šwb*) with him. But there is a second meaning that emerges in a later scene that echoes this one. In 13:29 the prophet again finds the man of God

on the road—this time as a corpse—and "brings him back" for burial. The two scenes are clearly parallel, though ironically so. In the first, the prophet brings the man of God back deceptively, and the prophet's hospitality is hypocritical; in the second, the prophet brings the man of God back sincerely, and his hospitality (the burial) is honorable. The deep irony is that the first "bringing back" was the cause of the second. If the man of God had not disobeyed, he would not have died. So when the reader arrives at the second scene and discovers the prophet "bringing back" the man of God's body, the reader realizes that the phrase "the prophet who had brought him back" pointed *forward* to this scene as well as backward to the first one.

The metaphorical meaning is also operative. The man of God's acceptance of the old prophet's invitation to eat and drink was an act of disobedience to God (even if the man of God was misled). In other words, it was an act of "turning back" from God's commands. Since the old prophet instigated this behavior, he is rightly described as "the prophet who caused the man of God to *šwb*," that is, caused the man of God to disobey Yhwh.

Finally, the literal and metaphorical meanings converge to form a fourth way of understanding the term. God's commands to the man of God forbade three things: eating, drinking, and (literally) "returning [*šwb*] to go by the road on which you went" (13:17). It is not entirely clear what that third command means. Perhaps the man of God is being enjoined to return to Judah by a route other than the one he took to go north to Bethel; or perhaps he is being told to keep moving onward at all times, to Bethel and back, and never to retrace his steps. What is clear, however, is that he is forbidden to *šwb* in some sense or other. When the narrator tells us, then, that the man of God *šwb* with the old prophet (13:19), the narrator is already describing how the man of God broke one of the divine commands. His eating and drinking with the old prophet will break the other two. Note how, when the old prophet is seized by the word of God, he condemns the man of God for violating *all three* of the commands (13:21–22: "Because you have disobeyed . . . you *šwb* and you have eaten and you have drunk . . ."). So to say that the man of God *šwb* is not only to say, in a general way, that he has turned away from God's command; it is also to say that he has directly and specifically disobeyed a command not to *šwb*. And he was led to this explicit disobedience by the old prophet who claimed that he was commissioned to "cause him to *šwb*" (13:18).

Note: For several other examples of important gaps and ambiguities in the Jeroboam story, go back to the discussion of question 3 under "Characterization."

REPETITION AND VARIATION

1. The first repetition I detect occurs when Rehoboam asks for the youngsters' advice by quoting the objection voiced by the leaders of Israel (12:9, quoting 12:4). There are two indications that the repetition is not needed. First, when

Rehoboam spoke to his elder advisers (12:6), he did not cite the Israelites' demands at all. This implies that his elder advisers were already familiar with them, either because the elders were present when the demands were presented or because the demands had since become common knowledge. Second, when the youngsters repeat the objection in their turn (12:10), they include elements of the Israelites' words that Rehoboam did not use. They begin with a direct accusation against "your father," as did the Israelites;[25] Rehoboam mentions "your father" only at the end of his quotation. They use the word "heavy."[26] And they also preserve a wordplay that Rehoboam weakened.[27] In this way they show that they too are already familiar with the original wording of the demands. Rehoboam's repetition, then, is unnecessary and may well be intended to convey subtler implications.

There are several variations between the Israelites' words and Rehoboam's version of them. He eliminates the direct accusation against Solomon; he eliminates the reference to "the hard service of your father"; he eliminates the adjective "heavy" in the Israelites' demand that he lighten "the . . . yoke";[28] and he leaves out the Israelites' conditional promise to serve him. It appears to me that most, if not all, of these changes are attempts to weaken the force of the Israelites' complaints. Solomon's favoritism for Judah would have been well known;[29] ignoring the Israelites' mention of it is tantamount to dismissing it as insignificant. Revising "heavy yoke" to "yoke" amounts to the same sort of weakening. And eliminating the Israelites' conditional promise leaves the tone of their language entirely confrontational, with no openness to compromise. As I read it, then, Rehoboam is signaling to his young advisers that he has no patience with the Israelites' complaints; and the youngsters, sycophants that they are, reply accordingly.

In this light, it is also worth speculating why there is *no* repetition when Rehoboam consults his elder advisers. Their prior knowledge of the Israelites' demand is not a sufficient explanation, since Rehoboam did not hesitate to repeat at least parts of that demand to the youngsters. To my mind, the answer to this question is made clear by a second case of repetition. In 12:8 the narrator tells us that Rehoboam "disregarded the advice that the elder men gave him." And in 12:13 the narrator repeats the same words verbatim, and adds that he "spoke to them [the Israelites] according to the advice of the young men." The words are entirely appropriate in 12:13. But why does the narrator anticipate them already in 12:8? He seems to be telling us that Rehoboam had decided to disregard the elders' advice *even before* he heard the youngsters' ideas. This is especially plausible in view of the way he prompts the youngsters for the advice he wants. If that is the case, then he may well have made up his mind even before he consulted the elders. Having done so, he had no need to prompt them; he already knew he was going to ignore them. His consultation of them was little more than a formal gesture, owed to them because they "had attended his father Solomon while he was still alive" (12:6); the youngsters, by contrast, "had grown up with him and now attended him" (12:8).

Another repetition in the same scene is, to my mind, rather less significant. Rehoboam had told the Israelite leaders, "Go away for three days, then return to me" (12:5). The narrator will quote part of this command again, "Return to me on the third day" (12:12b), after recounting that the Israelite leaders "came to Rehoboam on the third day."[30] The second and third occurrences telescope the two parts of Rehoboam's directive by incorporating their equivalents of "three days" and "return to me" into the same clause. The narrator's citation of the directive uses the same verb Rehoboam used ("return")—the narrator is "reliable"[31]—but his account of the leaders' behavior changes it to "came." This variation may simply be stylistic ornamentation, but there is another possible reading. Very tentatively indeed, I suggest that this is the narrator's way of implying something about the Israelite leaders' attitude. They do not see themselves as subjects *obeying* a royal command to "return" to him, since they have not yet recognized Rehoboam's authority; they are "coming" to Rehoboam on their own terms, as negotiators intent on establishing a changed relationship between him and their people.

I find two other instances of repetition in 12:1–20, neither of which strikes me as having any special surplus of meaning. In 12:15 the narrator says that "the king did not listen to the people," and in 12:16 he repeats, "When all Israel saw that the king would not listen to the people." The repetition is somewhat fuller than it needs to be, but that is probably because the narrator feels a need to pick up the story again after his aside in the remainder of 12:15.[32] Alternatively, it might be a subtle way of pointing out that, in contrast with Rehoboam, the Israelites had negotiated in good faith, and break off negotiations only when Rehoboam's intransigence becomes evident.[33] The last example of repetition is when the narrator, at the end of 12:16, quotes a few words from the Israelites' brief poem. The poem said, "To your tents, O Israel," and the narrator confirms that "Israel went away to their tents." Here I see no special significance to the repetition other than the narrator's assurance to us that the Israelites acted *exactly* as they said they would.

2. There are several variations to be considered. The first is the reversed order of the corresponding verses: 12:30 matches 13:34; 12:31 matches 13:33. This, as we see in chapter 10 on structure, strengthens their function as an inclusion, because in effect it turns the repetition into a *double* inclusion: 12:31 and 13:33 form an inclusion around 12:32–13:32, and 12:30 and 13:34 form a further inclusion around 12:31–13:33. Let's consider each pair of corresponding verses separately (the translation is from the NRSV).

> 12:30. And this thing became a sin,
>   for the people went to worship before the one . . .[34] as far as Dan.
> 13:34. This matter became sin to the house of Jeroboam,
>   so as to cut it off and to destroy it from the face of the earth.

The change from "thing" to "matter" is trivial. They mean about the same thing in English, and in fact they render the same word in Hebrew (*dābār*).

The English language variance is simply a translator's stylistic choice. There is, however, a difference in Hebrew that is not reflected in the NRSV. In 12:30 the narrator says, "this thing (*haddābār hazzeh*)"; in 13:34 he says, "*in* this thing" (*baddābār hazzeh*). Though minor, the change makes a difference. It is best understood together with a second change, namely, the addition of the words "to the house of Jeroboam" in 13:34. In 12:30 *the* "thing" is what was mentioned in 12:29, the cult of the golden calves. Since "the people went to worship" them, the "sin" referred to in 12:30 is a national offense on the part of the populace. In 13:34 the thing *in which* the sin arose is Jeroboam's "evil way" (13:33), specified as installing unqualified individuals for priestly service at the high places. The offense was Jeroboam's, but the destruction that would result from it was to extend to his whole house. The shift is from a focus on Israel's sin, at Jeroboam's instigation, to Jeroboam's sin from which grew dynastic disaster. The variations, then, strengthen the focus on Jeroboam and his intransigence that the inclusion itself creates.

The second pair of corresponding verses reads as follows.[35]

12:31.   He also made houses on high places
and made priests from among all the people
who were not Levites.

13:33.   Even after this event Jeroboam did not turn from his evil way
but made priests for the high places from among all the people;
any who wanted it he installed to be priests for the high places.

The first line of 13:33 achieves the shift I mentioned a moment ago, and focuses this second part of the inclusion on Jeroboam. The second line of 13:33 telescopes the first two lines of 12:31 ("high places" from the first line, "made priests from among all the people" from the second). The only variation is that 13:33 eliminates the word "houses" (i.e., temples or sanctuaries). This is probably simply due to the telescoping of the two sentences into one. The word is necessary in 12:31, since Jeroboam made the *building* but not the high place itself. (A "high place" was a hilltop where worship of some deity took place regularly. It is likely that the high place in 12:31 was an already existing cultic site to which Jeroboam gave royal approval by building a temple there.) The word "house" is not necessary in 13:33 since "high place" was shorthand for the whole cultic installation on the hilltop including the building and the cult practiced there.

The third line of 13:33 represents the most significant variations: it specifies that he made the priests by "installing" them, and it changes the description of the illegitimate priests Jeroboam installs from "not Levites" to "any who wanted it."[36] Attributing the installation of the priests to Jeroboam strengthens the impression that his support of the cult place at Bethel was not simply a matter of royal administrative pragmatism but involved his personal participation as well. He did not just commission a building and appoint ("make") its personnel, he presided at their installation.[37] The final change, from "not Levites" to "any who wanted it," emphasizes substituting the human will of the priests themselves for the divine will of Yhwh, who had entrusted Israelite priesthood to the descendants of Levi.[38]

3. When he has buried the man of God from Judah, the old prophet of Bethel takes up the man of God's original prophecy (13:32a), and then embellishes it by extending it to the houses of the high places "that are in the cities of Samaria."[39] Despite his earlier lie to the man of God (13:18), the old prophet has become a bearer of God's true word (13:20–22, fulfilled in 13:23–30). The death of the man of God, however, could jeopardize the effectiveness of the prophetic condemnation he uttered against Bethel in 13:2. By reiterating that condemnation, the old prophet makes it his own and assures its ultimate fulfillment; and when he extends it to the "houses of the high places that are in the cities of Samaria," he utters his own original oracle. The fulfillment narrative in 2 Kings 23:19–20, therefore, confirms the old prophet's credentials as much as it does those of the man of God from Judah. Together the whole complex of prophecies, lies, infidelities, and fulfillments adumbrates a theology of the prophetic word that subordinates the prophet to the word, the vehicle to the message. Yhwh's word will prevail, despite the unworthiness of its bearers.

VOICE(S) OF THE NARRATOR

1. It is truly tempting to attribute these passages to the implied author rather than to a narrator, particularly in view of the mentions of other written source documents; they are like erudite reference footnotes in a modern textbook. In my opinion, however, this is simply another example of the misleading transparency of the narrator. It is not difficult to conceive of the (oral) narrator including such a statement in the tale. When we tell stories, we often cite our sources ("I heard from so-and-so that . . ." or "I read somewhere that . . ."). Moreover, the decision whether to attribute these passages to the narrator or to the author has a very important implication. If we attribute them to the author, we understand the source documents to have existed in our primary world, and the author to have consulted them in preparing the text.[40] If we attribute them to the narrator, we understand the source documents to have existed in the secondary world as literary creations of the author (just as the characters "Jeroboam" and the "man of God from Judah" and the donkey and lion of 1 Kgs. 13:24 and 28 exist in the secondary world as literary creations); and we leave open the question of whether something corresponding to them existed in our primary world (as Jeroboam certainly did) or not (as the donkey and lion—stereotypical "story animals"—may not have).[41]

Personally, I find little in either passage that I would describe as "opinion" or "evaluation." (This is not true of all such regnal formulas; sometimes approval or condemnation of the king in question is clear.) In the Solomon passage, mention is made of his "wisdom" (11:41). In most of its appearances in the Solomon story "wisdom" is praiseworthy; but, as we have seen above, this is not always the case (see p. 72). As a result, its mention here is not merely informational but reawakens all the ambivalence the narrative has shown toward the classic claim of Solomon's wisdom. The rest of 11:41–43 is simple factual data. In 14:19–20, the concluding formula for Jeroboam's regnal account, only the phrase "how he warred and how he reigned" could conceivably carry any evaluative force. But there is not, to my mind, a clear positive or negative valence. Even "how he warred," by not specifying whom he warred against (and there is nothing about his wars elsewhere in the Jeroboam story), leaves open the question whether these wars were good for Yhwh's people.[42]

For me, the main effect of these passages is *distance* from the action of the story. The concluding regnal formulas are retrospective summaries. They invite me to step back from the flow of the plot and consider the entirety of the king's reign—its dynamics, its events, its results. Personally, I cannot undertake that reflective consideration without coming to some sort of evaluation of the king, perhaps moral, perhaps political. And so I am urged to judgment. In the case of the two passages under consideration at the moment, I do not feel that I am being urged to one judgment rather than another. Of course, my negative or positive evaluation will ultimately emerge not just from this concluding regnal formula, but from the whole story of the king's reign; and on that level the stories of Solomon and of Jeroboam have both done their best to shape my opinion. The neutrality of the concluding formula may simply reflect the narrator's confidence that he has made his case convincingly.

2. One cannot really consider 13:3 in isolation, since it prophesies an event whose fulfillment is recounted in 13:5. It is certainly possible to see these verses as part of the story; in that case the prophecy is a flashback to some earlier moment ("he *had* given" the oracle) when the man of God uttered the words attributed to him here, and 13:5 apparently recounts its almost immediate fulfillment. But that paints a bizarre picture (one that has bewildered many historical critics). It portrays the man of God announcing the utter destruction of the altar at which Jeroboam is standing,[43] and the crumbling of that altar apparently on the spot. Yet Jeroboam makes no reference to such a spectacular demonstration of power.

On the other hand, if we take the verses as a two-part frame break, they are the narrator's asides to the narratee. In other words, they are not part of the story's events, and it is irrelevant whether Jeroboam or anyone else at Bethel actually heard the "sign" or witnessed its fulfillment. They are the narrator's way of linking the events of the story (the man of God's oracle against the Bethel altar in 13:2) to the present of the narrator and narratee. In this reading, the narrator informs the narratee that, in addition to the oracle of 13:2, the man of God *also* delivered a prediction that the altar would crumble; and, by the time the narrator tells the story to the narratee, this has in fact occurred (13:5).

3. There are two parts to 1 Kings 12:15. The first clause, "So the king did not listen to the people," hardly breaks frame at all. It summarizes the action of

12:13–14 and characterizes that action with reference to the earlier requests of the Israelite leaders in 12:4. On the other hand, precisely because it does not advance the story but merely rephrases what has already taken place, it slows the pace, distances the narratee from the action, and affords the narratee and the reader some time for reflection and consideration. Further, by summarizing the story in terms of the tension between the Israelites' request and the king's response, it invites the narratee (and the reader) to take a position vis-à-vis those conflicting stances.[44]

I suspect that this clause will affect some modern, Western readers quite differently from the way it would an ancient Israelite implied reader. To "listen to the people" is ideal behavior for leaders in a democracy; a reader raised on the values of modern democratic society may well understand the narrator's words as a criticism of Rehoboam's unwillingness to negotiate seriously with popular opinion. But would the ancient Israelite reader share that political ideology? We do not know enough about the operations of monarchy within Israel to answer that question with full confidence, but the impression we get from other ancient Near Eastern polities is that attention to popular opinion would not have figured significantly in the king's job description.[45]

The remainder of the verse is a classic frame break (from "because it was a turn of affairs . . ."). No one in the story is aware of this; it is an aside to the narratee by the narrator, interpreting the events at Shechem in the light of the oracle of Ahijah (11:31, 35). As such, it also implies an evaluation: since it is God's doing, foretold by a prophet, it is good.

4. The frame break I have in mind is in 12:19: "So Israel has been in rebellion against the house of David to this day."[46] The narrator's disapproval is clearly revealed in the words "rebellion against the house of David." I detect considerable tension between this attitude, which condemns the Israelite secession as "rebellion," and that of the narrator in 12:15, which reminds the narratee that Rehoboam's obduracy (the immediate cause of the secession) was "brought about by Yhwh." It is entirely plausible to see these very different attitudes as signs of conflicting narrative voices. However, I do not think that such a conclusion is inevitable. The reason for my hesitation lies in the very similar situation in 2:26–27. As I read that passage, the narrator considers Solomon's actions against Abiathar to be unjustified (see chap. 9, n. 11). At the same time, however, the narrator sees it as the fulfillment of a divine prophecy (2:27b). There the narrator seems to be saying that the prophecy was fulfilled (and that is good, since it is God's will), but that *Solomon's motives for acting*—which certainly did not include fulfilling ancient prophecies—were unworthy. Similarly, here in 12:15 and 19, the narrator may be saying that Rehoboam's actions precipitated the prophesied schism and were therefore according to God's will; but that *the Israelites' reasons for seceding*—namely, Solomon's injustices and their threatened perpetuation by Rehoboam—were not sufficient to justify turning their backs on the divinely chosen house of David.

Nevertheless, whether one thinks of a single narrator whose opinion is complex and carefully nuanced or of an implied author who creates conflicting narrative voices as a way to express a coherent vision, the reader still must ponder how to resolve the tension and find the unified view that transcends it. The introduction of the term "rebellion" in 12:19 suggests a possibility. In 12:15 the narrator refers to Ahijah's oracle, which prophesied the *separation* of ten tribes from the house of David (11:31) but did not characterize this separation as "rebellion."[47] One might well surmise that the coherent authorial vision lying behind this passage is a sociopolitical arrangement in which the tribes formed two independent polities living in harmony with one another but united only by their worship of Yhwh (no matter how unlikely, humanly speaking, such an arrangement would be).

STRUCTURE AND SYMMETRY

1. In 12:1–20 the repeated element is both verbal ("all Israel"[48] in both passages [twice in 12:20] and "to make him king"/"made him king") and thematic (the leaders of "all Israel" choose their king). As I mentioned in passing (see n. 5), this echo adds a note of irony to the whole story: the leaders of Israel came to Shechem to make Rehoboam king, but eventually chose someone else. Although the story is, in the main, a story of the disintegration of Solomonic hegemony, the irony also points up that Rehoboam himself, by perpetuating the injustices of his father, shares responsibility for the political secession of the northern tribes from the house of David. Yhwh promised Jeroboam the throne of Israel because of Solomon's sins (11:31–39), but "all Israel" fulfilled the promise because of Rehoboam's own folly.

In the case of 12:30–13:34, the inclusion has several repeated elements arranged chiastically; and the inclusion surrounds two relatively autonomous stories (13:1–10, 11–32), both of which, the inclusion suggests, demonstrate Jeroboam's intransigence. (See the discussions above on pp. 135–36 and 150–52.)

2. The inclusion is chiastic, with two sets of repeated elements in inverse order. The speech begins and ends with "day": "if today"[49] and "all days." (Notice, however, that this repetition entails a potentially ironic *contrast* between "now" and "always"; see p. 140 above.) Immediately inside that inclusion come the parallel phrases "you will be servant to this people"/"they will be to you servants." The inclusion surrounds the elders' advice, which is given in three clauses: "you serve them, you answer them, you speak to them good words."

Since the three clauses are of unequal length (the first two clauses are one word each in Hebrew; the third is much longer) and contain no verbal links, they do not clearly continue the reverse symmetry. However, if one were to put the first clause last ("you answer them, you speak to them good words, you serve them"), the balance of the whole unit would be symmetrical, focusing attention on the central element, where the elders advise Rehoboam to "speak good words" (be conciliatory?) to the Israelites. And the sequence of clauses would make much better sense: "answer them" (answer them how?); "speak good words to them";

and then, having spoken to them, "serve them." Even more importantly, putting "serve them" last, after a clear midpoint, would link this "serve" with the word "servants" in the final clause of the verse and imply that the Israelites will be his "servants for all days" if Rehoboam "serves them [for all days]." In the text as we have it, however, "you serve them" comes *before* any possible midpoint. That suggests two things. First, it links Rehoboam's service with the word "servant" that *begins* the verse, where the elders advise him to be the Israelites' servant "today." Second, it implies that the nature of Rehoboam's service is spelled out in the next two clauses—"answering" and "speaking"—and is therefore literally "lip service," telling the Israelites what they want to hear. In short, the present wording of the text supports the "cynical" reading I proposed above better than a hypothetically reworded and symmetrically more satisfying version would.

3. Let's begin with a series of very noticeable repeated elements: "tear the kingdom from the hand of Solomon"/"take the kingdom away from his son"[50] (11:31b, 35a); "give you ten tribes"/"give it to you, that is, the ten tribes" (11:31c, 35b); "one tribe will remain his"/"to his son I will give one tribe" (11:32a, 36a); "my servant David" (11:32b, 34b, 36b, 38e); "Jerusalem, the city I have chosen" (11:32c, 36c); "walk in my ways" (11:33c, 38b); "what is right in my sight" (11:33c, 38c); "my statutes and my ordinances/commandments" (11:33d, 38d); "his father David did/David my servant did" (11:33e, 38e). These repetitions are more than sufficient to reveal the forward symmetry. The layout that follows includes a few more subunits, some unmatched and some based on thematic rather than verbal parallels.[51] I will make several comments below.

    a. I am tearing the kingdom from Solomon's hand (11:31a)
      b. and I will give you ten tribes (11:31b)
        c. one tribe will be his (11:32a)
          d. for the sake of David my servant (11:32b)
            e. and for the sake of Jerusalem, my chosen city (11:32c)
              X. *(unmatched subunit)* (11:33a)
                f. because they did not walk in my ways (11:33b)
                  g. and do what is right in my sight (11:33c)
                    h. my statutes and my ordinances (11:33d)
                      i. as David his father did (11:33e)
                        j. I will not take the whole kingdom from him (11:34a)
                          k. make him ruler all the days of his life (11:34b)
    a'. I will take the kingship from his son's hand (11:35a)
      b'. and I will give you ten tribes (11:35b)
        c'. one tribe will be his son's (11:36a)
          d'. for the sake of David my servant (11:36b)
            e'. before me in Jerusalem, my chosen city (11:36c)
              Y. *(unmatched subunit)* (11:37)

> f'. if you walk in my ways (11:38b)
>> g'. and do what is right in my sight (11:38c)
>>> h'. my statutes and my commandments (11:38d)
>>>> i'. as David my servant did (11:38e)
>>>>>> k'. I will build you an enduring house (11:38f)
>>>>> j'. I will not punish David's seed forever (11:39)

The forward symmetry points to progression rather than contrast. This is borne out when we notice that the first half of the oracle speaks of Solomon and the past; the second half speaks of Solomon's son and the future. But there are some asymmetries in the pattern as well. The subunits I have marked *X* and *Y* correspond in their locations in the pattern, but there are no verbal links or even thematic parallels connecting them. There is only a vague contrast between Solomon's sins of idolatry (which constitute disobedience to Yhwh) and a promise to Jeroboam contingent on his obedience. A further asymmetry is the reversed order of subunits *j/k* and *k'/j'*. Each of the corresponding pairs lacks verbal links, but displays thematic ones. Subunits *j* and *j'* both speak of limits Yhwh has set on the punishment of Solomon's line: the punishment will not involve loss of the *entire* kingdom (subunit *j*), nor will it last forever (subunit *j'*). Subunits *k* and *k'* compare the endurance of Jeroboam's "house," that is, dynasty (subunit *k*)—contingent, of course, on obedience (11:38bcd)—to the prolongation of Solomon's reign to the end of his life (subunit *k'*). However, there is a bitter irony concealed here. First, what does it mean to promise Jeroboam "an enduring house, as I built for David," at the end of an oracle that announces the disastrous failure of David's dynasty in its second generation?[52] Second, the reversed order of subunits *k'* and *j'* means that the promise of endurance for Jeroboam's house is overshadowed (and thereby undermined, if not nullified) by the announcement that the punishment of David's line will not last forever.

Appendix 2

The Elijah Story

A reminder before you begin. What follows are not answers to the questions in the sense that these are the answers you should have come up with or the analyses you should have produced. They are only examples of the *sort* of answers you might have found. They are examples that, for one reason or another, I find particularly appropriate or interesting; but there are almost always other examples that you could have cited. And my analyses may often go deeper than yours do. (I should hope so! Thirty years of working through 1 Kings ought to give me something of a head start!) When my explanations do go more deeply into the text, ask yourself whether they appear plausible to you (that is, whether they enable richer readings of the text that account for more details than another reading might). If they do, they may help you hone your own analytical skills; and if they do not appear plausible, they may demonstrate ways of *misreading* that you ought to avoid.

PLOT

Simple Arc of Tension

The main arc of tension is Ahab's summons and command to Obadiah and Obadiah's obedience to the command. The end of the arc is clear, with the double departure notice in 18:6: Ahab leaves the scene in one direction, Obadiah in the other.[1] Where the arc begins, though, may be less clear because of the traditional verse numbering. In 18:2a Elijah's obedience to Yhwh's command in 18:1 brings that brief arc of tension to partial resolution.[2] In 18:2b the mention of famine is not a continuation of the tension of Yhwh's command and Elijah's obedience, but a note of background information for what follows, Ahab's and Obadiah's quest to find fodder for the royal livestock. So 18:2b describes the beginning situation of relative stability, which is destabilized by Ahab's summons to Obadiah in 18:3a. After the interruptive description of 18:3b–4, Ahab's command continues the movement of the plot.

The lengthy interruption that describes Obadiah's faithfulness to Yhwh and his prophets serves primarily to characterize Obadiah, as we shall see again in later chapters. But it also contributes to the development of the plot in at least two ways. First, characterizing Obadiah as caught between his Yahwist loyalties and a Baalist king lays the groundwork for the next scene, where Obadiah will make the dangers of his position clear. Second, the description of Obadiah also affects the movement of the plot by changing the tensive question.[3] Ahab and Obadiah are searching for water; but Obadiah already knows where water can be found, since he supplies it to the hidden prophets. This changes the tensive question from, Will Ahab and Obadiah find water? to, Will Obadiah reveal his source of water to Ahab? (Neither question is ever answered.)

A More Complex Example

The easiest way to approach this question is to leave 17:1 aside for the moment. Beginning with 17:2, Yhwh gives Elijah a command. What will Elijah do? And will Yhwh's promises come to pass? The tension is resolved when Elijah not only obeys, but his compliance is described in almost identical terms to the command. His obedience is letter-perfect, and Yhwh's promises are fulfilled in even more lavish terms than they were expressed (17:6). The next arc of tension begins with 17:7 and Elijah's renewed need for sustenance. It ends in 17:15–16, where he obtains sustenance, and a divine promise he uttered in the course of the story is confirmed and fulfilled. The third story unit begins when the woman's son falls ill in 17:17 and she understandably upbraids Elijah in 17:18. Both of these sources of tension are resolved when the lad is restored to her in 17:23, and she professes her faith in Elijah's prophetic identity in 17:24.

The most interesting aspect of the analysis so far is the odd position of 17:7. Thematically, it has to do with the setting of 17:2–6, the Wadi Cherith, where

Elijah has taken refuge at Yhwh's command. In terms of plot dynamics, however, it disturbs the situation of stability there, and thus initiates the tension that is developed and ultimately resolved in the next story unit.

This leaves us with 17:1. The most obvious effect of this verse is to raise the issue of the drought and its duration. How long will the drought last? What will have to occur in order for Elijah to decree rainfall again? The fact of the drought and the famine it causes forms the background for the stories in 17:2–6 and 17:7–16; but the question of its ending, and of what it will take to bring it about, is not resolved in chapter 17.

On the other hand, the verse raises another question that many of us are prone to overlook, though it would strike the implied reader with great force. It is more properly a question of characterization than of plot dynamics, but its answer is worked out in the cumulative effect of the plot. (It operates in the background, almost like a subtext, with its own arc of tension that begins in 17:1 and ends in 17:24.) The question is, Who is Elijah? Notice what the narrator does *not* tell us: he does not call Elijah a "prophet" or "man of God"[4] or anything of the sort, nor does he show us Elijah being divinely commissioned to deliver the prophecy of 17:1 and the power it asserts over the rain. Elijah himself claims to be a servant of Yhwh ("before whom I stand"); but since he has never previously appeared in the biblical text, we have no basis on which to judge the truth of his claim. And he claims *for himself* (not for Yhwh) authority to end the drought ("except by *my* word," as the NRSV renders it [italics added]). Just who is he to make such claims?[5] This question simmers in the background of the entire chapter, and reaches resolution at the very end. In 17:2–6 we learn that Elijah is a faithful and obedient servant of Yhwh. In 17:7–16 we learn that Elijah can indeed speak a word of divine power, and that loyalty to Elijah wins Yhwh's favor. In 17:17–23 we learn that Elijah can also speak a word of powerful intercession, and Yhwh will respond to him. Having seen all these sides of his relationship with Yhwh, we can accept the woman's judgment in the last verse of the chapter that Elijah is a "man of God."

The Whole Elijah Story

The previous answers have already indicated some of the major units of the Elijah story: 17:2–6 (Elijah at the Wadi Cherith); 17:7–17 (Elijah and the widow of Zarephath); 17:18–24 (Elijah raises the woman's son); 18:2b–6 (Ahab and Obadiah). Following that same trajectory, we can see 18:7–16 as a self-contained scene (Obadiah and Elijah), ending with another double-departure notice; and the scene of encounter between Elijah and Ahab begins in 18:17 and ends in 18:20.[6] The next scene begins with Elijah's challenge to the people in 18:21 and his proposal of a contest to the prophets of Baal in 18:22; the latter is resolved with Elijah's victory over the prophets in 18:38 and the former with the people's profession of faith in 18:39. But 18:40 should be reckoned with this scene as well, since it describes the aftermath of the contest and establishes a new situation of stability. The next scene begins with Elijah's announcement that rain will come

(18:41), and the arc of tension ("Will it happen?") ends when the rain falls in 18:45a. The last sentences (18:45b–46) bring the scene to a close with yet another double-departure notice, this one more elaborate than such notices usually are.

Before we move on to chapter 19, consider larger arcs of tension that encompass the first two chapters. The unresolved question of 17:1—when will the drought end, and what will bring that about?—comes to resolution at 18:45. Similarly, Yhwh's words to Elijah in 18:1 reach final fulfillment at the same point. Yhwh had said, "Go, show yourself to Ahab, that I may send rain upon the earth."[7] Elijah went (18:2), showed himself to Ahab (18:17), and now Yhwh sends rain upon the earth (18:45). Thus the arc of tension centered on the drought unifies the whole of chapters 17–18. Note, however, two parts of that narrative block that are only loosely and, one might say, only extrinsically connected to the drought theme. The first, 17:17–24, does not presuppose the drought at all. And the second, 18:21–40, not only has no direct reference to the drought; even the dramatis personae change almost completely, from Ahab and Obadiah in 18:1–20 to the prophets of Baal and the people of Israel in 18:21–40.[8] Nevertheless, from a literary point of view both of these narratives play an integral if rather subtle role in the thematic development. The story of the resurrection of the woman's son, though it has nothing to do directly with the drought, is the climactic event that leads the woman to answer the less obvious question raised in 17:1, Who is Elijah? And the story of the contest on Mount Carmel gains a new dimension from its insertion into the drought story since, quite surprisingly, the people of Israel are able to produce twelve large vessels of water (18:33–35) where the king himself could find none.[9]

Chapter 19, too, has nothing directly to do with the drought theme. Its attachment to what precedes is very loose: events that happen to Elijah as he flees from Jezebel's threat to his life. Only by depicting Jezebel's threat as resulting from Ahab's report about the events on Mount Carmel is there any link at all between the theme of the drought and Elijah's theophany on Mount Horeb.[10] Although chapter 19 comprises many individual scenes, some very short indeed, and could be analyzed in terms of the arcs of tension that demarcate each of them, the whole chapter is, by and large, unified by the single question, What purpose lies behind Elijah's journey? Partial answers are scattered throughout the chapter (flight from Jezebel's threat [19:2], desire to die [19:4], intent to journey to Horeb [again, why?], and so on). But these all culminate in Elijah's dialogue with Yhwh and the commands that Yhwh gives Elijah (19:9–18),[11] and in Elijah's first efforts to fulfill those commands (19:19–21).

CHARACTERS

1. In 18:3–6, Ahab is named first, but Obadiah is named more often (Ahab three times, Obadiah five). The scene closes with a line that balances the two perfectly (18:6). Ahab is clearly the dominant figure in the relationship (king to

steward), and has a lengthy speech in the scene (18:5), whereas Obadiah is silent throughout. On the other hand, the narrator interrupts the scene with a detailed aside (18:3b–4) that focuses on Obadiah and displays his courageous initiatives outside the royal court. In short, the two figures are so carefully balanced that either could be construed as central; or perhaps it would be more accurate to say that the narrator leaves the reader undecided. Both possibilities remain open, and the reader looks for further clarification in later scenes.

In 18:7–16, however, things only get more complicated. Again only two characters are on stage—now Obadiah and Elijah—but the narrator effects a similar balance. Obadiah is named first, but Elijah is named more often (Obadiah twice by name[12] and twice as "your servant" [18:9, 12], Elijah seven times by name and once as "my lord" [18:13]). Elijah is the dominant figure in the relationship: he commands Obadiah to do things, and Obadiah calls him "my lord"; but Obadiah's lengthy speech dominates the scene (18:9–14). Moreover, *Ahab*, though he is not present, is named eight times (four times by name, three times as "your lord" [18:8, 11, 14], and once as "my lord" [18:10]); and all of Obadiah's speech except one verse is about Ahab. Finally, also absent from the scene but named (by name) six times is *Yhwh*, who, after all, is the moving force behind Elijah's attempt to meet Ahab in the first place (18:1–2). Considered in itself, the scene seems to put forward several candidates for main character.

At least one interesting question emerges from all this. Obadiah appears nowhere in the Hebrew Bible except these two scenes. Why is he so prominent? (We will pursue this question a bit more below.)

2. The first flat character in the chapter is Jezebel herself. In this passage she is simply the threat that triggers the movement of the plot. Even in the larger Elijah story (17:1–19:21), she is only slightly more rounded by the mention of her pogrom in 18:4 and 13. She will not become a fully rounded character until 1 Kings 21.

The second flat character is the messenger (*mal'āk*) Jezebel sends to Elijah. He is little more than an embodied message; even the words he speaks are Jezebel's. The next flat character is even less substantial: the servant that Elijah leaves behind in Beer-sheba (19:3). He has a narrative effect in that he establishes a link to the preceding chapter, where Elijah also had an unnamed servant (18:43–44), and a dramatic effect in that, by being left behind, he emphasizes Elijah's solitude on his journey to Horeb.

The next flat character appears twice (19:5, 7). Most English translations call him "an angel" (19:5) and "the angel of the LORD" (that is, "the angel of Yhwh," 19:7). However, there is no distinct Hebrew word for "angel"; this figure too is a "messenger" (*mal'āk*). It has become traditional to translate the word as "angel" when the master that the messenger serves is God, but the word actually connotes nothing about the *nature* of the messenger. He is God's errand boy, just as the messenger of 19:2 is Jezebel's.

The dramatic effect of this messenger's appearances is considerable. Put yourself in Elijah's sandals: alone, in the desert, fleeing royal death threats that were brought to you by a "messenger." You fall asleep exhausted and are suddenly shaken awake by . . . a "messenger"! Immediate panic would seem appropriate. The messenger's gift of food is reassuring; but notice that, once Elijah has eaten, he lies down again but apparently does not sleep this time. When "the" (therefore the *same*) messenger rouses him once more, Elijah is more alert: he readily recognizes him as "the messenger of Yhwh" and is able to grasp that the food the messenger gives him is "for the journey."

3. One group character is the people (18:21–24, 30–35, 39–40). They move from silence (18:21) to consent (18:24) to compliance (18:30, 33–34) to acclaim (18:39) to active partisanship (18:40).[13] A second group character is the prophets of Baal (18:25–29, 40). There is a bit of subtle sarcasm when Elijah, without consulting them, decides the rules of the contest (18:23–24) and tells them what to do (18:25), and they do it (18:26). The sarcasm becomes much more obvious when Elijah mocks Baal and the prophets comply word-for-word with his advice ("cry aloud," 18:27–28a). Their compliance turns gruesome (18:28b) and frenetic (18:29a)[14] but to no avail (18:29b). Finally, they die at Elijah's hand (literally, he "slaughters" them, 18:40).

Both group characters are clearly important in the dynamics of 18:21–40. They are not, as group characters often are, relatively flat. In both cases the groups change notably: the people from neutrality, if not Baalist proclivities, to exclusive worship of Yhwh; and the prophets of Baal from numerical supremacy and royal patronage to defeat and death. It is worth speculating why the narrator chose to emphasize the group nature of these major characters, and did not choose to give either group a representative spokesperson. In the case of the people of Israel, a representative individual would have drawn the reader's attention away from the people *as people*; but the stakes of the struggle between Yhwh and Baal are precisely the loyalties *of the people*. Maintaining "the people" in the foreground preserves this focus. In the case of the prophets of Baal, a representative spokesperson would have situated the struggle on the level of individuals—Elijah versus Other Prophet—rather than on that of the deities behind the prophetic antagonists. Constant repetition of the phrase "prophets of *Baal*," however, forces the divine antagonists to the forefront of the reader's attention. Further, emphasizing the *group* of prophets keeps alive the reader's awareness of the striking disparity between a single prophet of Yhwh and 450 prophets of Baal.

4. The convention is almost preserved intact, but it is violated at the very last moment. At first the only characters on the scene are Elijah and the people. Elijah's speech to the people talks *about* the prophets of Baal, and even goes so far as to identify the people with the prophets ("you" in 18:24), but the prophets do not participate in the conversation, even if they might be present. Once Elijah turns to address the prophets of Baal (18:25–29), the people more or less fade into the background, though they are presumably present as witnesses to all that is happening.

The definitive failure of the prophets of Baal (18:29) marks their departure from the scene as active participants. Elijah turns once again to the people, who comply with his commands (18:30–35). Elijah then "draws near" to address Yhwh, who responds to his prayer with the theophany of lightning. The people, present as witnesses, respond (18:39), but their response is directed to Elijah in the terms of his original ultimatum (18:21). Thus, even here, with three active characters on stage, two of them (Yhwh and the people) interact with the third (Elijah), but not directly with each other.

Finally, however, the rule is broken in 18:40: three characters are on stage, and each interacts with the other two. Elijah orders the people, the people seize the prophets of Baal, and Elijah slaughters the prophets of Baal. The limited extent of this departure from narrative convention means that an audience will have no difficulty following what is happening, but the departure should be noted nevertheless. It is as if the chaotic violence of the bloody scene has spilled over and been reflected in the narrator's unconventional staging.

5. Obadiah is caught in a cleft stick. He is literally "over the house" ("in charge of the palace," says the NRSV) of the Baalist King Ahab—that means that he is in a position of great authority and responsibility (perhaps something like a secretary of the interior). At the same time, he himself is a worshiper of Yhwh and strives clandestinely to thwart the queen's pogrom against prophets of Yhwh. (His very name, "Obadiah," means "servant of Yhwh.") His language reflects his conflicted situation: he addresses Elijah as his "lord" (18:7, 13), but he uses the same term to refer to Ahab (18:10). Elijah has no patience with Obadiah's divided loyalties. He calls Ahab Obadiah's "lord" (18:8), and demands that Obadiah make a public profession of faith in Yhwh.[15]

Obadiah's religious compromises—which Elijah dismisses as unacceptable—make him the foreshadowing of the group character "the people" in 18:21–40. As far as Elijah is concerned they, like Obadiah, "limp with two different opinions" and must make a choice (18:21). In this way the tense triangle of Ahab (the Baalist), Elijah (the Yahwist), and Obadiah (in between) in 18:1–20 foreshadows in 18:21–40 the struggle of the prophets of Baal and Elijah for the loyalties of the people.

CHARACTERIZATION

1. Among the examples of things the narrator "tells" us in the Elijah story are: that Elijah is a "Tishbite"[16] and that he hails from Gilead (17:1); that his hostess in Zarephath is a widow (17:8), that she has a son (17:12), and that she owns a two-story house (17:17, 19); that Obadiah is Ahab's majordomo[17] (18:3a); that Elijah's opponents on Carmel are prophets, and that the god they serve is Baal (18:25; Elijah has described them this way before, but this is the first time the narrator does so); that Elijah is a "prophet" (18:36, for the first time in the narrator's voice!); that Elijah has, unexpectedly, a servant (18:43); that Elijah was afraid (19:3). With a little strain, one might also list as "telling" the narrator's

statements about where Yhwh was *not* to be found: "not in the wind . . . not in the earthquake . . . not in the fire" (19:11–12).[18]

Most of the qualities the narrator tells us about are lasting traits. The only truly transitory one is that Elijah is "afraid" (19:3).

2. Elijah's first prayer is in 17:20–21, preceding the raising of the woman's dead son. His words in 17:20 are particularly interesting, because they echo to a large degree the woman's reprimand of Elijah in 17:18. They reveal Elijah as someone whose relationship with Yhwh is open and free enough that he feels justified in rebuking Yhwh when he believes God is responsible for an injustice. They also demonstrate a sense of compassion for the woman and gratitude for her hospitality.

Elijah's next prayer is found in 18:36–37. Here we must be a bit more circumspect in our interpretation. Elijah is not speaking to Yhwh in solitude; he is being overheard by the people of Israel, whom he is trying to win over, and perhaps as well by the prophets of Baal, his adversaries. This may explain the much more formal character of his prayer, and it certainly explains his choice of the key verb "answer (me)," to contrast with the ineffective prayer of the prophets of Baal in 18:26. However, his prayer does make one particular impression on me, though it is not all that admirable: Elijah seems at least as concerned that he himself be acknowledged as a prophet as he is that Yhwh be acknowledged as God (18:36).

Elijah's next prayer, if it is that, is wordless. On top of Mount Carmel, waiting for rain, he "bowed himself down upon the earth and put his face between his knees" (18:42). Nowhere else in the Hebrew Bible does anyone do anything like this, so it is impossible to know whether it is intended as a form of prayer (intercession? profound humility? faith-filled waiting?). The mysteriousness of the posture plus the lack of accompanying words mean that we can infer nothing definite about Elijah from this scene.

In 19:4 Elijah utters a brief prayer of despair. It reveals his current emotional state, but tells us little about the core of Elijah's personality. The principal irony here is that Elijah's words and behavior are a bit self-contradictory (don't we often find this about ourselves, too?): he flees from Jezebel's threat of death in order to save his life, then asks God to let him die!

Finally, Elijah twice speaks to Yhwh in exactly the same words (19:10 and 14).[19] The elements that emerge most saliently from his words are self-justification, recrimination against the Israelites, and self-pity for his isolation. Equally striking is what is lacking: any intercession for Israel, or even for himself. The prayer is a prayer of *complaint*, but not of hope. Elijah is, to borrow a wonderful Yiddish word, kvetching.

I am not sure that any one of these utterances reveals more of Elijah than all the others; but I am struck by a progression from compassion for others in 17:21 to focus on self in 18:36 to closed-minded self-righteousness in 19:10, 14.

3. Some of the prayers discussed in the preceding remarks could just as easily be treated as examples of direct showing, since, technically, Elijah is speaking to

someone (God) and revealing himself in the process. Here, however, I will explore self-revealing speeches by other characters. Almost any speech is going to reveal something about the speaker. I have chosen three speeches where quite divergent inferences are possible about precisely what the speech reveals of the speaker.

Obadiah's lengthy protest to Elijah (18:9–14) tells us a great deal about Obadiah (even apart from his self-description in 18:12–13). First, it expresses his utter panic. Three times in six verses he objects that what Elijah demands is tantamount to a death sentence for him (18:9, 12, 14).[20] He also reveals his conflicted loyalties: earlier he addressed the prophet of Yhwh as "my lord" (18:7), and here he does so again (18:13); but he also uses the same term to refer to the Baalist king (18:10). As we discussed in the last section, Obadiah's status as an overdeveloped secondary character is probably to be explained by this internal religious division, which prepares the reader for the analogous position of the people of Israel in the scene atop Mount Carmel. Having Obadiah himself reveal his conflict (subconsciously?) is a potent way to construct his character.

When Ahab finally encounters Elijah, he greets him with hostility: "Is it you, you troubler of Israel?" (18:17). There is certainly no doubt about the hostility, but one could explain the accusation in two different ways. Some readers will take it as meaning that Ahab holds Elijah responsible for the drought and therefore tacitly admits that Elijah has the power over the rain that he claimed in 17:1. This, however, seems unlikely. The point of the conflict between Baal and Yhwh is that they *both* claim sovereignty over the rain.[21] If Ahab is a worshiper of Baal, he cannot recognize that Yhwh has any such power. It is more likely that Ahab sees Elijah's claim as an insult to Baal and that, until Elijah has been punished for his blasphemy, *Baal* will withhold rain from Israel.

A third example is relatively peripheral in the development of the plot, but presents an intriguing puzzle nonetheless. In 19:1–2 Ahab has reported to Jezebel the results of the contest on Mount Carmel, including the execution of her protégés, the prophets of Baal. Jezebel in turn sends Elijah a death threat. The meaning of the message is unequivocal. But what it says about Jezebel is baffling. If Jezebel intended to have Elijah killed, why did she not send an assassin to do the deed instead of a messenger to warn him? After all, she has been "killing prophets of Yhwh" right and left for some time now (18:4), so she ought to have no compunction about one more. Yet, instead, she forewarns him, giving him a chance to flee her sphere of control. Are we to infer that she harbored some suspicion that Elijah did have a powerful deity on his side, and that killing Elijah might in the long run prove more dangerous to her than urging him into self-imposed exile?

4. In 17:9 Yhwh tells Elijah that he has "commanded" the widow of Zarephath to feed Elijah. When Elijah arrives at Zarephath and encounters the widow, however, neither of them alludes to Yhwh's command. Elijah simply requests a drink of water, and the widow turns to fetch it without a word. That action is, in context, ambiguous. It could simply demonstrate that the widow has, indeed, been commanded by Yhwh to care for Elijah, and that she is obedient to the

divine will.[22] Or it could bespeak her extreme compassion and commitment to hospitality even in the midst of a drought. The issue becomes a bit clearer in the next verses. Elijah adds a request for food, and the woman retorts that she and her son are about to starve to death. In other words, she seems to know nothing of a divine command to provision Elijah. Her willingness to supply water therefore arises from compassion, and would extend to food if she had any. In this way the narrator disposes us to a sympathetic feeling for the widow, despite the fact that she is at first unwilling to bring Elijah food.

Another obvious example is the narrator's description of Obadiah in 18:4. This still qualifies as direct showing, even though it is a flashback to something that happened earlier in the story world, because in it the narrator shows Obadiah *acting*. We infer from it qualities of courage, willingness to take serious risks in service to Yhwh; and we learn (surprisingly, in view of the present scene) that Obadiah has access to water, since he can supply it to the prophets he has hidden. Some readers will, like Elijah, see Obadiah's willingness to stay in service to Ahab as negating any other good he may accomplish and will insist that the only remedy for such hypocrisy is suicidal honesty.[23]

Elisha undertakes some puzzling activity in 19:21. My inferences from his behavior here are very tentative indeed. Certainly his slaughter of one yoke of oxen[24] and destruction of their tackle betokens a radical break with his former way of life. But the phrase "twelve yoke of oxen" may indicate the great wealth of Elisha's family; or, on the contrary, it may indicate that in Abel-meholah (see 19:16) agricultural work was undertaken as a communal activity. That Elisha serves the boiled oxen to "the people" may indicate this communal setting. On the other hand, it may also be a foreshadowing[25] of later stories in which Elisha will guarantee food for hungry people (see, for instance, 2 Kgs. 4:38–41, 42–44; 6:24–7:20).

5. In 17:14 Elijah promises a miracle in Yhwh's name. As I mentioned above, Elijah's reliability has not yet been established, and so his claim of Yhwh's miraculous benevolence remains uncertain until the narrator assures us that the promise was fulfilled (17:16).[26]

A very clear example is 18:10, where Obadiah tells Elijah about Ahab's fruitless quest to lay hold of the prophet. Obadiah does not tell us precisely *why* Ahab seeks Elijah, but it hardly seems likely that Ahab's motives are benign.[27] The remark contains a priceless double irony of which Obadiah is completely unaware. But Elijah would see it, and so would the implied reader. Ahab's search has been international, and he has elicited an oath from foreign lords that Elijah is not in their territory. Where has Elijah been? In Zarephath of Sidon. Who is the king of Sidon? Ahab's father-in-law (see 1 Kgs. 16:31)! And who is the god of Sidon? Baal! Neither the Sidonian king Ethbaal nor the god he worships is able to locate the prophet of Yhwh, even when he is in their own territory!

In 19:19 Elijah throws his mantle over Elisha while the latter is engaged in plowing. This certainly tells us something about Elisha: that Elijah has selected him for a special role. But it is not exactly what Yhwh told Elijah to do. In 19:16 Yhwh commanded Elijah to "anoint" Elisha. An investiture is not the same as an anointing. So we are left a bit unsure of exactly what Elijah is calling Elisha to: Is Elisha to become Elijah's *successor*, or simply his *servant*? Even the language does not help: Elisha "attends" (Hebrew šrt) Elijah. This is the same verb used of Joshua's relationship to Moses, whom he later succeeded (Josh. 1:1), but it is also the term used to describe Abishag's service to David (1 Kgs. 1:4).

POINT OF VIEW

1. The point of view is omniscient. First, we are able to follow the action as it unfolds in the upper chamber, when Elijah is the only character present. Second, we know Yhwh's reaction to Elijah's prayer—he "listened to the voice of" Elijah (17:22)[28]—a reaction Elijah himself becomes aware of only when the boy comes back to life. This point of view allows us a bit of distance. We watch with interest as Elijah takes the boy upstairs, but we do not really have any doubt what is going to happen: the prophet's failure is unthinkable. So we can concentrate on other aspects of the story, such as the strongly admonitory tone Elijah takes with Yhwh (Elijah's complaint to Yhwh is no less angry than the woman's complaint to Elijah), Elijah's odd (magical?) behavior with the boy's body, and the (chastened?) response of Yhwh to Elijah's request.

2. We must keep in mind a couple of factors here. The implied reader is an ancient Israelite and, presumably, a Yahwist. So right from the start there is impetus for the reader to identify to some degree with "the people [of Israel]" and to distance himself or herself from the prophets of Baal. This tendency is immediately undermined by Elijah's accusation to the people that they are "limping with two different opinions" (18:21)—in other words, trying to worship Yhwh and Baal both. So, at first, I find myself in a relatively neutral position, not because *my* Israelite and Yahwistic identity (I speak here as the implied reader) is in question, but because the "people's" is. The people's silence (18:21b) does nothing to counteract this sense of distance between me and them. However, when Elijah proposes the terms of the imminent contest, I find myself sharing, at least to some extent, the people's enthusiasm (18:24b). After all, everybody likes a contest; and one that promises to be this spectacular is especially exciting. So even though I have not identified myself with the people (they are still not true Yahwists, like me!), I am at least seeing some things from their perspective. With them, I watch the prophets of Baal follow Elijah's directions and fail (18:26). With them, I hear Elijah's mockery ("Cry louder!" 18:27) and perhaps chuckle as the prophets take Elijah seriously ("They cried louder," 18:28).

Then Elijah calls the people to "draw closer" to him (18:30). Since my Israelite, Yahwist sympathies are with Elijah (though my point of view is not), this brings the people closer to me as well. I continue to observe, as they do, while Elijah undertakes his part of the contest.

Things get complicated here. What is the point of view in 18:31? First, Elijah takes twelve stones—everybody can observe that without problem. But then the narrator tells us that these twelve stones equal "the number of the tribes of the sons of Jacob." Who is thinking that? Elijah? The Israelites? The narrator? Certainly the last, but quite possibly Elijah and the Israelites as well. This reminder of a common heritage creates—or, perhaps better, recalls—a bond between me and the people, and maneuvers me closer to them in loyalty, although not in sympathy for their divided religious allegiances. The narrator continues by reminding me that Yhwh renamed Jacob "Israel." It seems rather less likely that this represents what is consciously in the mind of either Elijah or the people—it is almost certainly an aside from the narrator to the narratee. Its effect on me is to affirm the distance I have from the religiously disloyal "people" and simultaneously to strengthen the bond of unity I have with them as "Israel." (Notice how smoothly my attention has been diverted temporarily from What happens next? to my identity vis-à-vis the group character "people of Israel.") I soon return to watching the action from a perspective that is, presumably, not too different from the people's, now that the narrator has focused my attention on the bonds that connect me to them. Their immediate and extravagant[29] obedience to Elijah aligns my point of view even more strongly with theirs, both because it identifies their attitudes more closely with my own Yahwism and because I (like the people, I'm sure) wonder why Elijah wants all that water drenching the sacrificial site.

3. In 19:1 I am at a considerable distance from the conversation Ahab has with Jezebel. I do not hear Ahab's actual voice, and I have no clue what the *tone* of his message is. It is likely that he is recounting the slaughter with chagrin, since he has been described previously as a supporter of Baal; but it is not inconceivable that Elijah's triumph on Mount Carmel has had its intended effect, and that Ahab, now won over to Yahwism, is telling Jezebel that her side has lost to a stronger deity. (I pursue the implications of this uncertainty about Ahab in the section below on "Gaps and Ambiguities.")

My sense of distance continues until Jezebel's messenger reaches Elijah, and I actually hear him deliver the queen's message. I stand more or less close to Elijah, watching and hearing the messenger as he speaks. My closeness to Elijah intensifies briefly as I perceive his emotion and motivation ("he was afraid . . . and fled for his life"). But his flight is so rapid (from Jezreel to Beer-sheba—around one hundred miles, as the crow flies—in less than half a verse) and so lacking in detail that I almost feel like I am following a map, rather than a journey, or perhaps tracking him from the air. Once he stops in 19:4, I catch up with him and come close enough to hear him say his night prayers. I watch and listen to his two encounters with the "angel," then see him walk slowly away from me toward the south. (I do not follow, because I do not see him for the next forty days, when I find him again at Horeb.)

4. The principal effect of the two occurrences of *wĕhinnēh* is a strong identification of my point of view with that of Elijah.[30] I am standing nearby watching when he lies down the first time and falls asleep. But the *wĕhinnēh* means that I experience the "messenger" just as Elijah does: I can almost feel him shake my

shoulder. That, combined with the ambiguity of the word *mal'āk*, gives me a jolt of adrenaline comparable to what Elijah must feel as he wakes up in panic. Then I see the food (still through Elijah's eyes), and that calms me down. When Elijah lies down a second time (this time without falling asleep), I find myself back in my original position, watching from nearby.

MANIPULATION OF TIME

1. It seems to me that Elijah's journeys up to his chamber and back down (17:19, 23) move more quickly than his actions with the boy's body in the upper chamber (17:21a), even though the latter remark is shorter. His journeys each involve several action verbs (took, carried up, laid; and took, brought down, gave), while his raising of the child only has one, "he stretched himself out." In addition, the enlargement of the scene in the upper room by two relatively wordy speeches (17:20, 21b), and the detailed narrative of Yhwh's response (which unnecessarily repeats several words from Elijah's prayer) also slow the tempo noticeably. The effect is to focus my attention on the climactic event, the child's resuscitation, and the mysterious gestures Elijah performs in accomplishing it. It also focuses my attention on Yhwh's startling compliance[31] with Elijah's prayer.

In addition to his two speeches to Yhwh, Elijah also engages the woman in dialogue twice (17:18–19a and 23b–24). His remarks are brief and pointed. Her longer speeches, on the other hand, pose one serious theological dilemma (is the boy's death just, given the self-sacrificing hospitality the woman has shown Elijah?) and resolve another (the identity of Elijah as a "man of God"; the phrase occurs in both of the woman's speeches).[32] The length of the speeches slows the tempo and affords the reader time to reflect on the issues they raise.

2. The point of very slow movement is 17:6. Its wordiness retards the tempo considerably, and that it seems to portray a repeated pattern rather than a single event makes it function more as description than as action. For the *narratee*, the effect is probably little more than an emphasis on just how lavishly Yhwh provisioned Elijah in the midst of a drought. Few Israelites, and then only the richest, would have enjoyed meat twice a day. For the *implied reader*, however, there is more. The divine command and the last words of 17:6 are strikingly repetitive ("turn eastward and hide yourself by the Wadi Cherith, which is east of the Jordan"; "he went and lived by the Wadi Cherith, which is east of the Jordan"). This sets up an expectation that Elijah's compliance with Yhwh's command will continue to repeat the command almost verbatim. But all the details in 17:6 violate that expectation considerably. "Morning" and "evening," "bread" and "meat" are all unexpected words; they therefore draw attention to themselves. The implied reader who is familiar with the broader biblical context will note in them a clear allusion to the traditions of Moses.[33] There will be a whole series of parallels drawn between Moses and Elijah in 1 Kings 17–19.[34] This passage alerts the reader early on to watch for them.

3. Yhwh informs Elijah that there are "seven thousand" Israelites (that is, many thousands; "seven" can be used for "an ample number") who have not worshiped Baal. This divine claim stands in considerable tension with Elijah's claims in chapter 18 that (1) he was the only prophet of Yhwh left (18:22)[35] and (2) the people were "limping with two different opinions" (18:21)—that is, they were trying to worship both Yhwh and Baal, a course of action Elijah deemed unacceptable.[36] This tension leads us to consider the possibility that Elijah was exaggerating the situation (perhaps to aggrandize his own role?). When we take note of the fact that in 18:1 Yhwh's instructions to Elijah merely tell him to "show yourself to Ahab so that I may send rain upon the earth"[37]—in other words, Yhwh gave Elijah no command to confront the Baal prophets on Mount Carmel—we may even wonder whether Elijah might have engineered the whole contest on his own initiative.

4. The actions of the prophets of Baal take all day, from morning till noon (18:26), then from noon till the time of the afternoon offering (around sunset; 18:29). Elijah's actions seem to progress much more quickly. We do not know when he starts his preparations, but the impression is that he does not begin them until the Baal prophets' failure is clear. On the other hand, he has finished his preparations at about the same time the Baal prophets have apparently given up, the "time of the afternoon oblation" (18:36). So the prophets' all-day exertions are condensed into four verses; Elijah's briefer actions take six verses. In itself, this has only a small effect on the reader's experience of the tempo of the story. But the prophets' actions are described much more laconically than Elijah's comparable deeds: the prophets "prepared" their bull (18:26); Elijah "cut the bull in pieces and laid it on the wood" (18:33). And Elijah performs detailed preparations unmatched by the prophets (see 18:30b–33a). The account of the prophets' deeds slows down only in 18:27–28, where the reader is invited to mock them as the narrator does.[38] In 18:29 it picks up again, when the entire afternoon passes in a single verse. By contrast, Elijah's deeds are paced slowly throughout. We are not only told that he repairs the altar; we are told how many stones he used, and why, and the location and size of a mysterious trench he digs around it. After he has prepared his sacrifice, we see him have the people drench the whole thing with water, and they do. And they do it again. And they do it again. The attention to even the tiniest features, such as the size of the trench, allows us time and leisure to imagine the whole scene in vivid detail. Where our point of view was distanced from the Baal prophets by their bloody self-mutilation, it is drawn near to Elijah when he tells the people to "come closer to me" (18:30). Everything works together to focus our attention and our favor on Elijah's undertaking.

GAPS AND AMBIGUITIES

1. Since the narrator tells us of Ahab's report rather than presenting Ahab's own words to Jezebel, we ought to assume that Ahab's report was accurate, though

perhaps brief.[39] So we can rule out any motivations that imply Ahab's attempt to manipulate Jezebel by skewing the information. One possibility—perhaps the most obvious one—is that Ahab, angry and frustrated by Elijah's victory, is informing Jezebel that Elijah has killed her protégés. Ahab sees this as the beginning of open hostilities between the prophet and the royal couple; his report brings Jezebel up-to-date and enlists her cooperation in the conflict. In response, Jezebel takes the next step in violence and threatens Elijah's life (19:2). Alternatively, one could conjecture that Ahab has been suitably impressed (perhaps even converted?) by Yhwh's spectacular display on Mount Carmel, and he realizes that the slaughter of the Baal prophets marks the *end*, not the beginning, of the conflict. Yhwh has won. His report to Jezebel, in this case, would have to be read as a warning: "Beware of angering Yhwh. He is stronger than Baal." Jezebel's threat, then, arises from her own pique, not from the urging of her husband.

The two readings do not produce much difference in our appreciation of Jezebel's character. She supported the cult of Baal in the past (18:19) and persecuted prophets of Yhwh (18:4); now that her favorites are dead, she lashes out at the Yhwh prophet responsible for their death. The character of Ahab, by contrast, is significantly different in the two readings. In the first case, he remains a supporter of Baal, allied to his wife in her campaign to extirpate anyone who opposes her deity. In the second case, he is at least neutral toward the cult of Yhwh, if not positively disposed toward it (out of fear, if not out of devotion).

This gap creates a real tension in the reader who is aware of it. Since Ahab is not mentioned again in chapter 19, the gap remains open through the chapter, making the reader somewhat impatient to get some further clarification of precisely where the king now stands.

Elijah's journey to Horeb is more problematic. One possibility is that he is journeying back to the roots of Israelite faith—the site where Yhwh appeared to the people and established the covenant through Moses—in order to renew his own commitment. Perhaps he even seeks to remind Yhwh that the covenant demands divine fidelity as well. Israel's sinfulness (as Elijah portrays it) required divine response, and Elijah seems to opine that Yhwh has been negligent in not acting to support Elijah's own preaching and prophetic ministry. Elijah seeks to become a new Moses, credentialed by Yhwh to lead the people from paganism (Baalism understood as an analogue of Egypt) to fidelity (Yahwism understood as an analogue of the promised land).

This is the way the story is most commonly understood by professional biblical scholars and lay readers alike. It is important to note, however, that little or nothing in the text itself would either sustain or counter such a reading.[40] An alternate reading is possible. Though it too is neither sustained nor countered by specific elements in the text, it is equally successful in accounting for those data the text does supply.

This alternate reading is that Elijah has reached the breaking point and makes his journey to Horeb *in order to resign his prophetic calling*.[41] The despair he voices in 19:4 is hard to reconcile with his miraculous victory in 1 Kings 18;

nevertheless, it is the despair that sets the context for his flight to Horeb and encounter with God there. Beyond that, the absence from his complaints (19:10 and 14) of any specific requests for divine action may well mean that he has no plans for the future that would require Yhwh's assistance. Finally—and, for me, the most telling bit of evidence—is that, indeed, Yhwh tells Elijah to anoint a prophetic replacement (19:16).

2. In terms of the simple story line, of course, "Elijah is here" is the necessary reading: Elijah is sending Obadiah to fetch Ahab so that Elijah can carry out Yhwh's instruction to present himself to Ahab (18:1).[42] This does not mean, however, that the second reading is to be rejected. There is nothing incompatible about the readings. As we have seen in discussing Obadiah's character, his divided loyalties make him an apt foreshadowing of the people, whose divided loyalties Elijah condemns on Mount Carmel (18:21). Obadiah is caught between his position in the court of a Baalist king and his loyalty to Yhwh. He resolves his personal conflict by using his political influence to give clandestine support to Yhwh's prophets. For Elijah, this is unacceptable; like the people, Obadiah is "limping with two different opinions." If we read 18:8 in its second meaning (*hinnēh 'ēlî yāhû* = "Look! Yhwh is my God"; see n. 15 this appendix), Elijah presents the same ultimatum to Obadiah that he will later lay before the people; he requires a public and exclusive profession of faith in Yhwh.

The whole situation produces a gap in the text, too. Obadiah delivers the message to Ahab (18:16), but we do not know whether his version of it remains ambiguous. We know that, in response, Ahab "goes to meet Elijah," but we do not know how he deals with Obadiah. However, since Obadiah never again appears in the Bible, the fact that the gap, intriguing as it is, remains unfilled is inconsequential to the story.

3. The plain reading is about the geographical movement of the two characters; they "divide up the land" and go in different directions in their quest for fodder. But the absolutely balanced language is striking,[43] and it alludes to the fact that Ahab and Obadiah move in opposite directions in their religious loyalties as well.

4. One thing that the two translations leave wide open is whether this is an *articulate* reality: Is it a "sound" or a "voice" in 19:12? The Hebrew does not help here, since *qôl* can mean either; so the implied reader would be just as much at sea as we are. Although "sound," as the more general term, could include an articulate "voice," *qôl* appears in the immediately following verse in the more specific sense ("Then there came a *qôl* to him that said . . . ," 19:13b). That could argue for taking *qôl* in the same sense in both places. However, the two manifestations are clearly not the same *qôl*: the second one arrives *after* the first, and is not identified as "the" *qôl*, as it would have been were it the same. So the reader is left to choose between an inarticulate "noise," like those of the wind, earthquake, and fire that precede, or an articulate "voice," like the *qôl* that follows.

Whatever choice one makes, though, it is a diametric contradiction to "silence" (or the adjective "still" of the KJV).[44] How does one conceive of a "silent sound"? Is it the inner voice of conscience? Or of the Deity speaking in one's heart? Is it the sudden, terrified realization that one has encountered the ineffable *mysterium tremendum*? Is it the very presence of the "ineffable"?[45] Or, taking it as part of a series of disastrous theophanies (wind, earthquake, fire), is it the ultimate disaster, a return to the silence of precreational chaos that was before the word that brought forth light (Gen. 1:1–3)? An oxymoron, by definition, gives us no conceptual terra firma on which to construct an understanding. Each reader, then, will need to find his or her own footing. Such is the power of paradox.

What about the third element: "sheer" (NRSV) or "small" (KJV)? Can this help us clarify the meaning of the phrase? Unfortunately, no. The term in Hebrew (*daqqâ*) is a physical word, primarily tactile or visual. Its other occurrences describe "thin" fabric, or "sparse" hair, or "emaciated" cattle, or "fine" (as opposed to "coarse") grain, and the like. It is used in a metaphorical sense only here.[46] One problem here, as with many metaphors, is discerning precisely what aspect of the physical term is being attributed to the target. And is it the *qôl* that is *daqqâ* or the silence? (Grammatically, it is the silence; but in this sort of paradoxical phrase we may need to strain the grammar a bit to come up with any meaning at all.) If it is the *qôl*, perhaps the silent sound is "thin" (like a note on the oboe, or a nasal voice), or "soft" (like a whisper), or "unwontedly small" (like the rasping of a person with laryngitis). If it is the silence, perhaps the silence is only "tenuous," or is portentous (like "holding one's breath in anticipation"), or is portentous in the opposite sense (like "empty"). Again, *daqqâ* allows any of these senses, and different readers will choose differently.

For what it is worth, I offer here my personal reading of the phrase. Since the context, for me, is a story in which Elijah has come to Horeb to resign his prophetic office, I see the theophany Yhwh grants him as one that promises that Yhwh has power (wind, earthquake, fire), but is more than power ("Yhwh was not in . . ."). Yhwh awaits Elijah's response, for he is willing to let Elijah resign if he insists. Yhwh's waiting presence is silent, but it is full of meaning (it is a *qôl*); and the silence is "slender," that is, it is tenuous: Yhwh is eager and impatient to hear Elijah's response.

Note. For another example of ambiguity see the earlier discussion of Ahab's hostile words to Elijah in 18:17, calling him "troubler of Israel" (p. 167 above).

REPETITION AND VARIATION

1. The first instance is Yhwh's command to Elijah in 17:3 and the account of Elijah's compliance in 17:5b. Yhwh's speech has three imperatives—go from here, turn eastward, hide yourself—plus two sentences of explanation in 17:4. Elijah's

compliance telescopes the commands by citing the first word of the first and the last phrase of the third, implying that he complied with the whole thing.

> 17:3. *Go* from here
> and turn eastward
> and hide yourself by *the Wadi Cherith,*
>   *which faces*[47] *the Jordan.*
>
> 17:5b. *He went,*
> and lived in *the Wadi Cherith,*
>   *which faces the Jordan.*

Note too how the narrator emphasizes the exactitude of Elijah's obedience by adding the unnecessary comment, "He went and did according to the word of Yhwh."

The two sentences of explanation Yhwh had offered Elijah the narrator expands with much detail, whose significance would without doubt have been clear to the ancient Israelite implied reader. To understand it ourselves, we must make something of a detour here. Take a look at Exodus 16:8 and 12.[48] The echo of those verses here is unmistakable. Elijah, like Israel under Moses, is provisioned by God himself with bread and meat. In fact, Elijah is provisioned more richly, since he has meat twice a day! This is the first appearance of a long series of allusions linking Elijah with Moses. The most obvious is the theophany that Elijah will experience on Mount Horeb in 1 Kings 19, just as Moses and the Israelites encountered Yhwh at Horeb/Sinai. That theophany will climax the series, but a number of more subtle Mosaic allusions lead up to it, of which 17:6 is the first.

The second instance of repetition in 1 Kings 17 is another command-and-compliance pattern. Yhwh orders Elijah to "get up, go to Zarephath, which belongs to Sidon" (17:9); Elijah "got up and went to Zarephath" (17:10).[49] His compliance is abbreviated, but exact. The third instance is not a command-and-compliance situation, but a promise-and-fulfillment. In Yhwh's name, Elijah makes a miraculous promise to the widow (17:14); when she complies with his wishes, the promise is fulfilled exactly (17:16). Throughout this scene the narrator punctuates the action with a refrain, though the NRSV obscures it by varying the translation. Elijah tells the widow, "do according to your word" (17:13; NRSV, "do as you have said"); when she acts "according to the word of Elijah" (17:15; NRSV, "as Elijah said"), the divine promise is fulfilled "according to the word of Yhwh that he spoke by Elijah" (17:16).

So, to this point, the use of repetition has underscored (1) that Elijah's obedience to Yhwh's word of command is letter-perfect; (2) that Elijah has the authority to speak a word of divine promise; (3) that obedience to Elijah wins divine favor. There is more to come.

In the third story of the chapter, Elijah utters a prayer (17:21b) and Yhwh grants his prayer in exactly the same words (17:22b). This is tantamount to a command-and-compliance pattern transposed into the key of intercession.[50] Elijah is not only obedient to Yhwh, he is not only a bearer of a word of promise *from* Yhwh, he can also speak a word of power *to* Yhwh that evokes divine favor.

In the light of these careful uses of verbatim repetition to indicate the exactitude of conformity between word and fulfillment, what can we infer from the variations in 18:19–20 and 18:41–42? In the first case, Elijah has ordered Ahab to "send and assemble all Israel"[51] at Mount Carmel, along with "the four hundred fifty prophets of Baal" and "the four hundred prophets of Asherah." Ahab complies, but his compliance is not phrased in those precise terms. He "sends" to all the Israelites, but we are not told that he "assembles" them (though this may simply be a case of abbreviation); and he assembles "the prophets," but with no further specification. Since only the prophets of Baal figure in the remainder of the chapter, we are entitled to wonder whether Ahab gathered those of Asherah. (He does gather all 450 prophets of Baal; Elijah will confirm this in 18:22.) The bottom line is that the less than exact repetition allows us to *consider*, but not to *conclude*, that Ahab's compliance with Elijah's command was halfhearted and incomplete.

And what about 18:41–42? The variation is quite subtle. Elijah orders Ahab to the top of Mount Carmel for a meal: "Go up, eat and drink." Ahab's compliance is not phrased, "he went up and ate and drank," but "he went up *to eat and to drink*." Infinitives of purpose substitute for past tense verbs, leaving the question open whether Ahab ate and drank as he was told to. This would be an utterly trivial variation, were it not for the Mosaic allusions I mentioned a moment ago. In Exodus, after Moses has experienced his encounter with Yhwh at the top of the mountain, Yhwh orders him to bring up to the divine presence seventy elders of Israel—in other words, leaders of the people—for a covenant meal in God's presence. We are told, "Moses and Aaron, Nadab, and Abihu, and seventy of the elders of Israel *went up* . . . they beheld God and *they ate and drank*" (Exod. 24:9–11). The pervasive links drawn between Moses and Elijah would suggest to the ancient Israelite implied reader that Ahab, like the seventy elders, was being invited to a meal to renew the covenant between Yhwh and the people. That we are not told whether he in fact "ate and drank" means that we do not know whether he renewed the covenant (that is, returned to fidelity to Yhwh).

2. Since we assume the reliability of the narrator, his characterization of Obadiah is the standard against which we judge Obadiah's self-description. The latter is almost exactly the same as the narrator's words, so we conclude that Obadiah is honest and reliable himself, despite the compromising position he holds in Ahab's court. Moreover, Obadiah would have every reason to exaggerate his good qualities to Elijah, since he is desperately trying to persuade Elijah not to send him into danger by making him confess his Yahwistic loyalties to the king (see above, p. 165, and especially n. 15). Since he does not exaggerate, his integrity is evident.

The important differences between the narrator's words and Obadiah's are two. First, where the narrator said that Obadiah revered Yhwh "greatly" (18:3),

Obadiah says that he has revered Yhwh "from my youth" (18:12). By locating the index of his loyalty in its duration rather than in its intensity, Obadiah seems, if anything, to downplay its significance out of modesty. Second (though this is not clear in the NRSV), the verb for Jezebel's pogrom is different. The narrator says that she was "cutting off" (*hakrît*, from the verb *krt*, "to cut"; NRSV "killing off") the prophets of Yhwh (18:4); Obadiah says that she was "killing" (*hărōg*) them (18:13). There is no real difference in meaning at all.[52]

3. I have already mentioned that the tone of recrimination and the absence of any request for Yhwh to act have led some scholars to see Elijah's complaint as tantamount to an attempt to resign his prophetic commission. When Elijah first complains, Yhwh responds with an unparalleled display of power. There are echoes of the theophany on Mount Sinai to Moses and the Israelites in Exodus, but Elijah's experience seems even more impressive. Elijah witnesses wind that splits mountains and shatters rocks, earthquake, and fire—yet Yhwh (who clearly controls all these manifestations) "was not in" any of them: Elijah's Deity transcends all such powers, overwhelming as they may be. Elijah then experiences the self-contradictory "sound of sheer silence"—the ineffable paradox in which Yhwh himself may (or may not; see n. 45 this appendix) be found. And all of this has no effect whatsoever on Elijah. He repeats his complaint without a jot or tittle of difference. The effect of the verbatim repetition is to highlight starkly Elijah's refusal to budge from his position. Nothing Yhwh does makes any difference to him.

The question Yhwh poses to him in 19:9 and "a voice" repeats in 19:13 is a different matter entirely. The change from "word of Yhwh" to "a voice" (*qôl*) is, frankly, a puzzle to me. It is difficult to understand the second question as asked by anyone except God, so perhaps the mysterious anonymity of "a voice" is simply the narrator's way of prolonging the unimaginability of a "*qôl* of sheer silence." On the other hand, the questions, identical though their wording is, take different meaning from their different contexts. Both question Elijah's reasons for appearing at a particular location: "Why are you *here*, Elijah?" In 19:9 Yhwh is asking about Elijah's presence at Horeb. In other words, "Why have you made this journey, instead of remaining in Israel where your prophetic calling requires you to be?" In 19:13b the voice is asking about Elijah's location "at the entrance of the cave" (19:13a). Yhwh had instructed Elijah to "go out and stand on the mountain before Yhwh" (19:11)—a command that the obedient Elijah of chapter 17 would have complied with in identical terms: "He went out and stood on the mountain before Yhwh." But that is not what happens. After witnessing the divine manifestation of power, Elijah "went out and stood at the entrance to the cave" (19:13a). The prophet's compliance diverges in two significant ways. He does not stand "before Yhwh" (a standard Hebrew idiom for being a servant of Yhwh; see 17:1 and 18:15), and he does not stand "on the mountain."[53] When the voice challenges the incompleteness of his obedience, Elijah merely repeats his original complaint.

VOICE(S) OF THE NARRATOR

1. The words I have in mind are the last words of 17:16, "according to the word of Yhwh that he spoke by Elijah." In one sense, they confirm to the narratee that the word of promise Elijah spoke in 17:14 was truly, as he claimed, a word of Yhwh. But that was already obvious, since the fulfillment of the promise had been recounted in 17:15. The narrator seems here to go to unnecessary lengths to emphasize Elijah's authenticity as a bearer of the divine word of promise. I have spoken briefly above of how chapter 17 progressively reveals Elijah's prophetic credentials. That revelation is reflected textually by several appearances of the Hebrew word "word" *dābār* (although the NRSV obscures that key word in several places). The question of Elijah's authority is posed in 17:1 when he claims power over rain and says it will not fall "except at the *mouth* of my *word.*"[54] His authority to make such a claim unfolds in stages. First, Elijah's letter-perfect obedience to Yhwh is affirmed in 17:2–7, when he acts "according to the *word* of Yhwh" (17:5a). Next, his role as a bearer of divine power emerges in a series of three statements: he urges the woman to act "according to your *word*" (17:13; NRSV "as you have said"); she acts "according to the *word* of Elijah" (17:15; NRSV "as Elijah said"); and the promise is fulfilled "according to the *word* of Yhwh that he spoke by Elijah" (17:16b). Third, although the word *dābār* does not appear in 17:17–23, the scene demonstrates that Elijah can also speak a *human* word of powerful intercession to Yhwh.[55] Finally, the climax of this development comes in 17:24, when the woman acknowledges what the narratee and reader have also come to recognize, that Elijah is a "man of God" (that is, a prophet), and that—notice the echo with 17:1 here!—"the *word* of Yhwh in your *mouth* is truth!"

The primary effect, then, of 17:16 is not to advance the narrative, but to help develop the motif of "word and obedience" that gradually confirms Elijah's prophetic credentials. For the first time the narrator explicitly asserts that Elijah is a bearer of the divine word. It is less an element of *story* and more a narrator's comment, drawing out the implications of 17:15 for Elijah's characterization.

2. Flashbacks can have much the same impact on a narratee or reader as frame breaks. Both categories of aside interrupt the smooth flow of the story and in that way point up the fact that this is a *story*, not an actual, ongoing sequence of events. Here the narrator's decision[56] to use "greatly" at 18:3 and to have Obadiah say "from my youth" at 18:12 is meaningful at both points. I have discussed the impact of Obadiah's words above. The narrator's use of "greatly" adds a dimension of *evaluation* to what is otherwise a descriptive and informational flashback. It implies the narrator's admiration for Obadiah—an admiration that, interestingly, Elijah does not seem to share.

3. The frame break I am thinking of is 18:31b, where the narrator interprets the twelve stones as referring to the twelve tribes of Israel, and recalls the Genesis tradition of God's renaming of the patriarch Jacob. We discussed this at some length above (see pp. 169–70).

STRUCTURE AND SYMMETRY

1. The repeated elements[57] include "the woman" (17:17, 24); "man of God" (17:18, 24); "to kill my son"[58]/"to kill her son" (17:18, 20); "give me *your son*"/"*your son* is alive" (17:19a, 23d); "took him from her bosom"/"gave him to his mother" (17:19b, 23c); "carried him up to the upper chamber"/"brought him down from the upper chamber" (17:19c, 23b); "laid him on his bed"/"took the child"[59] (17:19c, 23a); Elijah speaks to Yhwh with identical introductory words (17:20, 21b).[60] All in all, these repetitions point to a concentric structure with a slightly complicated center.[61]

    a. Speech by the woman (17:18; "man of God")
        b. Speech by Elijah (17:19a; "give me your son")
            c. Elijah takes the boy from his mother's lap (17:19b)
                d. He carries him up to the upper chamber (17:19c)
                    e. He puts him on the bed (17:19d)
                        f. *Central unit; see below (17:20–22)*
                    e'. He picks the child up (17:23a)
                d'. He brings him down from the upper chamber (17:23b)
            c'. He returns him to his mother (17:23c)
        b'. Speech by Elijah (17:23d; "your son is alive")
    a'. Speech by the woman (17:24; "man of God")

The reverse symmetry underscores the contrasts between the two parts of the scene. The woman accuses Elijah, then professes faith. The child is dead, then is alive. Elijah takes the child from his mother, then gives him back. Elijah carries the child up, then brings the child down. The turning point, of course, is the miraculous central subunit, where Yhwh restores the child's life. That subunit, however, has an alternating structure.

    f_1. "He cried out to Yhwh, 'O Yhwh my God. . . .'" (17:20)
        f_2. narrative: Elijah attempts to revive the boy (17:21a)
    f'_1. "He cried out to Yhwh, 'O Yhwh my God. . . .'" (17:21b)
        f'_2. narrative: Yhwh revives the boy (17:22)

This central subunit displays elements of both reversal and progression. Reversal is evident in the death/life of the boy. Progression is evident in the prayer/fulfillment sequence. But the precise relationship of these four central acts remains ambivalent. One could read reversal as the principal dynamic. In that reading, Elijah's first speech is accusatory of Yhwh (note how similar it is to the woman's accusation of Elijah in 17:18), whereas his second speech is a submissive entreaty. Likewise, Elijah's attempt to revive the boy fails, but Yhwh's power succeeds. Alternatively, one could equally well read the four acts as a gradual progression. Elijah points out to Yhwh that the child's death was an injustice, begins the process of revivification by his ritual act, calls on Yhwh's power as part of that ritual act, and Yhwh makes the ritual efficacious.

The relationship between Elijah and Yhwh, then, can be read in two ways: as a collaborative convergence of prophetic prayer and divine power in the service of justice or, more tensively, as a struggle that pits prophet and Deity against one another on some level. To ask which of these readings is "right" is, in my opinion, to ask the wrong question, since both readings are equally adequate to the text. A more *self*-revealing question for the reader is to ask Why do I lean to *this* reading rather than that one?[62]

2. The pattern established by the repeated elements displays forward symmetry.[63]

   a. Elijah spends the night *in a cave* (19:9a)
      b. Yhwh questions him: *"What are you doing here, Elijah?"* (19:9b)
         c. *Elijah answers at great length* (19:10)
            d. Yhwh gives Elijah a command (19:11a)
               e. The narrator describes a powerful theophany (19:11b–12)
   a'. Elijah stands at the entrance *of the cave* (19:13a)
      b'. A voice questions him: *"What are you doing here, Elijah?"* (19:13b)
         c'. *Elijah answers at great length* (19:14 is identical to 19:10)
            d'. Yhwh gives Elijah commands (19:15–16)[64]
               e'. Yhwh describes his coming victory over Baal (19:17–18)

Forward symmetry tends to point to progression rather than contrast, and both of the interpretations suggested in earlier sections are progressive. The commoner interpretation sees Elijah as seeking renewal in his struggle against Baal and Yhwh granting him this with a powerful theophany. This leads to Elijah's recommissioning to undertake actions that will assure Yhwh's ultimate victory over Baal. The alternative interpretation sees Elijah as seeking to resign his prophetic office and Yhwh accepting his resignation and instructing him to anoint a successor. Forward symmetry would support either of these interpretations. But an interpretation that highlights contrast—for instance, Elijah comes to Horeb seeking to resign his prophetic office, but Yhwh refuses and sends him back to take up the struggle once again[65]—would be more compatible with a reverse symmetrical pattern.

3. The pattern, as I read it, flows like this.[66]

   a. *"To kill me"* (18:9)
      b_1. Obadiah's first argument: Ahab has been looking for Elijah (18:10)
         c. He quotes Elijah's command from 18:8 (18:11)
      b_2. He continues his first argument (18:12a)[67]
   a'. *"He will kill me"* (18:12b)
      b'. Obadiah's second argument: I have been faithful to Yhwh (18:12c–13)

       c'. He quotes Elijah's command from 18:8 (18:14a)
a". *"He will surely kill me"* (18:14b)

Two symmetries conflict here, because subunit b_2 has no counterpart in the second half. If it did, then the symmetry would be balanced, and reverse ($ab_1cb_2a'b'_1c'b'_2a"$). Or, if the first argument were not divided (that is, if there were no subunit b_2 at all), the symmetry would be balanced, and forward ($abca'b'c'a"$). Obadiah is a highly placed official in the court ("in charge of the palace," as the NRSV puts it in 18:3). Rhetorical excellence was expected of such officials; and Obadiah here demonstrates his control of rhetorical forms, yet fails to craft a coherent, well-structured speech. This failure is best seen as a measure of the absolute panic he feels in the face of Elijah's uncompromising command to confront Ahab.[68]

Appendix 3

The Ahab Story

A reminder before you begin. What follows are not answers to the questions in the sense that these are the answers you should have come up with or the analyses you should have produced. They are only examples of the *sort* of answers you might have found. They are examples that, for one reason or another, I find particularly appropriate or interesting; but there are almost always other examples that you could have cited. And my analyses may often go deeper than yours do. (I should hope so! Thirty years of working through 1 Kings ought to give me something of a head start!) When my explanations do go more deeply into the text, ask yourself whether they appear plausible to you (that is, whether they enable richer readings of the text that account for more details than another reading might). If they do, they may help you hone your own analytical skills; and if they do not appear plausible, they may demonstrate ways of *misreading* that you ought to avoid.

PLOT

Simple Arc of Tension

The state of stability that sets the context for the confrontation of prophet and king is Ahab's victory over and treaty with Ben-hadad in the earlier part of the chapter. Ahab is apparently on his way home from the battlefield. This joyous return is interrupted by the cry of the bandaged bystander. There are two arcs of tension in the scene. The first arises from the case the disguised prophet lays before the king, which we, the readers, assume to be a deceptive ploy, though we do not know what the prophet is really after. The tension is, What will the king's judgment be? Once Ahab renders his judgment, thus resolving the first arc of tension, the judgment immediately becomes the starting point for the next arc of tension. The prophet reveals himself and turns Ahab's own words back on him as a condemnation of the king. The tension now is, How will Ahab respond? The resolution lies in the two descriptive adjectives applied to Ahab in 20:43 ("resentful and sullen," NRSV[1]), which otherwise is simply a departure notice that brings the scene to an end.

A More Complex Example

The first verse sets the background. "Siege" is certainly not what one would call a situation of political "stability," but in this literary context, it is the stable situation within which the events of 20:1–11 take place. The first arc of tension is clear: Ben-hadad sends a challenging message to Ahab (20:2–3). How will Ahab respond? He capitulates (20:4).[2] The second arc of tension begins in the next verse, when Ben-hadad raises the stakes, so to speak, by turning his original demand for a profession of loyalty into a demand for delivery of tribute (20:5–6).[3] Again, how will Ahab respond? The answer does not come until 20:9, with Ahab's polite ("my lord the king") refusal. Within that arc of tension is contained another: Ahab consults "elders of the land" about Ben-hadad's demands (20:7). How will *they* respond? That arc of tension resolves in 20:8, when the elders (and "all the people") urge Ahab to refuse. Finally, another arc of tension begins in 20:10 when Ben-hadad threatens Ahab with obliteration. Ahab's response in 20:11 (no longer polite; it is, rather, an insolent taunt) resolves that tension, though it clearly points forward to new questions (How will Ben-hadad respond to Ahab's impertinence?) that will develop into pitched battle in 20:12–21.

The Whole Ahab Story

The material from 1 Kings 20:12–21 is the first arc of tension. In 20:12 Ben-hadad orders an attack. Who will prevail in all-out war? The question is resolved in 20:21 when Ahab "defeated the Arameans with a great slaughter." The next verse opens new tension by predicting another military campaign by Ben-hadad in the next year. Both kings receive advice (Ahab from a prophet in 20:22, Ben-hadad from courtiers in 20:23–25). These counsels destabilize the situation of peace (or at least absence of war) reached in 20:21. That arc of tension resolves in 20:30 with another defeat of the Arameans and the flight of Ben-hadad from the battlefield. That situation, however, is hardly stable, since Ben-hadad is hiding in a city Ahab has just conquered (20:30b). So a new arc of tension begins: What will happen to Ben-hadad? Negotiations for his safe conduct are successful, and the two kings sign a treaty (20:34) that brings about a new situation of stability.

In chapter 22 the first verses supply background information that describes the situation of stability before the events of the chapter take place. Ahab's question (22:3) and Jehoshaphat's acquiescence (22:4) constitute the first arc of tension. The second begins with Jehoshaphat's desire to consult a prophet of Yhwh. Although it is possible to discern several low-level arcs of tension in what follows (e.g., 22:5–7, first consultation), the whole narrative is so tightly woven that these low-level arcs intersect with one another and the tension is not really resolved until 22:27–28a,[4] when Ahab incarcerates Micaiah and Micaiah utters his final word of condemnation. The battle begins in 22:29 with its inevitable question, Who will win? But in view of the preceding scene and Micaiah's prediction of Ahab's death, that question carries a more specific point: Will Ahab die as Micaiah prophesied? The second question is resolved in 22:37. The first question is, surprisingly, not answered. It is unclear who won the battle. With Ahab's fatal wounding, the Israelites seem to have abandoned the battlefield (see 22:36, and compare it to 22:17). Oddly, 22:38 does not seem to belong to this arc of tension. The washing of Ahab's blood from his chariot could simply be a note on the aftermath of the battle, but in this context it is clearly more. It leads into the remark about dogs and prostitutes (22:38b), which is in turn identified as originating in a prophetic word (22:39c). One would expect a reference back to Micaiah's prophecy, but that is not the case. The only earlier prophetic word that is anything like this verse is in 21:19,[5] and that is different enough from what we have in 22:38b that, if 22:38b is intended to allude to 21:19, the allusion is distorted indeed.[6]

The first part of chapter 21 begins with a simple, short arc of tension. After some background information (describing the situation of stability) in 21:1, Ahab's offer to purchase Naboth's vineyard destabilizes the situation. Naboth's refusal[7] of the king's offer (21:3) resolves that tension. The beginning of the next verse is a departure notice that ends the scene with Ahab returning home, muttering about Naboth's refusal.[8] The last words of 21:4 situate Ahab in his private chambers, where he indulges in a fit of pique. This is background for the next arc of tension, which begins with Jezebel's solicitous question (21:5) and ends with her promise to acquire Naboth's vineyard for Ahab (21:7). This, however, immediately opens new questions: Will she succeed? *How* will she succeed? The second question points forward to 21:8–14, where Jezebel's plot is detailed in her letter, carried out by her henchmen, and succeeds in encompassing Naboth's murder.

(One could describe this arc of tension, *How* will Jezebel succeed, as starting with her promise in 21:7 or with her letter writing in 21:8.) The other question that begins in 21:7, Will she succeed? surrounds the arc of tension about *How* will she succeed? and is resolved in 21:15–16, when Jezebel announces the achievement of her promise to Ahab and Ahab realizes his desires by taking possession of the vineyard.

The second part of the chapter (21:17–29) begins with a command from Yhwh to Elijah to deliver a condemnation to Ahab for the murder of Naboth. That initiates an arc of tension: Will Elijah obey the command? After the story of Elijah in 1 Kings 17–19, the implied reader is unlikely to think this is much of a question: Elijah's prophetic credentials are well-established, and his pattern of obedience to Yhwh has been demonstrated. It comes as a bit of a shock, then, to see that, when Elijah finally meets Ahab and speaks to him (21:20b–22[9]), the message he delivers is quite different from what he was commissioned to say.[10] So one arc of tension is partially resolved (Elijah obeys, but not perfectly), but another arc of tension is originated: Why does Elijah change Yhwh's message so considerably? This arc of tension is never resolved. A second arc of tension begins with Elijah's speech: How will Ahab react? (He has already called Elijah his "enemy" in 21:20.) That arc of tension resolves in 21:27, where Ahab's behavior "when he heard these words" is described. Since that behavior is apparently penitential, the question arises, Will Yhwh respond to Ahab's repentance? That is answered in 21:28–29, with Yhwh's decree commuting Ahab's punishment by deferring it to the next generation.[11] That decree, in turn, begins a new arc of tension (Will it happen as Yhwh decrees?) that is not resolved within this chapter.[12]

Clear connections between the two chapters about Ahab's wars with Aram are scarce. In 22:1 the remark that the two nations were at peace for three years can be read as a reference back to the treaty in 20:34; but since nothing in chapter 20 points forward to a three-year peace, the connection is only implicit. A clearer connection begins in 20:34, where Ben-hadad promises to return to Ahab "the towns that my father took from your father." In 22:3 Ahab complains to his servants[13] that "Ramoth-gilead[14] belongs to us, but we are doing nothing to take it out of the hand of the king of Aram." Together these statements sketch a situation where Ben-hadad has not honored the terms of the treaty he made, and Ahab (who, after chap. 20, now believes himself militarily superior to Ben-hadad) intends to compel compliance by force.

CHARACTERS

1. Ahab, Jezebel, and Naboth all have a claim on precedence in 21:1–16. Ahab is mentioned slightly more often than Jezebel (eight times as against six), but Jezebel is more active and occupies the center of the story as she designs and implements the plot against Naboth. On the other hand, the basic complication and resolution of the plot has Ahab in view: he wants the vineyard, he gets

it. But over against all this stand several elements that point to Naboth. He is mentioned first, and he is named more often than Ahab and Jezebel combined (seventeen times, including six times with the full title "Naboth the Jezreelite"). He is even named six times in the three verses after he is dead! And his destiny changes even more than Ahab's: he loses not only his vineyard but his life. It is not without reason that readers regularly refer to this story as "Naboth's Vineyard," rather than "Ahab's [or Jezebel's] Crime."

2. At least two traits stand out about this unnamed prophet. First, he disobeys a divine word (perhaps unintentionally); second, he is killed by a lion. In the present narrative, his death in fulfillment of his confrere's prophecy serves to guarantee that the confrere truly speaks a divine word. Elsewhere in 20:35–43 nothing verifies the credentials of the prophet who condemns Ahab; we know that his claim to speak for Yhwh is reliable only because we have this bizarre example of his word being miraculously potent.

In a larger context, another story of a prophet who disobeys a divine word (perhaps unintentionally) and is killed by a lion occurs in 1 Kings 13:11–32.[15] There the story is used to evidence Jeroboam's intransigence and justify Yhwh's subsequent rejection of him. Here the story functions similarly. Ahab becomes, in the words of the NRSV, "resentful and sullen"; as I said in the preceding section (see n. 1), "fuming and furious" is a little closer to the mark. However one translates the phrase, it bespeaks obduracy. The story also begins a series of prophetic condemnations of Ahab that will culminate in the divine rejection of his whole dynasty (21:21–24) and the decree of Ahab's own death (22:13–23).

3. The representative spokesperson for the prophets of 1 Kings 22 is Zedekiah, son of Chenaanah (22:11, 24–25). In the first part of the scene, 22:5–12, before the appearance of Micaiah, son of Imlah, Zedekiah is associated with the group of prophets and acts as their representative. However, once Micaiah appears (22:15–28), the group is not mentioned again and Zedekiah emerges as an individual character. By individualizing him and giving him both a name and a patronymic, the narrator makes him a more apt adversary for the individual prophet Micaiah, son of Imlah. Their antagonism takes on the dimensions of a personal struggle. In 1 Kings 18:21–40 the prophets of Baal versus Elijah stood for the deeper struggle between the deities Baal and Yhwh. Here all the prophets claim Yhwh's name, not Baal's (see 22:11–12); so the struggle is between prophets, not gods. Individualizing the group character enables this personal dynamic to emerge more clearly.

4. In 22:15–28 there is a very slight, technical violation of the convention. Once Micaiah appears, there are three principal actors—Ahab, Micaiah, and Zedekiah—who interact in accord with the convention: Ahab and Micaiah interact, Micaiah and Zedekiah interact, but Ahab and Zedekiah do not. There is, however, a fourth figure, Jehoshaphat, to whom Ahab speaks in 22:18. Were Jehoshaphat a completely flat character (like the unnamed individual to whom Ahab gives an order in 22:26), this would not constitute a real violation of the convention. Characters so flat as to be little more than animated props do not

count. But Jehoshaphat was a major character in 22:1–12, and will be again in 22:30–33. He cannot be dismissed in 22:18 as a nonentity.

The narrator, however, lessens the infraction in a clever way. First, he reduces Jehoshaphat to silence: the king of Judah says and does nothing in the scene (contrast his active, even contentious presence in 22:4–8). Second, he modifies Ahab's language to include Jehoshaphat: contrast 22:6 ("Shall *I* go . . . ?") with 22:15 ("Shall *we* go . . . ?"). In effect, he collapses Ahab and Jehoshaphat into a royal *group character*, with Ahab acting as spokesperson.

The narrator achieves a difference in focus by shifting the pivotal role from king to prophet. In 22:1–12 Ahab is the central character; both Jehoshaphat and the four hundred prophets interact with him, but not with each other. In 22:15–28, though Ahab remains on stage, the central character is Micaiah; both Ahab and Zedekiah interact with him, but not with each other. The reader's attention, therefore, is transferred from Ahab's political and military ambitions to Yhwh's machinations against the king.

5. The first thing a reader notices is that the kings of Israel and Judah seem to be on friendly terms. This is unexpected, since there has been no sign of reconciliation between the kingdoms since the northern tribes rejected the house of David and elected Jeroboam their king. The reader cannot help but wonder how and when the breach was healed.

Jehoshaphat's relationship with Ahab is also unclear. There are indications that Jehoshaphat is Ahab's vassal, as I have previously suggested (see above, p. 22). However, Jehoshaphat's repeated insistence on consulting Yhwh does not seem to be behavior typical of a vassal but more characteristic of discussion between monarchs who consider themselves equals. What exactly is their relationship?

When Jehoshaphat was introduced in 15:24, the story of Israel was at the beginning of a period of catastrophic chaos.[16] In the thirty-six years that pass between 15:25 and the accession of Ahab in 16:29, Israel sees five kings, three of whom reign a total of about two years, and one of whom spends much of his twelve-year reign embroiled in a civil war. Judah, by contrast, apparently flourished under Jehoshaphat's father Asa: "Now the rest of all the acts of Asa, all his power, all that he did, and the cities that he built, are they not written in the Book of the Annals of the Kings of Judah?" (15:23). The reader expects Judah to be strong, Israel to be recovering but probably still weak. If Jehoshaphat is Ahab's vassal, as the text intimates, how did this reversal of fortunes come about?

Finally, Jehoshaphat's odd situation in the battle (taking Ahab's place as a rallying point in a position of safety, yet being specifically targeted for attack), along with the fact that chapter 22 leaves the overall outcome of the battle unresolved, raises the question of what happened to Jehoshaphat. The king of Israel was killed in battle; did the king of Judah perish at the same time?

In short, Jehoshaphat's presence in chapter 22 raises several questions about the political and military relationship of Judah and Israel as well as about Jehoshaphat's own story. The reader is drawn forward beyond the account of Ahab to look for further information about affairs in Judah at the time.[17]

6. The basic story line is fairly straightforward. Ahab and Jehoshaphat attack Aramean forces at Ramoth-gilead, and Ahab is slain in the battle. This, however, does not require Micaiah. The narrator could have moved directly from plan (22:4) to execution (22:29) or, to introduce a theological dimension, could have allowed the four hundred prophets to convince both kings at 22:6.

The plot-behind-the-plot, so to speak, is that all of this is happening at Yhwh's behest, and that Yhwh assures the success of his plans by using Ahab's prophets to deceive the king into undertaking the battle. But even this does not require Micaiah. The narrator could simply inform the reader in an aside: "but the prophets were lying; all this happened because Yhwh willed evil for Ahab," or something like that (compare, for example, the narrator's similar asides in 12:15 and 13:18b). What Micaiah accomplishes is twofold: he *informs both Ahab and the reader of Yhwh's deceptive plot*. In this way, he creates major dilemmas for both Ahab and the reader. By explaining Yhwh's stratagem to Ahab, he deprives the king of any opportunity to blame his downfall on divine deception. By explaining it to the reader, Micaiah forces the reader to deal with a God who lies and with prophets who are truly divinely inspired to speak those lies. In terms of the story line, then, Micaiah is a tool of the narrator to weave deep and disturbing dramatic and theological subtexts into the text.

Micaiah as tool is different from Micaiah as developed character. The narrator gives us aspects of Micaiah's individuality that point beyond the immediate story. First, there is backstory. Ahab's complaint that his so-far unnamed prophetic nemesis "never prophesies anything favorable about me, but only disaster" (22:8), implies a long history of hostile confrontation. We expect him to name Elijah, and are surprised when he names a prophet we have never heard of before. We recall then that Ahab has had dealings with other unnamed prophets (see chap. 20), and at least one of them was antagonistic to him (20:35–43). We infer from these glimpses a much broader intercourse between king and prophetic figures, and in particular between king and *hostile* prophetic figures, than we had previously suspected.

We learn that Micaiah is obedient to the spirit of God. He insists on his fidelity to Yhwh in 22:14 and his first prophecy (22:15) *agrees* with the prophecy of the four hundred prophets—which, according to Micaiah's subsequent story, is truly inspired by the (lying) spirit from God. In this way, Micaiah's own prophetic credentials are demonstrated, and his stories about his visions portending Ahab's death (22:17) and of the heavenly court deliberations (22:19–23) are substantiated.

Finally, we learn that Micaiah has more to say. In the present text, 22:28b announces further oracles ("Hear, you peoples, all of you"), although they do not appear in the text; in fact, the words point to the book of Micah in the Minor Prophets (see Mic. 1:2).[18] These words may well be a later accretion to the text,[19] but in the present text they leave the impression that Micaiah's career is not ended. Ahab's threat (22:27) means that, when the king "returns in peace," the falsity of Micaiah's prophecy would have been demonstrated and his credentials as a prophet would have been nullified (see Deut. 17:22). By attributing to Micaiah a continuing prophetic career, the narrator foreshadows that Ahab's threat will never materialize because, as the remainder of the chapter shows, he will not "return in peace."

CHARACTERIZATION

1. In several instances titles are equivalent to the narrator *telling* us something about the character. Ben-hadad is a king, and he is from Aram (20:1); Ahab is a king, and he is from Israel (20:2 and frequently); Jehoshaphat is a king, and he is from Judah (22:2); Naboth is a Jezreelite (21:1 and frequently); Micaiah's father's name was Imlah (22:8 and frequently); Zedekiah's father's name was Chenaanah (22:11, 24); and so forth. One instance of such a title would strike the implied reader as especially startling, though most modern readers might overlook its significance. Ahab, king of Israel, is called "king of Samaria" in 21:1. This title appears only one other time in the book of Kings, in 2 Kings 1:3; and it is inappropriate. "Samaria" was not used as a term for the territory of the northern tribes until much later. At the time of Ahab, it was the name of his capital city. To call Ahab "king of Samaria" is like calling the monarch of England "king [or queen] of London."

Other examples of telling can be found in 20:16 (Ben-hadad is drunk; in 20:12 we were already shown that he was drinking; now the narrator informs us that he has been drinking to the point that he is drunk) and in 20:43 (Ahab is "resentful and sullen";[20] the same description will appear again a few verses later, in 21:4). Perhaps most striking of all is the lengthy and, for Hebrew narrative style, relatively florid description of the kings in their regalia, surrounded by the four hundred prophets, in 22:10.[21]

2. The difference between the two readings is very slight. If the captains say this to one another, it reveals coordinated planning. If they say it individually to themselves, it may simply reflect their readiness to obey to Ben-hadad's command in 22:31. (Or it may reflect each individual's desire for the glory of killing the enemy king.) In terms of the larger narrative, the effect is the same in either case: Ahab's ploy of disguising himself has worked and has drawn hostile attention to Jehoshaphat instead. This sets up the background for the ironic random arrow that mortally wounds Ahab despite his machinations.

3. I have already mentioned how Ahab's polite replies to Ben-hadad in 20:4 and 20:9 reveal that Ahab is probably Ben-hadad's vassal. Ben-hadad's words in 20:18 offer an amusing example of characterization. One could take them simply as Ben-hadad giving a military command, but his speech is not phrased the way people ordinarily talk. One would expect Ben-hadad to say, "If they have come out for peace, take them alive; if they have come out for war, kill them." Or perhaps, "Whether they have come out for peace or for war, take them alive." The overblown repetition, however, is awkward and unnatural.

Then we remember 20:16: Ben-hadad is *drunk*! This is precisely the sort of thing someone would say if their thought processes were sodden with alcohol. Ben-hadad's inarticulateness reveals his condition.

Ahab's words to Naboth in 21:2 indicate the king's goodwill in offering to purchase Naboth's vineyard. He offers a *better* vineyard; or, in the unlikely event that the landowner will prefer silver to land, he offers full value. At the same time, Ahab's reasons for the purchase seem shoddy. Having a vegetable garden near his palace might be a convenience, but a vegetable garden is a relatively simple bit of agriculture. A productive vineyard, on the other hand, requires years of careful cultivation and maintenance. There is a certain lack of feeling in Ahab's willingness to offer Naboth this purpose to justify the sale. So we can infer from this speech that Ahab is the sort who wants what he wants; he is willing to be generous to get it, but he is rather insensitive to what impact his desires will have on others.

Micaiah's words to the messenger (22:14), on the surface, imply that he is (or claims to be) one who is unswervingly obedient to Yhwh's word and will. Since we have never encountered Micaiah before, we cannot be certain that his claim is reliable; but Ahab's hostility toward him (22:8) implies that Micaiah is certainly not a yes-man. And so we move further into the story inclined to assume the validity of Micaiah's prophetic word. Imagine our surprise, then, when the first words out of Micaiah's mouth are the same as those of the four hundred prophets (22:15)—words that Micaiah himself will later label a lie (22:23)! The complexity of Micaiah's character requires much from the reader if he or she is to make sense of it.

4. In 20:7 Ahab consults the "elders of the land" about what response he should give to Ben-hadad. Since Samaria is under siege, and the phrase "elders of the land" refers to the chief people in the outlying villages, Ahab is consulting those most affected by the situation. If he refuses Ben-hadad's demands, the villages will suffer first from the Aramean depredations. From a modern, Western point of view, this is admirable behavior: the right of the people affected to have a voice in their own destiny is one of the fundamental pillars of democracy. But at least some ancient monarchical societies are likely to have seen things differently. For them, decisions like this are the king's responsibility, and involving anyone else (except his immediate political advisers) in the decision could be construed as an attempt to shirk his duty. In the present context, however, I see no indication that the narrator (or the implied author) wishes the narratee (or the implied reader) to judge Ahab negatively. The "elders" (and note that the narrator even adds "and all the people" [20:8]) do not simply throw the decision back to the king. On the contrary, they support his position and urge him to maintain it.[22] My inferences from this scene add very positive notes to the portrait of Ahab. He is concerned about his people and is not willing to endanger them needlessly. He is even willing to undergo severe personal deprivation to protect them.[23] Conversely, his people respect and trust him, and are willing to run the risk of severe suffering out of loyalty to him.

In 20:33 Ahab has Ben-hadad "come up into the chariot." Is this simply a trivial detail, or does it carry significant overtones? In my reading, it is very significant, though only part of its significance survives translation. At the beginning of the chapter, Ahab was vassal and Ben-hadad was overlord. Now, Ahab has defeated Ben-hadad definitively twice in two years (20:21 and 20:29–30). We have every right to expect Ben-hadad to sue for vassal status to Ahab as overlord. Before he can do so, however, Ahab has called him "brother" (20:32), a term that implies a readiness to treat Ben-hadad as an equal (notice how quickly Ben-hadad's servants pick up the signal: 20:33a). When Ben-hadad finally comes before Ahab, the latter's gesture of bringing him up into the royal chariot seems to continue this offer of equality: it means that Ahab is treating with Ben-hadad on level ground rather than looking down on him. A further, more subtle signal to the reader (though it does not always survive translation) is in the verb. Ahab "had him come up" (NRSV). In Hebrew that is a form of the verb "to go up," which is the same verb used twice already to describe Ben-hadad's attacks on Israel. In 20:1 Ben-hadad "*went up* and besieged Samaria" (NRSV "marched against Samaria and laid siege to it"); in 20:26 he "*went up* to Aphek to fight against Israel." Both of those "goings up" failed, and Ben-hadad was defeated. Now, at the moment of Ben-hadad's greatest submission, Ahab himself enables his erstwhile enemy to "go up" successfully, into Ahab's chariot. The verbal echoes are ominous. Has Ahab inadvertently undermined the results of his own victories?

Jezebel's actions in 21:9 are very revealing but at the same time leave an important question unanswered. (Note that here I am concerned only with her actions in 21:9, not with the content of the letter she writes in 21:10.) Jezebel is clearly unscrupulous in her readiness to assume and exercise authority in Ahab's name: "she wrote letters in Ahab's name and sealed them with his seal." It is presumably this claim of royal authority that motivated the "elders and nobles" of Jezreel to undertake their part in this legal charade. What is unclear, however, is how much of this was known to Ahab. Did he freely allow Jezebel to use his seal,[24] or did she appropriate it on her own initiative? Did he have any idea what she intended to do with it? Was he perhaps willing to sit back and let her do his dirty work for him, or was he naively unaware that she was about anything at all? So the verse shows us much about Jezebel ("direct showing"), but what it implies about Ahab ("indirect showing") is ambiguous in the extreme.

5. The immediately preceding example of direct showing of Jezebel has also involved some indirect showing of Ahab, though it is of a particularly ambiguous nature. The text of Jezebel's letter in the next verse (21:10) contains another particularly clever instance of both.[25] In the text of her letter, Jezebel demands two false witnesses to accuse Naboth, and she calls them "scoundrels." That is an instance of indirect showing about the witnesses, and it indicates Jezebel's low opinion of them. Even though the whole scene demonstrates clearly that Jezebel is hardly a paragon of honesty, it is difficult to imagine any reason why she would malign her own hirelings in this way if the description were not accurate. That she is willing to put such an insult into writing tells us something about her

as well (direct showing): she has no qualms about making use of "scoundrels" to help her get what she wants, she has no illusions about their moral character, and she even has the arrogance to put her insulting opinion into writing.

In 20:23 Ben-hadad's "servants" advise him on how to win the second year's battle against Israel. One of their claims is that "their gods are gods of the hills,"[26] and on that claim they base the military strategy they propose to Ben-hadad. The implied reader (as well as the modern one) knows, however, that Yhwh's power is *not* limited to hill country and recognizes this indirect showing of Yhwh's character as utterly inaccurate. Ben-hadad's subsequent defeat demonstrates that the "servants" were very wrong indeed. Now fast-forward to 20:31, where Ben-hadad's "servants" (presumably the same ones) make a strong claim about the *kings* of Israel: "We have heard that the kings of the house of Israel are merciful kings."[27] Since the servants' track record for accuracy is pretty bad, we can readily wonder (and Ben-hadad ought to!) whether their appeal to Ahab's mercy will be any more successful than their military advice. In other words, the indirect showing of Ahab (he is one of the "kings of the house of Israel" and therefore a "merciful king") is of uncertain validity until we reach 20:32, where Ahab calls Ben-hadad "brother"; 20:33, where Ahab takes Ben-hadad up into his royal chariot; and 20:34, where the two kings make a treaty of equals.

Certainly the most shocking example of indirect showing in the Ahab story is Micaiah's speech in 22:19–23. He depicts Yhwh as approving a plot to trick Ahab to his death. The plot involves inspiring prophets to lie by putting false assurances in their mouths. There are two levels of scandal here. The first is theological: the indirect showing of Yhwh as condoning falsehood to get Ahab killed.[28] The second is religious: if Yhwh can inspire prophets to lie, then the entire institution of prophecy is called into question, since the reliability even of prophets whose credentials are impeccable can be no greater than the reliability of the Deity who inspires them.

POINT OF VIEW

1. The introductory bit of background information (20:1) is probably best seen as having a neutral external point of view. I hear the dialogues between Ahab and Ben-hadad's messenger (20:2–6) mainly from Ahab's point of view; nothing that Ahab says focuses my attention on him, and the severe and eventually outrageous demands the messenger utters evoke my anger by their tyranny. When Ahab consults the elders (20:7–8), my point of view remains Ahab's: his presentation of the problem to the elders tells me nothing new; and my attention is focused, as is Ahab's, on what response they will give him.[29] The next exchange between Ahab and Ben-hadad (20:9–10) continues to present Ahab's point of view. His message of refusal to Ben-hadad tells us nothing more than that he has accepted the elders' advice. But Ben-hadad's threatening response is calculated to strike fear into him, as it does into the reader. However, 20:11

changes things. To this point Ahab has been submissive, polite, and diplomatic (notice "my lord the king" in 20:4 and 9). We half expect something similar—perhaps a further effort to negotiate a compromise. We do not expect Ahab to respond with a laconic insult.[30] When he does, our surprise focuses us on him, rather than on Ben-hadad's messenger. In a sense, we step back from our position at Ahab's side and take a new look at this king whose inner strength we had underestimated. The effect is, paradoxically, a somewhat greater distance from Ahab and, simultaneously, increased empathy for him. Finally 20:12 takes us for the first time into the Aramean camp. We return to the neutral external point of view that we had in 20:1, but with an important difference. In 20:1 we were far enough from the scene to witness a large-scale military invasion and its march from Aram to Samaria. By 20:12 we have been brought very close to the action indeed, both physically (hearing all the speeches of messenger, elders, and King Ahab) and emotionally (by our empathy for Ahab); and now we find ourselves close enough to hear Ben-hadad's words from his own mouth.

2. In 20:35 the point of view is neutral external. It is not omniscient, because we have no knowledge that is not available to a neutral observer and, indeed, we definitely feel the lack. We wonder, for instance, about the motivation of the prophet who commands his confrere to hit him; and we may even wonder about the motivation for the confrere's refusal. This distances us from both, and gives us a neutral position. That continues in the next verse. Here there is slight touch of omniscience, since we know something that happened at a different location (the confrere's death). But since we do not *witness* the lion attack (that is, the narrator does not portray it as a scene), it feels less like omniscient knowledge and more like a report we have heard. The neutral external point of view continues through 20:37 and follows the prophet on his journey in 20:38. It remains neutral, however, because we still do not have any insight into the prophet's motivations, particularly when he goes to the trouble to disguise himself. The dialogue between prophet and king in 20:39–40 (the sham appeal and royal judgment) continue the same point of view, since there is nothing that cannot be observed by a neutral observer. There is, perhaps, some slight shift toward the king's point of view, since, like the king, we hear the prophet's claims for the first time and since the king's verdict seems reasonable.[31] There is not enough sense of royal deliberation, however, to bring our point of view into complete alignment with Ahab's; we still remain more or less neutral. By contrast, the next verses (20:41–42) move our point of view very close to Ahab's. We watch the prophet reveal his identity; and we sense Ahab's surprise as he recognizes the prophet (though we do not share that surprise; we have known the prophet's identity all along). From a position relatively close to Ahab, we hear the prophet's oracle of condemnation. Finally, in 20:43 we gain insight into Ahab's internal feelings[32] as we journey with him back to Samaria.

This last verse, however, poses a problem for an analysis of point of view, and offers us an opportunity to appreciate the impact *context* has on our responses.

The reader who comes to this story with an image of Ahab drawn from the larger context of 1 Kings 16:29–19:21 will fully expect Ahab to be condemned. The picture of Ahab in 16:29–19:21 is unrelievedly negative. This reader, then, will see Ahab's resentment as part of his characteristic opposition to Yhwh, and will tend to view Ahab's condemnation from a point of view hostile to Ahab and sympathetic to Yhwh—therefore approaching an omniscient point of view. On the other hand, the reader who reads chapter 20 as a self-contained story with no prior characterization of Ahab in mind will see something quite different. Such a reader will see a king who is considerate of his people, receives advice from Yhwh even to the point of specific tactical details (20:13–14), obeys without hesitation, is granted victory in two stunning military upsets, and implements that victory with mercy and restraint (20:31–34). That reader will come to this scene predisposed to admire Ahab and will be baffled by the prophet's oracle of condemnation. The reader cannot fault the prophet, whose prophetic credentials were assured by the little scene in 20:35–36; but he or she is unwilling to fault Ahab either, since there is nothing in the text to indicate to Ahab (or to the reader) that Yhwh had specific plans for Ben-hadad. Ahab's resentment will resonate with this reader's admiration and bafflement to make the reader's point of view very close to, if not identical with, the king's.

It is especially noteworthy that the narrator could easily have avoided this effect. The story of prophetic condemnation is, for all intents and purposes, completed in 20:42; and the chapter could have ended very satisfactorily with that verse. Indeed 20:43 opens a new arc of tension (What will Ahab do now?) that is not clearly resolved (unless the repeated mention of identical feelings in 21:4 is intended to continue that arc of tension); and the focus on Ahab's interior life is quite different from the focus on Ahab's deeds as king that characterizes everything else in the chapter.

3. The point of view in these verses does not fit well into any of the categories we have been using to this point. It does not seem to correspond to any particular character's point of view; nor is it a neutral external viewpoint, since it does not simply observe outward words and actions but makes moral judgments about them. It is perhaps closest to an omniscient point of view, but there is nevertheless a difference between making moral *judgments* and knowing *facts* no character could know. So whose point of view is expressed here? It is *the narrator's*.

It is important to remember that the narrator, too, is a figure within the narrative world. (We will spend a whole section on the narrator later.) The narrator may or may not be a *character* in the story (he rarely is in biblical stories), but he is nonetheless a personality in the narrative world. The narrator is not merely a disembodied voice telling the story but has opinions about the story he is telling. He usually injects those opinions implicitly into the narrative (for instance, by calling Jezebel's hirelings "scoundrels" in 21:13), but occasionally he will step outside the storytelling role, as here in 21:25–26, to make his moral judgments explicit.

MANIPULATION OF TIME

1. The narrative starts with background information to set the scene (22:29–30). Since this is background information rather than action, it does not establish any pace at all. Indeed, 22:30 is probably a flashback, since the king of Israel probably gave Jehoshaphat these instructions *before* they "went up to Ramoth-gilead" (assuming "went up" means, as it often does, "attacked"). In any case, 22:31 is clearly a flashback, revealing background information necessary for the reader to understand the action in 22:32–33. Note, though, that all the information in 22:30–31 relates to the action in 22:32–33, so the whole four-verse unit functions to portray the misdirected and aborted attempt on Jehoshaphat's life. By contrast, in the next half verse, Ahab is fatally wounded (22:34a). The abrupt change in tone (from escape[33] to mortal injury) is reinforced by the equally abrupt change of pace. After the comparatively rapid recounting of the attack on Jehoshaphat and its abandonment (the action of 22:32–33 must take several minutes at least to unfold), 22:34 shows us (almost in slow motion) an archer drawing his bow, looking around for a target, and shooting; then, in close-up, we see details of the king's armor and the design flaw that permits his wounding, and we hear his instructions to his driver. This sudden slowing of pace has the effect (on me at least) of an unexpected shock, like being blindsided. Then suddenly the pace slows even more (in fact, it stops completely for the brief descriptive words of 22:35a), and we watch as Ahab, propped up in his chariot, slowly, agonizingly bleeds to death.[34] Finally, 22:36 skips to the end of the day and the Israelite withdrawal from battle. It even neglects to tell us who won! Apparently all that is important for the narrator is Ahab's death.

2. The descriptive passage is 22:10, which portrays the kings in their regalia, sitting on thrones, surrounded by the four hundred prophets. What this unusually detailed description portends is not clear until 22:19, when Micaiah describes in very similar terms the scene he saw in heaven. He too witnessed a king on a throne, surrounded by his royal court. The implied contrast between the two scenes is stark: the two human kings *think* they are making important decisions, whereas all true decisive power is in the hands of the divine king enthroned above them.[35]

3. The flashback in 22:38 seems to point back to Yhwh's condemnation in 21:19b, with, perhaps, a secondary allusion to Elijah's words in 21:24a. However, the differences are considerable. First, Elijah is not mentioned by name in 22:38; the oracle is simply attributed to Yhwh.[36] Second, the place is wrong. In 21:19 Yhwh decreed that dogs would lick up Ahab's blood "in the place where the dogs licked up the blood of Naboth." Naboth was a Jezreelite (21:1), was tried by the elders of his own city (21:8), and was executed outside the city walls (21:13). Ahab's blood, however, was washed out of his chariot in Samaria (22:38), to be consumed there by dogs. Third, there was nothing in either the divine words in 21:19 or Elijah's oracle in 21:24 about "prostitutes

washing in Ahab's blood." Finally, and most importantly, 22:38 seems unaware that Yhwh's threat of disaster for Ahab in 21:19 had been abrogated by Yhwh himself in 21:29!

With so many differences, at least the last of which seems quite significant, I hesitate to consider 22:38 a simple flashback to 21:19 without further qualification. At the very least there seem to be two versions of the oracle in play. We might posit that, on some occasion that is not recorded in the Bible, Elijah delivered the condemnation of 21:19 in terms rather different from those that he had received; or perhaps we might postulate a second oracle (by a different prophet?) closer to what we see in 22:38.[37] (The situation would get even more complicated if we were to add 2 Kgs. 9:25–26 to the mix. There Jehu invokes a still different version of the oracle against Ahab to justify throwing the body of Ahab's *son*, whom Jehu has just killed, on to the plot of land that had belonged to Naboth.)

4. In 20:15–21 the narrator interweaves views of the Israelite army's sortie from Samaria with views of Ben-hadad getting progressively drunker in his tent. Like 1 Samuel 12:12–13, the portrayal is a split-screen technique.

Israel	Aram
The army goes out (20:16a)	Ben-hadad is getting drunk (20:16b)
The young men went out first (20:17a)	Ben-hadad sends scouts[38] (20:17b)
Report: "Men have come out . . ." (20:18a)	Ben-hadad says, "Take them"[39] (20:18b)
The whole army is now on the march (20:19)	
	Battle is joined: Each killed his man (20:20a)
	Arameans flee, Ben-hadad escapes (20:20b)
Finally, the king goes out (20:21a)	

The picture on the Aramean side watches Ben-hadad go deeper into his cups, and eventually sees the defeat of the Aramean forces. On the Israelite side, it watches the army come out of Samaria exactly as Yhwh had ordered in 20:14: the "young men who serve the district governors" first and Ahab last, with the rest of the army presumably in between.[40]

The main differences between this split screen and that in 1 Samuel 12:12–13 lies in the point of view. In 1 Samuel the two halves of the screen represent two different points of view on the same object. On one side we have Hannah's own point of view (only she knows she is praying silently); on the other we have Eli's more distant point of view. The differences between what Hannah knows and what Eli thinks he sees lead to his poignant misunderstanding of her situation. In 1 Kings 20 we have one neutral, external point of view of two widely separated objects, the Israelite sortie and the Aramean camp. We watch the two as they near one another, see the battle joined, and follow the aftermath as the surviving Aramean forces flee and Ahab destroys the materiel they leave behind.

GAPS AND AMBIGUITIES

1. The simplest possibility is to assume that Ahab knew that Yhwh had commanded Ben-hadad's death but ignored the command. This would make the situation comparable to that in 1 Samuel 15:17–23, where Samuel condemns Saul for sparing Agag the Amalekite and the best of the spoils of war despite Yhwh's command to Saul to "kill both man and woman, child and infant, ox and sheep, camel and donkey" (1 Sam. 15:3). As Saul was condemned, so too Ahab merits the condemnation the prophet issues. There is little in the text to rule out this conjecture, but there is little to support it either. Against it is the consistent portrayal of Ahab throughout 20:1–34 as attentive to Yhwh, unequivocally obedient to him, and favored by Yhwh with battlefield victories.[41] In support of the conjecture, it is possible to read the man of God's promise in 20:28 ("I will give all this great multitude into your hand") as implying that Yhwh, who gives the victory, claims the right to dispose of the spoils. However, this is scarcely the most evident meaning of the words. And if the narrator wished to be clear, he could easily have had the man of God go on to instruct Ahab to destroy Ben-hadad utterly. To my mind, the narrator's silence about the issue (contrast the explicit recounting of the command in the case of Samuel and Saul) is telling. Whatever we ultimately decide, the narrator wants us to wonder whether Yhwh gave Ahab such a command.

Another possibility is that the prophet made the whole thing up. Yhwh never intended Ben-hadad's death, but the prophet takes advantage of the situation to utter a condemnation of Ahab on his own initiative. In that case, the prophet deserves condemnation for lying about Yhwh's word and Ahab deserves some sort of vindication for having been the victim of a prophetic falsehood. The absence of both of those outcomes is a rather strong argument against this possibility. Furthermore, the only point that the odd story in 20:35–36 appears to have is to verify the prophet's divine credentials: when he speaks, Yhwh miraculously sustains his claims. If the rest of the story were about him speaking falsely in Yhwh's name, there would be no point to 20:35–36 at all.

Between these two extremes there is a much more complex possibility: Yhwh willed Ahab should kill Ben-hadad, but Ahab was unaware of it. Presumably Yhwh expressed his will to the prophet, since he knows of it; but the prophet did not convey the message to Ahab. This opens a further gap. Did the prophet withhold the information on his own responsibility, or did Yhwh not commission him to deliver it? The former case is somewhat similar to the second possibility we considered: the prophet is culpable and merits divine disapproval. Moreover, such malfeasance would undermine our confidence in the reliability of his claim in 20:42 that Yhwh has condemned Ahab. Like the second possibility, this one is weakened by the narrator's efforts to establish the prophet's credentials in 20:35–36.

The second variant—that Yhwh desired Ahab to kill Ben-hadad but did not send the prophet to inform the king of this desire—is perhaps the most awkward. It puts the onus of falsehood, or at least of deception by omission, squarely on Yhwh himself: Yhwh is condemning Ahab for not obeying a command that Yhwh himself kept Ahab from knowing about. For many readers, that alone is sufficient argument to reject this reading. However, when one reaches chapter 22 and encounters the story of Yhwh inspiring his own prophets with a lying spirit in order to trick Ahab to his death, one may look back to this passage and wonder whether Yhwh's unscrupulous tactics were not already at work.

2. One way to explain Micaiah's words is to imagine him delivering them in a vocal tone that reveals their insincerity. This in turn would explain why Ahab disbelieves him. It would not, however, explain why Ahab uses the word "truth" to describe what Micaiah did not say and why he insists that Micaiah prophesy "the truth" when he clearly wants prophetic endorsement for a course of action he has already decided upon. Furthermore, since we are dealing with a *written* text, vocal nuances are not preserved. A narrator, telling the story orally to a narratee, might be able to communicate them; but a written text would have to signal the insincerity some other way if the implied author intended it to be clear to the implied reader.

There is another possibility, but one that requires courage of the reader. What if we take Micaiah at his word in 22:14? This would mean that his prophecy of Ahab's victory in 22:15 is what Yhwh told him to say, notwithstanding its falsity. That entails a major theological problem, in that it means that Yhwh is inspiring his prophet to lie. Note, though, that that theological problem is present *no matter how we read Micaiah's words*: it is precisely the point of the story Micaiah will tell in 22:19–23! In other words, the four hundred prophets have been inspired by a "lying spirit from Yhwh" to prophesy Ahab's victory. If that is so, presumably Micaiah too, as a prophet of Yhwh, has received the same "lying spirit," and prophesies accordingly in 22:15. The difference is that the four hundred prophets do not know that their prophecy is a lie, whereas Micaiah, having been privileged to witness the divine council where the conspiracy was hatched, does know it.[42] In that case, Ahab's expectation that Micaiah will prophesy disaster as he usually does is not met; and Ahab's rebuke voices his suspicion that Micaiah is up to something, as well as a bit of embarrassment because the prediction Ahab made to Jehoshaphat in 22:8 has proven wrong. Ahab's retort would mean something like, "Well, Micaiah, I know you, and if you are prophesying *good* for me, you must be lying through your teeth! Tell me what you really mean!"

3. The more apparent meaning of Zedekiah's question would be, "What claim do *you* have, Micaiah, to possess the prophetic spirit? *We* are Yhwh's prophets, and you are nothing but a fraud." Against this view, however, is the history of Ahab's dealings with Micaiah (22:8), which implies that Micaiah has long-standing credentials as a prophet of Yhwh. An alternative meaning for Zedekiah's question emerges if he is picking up explicitly on Micaiah's claim that Yhwh has sent forth a "lying" spirit. The "spirit" that "passed from me [Zedekiah] to speak to you [Micaiah]," then, would be this *lying* spirit; and Zedekiah is saying,

in effect, "Well, Micaiah, that lying spirit you claim Yhwh has sent forth must have missed us and lodged in you." In both cases, Zedekiah is claiming that he is right, and that Micaiah's version of Yhwh's will is false. But in the second case Zedekiah manifests a greater degree of cleverness and rhetorical skill, which befits someone who functions as spokesman for a whole prophetic coterie, and admits, ironically, that Micaiah may be (truly) inspired (to lie).

4. If one applies the physical sense, then the archer draws his bow "to his full strength." This would explain the seriousness of the wound, once the arrow finds the literal chink in the king's armor. If one applies the moral sense, then the archer draws his bow "in innocence"—that is, he is simply targeting an anonymous enemy soldier, and does not realize that his victim is the king of Israel. Most translations prefer the second meaning (NRSV "unknowingly"; others: "at random" or "at a venture" or the like). Since neither meaning is more probable linguistically, this preference is no doubt because the second meaning is theologically richer: it permits the inference that the archer and his arrow were guided by divine providence to carry out the doom announced by Micaiah. The translator must make a choice; but for the reader of the Hebrew text, the two meanings are folded together in a delicious double entendre.

REPETITION AND VARIATION

1. The differences between Ben-hadad's first message and his second one lie, first, in what they demand of Ahab, and second, in the possessions they have in view. The first message is a claim to ownership. Since Ahab seems to be Ben-hadad's vassal (note how Ahab repeatedly calls Ben-hadad "my lord the king" in 20:4, 9), recognition of the overlord's right to claim ownership of the vassal's belongings involves nothing more than a profession of loyalty. Thus Ahab's words in 20:4 fully satisfy the demand as it is formulated in 20:3. In 20:5, by contrast, even though Ben-hadad claims that this is the same message ("I sent to you, saying . . ."), he now demands *delivery* of the goods, not just acknowledgment of his right to them. Further, his list of goods demanded is increased in one respect. Instead of "your fairest wives" he now demands "your wives."[43] At the very least, Ben-hadad has stepped across the bounds of what the ancient Near East would have thought acceptable behavior on the part of an overlord. We may speculate why he has done so and perhaps find an answer in 20:1. Ben-hadad gathered his army and marched against Samaria even before he opened negotiations with Ahab. In other words, he has decided on military action, and raising the ante of his demands until Ahab refuses will supply him with justification for attack.

In 20:7 Ahab reports to the "elders of the land" Ben-hadad's demands. The most significant modification he makes is that, instead of listing silver and gold first and wives and children second, as Ben-hadad did twice, Ahab lists wives and children first and silver and gold afterward. As I read it, this is a delicate and subtle characterization of Ahab (who, remember, is much more positively portrayed in this chapter than he was, for instance, in chaps. 17–19). The modification suggests to me that concern for family is in the forefront of Ahab's mind, and the threat to his material wealth takes second place to it.

2. The original conversation has two parts: Ahab's words to Naboth, and Naboth's reply to Ahab. They are each repeated through the course of 21:1–16, but not always together. The first repetition is in 21:4. Ahab is walking home angered by Naboth's rebuff of his offer. To explain Ahab's anger, the narrator reminds us of Naboth's words. In this reading the narrator's substitution of "I will not give you" for Naboth's original "Yhwh forbid that I should give you" can only be seen as a stylistic variation. We know what Naboth actually said, and we know that the narrator is reliable; so as far as the narrator is concerned, the two phrases—his and Naboth's—are equivalent. (However, this is not the only way to read 21:4. We will reexamine the verse in a moment.)

The second repetition of the conversation is in 21:6. In reply to Jezebel's query, Ahab repeats the offer he made to Naboth and Naboth's answer. There are several deviations from the original conversation. (1) In 21:2 Ahab explained to Naboth why he wanted the vineyard; in 21:6 he leaves that explanation out. (2) In 21:2 he offered a "better" vineyard; he drops this word in 21:6. (3) In 21:2 Ahab's first offer is of a vineyard for the vineyard, with money as an alternative; in 21:6 he reverses the order of what he offered. (4) In 21:3 Naboth said, "Yhwh forbid that I should give you"; in 21:6 this becomes "I will not give you" (as it had already in 21:4). (5) In 21:3 Naboth called the vineyard his "ancestral inheritance"; in 21:6 Ahab reports Naboth's words as "my vineyard."

Let's examine these variations in order. (1) Leaving out his reasons for wanting the vineyard could be simple abbreviation to avoid too much repetition. On the other hand, Ahab is talking to Jezebel, who—being of royal blood and a non-Israelite (16:31)—may have had very different ideas about how a king should exercise his power over his subjects (note her words in 21:7!). If Ahab thinks that she would scorn him for treating the landowner respectfully, he may choose to leave out the fact that he attempted to reason with Naboth. (2) For the same reason, Ahab may have neglected to mention to Jezebel that the vineyard he offered Naboth was a "better" one. A woman of the character Jezebel is about to demonstrate in this chapter is unlikely to have considered Ahab's fairness and generosity admirable. (3) Ahab offers land as the most likely form of compensation to appeal to Naboth; money is a conceivable alternative, but it is less likely to appeal to a landowner. When reporting the conversation to Jezebel, however, Ahab puts money first. This argument is likely to sound more persuasive to a wealthy princess/queen, for whom owning and working a vineyard would be outside her experience. (4) If the NRSV's rendering of 21:4 is correct, then this variation is of no consequence. The narrator has already shown that he considers the two phrases equivalent. On the other hand, if the NRSV's rendering of 21:4 is wrong, then this variation both there and here must be reconsidered. (See below.) (5) The term "ancestral inheritance" is a technical one in Israelite culture and law. It did not mean simply whatever one inherited from one's ancestors. It meant that specific plot of land that was considered Yhwh's gift to a particular family. There were laws governing the disposal of such property. For instance, a person could not sell his "ancestral inheritance" unless he was in desperate financial straits, and even then he could only sell the land temporarily. At the next jubilee year it reverted automatically to his family's possession. (See Lev. 25:8–10, 25–28.[44]) So Naboth is not *refusing* to sell the vineyard; he is claiming that he *cannot* sell it. Ahab's avoidance of the legal term could mean either of two things. It might suggest that Ahab cared nothing at all for the technicalities of Israelite law. Or it might suggest that Ahab opined that *Jezebel* neither understood nor cared for such technicalities.[45]

The last repetition of the conversation is in 21:15; it is considerably abbreviated and telescopes both parts of the original dialogue into a single phrase. Jezebel tells Ahab to take possession of the vineyard of Naboth, "which he refused to give you for money." Besides the abbreviation, two points are worth noting. Naboth's protest that he *could* not sell his ancestral inheritance (21:3) had become in Ahab's report to Jezebel a simple refusal to sell a vineyard (21:6); this is how Jezebel remembers it. Second, Ahab's original offer of another, better vineyard or perhaps of money (21:2) had become in his report to Jezebel an offer of money or perhaps another vineyard (21:6), on the king's assumption that money would impress Jezebel more than land. Apparently Ahab was right on this count, since Jezebel remembers the offer of money but ignores the alternative offer completely.

Now we must tackle the problem of 21:4. Despite the NRSV's rendering, the Hebrew text as we have it cannot mean "for he [i.e., Naboth] had said." Standard Hebrew syntax demands, "Ahab went home resentful and sullen because of what Naboth the Jezreelite had said to him; and he said, I will not give you. . . ." In that syntax, "he" can only be Ahab, despite the fact that the words that "he" said echo Naboth's speech.[46] It seems to me that the picture the narrator is painting for us is of Ahab returning home angry, *replaying Naboth's words* as he goes. So "I will not give you my ancestral inheritance" is Ahab's memory of the conversation. Since he is talking to himself, he is not shading or skewing his memory to impress or persuade a listener. It is Ahab, then, and not the narrator, who considers "I will not give you" equivalent to "Yhwh forbid that I should give you." Ahab is apparently unmoved by Naboth's sense of religious obligations to Yhwh. All Ahab hears is a refusal. On the other hand, Ahab *does* remember the legal obstacle—that the vineyard is Naboth's "ancestral inheritance." When he leaves that detail out of his report to Jezebel, then, it is not because Ahab is dismissive of its import (one of the options we considered above). Rather we presume he does so intentionally, deeming her uninterested in Israelite legal technicalities.[47]

At each step of the way, then, the variations in the repetition of the original conversation contribute to direct or indirect characterization of Ahab and Jezebel. We learn not only about qualities of each character, but we also learn something of what Ahab thinks of Jezebel (and, if we broaden our view to include 21:5 and 21:7, what Jezebel thinks of Ahab).

3. In general, the point-by-point correspondence between Jezebel's letter and the elders' compliance underscores the smoothness with which her plot works and the care with which the elders carry out her orders. Several of the variations nuance this basic impression. Where the narrator identifies the addressees of Jezebel's letter as "the elders and the nobles who were living in his city *with Naboth*"[48] (21:8), in describing their compliance he calls them "*the men of his city*, the elders and the nobles, who were living in his city" (21:11). The addition of "men of his city" emphasizes the relationship between Naboth and the elders and nobles who are going to betray him: they are not just royal flunkies, they are his fellow citizens. The elimination of the phrase "with Naboth" may simply be an abbreviation, but it may also be part of a strategy of *depersonalization* that the narrator uses to signal how Naboth is turned into an object to be disposed of rather than a person. The next variation is the insertion of a wordy statement, itself repetitive, that the elders and nobles did as they were ordered (21:11). Since the narrator is going to recount their compliance in detail, this statement is entirely unnecessary. It further points up the exactitude of their obedience ("as she sent," "just as it was written"[49]). In light of the earlier emphasis on the elders and nobles as Naboth's fellow citizens, their willingness to obey the queen so meticulously appears even more heinous.

The queen's directives about proclaiming a fast and seating Naboth in the assembly are carried out verbatim. The seating of the two "scoundrels," however, diverges. Instead of the elders *seating* them, as Jezebel had instructed, they "*enter and sit*" across from Naboth. It is probably a reasonable precaution on the part of the elders to distance themselves from the "scoundrels" in this way; any unusual attention they pay to them might give away the collusion between them.

The next sentence diverges considerably. Where Jezebel directed, "let them testify, saying," the narrator gives much fuller detail: "*the scoundrels* testified *against Naboth across from the people*, saying. . . ." Repeating the pejorative term "scoundrels"[50] emphasizes the narrator's low opinion of them. Spelling out details of the scene seems to do little except increase the vividness of the narrative for the hearer or reader. With some hesitation, however, I offer one possibility for subtler meaning. The two scoundrels sat "across from" (*neged*, 21:13; NRSV "opposite") Naboth; when they testify, they do so against Naboth and "across from" (*neged*, 21:14; NRSV "in the presence of") the people. This echo implicitly associates Naboth with the people on one side, and the scoundrels on the other. In this way, the scoundrels' attack is shown to reflect a deeper issue in the text, namely, that their testimony not only is a perjury against an individual landowner, but also represents a royal assault on both law ("ancestral inheritance") and religion ("Yhwh forbid," 21:3)—and therefore on the fundamental values upon which the identity of Israel as a people is founded.

The scoundrels' testimony too differs slightly from what Jezebel prescribed. She would have had them address it directly to Naboth ("*you* cursed . . ."); but they address the assembly and level their accusation *about* him ("*Naboth* cursed . . ."). Naboth is no longer a *subject*, in control of his own defense and destiny, but an *object* of others' perjury and condemnation.

Finally, the death sentence Jezebel required is carried out, with two additional phrases added: "They took him out, *outside the city,* and stoned him *with rocks,* and he died" (21:13b). "Outside the city" simply assures the reader that the execution was carried out according to the law, which required that such executions take place outside the city gates (see Deut. 17:5). The specification that they stoned Naboth "with rocks" sounds utterly redundant in English (which is no doubt why the NRSV leaves the words out); in Hebrew the verb "to stone" is used frequently both with (as here) and without (as in 21:10) the phrase. There is no discernible difference in meaning or emphasis. Why the narrator would choose to add the phrase here is unclear to me.

The uncommon repeated word is "scoundrels." It is certainly not surprising to hear the narrator refer to the pair of conspirators with such a negative term. But it is puzzling to see the queen put such an insult in her letter. First, these people are her hirelings. Good-for-nothing though they may be, Jezebel would be unlikely to put into writing her low opinion of those she relies on to do her dirty work. What could be going on here? First, consider the effect the word has in her letter. We see that Jezebel is fully aware of the ignominy of her plot and that she realizes she needs scoundrels to carry it out. We also see that she is either imprudent enough or arrogant enough to call them scoundrels in writing. Second, consider that we learn the wording of Jezebel's letter *only because the narrator reports it to us,* and the narrator demonstrates in 21:13 that "scoundrels" is *his* word for them! Could it be that the narrator has "invaded" Jezebel's letter, so to speak, and slipped his own opinion into it—and thereby condemned not only the scoundrels but Jezebel as well through her own words? If so, then the irony is delicious because, by putting one true word into Jezebel's mouth, the narrator has condemned her for putting false words into Naboth's!

VOICE(S) OF THE NARRATOR

1. It is truly tempting to attribute a passage like this to the implied author rather than to a narrator, particularly in view of the mention of another written source document; they are like erudite reference footnotes in a modern textbook. In my opinion, however, this is simply another example of the misleading transparency of the narrator. It is not difficult to conceive of the (oral) narrator including such a statement in the tale. When we tell stories, we often cite our sources ("I heard from so-and-so that . . ." or "I read in the newspaper that . . ."). Moreover, the decision whether to attribute this passage to the narrator or to the author has a very important implication. If we attribute it to the author, we understand the source document to have existed in our primary world, and the author to have consulted it in preparing the text.[51] If we attribute it to the narrator, we understand the source documents to have existed in the secondary world as literary creations of the author (just as the characters Jezebel and the anonymous prophet and the lion of 1 Kgs. 20:36 exist in the secondary world as literary

creations); and we leave open the question of whether they existed in our primary world (as Jezebel certainly did) or not (as the lion—a stereotypical story animal—may not have).[52]

Personally, I find little overt expression of opinion in this passage, though the reference to "the ivory house that he built and the cities that he built" may imply narratorial disapproval.[53] The rest of 22:39–40 is simple factual data.

For me, the main effect of this passage is *distance* from the action of the story. The regnal formulas that conclude each reign are retrospective summaries. They invite me to step back from the flow of the plot and consider the entirety of the king's reign—its dynamics, its events, its results. Personally, I cannot undertake that reflective consideration without coming to some sort of evaluation of the king, perhaps moral, perhaps political. The reflective tone urges me to judgment, but in 22:39–40 I do not feel that I am being urged to one judgment rather than another. Of course, my negative or positive evaluation will ultimately emerge not just from this concluding regnal formula but from the whole story of the king's reign; and on *that* level the stories of Ahab have done their best to shape my opinion.[54] The neutrality of the concluding formula may simply reflect the narrator's confidence that he has made his case convincingly.

2. It seems to me that there is some tension between the extraordinarily severe condemnation of Ahab in 21:25a and 26 and the blaming of Jezebel in 21:25b. If I read 21:25a and 26 by themselves, Ahab is the villain of villains; there was "no one like him" in his evil, he acted "most abominably." Phrases like this are absolute. Yet 21:25b seems to shift responsibility for Ahab's wrongdoing onto his wife Jezebel, who "urged him on." It is not impossible, I suppose, for a single person to hold both views—surely, in the context of the crime in 21:1–16, there is enough blame to go around!—but it strikes me as more useful to read these verses as expressing *two* narrators' opinions, one of whom considered Ahab the prime culprit, the other Jezebel.

Another, rather less serious tension can be seen in the crime for which Ahab is blamed in 21:25–26. In 21:25a he is simply blamed for "selling himself to do evil"—an idiom of very general meaning. In 21:26 he is blamed for "going after idols." The two statements are certainly compatible, as generalization about and specification of Ahab's sin; but I would hardly call the narrative flow "smooth."

In the larger context of the whole chapter, things are a bit more problematic. Take the condemnation of Jezebel in 21:25b. According to that remark, Jezebel's guilt was that she "urged Ahab on." Yet in the story of 21:1–16, where Jezebel is clearly guilty of arranging the judicial murder of Naboth, she did not urge Ahab on to anything. If any "urging" took place, it was Ahab's pique that urged Jezebel to action (21:5–7). Certainly both the story and the frame break portray Jezebel in a very negative light; but the two portrayals are hardly compatible. In one, Jezebel is the perpetrator of the evil action; in the other, she is condemned as a clandestine manipulator.

Perhaps more unsettling, at least to me, is that the crime against Naboth, which is the focus of 21:1–16, has no mention in 21:25–26. The specific crime for which Ahab is condemned in 21:25–26 is idolatry, not the murder of Naboth and illicit seizure of his vineyard. In fact, Yhwh's mention of the crime against Naboth in 21:19 is the last time it is an issue. Elijah does not mention it to Ahab when he reports Yhwh's words, Ahab does not mention it before or after Elijah delivers his oracle, the narrator does not mention it as explanation for Ahab's acts of mourning (21:27), and Yhwh does not mention it again in his mitigation of Ahab's punishment. One cannot help but conjecture that, even though both 21:1–16 and 21:17–29 portray Ahab very negatively, they reflect a variety of narratorial opinions about just what constituted Ahab's evil.

3. The main argument for reading 21:23–24 as a continuation of Elijah's words is silence. The narrator gives no indication at all that Elijah has stopped speaking; this, then, naturally inclines the reader to read the words as Elijah's. Secondary arguments grow out of the continuity of attitude between 21:21–22 and 21:24. Both verses condemn Ahab and his entire line in absolute terms.[55] Moreover, if you compare the oracle Yhwh told Elijah to deliver (21:19) with what Elijah ultimately says (21:21–22), it is clear that Elijah's condemnation of Ahab's "every male, bond or free," is far more sweeping than Yhwh's condemnation of Ahab alone.[56] That same extreme broadening of the scope of condemnation is evident in 21:24 ("*Anyone* belonging to Ahab . . .").

On the other hand, in 21:20–21 Elijah regularly refers to Ahab as "you" rather than by name.[57] The use of Ahab's name links 21:24 a bit more closely to the narrator's usage in 21:25 than to Elijah's practice in 21:20–22. Further, if we were to read the entirety of 21:20–24 as Elijah's words, we would not expect the condemnation of Jezebel (21:23) to interrupt that of Ahab; the passage would flow much more smoothly if 21:23 and 21:24 were in the reverse order. By interrupting that flow, 21:23 sets 21:23–24 apart as a more or less self-contained unit.[58] Finally, the opening words of 21:23 ("Also concerning Jezebel Yhwh said . . .") sound much more like the introduction to a frame break than like words that Elijah would have said to Ahab. (Notice, for instance, that Elijah makes no claim that his words in 21:20–22 come from Yhwh.[59] Only in 21:23 is there any claim of the oracle's divine origin.)

The uncertainty whether 21:23–24 should be attributed to Elijah or to the narrator confronts the reader with a serious ambiguity. If the words are Elijah's, then we must wonder whether he extends the condemnation to Ahab's entire household and lineage on his own authority or on Yhwh's.[60] If the words belong to one (or more) narrator(s), then they do in fact express divine displeasure (assuming narratorial reliability). But in that case the odd placement of 21:23 and the unexpected introduction of a condemnation against Jezebel reflect the same sort of tension we saw in 21:25: one narrator who imputes all the guilt to Ahab, another who attempts to shift blame onto Jezebel.

Perhaps the smoothest reading (and one that would converge with the historical-critical observation mentioned above in n. 55) would be to take 21:24 as Elijah's words, but 21:23 as a narratorial frame break expressing the same anti-Jezebel sentiment we see in the last words of 21:25. In this case, the legitimacy of Elijah's extending the divine condemnation to Ahab's entire line remains dubious, but the anti-Jezebel sentiment is identified as part of a *narrator's* agenda rather than Elijah's. In the last analysis, the syntactic ambiguities of the passage open up several different, ultimately incompatible understandings for the narratee and the implied reader. This inevitably enlists the reader in choosing among the possibilities and thus involves the reader deeply in the process of making real the meaning of the story.

STRUCTURE AND SYMMETRY

1. The servants speak two clauses to Ahab, and Ahab responds with two clauses. One repetition and a pair of comparable words suggest the pattern.[61]

    a. "*Your servant* Ben-hadad says,
        b. 'Please let me *live*.'"
        b'. "Is he still *alive*?
    a'. He is *my brother*."

The four-part reverse symmetry (a chiasm in the strictest sense) suggests *contrast* as the interpretive dynamic. Ben-hadad's servants expect Ahab to demand their master's submission ("your servant"), if not his execution ("let me live"); but Ahab seems (pleasantly?) surprised that his defeated enemy has survived and unexpectedly offers him a treaty of equals ("my brother"). This arrangement of the clauses also saves the surprise for the end (until we reach "my brother," we have no idea what Ahab intends), and positions the startling word "brother" to act as a bridge to the servants' next words, which immediately seize on Ahab's concession: "Yes, Ben-hadad is your brother" (20:33).

As the story goes on (particularly in 20:35–43), one begins to suspect that the dynamic of contrast has a second level of meaning as well. It is not only a contrast between what Ben-hadad expected and what Ahab did, but also a contrast between what Yhwh wanted Ahab to do (at least in the view of the prophet of 20:35–43) and what Ahab did.

2. The asymmetry of the line will draw any reader's attention, and therefore I surmise that the author wants me to find some particular significance in it. I suspect, though, that my personal response to it grows in large part, if not entirely, out of my experiences as a late-twentieth- and early-twenty-first-century American citizen whose country has been involved in one war or another for most of my life. I am struck by the sudden *anonymity* of the verse. It is no longer a question of Israelites versus Arameans, which forms the basis of the alternating structure to this point. It is a matter of "men" killing one another. On one very profound level, war is not a matter of *sides*. At its core it is mutual murder; both sides lose.

3. The most striking link is the almost verbatim repetition of the words of Jezebel's letter (21:9b–10) in the account of the elders' compliance with her

instructions (21:11–13). Immediately surrounding this are two scenes set in Ahab's chambers, with Ahab and Jezebel present in both (21:4b–7, 15). Finally, the outermost scenes take place in Naboth's vineyard. In the first (21:1–4a),[62] Ahab and Naboth are both present; in the last (21:16), Ahab is alone. (But notice that Naboth is named—twice—in that single verse, even though he is already dead!) The pattern, then, is a reverse symmetry.[63]

    a. Ahab tries to buy Naboth's vineyard, and is refused (21:1–4a)
       b. Ahab and Jezebel in Ahab's chambers (21:4b–7)
          c. Jezebel's letter outlines a plot (21:8–10)
          c'. Jezebel's plot is carried out (21:11–14)
       b'. Ahab and Jezebel in Ahab's chambers (21:15)
    a'. Ahab takes possession of Naboth's vineyard (21:16)

The reverse symmetry points to contrast, but this is obvious even without appeal to the pattern. At the beginning Naboth has the vineyard and refuses it to Ahab. At the end, Naboth is dead and Ahab gets the vineyard. But there are equally strong dynamics of progression: promise made (subunit *b*), promise kept (subunit *b'*); conspiracy plotted (subunit *c*), conspiracy carried out (subunit *c'*). The main effect of the reverse symmetry is to focus our attention on the central subunits and the conspiracy that brings about the reversal. This focus, of course, highlights Jezebel's culpability in the plot; but, equally, it highlights the culpability of the elders of Jezreel. Notice how, even though Jezebel dominates subunit *c*, the wordiness of the text also emphasizes the elders (21:8: "the elders and the nobles who lived with Naboth in his city"); and, conversely, even though the elders dominate subunit *c'*, similar wordiness there also emphasizes Jezebel (21:11: "did as Jezebel had sent word to them; just as it was written in the letters that she had sent to them"). Further, focus on these two central subunits points up that Jezebel's plot compromises both the religious and the social structures of Israel. She calls for a sacrilegious religious assembly; she misuses royal authority; she suborns elders to perjury and murder. In this way the story's meaning transcends its explicit plot and becomes more than a story of a callous act of injustice. It portrays a royal attack on the fundamental social and religious structures that make Israel the nation it is.

Notes

Introduction

1. Translated by William Weaver.
2. There are exceptions to all these generalizations, of course. Some early-twentieth-century biblical scholars had both interest and training in literary appreciation and analysis and applied their skills to the biblical text; conversely some literary scholars undertook analyses of biblical stories in translation or (much more rarely) in the original languages. But such cases were the exceptions rather than the rule.
3. It is perhaps needful to point out that the term "story" simply categorizes a work as a narrative with a plot in which characters are involved in events that take place in settings. It implies nothing about the historical accuracy or inaccuracy of the tale. An entirely reliable historical biography is just as much a "story" in this sense as a fantasy novel. Literary analysis of biblical narratives or stories, strictly speaking, prescinds from questions of history in favor of understanding the *narrative dynamics* of the text. Arguably, such an analysis ought to *precede* attempts to evaluate a story's historical reliability and theological import though, in practice, it has not often done so in conventional biblical scholarship.
4. The term "criticism," of course, is not negative. Although in common usage the word often means "saying something negative about something," its broader sense is neutral: "making judgments on the basis of evidence." This is its meaning when we speak of film criticism, literary criticism, biblical criticism, and the like.

Chapter 1

1. This is what distinguishes post-Enlightenment, critical, biblical scholarship from the precritical interpretation that preceded it. What is usually called "precritical" (that is, pre-Enlightenment) interpretation took as its primary focus what it saw as the divine author's intended meaning. Interpretation of the Bible thus amounted largely to an exposition of the interpreter's faith. Since faith premises are presuppositions and not subject to scientific verification and falsification, this approach was unacceptable to the rational (and often rationalist) canons of Enlightenment thought, which demanded that biblical interpretation, like any intellectual endeavor, be an exercise in critical reasoning based on objectively demonstrable evidence. In turn, most Christian churches mistrusted and opposed critical biblical scholarship, at least at first. By the mid-twentieth century, however, historical criticism had become the norm in almost all mainstream Christian churches.
2. Purely text-oriented methods understand "meaning" as inherent in the words of the text, and the act of reading as analogous to digging up this buried treasure (sometimes called "decoding" the text). However, some text-oriented

methods of interpretation, like reader-response criticism, allow that a reader's subjectivity inevitably contributes to the "meaning" that is realized when a reader encounters a text. For such methods, "meaning" is situated on our earlier diagram somewhat to the "reader" side of "text," reflecting its character as a product of the collaboration of reader and text.

3. This term is a source of potential confusion for the nonspecialist in biblical studies. In the days when historical criticism was the only game in town, historical critics used "literary criticism" to refer to the method that identified and extracted written source documents from the final form of the text. There were cogent reasons for this usage, but it must be admitted that it was idiosyncratic. Outside biblical studies, "literary criticism" was a synthetic discipline that aimed at the interpretation of whole texts, not a primarily analytic one that dismantled existing texts to retrieve earlier, lost documents. Nowadays the terminology has regularized itself; and biblical scholars, by and large, use "literary criticism" for methods analogous to those used by interpreters of literature and "source criticism" for the method that reconstructs written source documents. Older writings in the field, however—and occasionally more recent writing, too—preserve the idiosyncratic usage.

4. It is important to acknowledge the debt biblical studies owes to literary specialists whose interests extended to biblical literature even in the days before biblical scholars began to dabble in literary methods. One of the seminal works in this regard is Eric Auerbach's *Mimesis: The Representation of Reality in Western Literature*, trans. Willard R. Trask (Princeton: Princeton University Press, 1953), whose justly famous treatment of the story of Abraham and Isaac points up how, by contrast with most Western literary traditions, ancient Hebrew literature is "fraught with background."

5. And, in the last analysis, this would not resolve the question either. The commentary would simply be another text, whose "meanings" would be similarly diverse. This is the foundational paradox that is exploited and even celebrated by the reading method known as "deconstruction."

6. Terence J. Keegan, *Interpreting the Bible: A Popular Introduction to Biblical Hermeneutics* (New York: Paulist Press, 1985). The diagram is found on p. 94 and discussed over the several pages following. My presentation owes much to Keegan's lucid explanations.

7. This terminology is not universal, but it has noble precedent. In a lecture he delivered at St. Andrew's University in Scotland in 1938, J. R. R. Tolkien disagreed with those who describe the attitude required of a reader as a "suspension of disbelief" (in other words, as a willingness to treat an "unreal" world as if it were "real"). Rather, opined Tolkien, one should approach the world of the story as the object of an act of "secondary belief" (that is, as a "real" world, though distinct from the world where we live and breathe and have our being, but one that requires an effort of commitment to believe in). See "Tree and Leaf," in *The Tolkien Reader* (New York: Ballantine, 1966), 37 (paginated separately).

8. In *Aspects of the Novel* (New York: Harcourt, Brace, 1927), 130, the literary critic and novelist E. M. Forster put it this way: "a story [is] a narrative of events arranged in their time sequence. A plot is also a narrative of events, the emphasis falling on causality."

9. Although literary critics do not all employ the categories "implied author" and "implied reader," and even those who do often understand them in slightly different fashion, the terms supply the narrative critic with very useful analytical tools. The discussion here lays the foundation for how I will make use of them in subsequent chapters.

10. The concept of "implied author" has at least two distinct advantages. For a (real) author, it is a form of immortality: something of the author becomes immortal in the enduring existence of the text. For the (real) reader, it offers a way of speaking about "author's intention" without making unverifiable claims about (real) authors. As Richard S. Briggs has said, "Wherever there is an authorial intention, the implied author will usually be found to have been the one who was busy intending it" ("The Implied Author and the Creation of the World," *Expository Times* 113, no. 8 [2002]: 264).
11. The question of language raises an interesting peripheral issue. Most readers of this book will be using one or another translation of the Hebrew text of 1 Kings. That is, they will be reading a variety of different English texts, all called "1 Kings," but each of which reflects a different translator's reading of a single Hebrew text, *mĕlākîm a'*. In many cases, the translation differences will affect our interpretations minimally and can, for all practical purposes, be ignored. Often, though, one or another important aspect of the text will be overlooked in some (or even most) translations. In those cases, I will supply translations of my own that aim to preserve in English the particular feature of the Hebrew text under consideration. I urge anyone who wishes to pursue aspects of this problem in greater detail to compare a diversity of English translations; I would particularly recommend the New Revised Standard Version (NRSV), the New American Bible (NAB), the New International Version (NIV), and the New Jewish Publication Society Tanakh (NJPS). (Of course, you could always learn Hebrew!)
12. A note to teachers: If this book is used with a sufficient number of students, they can be assigned to a "Jeroboam" group, an "Elijah" group, and an "Ahab" group. Each group should concentrate on its own story, of course, but should also familiarize itself with the others' target stories and observe (and perhaps comment on) the discussions about their readings. This will afford all students the opportunity to appreciate the wide range of reader responses, as well as come to a fuller knowledge of 1 Kings as a whole.

Chapter 2

1. Literary criticism often and rightly discerns several stages in the destabilization. One common analysis is "rising action, climax, falling action, denouement"; a slightly simpler one might be "complication followed by resolution." Such analyses are more detailed than we need to undertake at this point. They also tend to be overkill for many narratives of the Hebrew Bible, whose compass is often much shorter than one biblical chapter.
2. The point of (relative) stability in which an arc of tension ends need not be significantly different from that in which it began. The dynamic of tension is still at work when the destabilization fails to create a fundamentally new situation. Whether the hero rescues the damsel or tries and fails, there is tension in the attempt, and the action arrives at a situation of relative stability. Compare the two biblical examples immediately below.
3. A warning: Do not be overly influenced by chapter and verse numbers, or by the headings and paragraphing inserted into your translations. Chapter and verse numbers in modern Bibles were not part of the original text and do not always correspond to the only—or even to the best—division of a story's units and subunits. Chapter numbers were first introduced into biblical manuscripts around the thirteenth century; verse numbers did not appear until the sixteenth. In other words, chapter numbers derive from a late medieval *reading* of the text, not from the author's *writing* of it. For this reason, it is sometimes useful

to read a translation like *The Jerusalem Bible* that prints these numbers in the margin rather than within the text: it restores some of the visual continuity of the original. Headings and paragraph divisions inserted into the translation are even more recent; they are the work of the modern translator. Comparison of different translations will make clear that such markers reflect the individual translator's reading of the text. There is nothing in the Hebrew text that corresponds to them.

4. The courtiers' suggestion is not without parallel in ancient Mediterranean medical practice. Much later, a similar therapy is found in Galen, the famous second-century CE Greek physician.
5. Some translations, such as the NRSV, make this explicit by adding the word "sexually" or the like. The NAB puts it that David "did not have relations with her." The Hebrew is simply that he "did not know her." Semantically, simple dementia is a linguistic possibility; but in the narrative context it is not the most likely reading.
6. As does English, Hebrew uses the word "to be hot" of temperature, of anger, and of sexual drive.
7. Note that some translations (notably the NAB) transfer the last words of 2:46 to 3:1. In the Hebrew text, the words "and he went out, and he struck him down, and he died" end the *first half* of 2:46.
8. The first command amounts to house arrest. The second command severs him from his home and family, which were located in Bahurim on the Mount of Olives, just across the Kidron Valley from Jerusalem.
9. The implied reader is likely to consider this a real, ironic possibility, since "Achish, son of Maacah, king of Gath," sounds suspiciously similar to "Achish, son of Maoch, king of Gath," with whom David, Solomon's father, took refuge when he was fleeing from Saul, Shimei's tribal leader (1 Sam. 27:1–4).
10. There is, of course, a great deal more to be said about this story. For instance, *why* does the narrator give us this information in the middle of the story? Or, to put it in other terms, why does the narrator choose to change our tensive question at this point? We look at the story in more detail in chap. 5 on "Point of View" and chap. 7 on "Gaps and Ambiguities."
11. The following example is intended to illustrate the thematic complexity Biblical Hebrew narrative can reach. You are unlikely to find anything so tightly interwoven in the stories you are going to explore later in this chapter.
12. In the Hebrew Bible, heroic figures often deliver "valedictory" speeches just before they die. See, for instance, Gen. 49 (Jacob), Deut. 32–33 (Moses), 1 Sam. 12:1–25 (Samuel, though he does not get around to dying until 1 Sam. 25:1). David gets two "last words," one speech at the end of 2 Samuel (23:17) and here. So it would not surprise the "implied reader" to find a final Davidic utterance here, and may well occasion surprise if it were lacking.
13. The question of whether Solomon will carry out David's dying wishes is only partially answered, however. David had also advised Solomon to conform to the requirement of God's laws (1 Kgs. 2:2–4) and to reward the sons of Barzillai (2:7). Solomon's obedience to Yhwh is a major thematic thread that will run through the entire Solomon story. We never hear whether Solomon obeyed David's wishes to reward the sons of Barzillai.
14. Note that some translations mask the repetition and even assign the words of 2:46b to 3:1 (notably the NAB; see n. 7 above). The Hebrew, however, reads at 2:12b: "and his royal dominion was established firmly," and at 2:46b: "and the royalty was established in Solomon's hand."
15. We have an anomaly in 2:35. The information is a sort of epilogue (what happened *after* the tension was resolved), but it belongs not only to the con-

tiguous story of Joab (2:28–34) but equally to the separate story of Abiathar (2:26–27).

16. Note that a scene consisting only of a *monologue* (e.g., 2:2–9) has little if any self-contained tension, since no action happens in the scene. It may indeed supply starting points for dynamics that go beyond it (as David's words point forward to the executions of Joab and Shimei later in 1 Kgs. 2), but as a self-contained scene the only tension it holds is, "David speaks; what will he say?" Solomon's monologue in 2:42–45 is an exception to this claim that we will consider in chap. 10.

17. "Man of God" is a synonym for "prophet." As the chapter continues, the actions of the "man of God from Judah" and the "old prophet from Bethel" will be the focus of attention, but "man of God" and "prophet" are not to be taken as distinguishing the two professionally or morally (see, for instance, the old prophet's words in 13:18: "I am a prophet as you are"). The distinction is maintained in the text because both figures are anonymous and varying the terms for them would cause confusion.

18. Note that this gives the Greek version of 1 Kings a narrative structure considerably different from the Hebrew one. Instead of three chapters dealing with Elijah (in which Ahab plays a minor role) followed by three chapters dealing with Ahab (in which Elijah plays a minor role), the Greek presents us with *four* chapters about Elijah (equivalent to chaps. 17–19 + 21), followed by two chapters about Ahab's Aramean wars (equivalent to chaps. 20 + 22).

19. Note that I am not reckoning 22:39–40 as part of the arcs of tension that structure chap. 22. This is because they comprise a stereotyped formula that occurs at the end of the reign of almost every king, and they correspond to the equally stereotyped formula that begins each regnal account (for Ahab, see 1 Kgs. 16:29–30). Together, these two formulas mark a very high level arc of tension around the question, "What happened during the reign of King X?"

Chapter 3

1. See chap. 1, n. 7.
2. *Aspects of the Novel* (New York: Harcourt, Brace, 1927), 103–18.
3. Forster remarks that "the test of a round character is whether it is capable of surprising us in a convincing way" (ibid., 118).
4. Consider the people you know in everyday life. The larger a role the person plays in your life, the more you will perceive his or her many facets and inner complexities. The person you encounter only in a single, limited context—say, the checkout clerk at the supermarket—will always seem less "rounded" to you.
5. We examine the significance of Bathsheba's modifications of Nathan's scripted speech in chap. 8 on "Repetition and Variation."
6. The echo is a bit stronger in the NRSV than in Hebrew, since what the NRSV translates "very beautiful" in both places involves two synonyms in the Hebrew text. Literally, 2 Sam. 11:2 says that Bathsheba was "very good-looking"; 1 Kgs. 1:4 says that Abishag was "very beautiful."
7. The narrator actually gives us *Bathsheba's* point of view in 1:15. We discuss this point later, in chap. 5 on "Point of View."
8. Abiathar can trace his ancestry back to Eli of Shiloh. See 1 Sam. 2:22–36, especially v. 33; 14:3; and 22:20.
9. In the New Testament, Jesus' "disciples" often function as a group character, and sometimes Peter acts as their spokesman.

10. The identification of an "other woman" in each part, of course, does not mean that they are the same person, and therefore that "first woman" is the "woman whose child was living." "Other woman" simply contrasts with the preceding description. In the second part, it is equivalent to "woman whose child was dead." Nor does the appearance of "first woman" in 3:27 (NRSV) establish an identification with "first woman" earlier in the text, because *these words are not in the Hebrew of 3:27*. The Hebrew text simply says "her"; translators, plagued by the ambiguity of the sentence (which we will consider in chap. 7), regularly attempt to clarify the issue for readers.

11. The Hebrew of 1 Kgs. 3:1 reads literally, "Solomon became Pharaoh's son-in-law." The relationship is an alliance between two monarchs, more than a marriage between a man and a woman.

12. The verse numbering here is quite different in the standard Hebrew text from that found in most English translations. This is because the Hebrew text begins numbering chap. 5 immediately after 4:20.

13. We will look more closely at this use of repetition in chap. 8, on "Repetition and Variation."

14. A warning to readers. There is an important textual issue that you need to be aware of in this passage. Some ancient manuscripts and versions lack 12:2–3a and the mention of Jeroboam in 12:12. In this reading, Jeroboam does not come to Shechem until 12:20. Some English translations, including the NAB, accept this reading. (The NAB also transfers 12:2 to follow 12:19.) Other English versions, such as the NRSV, follow the standard Hebrew text and retain 12:2–3a in place; Jeroboam thus returns from Egypt before the meeting at Shechem between Rehoboam and the elders of Israel and is present at that meeting. My questions above and my discussion of them in appendix 1 assume the standard Hebrew text, with Jeroboam present at Shechem. For this exercise, you will find it helpful to use a translation that follows the standard Hebrew text as the NRSV does. The textual reading underlying your particular English translation will usually be detectable if you look closely at the verse *numbers*, which will correspond to those of the standard Hebrew text. If the verse numbers are in sequence and include 12:2–3, then the translation follows the standard Hebrew. If the verse numbers are out of sequence or lack 12:2–3, the translation represents the tradition of variant manuscripts, which the translator deemed to contain the more original version.

15. An interesting paradox here is worth mentioning. Several characters are *named* in this passage without actually *appearing* (Hazael, Jehu, and Elisha in 19:15–16 for instance). So, while it is true that these characters are not present in the scene, they are present to the reader's consciousness. For the sake of this question, however, I am interested only in characters that actually *appear* in the passage.

16. Actually, there is one example, which I discuss in appendix 2. In 17:1 Elijah himself is presented with virtually *no* background information about him at all, and his prophetic credentials emerge only gradually in the course of the chapter. See p. 161.

17. The minor prophet Obadiah is someone entirely different.

Chapter 4

1. Actually there is considerable ambiguity here. The Hebrew word *yārā'* can be translated "to be in awe of" (as the NRSV renders it here), but more commonly it means "to fear." Whichever translation we prefer, the narrator is *telling* us something about the people.

2. The Hebrew text says literally that "there was no more *rûaḥ* in her." Since *rûaḥ* can mean either "breath" or "spirit," it is a translator's choice to understand the queen's reaction as depression in view of Solomon's magnificence ("there was no more spirit in her," NRSV) or as amazement at it ("she was left breathless," NJPS).

3. Not all biblical interpreters would agree with this assertion. For them, the biblical authors would never depict Yhwh in ways that were at odds with their faith or that of their audience. I agree that if a biblical author does so it is a shocking narrative tactic, and one must surmise that the author has a particularly radical reason for indulging in it. I disagree, however, that it never happens, and a fortiori that it *could* never happen. One of the advantages of including the implied reader in the structure of a text is that it allows us to cope with situations like this. The implied author can create a narrative world within which God's character is different from that of the God the implied author and implied reader worship. In the narrative world, the narrator and narratee acknowledge that God just as the characters do. But in the primary world, the implied reader, perceiving a disparity between the God he worships and the God of the narrative world, is thereby maneuvered into serious (and at times unsettling) theological reflection.

4. This is not always easily discerned in the text because, although in Hebrew there is a phrase that explicitly denotes internal thought ("he said in his heart"), Biblical Hebrew idiom often abbreviates the phrase to a simple "he said" (Adonijah's words in 1 Kgs. 1:5, for instance, are almost certainly not spoken aloud). In such a case, the reader must infer from the circumstances whether the character is speaking to someone else or only internally.

5. There is an important caution to be raised here. It is possible for a person to speak *ironically* to himself. In this passage, for instance, it is not inconceivable that Hiram is being cynical, seeing in Solomon a naive young man whom he may be able to take advantage of. (Compare Solomon's self-appraisal as "a little child" who "does not know how to go out or come in" [3:7]; of course, Solomon himself may be speaking with false humility here too!). If Hiram is being cynical, he may be using irony to celebrate the possibilities inherent in the fact that he now has a "wise" (read "naive") treaty partner who rules a "great" (read "rich") people.

6. I use the term "Adversary" rather than the traditional "Satan" to point out that the character in Job 2 is not presented as an evil being, but as a member of the "sons of God," that is, of the divine court. He is "*the* satan" (the word means "adversary" or "accuser"), the one whose job it was to make sure nobody put one over on God. (Think of a "prosecuting attorney.") This word is the same one used in 1 Kgs. 11:14 and 23, where the NRSV renders it "adversary" (see also 5:4 [= Hebrew 5:18]).

7. Perhaps more interestingly, it *directly* shows us Bathsheba's impressive ability to use language to promote her own cause.

8. There is one other possible case of internal monologue in the Ahab story, but scholars generally overlook it. Do not bother searching for it right now, since few if any English translations preserve it. I discuss it at greater length in chap. 8 on "Repetition and Variation."

Chapter 5

1. See Adele Berlin, *Poetics and Interpretation of Biblical Narrative* (Bible and Literature 9; Sheffield: Almond, 1983); Jean Louis Ska, *"Our Fathers Have Told Us": Introduction to the Analysis of Hebrew Narratives* (Subsidia biblica 13; Rome: Pontifical Biblical Institute, 1990).

2. Some literary critics call the omniscient perspective of the narrator a "divine" perspective. In my opinion, this is a mistake; it confuses the God worshiped in the real world, who is omniscient, with the character "God" of the story world, who may not be. In Gen. 3:9–11, when God poses several questions to the human couple, I do not think we are intended to read these questions as pretense, on the assumption that "God knows everything, so of course he knows the answers." The plain sense of the text is that God does *not* know, and needs an explanation from the human beings in order to learn what has happened.
3. We will consider the effects of "distance" in more detail later in this chapter.
4. This is actually a manipulation of the *temporal* dimension of the narrative—a technique we will look at in the next chapter. It is appropriate to mention it here because of its effect on the reader's point of view.
5. Since Abishag was a member of the royal harem, Solomon would have inherited her along with all of David's other wives, and she would have been under the authority of the queen mother, Bathsheba. In that case, Adonijah's request could be tantamount to continuing to maintain a claim on the throne. (This is the reasoning Solomon uses to justify Adonijah's execution.) On the other hand, since Abishag was still a virgin (see 1:4), she was not technically a "wife" of David, and Adonijah may have desired her for entirely innocent—or at least nonpolitical—reasons.
6. The NRSV slants its translation a bit in 2:18. In Hebrew, Bathsheba does not tell Adonijah that she will speak to the king "on your behalf"; she merely says that she will speak to the king "about you."
7. James A. Montgomery, *A Critical and Exegetical Commentary on the Books of Kings*, ed. Henry Snyder Gehman (International Critical Commentary; Edinburgh: T. & T. Clark, 1951), 92.
8. Note that identification does not necessarily mean *sympathy*. It is quite possible (though a bit difficult) for a narrator to manipulate the reader into identifying with a character the reader does not like. That is a powerful way of evoking a sense of inner conflict in the reader.
9. There may be an element of omniscience in the narrator's information that these women were prostitutes. That information may or may not have been known to the king and court.
10. We might *infer* that the true mother's willingness to give up the child in order to save its life is enough evidence for Solomon, but the narrator never confirms this inference. (And, at least in my opinion, the inference is wrong. More on this in chap. 7.)
11. It might even be considered an omniscient point of view, if one takes the popular sentiment as the unspoken opinion of the populace, or as a view expressed throughout the whole country.
12. Feminist criticism, for instance, has shown that female exegetes often have a deeper insight into women characters than male exegetes find easy to achieve; and readings of the biblical text using liberation and postcolonial approaches have shown the sensitivity that contemporary readers from underprivileged classes have to powerless and often overlooked minor characters in the text.
13. For a powerful New Testament example of how the reader's perspective can shift suddenly from distant to close-up, see Luke 10:30–35. In 10:30–33 we have a broad overview. We see the victim lying on one side of the road, the priest and the Levite who have passed him by on the other, and the Samaritan who approaches him. But in 10:34a we are suddenly close enough to see the Samaritan pour oil and wine on the victim's wounds. From that point on, we lose sight of priest, Levite, and surroundings, until we step back slightly to watch the Samaritan load the victim on his animal and take him to the inn.

Then we accompany them on the journey, since we are present to hear the Samaritan's instructions to the innkeeper.

14. Gihon is the "gusher," the spring that provided most of the water for Davidic and Solomonic Jerusalem. It lies much lower down the slope of the hill (called "Mount Zion" in the Hebrew Bible, though that name has in modern times migrated to a different hill just to the west) than the defensive walls around the city. En-rogel, where Adonijah's gathering took place, is another, smaller spring nearby, less than a half-mile south of Gihon.

15. Notice that this example is translation dependent. The Hebrew verb used here can mean "to be terrified" (an emotional state) or "to tremble" (a physical reaction to the emotion of terror). Translations that speak of the people "trembling" (like the NRSV) set the reader's point of view physically close to the action; translations that speak more generally of the people's terror or alarm (like the NAB and the NIV) afford the reader a point of view that glimpses the people's inner life, but the reader is not necessarily brought *physically* close to the scene.

16. Adonijah's approach to Bathsheba is anything but smooth. He asks permission to make a request (2:14a), then explains why he is making a request (2:15), then again asks permission to make his request (2:16). Bathsheba has to encourage him twice to make his point, and after two and a half verses he still hems and haws before coming out with it (2:17).

17. If our point of view were identical to Bathsheba's, we would already know why she deviates from Nathan's script. Furthermore, we would know the truth about the oath that Nathan "reminds" Bathsheba of in 1:13 and that Bathsheba presents to David in 1:17 as his words. Nothing anywhere in 2 Samuel or 1 Kings enables us to determine decisively whether David actually swore such an oath. Presumably Bathsheba knows, but we do not share this knowledge.

18. There is another layer of narratorial sleight of hand here as well. Jonathan cannot possibly know what he tells us in 1:46–48. He arrived at En-rogel just as the sound of the trumpet was fading into echoes (1:41–42). Therefore he left Gihon before the procession back up the hill into Jerusalem began, and he could not have witnessed the events he recounts that took place in Jerusalem after Solomon arrived there. Yet, because everything he says in 1:43–45 is an absolutely accurate recital of what we have already witnessed, we do not hesitate to credit what he says in 1:46–48.

19. This is why the words can be considered an allusion to 2 Sam. 11:2, where David first lays eyes on Bathsheba: "he saw from the roof a woman bathing; the woman was very beautiful" (see chap. 3, n. 6).

20. Note how this becomes a technique for characterizing David. We infer from 1:4 that David, frail and feeble as he is, has not lost his eye for female beauty.

21. There is a translation problem in 14:5. The standard Hebrew text and the ancient Greek translation (the Septuagint) disagree about whether the last half of 14:5 is part of Yhwh's speech to Ahijah. The NRSV follows the Greek and treats it as a narrative line ("When she came, she pretended to be another woman"). The standard Hebrew text includes it as the last sentence of Yhwh's speech: "And when she comes, she will be pretending to be someone else." This is not particularly important for establishing point of view, but in terms of the plot dynamics it is significant. In the Hebrew, Ahijah knows that the woman is in disguise (14:6) because Yhwh told him so in the preceding verse. In the Greek (and in the NRSV), there is nothing to explain how Ahijah knows about her disguise.

22. There are no punctuation marks in Hebrew comparable to those in English; the exclamation points are my own interpretive insertions.

Chapter 6

1. There are, of course, exceptions to this general rule. James Joyce's *Ulysses* takes place in a single twenty-four-hour day, but it is unlikely that anyone has managed to read the whole thing in that length of time.
2. By this term I do not mean verbs in the grammatical "active voice," but verbs that describe actions. This excludes "to be" (which is frequently not expressed in Hebrew even when it is necessary in English) and verbs that describe states or conditions. In Hebrew, verbs that describe states or conditions are frequently distinguishable from verbs of action grammatically (the former are called "stative verbs"). In English, these stative verbs often require translation with "to be" ("King David *was old*") and are therefore relatively easy to spot as well.
3. That is, without verbs in Hebrew. These are usually translated with a copulative "to be" in English. See the example from Gen. 3:6 discussed here; English grammar requires the addition of "was" in several places.
4. This is not to say that the narrator may not be manipulating us very subtly in other ways. Here, for instance, by describing Shimei's obedience as lasting "many days," then specifying that he has remained in Jerusalem for a full "three years," the narrator impresses us with the length of time Shimei has endured house arrest. Thus we arrive at the story of Shimei's disobedience (2:39–41) somewhat positively disposed toward him. The story's tempo is not affected, but the characterization of Shimei is deepened by direct showing of the extent of his obedience.
5. This comparison is complicated by a translation problem. The reaction of all Israel is to *yr'* Solomon, which in Hebrew can mean to "revere" him or to "fear" him. We will examine some of the ambiguities in this scene in the next chapter.
6. Sometimes the narrator comments directly to the narratee in an "aside"; the technical term for this is "breaking frame." We consider this tactic at greater length in chap. 9, "Voice(s) of the Narrator."
7. For the ancient Israelite implied reader the experience was, no doubt, the exact opposite. Note how the descriptions in chap. 6 progress from an exterior view of the structure into the building until they reach the Holy of Holies, with its gilded cherubim (6:23–28), then move gradually back out into the courtyard (6:36) and admire the decorated walls and doors on the way. The chapter is, in effect, a guided tour of the whole temple. Since the ordinary Israelite was never permitted to enter the inner parts of the temple, much less the Holy of Holies, the opportunity to know and visualize this most sacred enclosure would be of compelling interest to the ancient Israelite implied reader.
8. See chap. 4, n. 2.
9. I have already pointed out a similar strategy using Abishag's beauty to draw parallels between Bathsheba (2 Sam. 11:2b) and her (1 Kgs. 1:4a); see above, p. 25.
10. Literary critics will sometimes distinguish between the *story* (the events of the plot in the order in which they are recounted) and the *fabula* (the events of the plot in the order in which they happened). Chronology and cause and effect shape the fabula; the narrator shapes the story.
11. Remember, it is *the reader* who decides where to begin reading and where to stop. In other words, the reader chooses the horizon, the context, within which to understand the story he or she is reading. The narrator (or implied author) may urge a larger context by flashbacks, cross-references, allusions, or the like, but ultimately the reader makes the final decision. This is significant because in

different contexts a particular story element may come to mean quite different things. Look, for instance, at Solomon's decision to exile Abiathar (2:26). In itself, this is a blatant act of political retaliation: Abiathar supported Solomon's rival Adonijah, so Solomon punishes Abiathar. However, in view of the narrator's remark in 2:27b ("thus fulfilling the word of Yhwh that he had spoken concerning the house of Eli in Shiloh"), the reader can put this act of reprisal in a larger context that reaches all the way back to 1 Sam. 3:14 and realize that Solomon's political payback is *also* a working out of the divine will in the story of Eli and his descendants.

12. For example, the summary statement about David's reign in 1 Kgs. 2:11 harks back to a fuller version in 2 Sam. 5:1–5.
13. Interestingly, we knew that David had commercial relations with Hiram (2 Sam. 5:11), but that earlier passage gave no indication of a political treaty. So the flashback in 1 Kgs. 5:1 creates a new context and thus a new potential for understanding the earlier passage.
14. The NRSV's translation "dowry" could imply that Pharaoh actually gave Gezer to Solomon as part of the marriage arrangements. But the Hebrew word *šilluḥîm* simply means that Pharaoh gave it to his daughter as a going-away gift.
15. In the next chapter we will consider how the narrator manipulates our responses by withholding information.
16. The narrator is cleverly explicit about the political dimensions of the arrangement. In 3:1a the narrator does not mention either "marriage" or the woman, but simply says, "Solomon became Pharaoh's son-in-law." Not until 3:1b does the narrator say that Solomon "took" (that is, as wife) Pharaoh's daughter.
17. Presumably this is an unrealistic schematization. Since the temple and palace complex were contiguous, efficiency would dictate that they be under construction simultaneously. As the story is told, however, the narrator's presentation is clear and straightforward. Solomon built the temple first; that took seven years (6:37–38). Then he built the administrative complex; that took thirteen years (7:1). The two projects together took twenty years (9:10).
18. So the NRSV renders it. Actually, the Hebrew verb form is probably better translated, "Solomon was also to make a house . . . for Pharaoh's daughter." In other words, 7:8b is another explicit foreshadowing.
19. Meir Sternberg uses this example to illustrate the form of prolepsis he terms "deductive paradigm." See *The Poetics of Biblical Narrative: Ideological Literature and the Drama of Reading* (Indiana Studies in Biblical Literature; Bloomington: Indiana University Press, 1987), 269.
20. This is particularly the case when the prophecy is unlikely. See 2 Kgs. 6:24–7:2 for an example.
21. I have taken this example from Jan P. Fokkelmann, *Narrative Art and Poetry in the Books of Samuel: A Full Interpretation Based on Stylistic and Structural Analyses* (4 vols.; Assen: Van Gorcum, 1981–1993), 4:42–43.

Chapter 7

1. Conversely, of course, this means that the *presence* of such descriptive information would strike the implied (Israelite) reader much more forcibly than it will a Western reader. This is why the appearance of description, particularly physical description of characters, should alert the modern reader to its significance.
2. And, of course, multiple options are possible. The missing datum may not be a simple "true" or "false" dichotomy; it may allow of several different realizations.

3. It would take us too far afield to explore what criteria readers use to choose between the options, such as coherence with one's understanding of plot and character up to that point. However, it is very useful for the individual reader to reflect on what leads her or him to make this or that choice. This is one of the ways in which great literature can reveal us to ourselves.
4. See the remarks above, pp. 66–67.
5. Since David founded the dynasty, primogeniture (succession of the eldest son) was not yet established as the operant policy. It may have been expected, but until David acted it could not be counted on.
6. Scholars have been unable to identify precisely what "almug wood" is, despite its traditional translation (in some English Bibles) as "sandalwood." The issue is complicated by conflicting information about its provenance (Ophir in 1 Kgs. 10:11 and 2 Chr. 9:10; Lebanon in 2 Chr. 2:7) and even its name ("almug wood" in 1 Kings; "algum wood" in 2 Chronicles).
7. Note that only the fleets of 1 Kgs. 10:22 seem to make a regular circuit. Solomon's fleet of 9:26–28 and Hiram's of 10:11–12 seem to have been engaged in one-time journeys.
8. John Gray's commentary is representative of this approach. In *I & II Kings: A Commentary* (2nd ed.; Old Testament Library; Philadelphia: Westminster, 1970), 99, he calls 2:2–4 a "Deuteronomistic preface to David's last charges."
9. See also Deut. 6:5 for the classic formulation of the requirements of the covenant, including the term "soul" (*nepeš*, better translated "life" or "being" here), which does not occur in the Yhwh speeches in 1 Kings.
10. The Hebrew term *lēb* or *lēbāb*, "heart," does not carry the emotional overtones it does in English. In our usage, the heart is metaphorically the organ of feeling; in Hebrew anthropology, it is the organ of *thinking*. So, when *lēb* or *lēbāb* appears in the Hebrew Bible in a metaphorical sense, the better translation is usually not "heart" but "mind."
11. Notice how David must misrepresent his own words in order to clear the way for Solomon's action. Contrast the unconditional pardon David gave Shimei in 2 Sam. 19:23 with his limited, revisionist version of it in 1 Kgs. 2:8.
12. The classic study of literary ambiguity is William Empson's *Seven Types of Ambiguity* (3rd ed.; New York: New Directions, n.d. [1st ed., 1930]). Empson's operative definition of "ambiguity" is much broader than the common acceptation of the term. Since Empson is concerned with English poetry rather than Hebrew narrative prose, his categories and his exquisitely subtle analyses are not directly applicable to our concerns here. I am interested in the dynamic that occurs for a reader when a text is susceptible of two (or more) fundamentally different, often incompatible understandings.
13. An even prior judgment is whether the Hebrew text the translator possesses is accurate, that is, whether all the changes that have occurred in the centuries-long process of hand-copying the text have been identified and corrected. Strictly speaking, however, establishing an accurate text is not the translator's responsibility but that of the text critic. A translator may act as his or her own text critic, but the proper business of *translation* does not begin until the text-critical work is finished.
14. Note the hidden assumption here that the author could not have *intentionally* written ambiguously.
15. I leave out of consideration here those translators who disambiguate the original text not by invoking some presumed "original author's intention" but by simply choosing whichever meaning best substantiates their denominational doctrine. Such a procedure is a form of apologetics; it is not respectable as translation.

16. I must confess that not all scholarly translators would agree with the principle I articulate above. This is why, even in scholarly translations, "clarifying" the text has been the norm in past generations. Nowadays, as translators increasingly come to appreciate ambiguity as a literary *device*, not merely a literary *flaw*, there seems to be a growing awareness of the value of preserving such devices in translation.
17. To be completely accurate, we must say "probably" here, since our knowledge of the precise vowel sounds of ancient Hebrew is conjectural.
18. If we understand the narratee as receiving the story in oral form from the narrator, then the words would be ambiguous for the narratee as well.
19. Solomon's "wisdom" will also appear in the morally neutral though still admirable sense of "encyclopedic knowledge" (see 4:29–34 [= Hebrew 5:9–14]).
20. While the second alternative may seem far-fetched, there are other issues in the story that can support it. The Israelites' reaction is itself ambiguous: the verb *yr'* can mean "to stand in awe," as the NRSV renders it; but its more common meaning is "to fear." The latter sense could suggest that Solomon's exercise of the "wisdom of God" was not perceived as entirely reassuring. Furthermore, there is a much more serious syntactic ambiguity in the passage, equally subversive to the reader's positive evaluation of Solomon, that we will consider later in this chapter.
21. Technically, this is not the sort of ambiguity where two words with different meanings have the same form (like "desert," meaning "arid wilderness," and "desert," meaning "to abandon"). This is a case where a single word has two quite different meanings, like "to settle," meaning "to take up residence" and "to resolve a dispute."
22. That is, upon the cherubim that surmounted the ark of the covenant, which Solomon had placed in the Holy of Holies (8:4–7). (The cherubim were probably representations of winged lions or bulls; such protective figures are known from Assyria and Babylonia.)
23. See above, p. 14.
24. The NRSV disambiguates, certainly correctly, by moving the final verb to the beginning of 1:10, thereby separating those invited from those not invited. This clarifies the matter for the reader, but it also absolves the reader of any need to actively *discern* (create?) the meaning of the passage. Reading becomes a spectator sport, instead of a participatory endeavor.
25. I have intentionally eliminated punctuation from this translation to give the reader as close a sense of the Hebrew syntax as I can.
26. The NRSV inserts "Ben-hadad" at the beginning of v. 34 to resolve this ambiguity.
27. Here too the NRSV disambiguates by inserting, "The king of Israel responded." The identification of the speaker is clearly correct, but by inserting the phrase the NRSV has already made a decision that the Hebrew text requires its readers to make.
28. The word "baby" is key here. To this point the children have been called *yeled*, "child," or *ben*, "son." Here, for the first time, one of the women calls the living child *yālûd* (literally, "born one," like the Scots term "bairn"). I am assuming that the term carries strong emotional connotations here (the mother is, after all, "moved with compassion"), and requires an equally emotion-laden term in English, like "newborn" or "baby."
29. Solomon uses the mother's revealing term *yālûd* in his verdict. The only deviation in his speech is that he turns the woman's negative from a plea (*'al*) to a command (*lō'*); I have tried to capture this nuance by changing "don't" to "do not," though only a very generous reader will allow that I have succeeded.

30. Compare the rather similar situation in English where one can "go back home," or "go back on one's word," or "go back to one's old ways."
31. I discuss one important gap of fact in 17:1, namely, Who is Elijah? in appendix 2 on p. 161.
32. Since the pronunciation is identical, the ambiguity is inevitable for a hearer, that is, for Obadiah and for the narratee. But ancient manuscripts did not always separate words with a space as we do today. So the statement may have been ambiguous even for a reader.
33. In my opinion, translations that weaken the oxymoron, such as "tiny whispering sound" (NAB) or "soft, murmuring sound" (NJPS), do a serious disservice to the reader.

Chapter 8

1. Many literary scholars working in biblical studies have discussed repetition. Readers who wish to pursue this topic—or any others considered in this book—at greater length are urged to consult the many excellent works listed in the section "For Further Reading." Several books in that section discuss repetition and repetition with variation in biblical narrative; Robert Alter's treatment in *The Art of Biblical Narrative* (New York: Basic Books, 1981), 88–113, is particularly good.
2. One particular use of this sort of repetition is to point up the structure of a literary unit and the organization of its subunits. We consider this effect of repetition in chap. 10, "Structure and Symmetry."
3. This is a fundamental principle at least for our discussion of biblical narrative in this chapter. In modern and contemporary literature, the narrator's reliability cannot always be assumed. And we will see in the next chapter that, even in biblical narrative, the principle of the "reliable narrator" may sometimes need to be qualified just a bit. For our purposes here, however, we will assume a reliable narrator.
4. Again, this is *within the world of the narrative*. One cannot insist too strongly on this qualification. To accept the narrator's version of characters and events *in the world of the narrative* is not at all to assume that the narrator's version accurately represents historical characters and events *in the world of the real author and real reader*. As I said earlier, *in the secondary world* the reliable narrator tells us that Adonijah is handsome (1:6); this strengthens the parallels between him and Absalom, who was handsome (2 Sam. 14:25). But it does not necessarily mean that the *historical* Adonijah (or the historical Absalom, for that matter) was good-looking.
5. Even readers who are unaware of the function of the inclusion see the coherence of the four episodes. Look at the NRSV, for instance, which subsumes all four episodes under a single heading, "Solomon Consolidates His Reign," but ignores the inclusion by treating 2:12b as the end of the preceding paragraph.
6. This was David's concern in his dying advice to Solomon: "obey the law" (2:3), but "use your 'wisdom'" (2:6, 9). See the discussion above on pp. 69–70.
7. For example, 11:2 cites a divine warning to avoid foreign women, "for they will surely *incline* your *heart* to follow their gods." The narrator tells us that Solomon did not heed this warning, but married hundreds of foreign women, "and his wives *inclined* his *heart*" (11:3). By limiting the repetition to two words instead of four in Hebrew (e.g., "his wives *inclined* his *heart* to *follow* their *gods*"), the narrator says, in effect, "And that is what happened," but does not emphasize the point by unnecessary repetition.

8. And, conversely, when the wording of the fulfillment narrative does *not* correspond exactly to the words of the prophecy—in other words, when there is variation within the repetition—the reader has every right to speculate about what the variation implies.
9. In most of these cases, the narrator's repetition of character speech occurs reasonably close to the speech: a command is given, then carried out; a prayer is offered, then answered. In the case of prophecy and its corresponding fulfillment narrative, however, the narrator's account is sometimes very distant from the prophecy itself. A notable example is Joshua's prophecy about the rebuilding of Jericho (Josh. 6:26) and its almost verbatim narrative fulfillment in 1 Kgs. 16:34. A repetition like this is likely to be noticed only by avid and regular readers of the biblical text. For them, in addition to the effects mentioned above, such a repetition also highlights the overarching unity of the narrative between the two linked passages.
10. The NRSV has skewed the meaning of both Bathsheba's speech and the narrator's words by translating "on your behalf"/"on behalf of Adonijah." In English those phrases imply that Bathsheba agrees to support Adonijah's request and that the narrator corroborates that impression. In Hebrew both Bathsheba and the narrator say that she will speak "about" Adonijah; there is no indication of what she intends to say. To capture the precise degree of neutrality Bathsheba's words exhibit, English would have to resort to paraphrase: "I will speak to the king about your request."
11. Since "reader response" is one aspect of the approach to narrative criticism I am attempting to illustrate in this book, this note is primarily intended to reveal something about my own reader response and my critical recognition of its limitations. My reader response to Bathsheba's words contains a strong component that the implied Israelite reader's certainly would not have had, namely, my disagreement with a respected and admirable translation like the NRSV (see the previous note). Where, in my opinion, the implied reader would hear "I will speak to the king about you," I cannot help but hear "I will speak to the king *about* you [but not necessarily *on your behalf*]." The speech thus focuses my attention much more strongly on the noncommittal character of Bathsheba's words than it would the implied reader's. And that may blind me to the possibility that the narrator's repetition has some completely different agenda than the one I have described in the text above. This is why, ideally, literary criticism is a cooperative enterprise. We need to share our readings in order to have others confirm (or disconfirm) their plausibility.
12. The NRSV's translation of this verse is misleading. The words "at once" are a paraphrase of the Hebrew word *lĕkî*, which begins the verse. It also begins v. 12, where the NRSV more accurately renders it "come."
13. I discuss this shift to Bathsheba's point of view in chap. 5; see p. 50 above.
14. The two conspirators also change one of the animal terms. Instead of the narrator's *bāqār* ("cattle" in general, irrespective of age or sex), Bathsheba and Nathan both say *šôr* (a full-grown male bovine—bull, steer, ox). This may be simply stylistic ornamentation, but since a full-grown male—especially a breeding male—is usually more valuable than a female animal or an immature one, the change may also contribute to lending Adonijah's gathering more portentous significance than the narrator gave it.
15. The NRSV's commitment to gender-inclusive language has led it into an inconsistency. In 1:19 and 25 it translates *bĕnê hammelek* gender-inclusively ("children of the king"), but in 1:9 it is constrained by the preceding phrase, "all his brothers," to translate the same words "sons of the king."

16. Some of the ancient translations suggest that there was an alternative text tradition wherein Nathan too said "Joab, the commander of the army"; but I am reading the standard, extant Hebrew text, not a conjectural reconstruction of an earlier one. The plural "commanders" is puzzling, unless it is a further attempt on Nathan's part to obscure the similarities between his words and Bathsheba's.
17. I find it hard to determine why Nathan avoids mentioning "the warriors" among the uninvited. (The warriors in question are almost certainly the king's private guard of mercenaries, the Cherethites and Pelethites, since they are so closely associated with Benaiah in 1:9. See p. 87 above.) With some hesitation, I propose this possibility. If Nathan *had* mentioned them as uninvited, it might have suggested to David that Adonijah's gathering was not, after all, an attempt to usurp the throne, since he had not laid claim to the king's private guard. This would have lessened pressure on the king to act immediately, which would have been counterproductive to Nathan's project.
18. For an example of a character repeating himself, with very significant changes, see the remarks on David's words in 2 Sam. 19:23 and in 1 Kgs. 2:8 above, chap. 7, n. 11.
19. I have changed the NRSV translation here to show that the Hebrew of the relevant phrases in 1:13 and 1:18 is identical, except for word order and the introductory "why" in 1:13. In 1:13 Nathan says, *maddûaʿ mālak ʾădōnîyāhû*; in 1:18, Bathsheba tells David, *ʾădōnîyāh mālak*.
20. See the discussion above, pp. 73–74. Note that, in his own audience with David, Nathan will go even further and claim that Adonijah's guests have *acclaimed* him king: "Long live King Adonijah!" (2:25).
21. The NRSV makes the allusion verbal by using "beautiful" in each place. It is more subtle in Hebrew, since the Hebrew words are different. In Hebrew the allusion is situational. In both cases, the narrator describes (without saying so explicitly) David's observation of the woman's attractiveness. There is also a contrastive dimension to the allusion. In Bathsheba's case, David's attraction leads to illicit sexual intercourse; in Abishag's case, though sexual intercourse would be licit, it proves to be impossible.
22. Although the English word "Satan" comes from this Hebrew word, the basic meaning of the word in Hebrew has nothing to do with evil beings or supernatural powers. It means "opponent," somebody who wishes to see another lose at something. The *śāṭān* who accuses Job before God, for instance, is not a tempter who tries to lead Job into sin. He is the resident cynic in the divine court, the "devil's advocate," whose job it is to make sure that nobody on earth gets away with anything. His attacks on Job are an endeavor to prove to God that Job's piety and integrity are ultimately a form of self-serving behavior.
23. It also occurs once to describe Joab's earlier murder of "two righteous men" (2:32).
24. The correspondence is even a bit closer than the NRSV shows. The NRSV leaves Jeroboam's word "favor" out of the narrative fulfillment ("the man of God entreated [. . .] Yhwh"), but it is in the Hebrew. I suspect this was a stylistic decision on the part of the NRSV translator, who found the repetition too wordy. The additional phrase in 13:6, "became as it was before," simply emphasizes the completeness of the restoration.
25. The NRSV changes the verb from "sacrificed" to "slaughtered," but this is misleading. It is exactly the same verb in Hebrew. In the Hebrew of 2 Kgs. 23:20 there are three variations: "all" the priests are killed; the description of the priests is abbreviated by eliminating the phrase "who offer incense on you"; and "altars" is plural instead of singular, presumably because more altars and

high places have developed in the three centuries since the prophecy was first announced.
26. My remarks in the appendix about the variation in 18:41–42 will bring in information that most of the readers of this book are not likely to be aware of. What is important for you at this point is to identify the variation and its simplest and most literal implication.

Chapter 9

1. Even in narratives where the first-person narrator is never actually named, references to "I" and "me" distinguish the narrator clearly from other figures in the text.
2. Even this restriction is true, of course, only when the narrator is actually telling the story. A third-person narrator can step out of the storytelling role to address the narratee directly (this is called "breaking frame"). In that case, the narrator speaks in his own persona and will sometimes use first-person pronouns, even though he does not always do so. We will examine examples of "breaking frame" later in this chapter.
3. Although the narrator's reliability may seem a foregone conclusion, it is not always so in contemporary literature. Some nineteenth- and twentieth-century authors, for instance, experimented with stories told by insane narrators or by narrators who lie to the narratee. When something like that happens, it becomes part of the reader's task to infer the narrator's imposture and to see through the deception the narrator practices upon the narratee. Fortunately, there do not seem to be any insane or lying narrators in biblical narrative.
4. It is important to recognize that biblical history writing, with its pervasive use of dramatic scenes, dialogue, and the like, is rather closer in style and in tone to modern historical novels than to modern history textbooks.
5. When the author creates a first-person narrator, the author will usually limit the narrator's knowledge to that possessed by the character who acts as narrator. But first-person narrators are very rare in the Bible.
6. When information from a biblical narrator conflicts with information from a *character*, the principle of the narrator's reliability ordinarily takes precedence. We assume the narrator's accuracy and evaluate the character's information in that light. (Remember, though, that while this is true of *information* it is not necessarily true of the narrator's *opinions*. As we will see later in this chapter and again in the final chapter of this book, there is room for a critical reader to disagree with the narrator's evaluations and value judgments.)
7. Conversely, the narratee's job description includes *being manipulated*. In other words, if the narrator's attempts to evoke a response from the narratee fail, then the narrative "contract" has aborted, and the story has no "meaning"—at least for that narratee. A reader who wishes to experience the story fully must submit—though with critical awareness—to the narrator's manipulations of the narratee. We will examine this more closely in the last chapter.
8. It is important to remember that "this day" is the "today" of the *narrator and narratee*—the day on which the narrator tells the story to the narratee. It is obviously not the "today" of the real reader (us), since neither the temple nor the ark stands in the Jerusalem of our day. But it is also not the "today" of the *implied author and implied reader*. Despite the reasoning of some historical critics, an aside like this does not constitute conclusive proof that the text was *written* prior to the destruction of the temple. It proves only that the author *set the narrative* (that is, the moment of storytelling) in a time when the temple still stood.

9. This sort of device is not uncommon in biblical narrative, and it is very common indeed in one relatively short section of the Solomon story. See 9:13, 21; 10:10, 12, 20b.
10. Of course, the narrator can also incorporate evaluations into the story without breaking frame. Characterization by "telling" and by "showing" often involves explicit or implicit value judgments. See, for example, the positive evaluation of Solomon in 3:3a and the contrasting negative one in 11:2–4.
11. To me at least, supplying this theological justification also points up by contrast the speciousness of Solomon's claim that Abiathar "deserves death" (2:26). What was his crime? He supported Adonijah, who was David's eldest surviving son and the heir apparent. But such support can be construed a crime only if Solomon deems any opposition to himself blameworthy—a tyrannical attitude much in evidence throughout 1 Kings 2.
12. Even if, as a few critics suggest, Ishmael embodies some of the experience Melville had on whaling ships, Melville never sailed with a one-legged captain obsessed with a white whale! Ishmael did.
13. This is fairly rare, since it is truly challenging to write prose the way an animal would and be convincing about it! One familiar classic of this sort is Anna Sewell's *Black Beauty: The Autobiography of a Horse* (New York: Grosset & Dunlap, 1945).
14. In theory, of course, one could attribute the ironic intent to the narrator himself, since whatever clues there are to the subversion of surface meaning also come to us in the narrator's voice. For ease and clarity of analysis, however, it is simpler to assign the surface meaning to the narrator and the clues that subvert it to the (implied) author.
15. Note the difficult line a successful ironist must walk. If the narrator's point of view is presented too consistently and cogently, the author's contrary point of view will never be suspected; but if the narrator's point of view is presented feebly and unpersuasively, then the author will appear to be setting up a specious argument and the author's contrary point of view will fail to convince.
16. The NRSV renders the verb "supplied" here, but the Hebrew verb is *nātan*, "to give," as it is also in the next three sentences.
17. My calculation is based on the figures in 4:22 and on expert estimates that ancient methods of milling wheat produced three measures of flour and meal for every four measures of wheat. The cor is usually a liquid measure. Its size is uncertain, but it is generally estimated to be between 75 and 100 gallons. As a dry measure it was probably 10–15 bushels. Ninety cors of flour and meal daily (4:22) would require 120 cors of wheat. This means Solomon's annual income was 43,800 cors of wheat, versus an annual payment to Hiram of 20,000 cors.
18. The quantity is unsure. The Hebrew text reads "twenty cors," or about 1,500 to 2,000 gallons. The ancient Greek translation, however, reads "twenty thousand baths," or over 200,000 gallons, which seems beyond credibility.
19. "Fine oil" (as the NRSV translates it) was very precious and its production very labor intensive. The olives were crushed by hand, not in an olive press; and then the oil was filtered, so that it would not be contaminated by fragments of the olive pits or other impurities. It would have been extremely costly.
20. This is where the analogy breaks down. The daughter can always ask questions of her parents. The narratee (who, like the narrator, is a creation of the author and exists in a fixed text and who therefore cannot speak for the reader) cannot question the narrator(s).
21. Note that this is not simply a matter of having different narrative voices recount *different* events. Many narratives—especially those with first-person

narrators—use multiple narrative voices (for example, in different chapters) to compensate for the limitations of each individual narrator's knowledge or point of view. Here, however, I am talking about multiple narrative voices recounting a *single* story to the narratee.

22. The most ambitious project of this sort to date is Robert Polzin's series of volumes that study the books of Deuteronomy, Joshua, Judges, and 1 and 2 Samuel: *Moses and the Deuteronomist* (New York: Seabury, 1980); *Samuel and the Deuteronomist* (San Francisco: Harper & Row, 1989); *David and the Deuteronomist* (Bloomington: Indiana University Press, 1993). For an introduction to the some of the theoretical ideas underlying such readings, see Barbara Green, *Mikhail Bakhtin and Biblical Scholarship: An Introduction* (Atlanta: Society of Biblical Literature, 2000).

23. That is, the meaning that the implied author intends to communicate to the implied reader.

24. Many readers of this book will have some familiarity with historical criticism and its identification of multiple sources that have been editorially combined to produce the biblical text we have today. The Pentateuch, for example, is thought to contain material from several narrative documents ("Yahwist," "Elohist," "Priestly"), legal codes ("Book of the Covenant," "Holiness Code"), and so on. The starting point for such theories is the presence in the text of what historical critics perceive as inconsistencies and sometimes outright contradictions. Were human beings created after the animals (Gen. 1:24–27) or before them (Gen. 2:18–20)? How many animals of each sort did Noah take on the ark (Gen. 6:20; 7:2, 8)? The historical critic explains these discrepancies by assigning the conflicting details to originally independent stories; when the stories were later combined, the editor did so in a manner that did not smooth over all of the disagreements.

There is an interesting convergence here between historical criticism and a literary theory of multiple narrative voices; and there is an equally interesting difference. On the one hand, both historical and literary criticisms attempt to explain unevenness in the text in terms of a multiplicity of origins: the historical critic infers multiple sources and the narrative critic identifies multiple narrators. On the other hand, the historical critic locates that multiplicity in the primary world (the "Yahwist," the "Elohist," etc., are deemed to have been historical figures, or at least extant documents), whereas the narrative critic locates multiple narrators in the secondary world, the "world of the narrative." An important corollary of this difference is that, for the historical critic, identification of independent, primary-world sources renders holistic interpretation of the composite text unnecessary, if not impossible, since the text is not a true authorial unity. For the narrative critic, the presence of multiple and divergent narrative voices does not negate the meaningful unity of the text, since that unity is rooted in the singularity of the (implied) author.

25. This already poses a problem of narrative coherence for anyone who has read the Elijah story in 1 Kgs. 17–19. Those chapters regularly condemn Ahab. How to reconcile that picture with the glowing portrayal of Ahab in 20:1–34 is a challenge to any attempt to read the account of Ahab's reign (which stretches from his accession in 16:29 to his burial in 22:40) as a coherent, meaningful unity.

26. Those who are familiar with the methods of historical criticism will see that my reasoning here is parallel to that by which a historical critic would identify 20:35–43 not as an independent source but as a later redactional (that is, editorial) embellishment of a preexisting story.

27. Notice that this is a *literary* analysis and refers to what happens *in the narrative world*. It says nothing about actual historical conditions during the ninth

century BCE. The text's historical accuracy is a matter for historical investigation, not for narrative criticism.

28. In this way the negative attitudes of the narrative voice in 20:35–43 echo the anti-Ahab sentiments that prevail in 1 Kgs. 17–19.
29. The situation is somewhat analogous to the claim of Nathan and Bathsheba that David had previously sworn that Solomon would succeed him. Absent any narratorial confirmation of the claim, especially when such confirmation would be easy to supply, the reader is entitled to wonder whether the silence is subversive.
30. To justify my disagreement with the NRSV here would plunge us too deeply into the technical arcana of Hebrew grammar. For the sake of this example, use the translation I propose above, though I admit that not all Hebraists would accept my argument.

Chapter 10

1. It is clear from the study of ancient manuscripts (for example, the Dead Sea Scrolls found at Qumran) that a few visual marks of punctuation were used: indentations to mark the beginning of some thematic units, long blanks in the middle of a line to separate thematic units, even longer blanks that extend to the end of a line to indicate the end of a major thematic unit. Careful study of such graphic devices is still relatively young. But the limited extent of literacy in ancient Israel and the oral nature of most narrative communication would imply that such devices were for the attention of the one who read the text aloud. It is not clear whether the literate reader would communicate such signals to the listeners and, if so, how. By contrast, structural and thematic signals embedded in and communicated by the words themselves would be both visible to the reader and audible to the hearers.
2. The material in this chapter is based in large part on my *Style and Structure in Biblical Hebrew Narrative* (Collegeville, MN: Liturgical Press, 2001) and on the work of many earlier scholars on whom I relied in that book. It is important for the student to realize that the conclusions reached in such studies remain provisional, though they offer promising starting points for further investigation. Until there is more widespread scholarly agreement on both the *criteria* for identifying meaningful verbal signals in the text and on the *interpretation* of such signals, we are still in the preliminary stages of exploration. My readings in this chapter may not always be convincing either to the student or to all of my colleagues in the guild of biblical scholars. I offer them as readings that illuminate the narrative for me and that seem to point to the sorts of structural devices ancient Israelite authors used.
3. Even chapter and verse numbers are comparatively late. Chapter numbers were first introduced into biblical manuscripts in medieval times (sometime during the thirteenth century), and verse numbers were introduced still later than that.
4. It seems reasonable to assume that ancient Israelite listeners, attuned as they were to the conventions of oral literature, were both more attentive to and more retentive of such aural signals than we are. The fact that we must pore over texts to discern these signals visually does not diminish the likelihood that the ancients would have noticed them much more readily.
5. For example, in 1:1–53 Nathan the prophet instigates Solomon's succession to David's throne; in 11:26–40 Ahijah the prophet instigates Jeroboam's succession to Solomon's throne. These two passages mark the beginning and end of the Solomon story. In 2:13–46a Solomon eliminates three people who pose a

threat to his rule, Adonijah, Joab, and Shimei. In 11:14–25 Yhwh "raises up" two men who pose threats to Solomon's security, Hadad and Rezon.

6. Conversely, a translator may inadvertently *create* links, too. The words the NRSV translates "eastward" and "east" in 1 Kgs. 17:3 are entirely different from one another in Hebrew.
7. The examples just given in n. 5 ought to make this clear. It has long been recognized that, in Hebrew poetry, parallelism of lines can be based on similarity as well as on repetition: "Happy the one who does not *go* in the *advice* of the *wicked* / nor *stand* in the *road* of *sinners* / nor *sit* in the *seat* of *scoffers*" (Ps. 1:1; my translation).
8. Such patterning is not always present; that is, it does not seem to be a necessary element in Hebrew prose style. Nevertheless, it is found frequently enough to warrant notice.
9. Many scholars use *inclusio*, the Latin form of the term.
10. See above, p. 84. This unifying thread will come as no surprise to most readers. I am not claiming that *only* the inclusion enables us to discern it. The effect of the inclusion is to help support that reading of the text, not to create it.
11. In Hebrew as in English "after him" follows the final "my lord the king." To my ear, this slight deviation does not noticeably diminish the unifying effect of the inclusion. Given the constraints of language, one must allow the author a bit of flexibility. The observant reader will also note that Nathan uses the phrase "my lord the king" *within* his speech as well (1:27a). This does not strike me as undermining the inclusive effect of the two other appearances of the phrase. Whether in the literary conventions of ancient Israel it might actually have strengthened that effect (like a key word or leitmotiv) is not clear.
12. From the Greek letter *chi*, which looks like a capital *X*. Narrowly defined, a "chiasm" would then have only four elements: *AB/B'A'*. But the term has come to be used of any reverse pattern with a double center and, even more broadly, of any reverse pattern at all.
13. Often, especially when the center comprises only a single element, there will also be a verbal link between the central element and the first and last elements.
14. The range could be extended much further. Elsewhere I have argued that the entire Solomon story (1 Kgs. 1:1–11:43) falls into a single, very complex chiastic pattern. See *Style and Structure*, 92–93, and *1 Kings* (Berit Olam: Studies in Hebrew Narrative and Poetry; Collegeville, MN: Liturgical Press, 1996), 151.
15. I have previously presented this pattern, in different words, in *Style and Structure*, 15, and *1 Kings*, 25.
16. I confess that most of these are repetitions only in a very vague sense. In *a* and *a'*, for instance, Solomon is seated on something that David speaks of as his own; in *b* and *b'* there is a contrast between "leading Solomon down" and "following Solomon up"; only in *c* and *c'* is there an explicitly repeated word, "king."
17. *Style and Structure*, 48–49; *1 Kings*, 61.
18. Ancient Hebrew texts do not include written vowels. In the grammatical forms used here, both the verb "to remain" and the verb "to return" have exactly the same consonants. It seems likely that, despite the difference in pronunciation, a listener would notice the similar succession of consonants.
19. *Style and Structure*, 25; *1 Kings*, 3; slightly modified.
20. In theory there is another form of forward symmetry that might be symbolized *AA'BB'CC'*, etc. This pattern is attested in Hebrew poetry (though even there it is not overly frequent), but it is not commonly seen in narrative prose. For a

plausible attempt to identify this form of symmetry in the Joseph story (Gen. 37–50), see David A. Dorsey, *The Literary Structure of the Old Testament: A Commentary on Genesis–Malachi* (Grand Rapids: Baker, 1999), 59.
21. See my *Style and Structure*, 38; *1 Kings*, 133–34.
22. Despite the NRSV's use of "incline" in element *c* and "turn away" in element *c'*, the Hebrew text uses the same verb in both places.
23. If my reader will forgive a gratuitous speculation on my part, I conjecture that, if the narrative development had been "warning of danger/danger averted," then reverse symmetry would have been more likely.
24. *Style and Structure*, 84–85. Some of the elements of this analysis originate in an article by Bezalel Porten, "The Structure and Theme of the Solomon Narrative (1 Kings 3–11)," *Hebrew Union College Annual* 38 (1967): 93–128. See also Jerome T. Walsh, "Symmetry and the Sin of Solomon," *Shofar* 12 (1993): 11–27.
25. I have made slight modifications to the NRSV to reflect the Hebrew wording and its patterns of repetition more precisely. See my *Style and Structure*, 48; and *1 Kings*, 63.
26. The Wadi Kidron runs east of Jerusalem and separates the city from the Mount of Olives. Shimei's home town, Bahurim, was on the Mount of Olives (see 2 Sam. 19:16). The purpose of Solomon's more stringent command in 2:37, then, was to prohibit Shimei from returning to his home.
27. And David's instructions too contain the same sort of self-serving misrepresentation as Solomon's. See chap. 7, n. 11.
28. This is not to imply that corresponding subunits must be close to equal in length. The balance is a relative one. One subunit's length relative to the subunits that surround it will usually be similar to the length of its corresponding subunit relative to the subunits that surround it. In other words, if *c* is longer than *b* but shorter than *d*, then *c'* will usually be longer than *b'* but shorter than *d'*.
29. There is also an ironic force to these words that will be picked up only by the erudite Bible reader. In 1 Sam. 21:10 (= Hebrew 21:11), "David rose and fled that day from Saul; he went to King Achish of Gath." Where David once fled to take refuge from Saul, now Shimei—a member of Saul's clan (2 Sam. 16:5)—also travels, but then returns (trustingly?) to the control of David's son.
30. The Hebrew is literally, "A man killed his man."

Chapter 11

1. It may seem to the reader of this book that my agenda has been to expose the narrator's operations so as to escape their influence, but nothing could be further from the truth. If the student finishes this book *immune* to the narrator's effects, one of us has failed. Understanding the narrator's manipulations must illuminate (and, if possible, deepen) our experience of them, not replace it.
2. In cases where the narrator's presentation is inaccurate, because the author has created either a narrator whose knowledge is limited or (at least in nonbiblical texts) one who is unreliable, the responsibility to infer that unreliability is better assigned to the implied reader than to the narratee.
3. For whatever reason, any given reader may be unable to accept the secondary world of a particular story on its own terms. This happens to all of us from time to time. It may be due to inferior writing—an incoherent secondary world holds little attraction for an experienced reader. (But this is unlikely to be the case in a text like the Bible, whose stories have compelled intelligent readers for millennia.) Alternatively, it may simply be that one finds the values operative in the secondary world insupportable. (Many people choose not to

read especially violent, or especially profane, or especially tragic stories for this reason, no matter how well-crafted they may be as literary artifacts.) Or it may be that the story evokes strong and powerful responses from us that we find unendurable. (In that case, the intensity of our response actually testifies to the success of the author's art and the power of the secondary world he or she has created.)

4. This does not mean, of course, that we have failed as readers when we do not have such intense responses. Not every narrative is pitched at the level of laughter or tears. Some seek to elicit only a smile, a sigh, or a sense of mild regret or satisfaction.

5. Strictly speaking, fluency in ancient Hebrew is probably not necessary for the implied reader of your text. This is because, by and large, readers of this book will not be reading the Bible in Hebrew. Rather, most of you will be using a *different text*, namely, a *translation* of the Bible into English, written by a modern "author" (the translator). So the implied reader of the text you are using is expected to be fluent in English, but not necessarily in Hebrew. That you are reading "a different text" also means that, even though the translator has done his or her best to create an English text that says just about the same thing as the Hebrew, there will be inevitable differences between the text you are reading and the text of the Hebrew Bible and therefore between the responses your text evokes from you and the responses of the ancient Israelite implied reader to the Hebrew text.

6. This certainly does not mean that, as readers, we cannot disagree with the views and values of the authors we read. But that disagreement is between us *as real readers* and what we perceive as positions held by the implied author. The implied reader by definition accepts the views and values of the implied author without question. Taking on the implied reader's role in this matter is necessary for the real reader, since the experience of successfully reading a text with whose values we disagree is an experience of an *inner conflict*, not merely of dismissal. We do not find ourselves simply *ignoring* the proposed values; wearing the implied reader's hat, we internalize them, and then we debate them within ourselves.

7. There seems to be an erroneous assumption among some modern religious readers that, at least as far as the biblical text is concerned, "history" is a privileged category over "fiction," and that we must presume the reliable historicity of a text unless its fictional character can be demonstrated beyond doubt. Concealed behind this assumption are two more on which it rests, neither of which is theologically defensible: first, that God cannot "inspire" fiction as readily as he can "inspire" history writing; second, that the "truth" of divine revelation consists essentially in historical data, rather than in divine *self*-revelation.

8. There are no unchallengeable answers to questions like these and the ones in the next paragraph. Since we have no treatises on literary style or on historiography from our ancient Israelite authors, any answers we propose are judgment calls based on how we read the biblical texts we possess. Our reasoning, then, is inevitably circular; but we have little alternative in this matter.

9. Later narrative texts of the Hebrew Bible that purport to be histories (specifically, 1 and 2 Chronicles) are much closer in this regard to Greek models (to which they are also roughly contemporary) than to the older biblical narrative books.

10. To be completely candid, the jury is still out on this issue. The idea that the Bible may house unreliable—or at least limited—narrators is recent, and the terrain has not been widely explored as yet. The results to date, however, suggest that disjunction between implied authors and the narrators they create,

while not unknown, is not common. See pp. 101–4 for examples of this sort of disagreement: subversive or ironic writing, limited narrators, and multiple narrative voices—all cases where the views expressed by the narrative voice(s) are not identical to those that the implied author wishes the implied reader to accept.

11. We should note, however, that a later passage in the Solomon story displays some signs of discomfort with the system—at least with the conscription of *Israelites* into the forced labor gangs. In 9:21–23 the narrator tells us that only non-Israelites were conscripted; Israelites served in higher-status positions, apparently including as foremen in the labor gangs (9:23).
12. Remember also the ambiguity about whether Yhwh "dwells" or "is enthroned" in the temple; on this, see the remarks above, p. 73.
13. Jonathan Culler, *Structuralist Poetics: Structuralism, Linguistics, and the Study of Literature* (Ithaca: Cornell University Press, 1975), 124.

Appendix 1

1. One must remember that, since the northern tribes have now separated from Jerusalem, and there is animosity between the two sovereignties (12:21–25), in Bethel the man of God *from Judah* would be considered a foreigner at best, and an enemy sympathizer or agent at worst.
2. This is likely to be more obscure to the modern reader than to the implied reader. Solomon had built a temple as well, and dedicated it in the seventh month (8:2), even though he would not finish it until (or had already finished it a year previously in) the eighth month (6:38). The specification of Jeroboam's feast as the "fifteenth day of the eighth month" suggests that it was intended as a dedication feast like Solomon's, and that it points forward to the unique event of Jeroboam offering sacrifice on the day of the Bethel altar's consecration, rather than backward to a listing of all the illicit and innovative religious policies Jeroboam practiced.
3. Actually, it is resolved, but only much, much later in the text: Josiah's destruction and desecration of the altar are described in almost the same words in 2 Kgs. 23:15–16. This is one of the threads that point to the literary unity of 1–2 Kings.
4. We explore the possible meanings of this invitation in the section on characterization.
5. I am a bit puzzled by the translator of the NRSV, whose paragraphing and heading link 12:20 more closely with 12:21–24 than with 12:1–19. It seems to me that the ironic echo of 12:1 in 12:20a ("they came to make Rehoboam king" versus "they made Jeroboam king") marks those verses as opening and closing the same scene, with 12:20b being a brief epilogue spelling out the dimensions of the irony.
6. The odd thing is that the intervening verses do *not* tell the story of Jeroboam's rebellion, but only recount the prophetic word that may have instigated it. One way to take account of this is to translate 11:27 more literally. The term *dābār*, which most versions at this point render "reason" or the like ("The following was the *reason* he rebelled against the king . . . ," NRSV), literally means "word." It would be quite possible (and more appropriate to the literary context) to translate 11:27a: "This was the *word* that caused rebellion against the king."
7. Note that I do not reckon 11:41–43 as an episode within the Jeroboam story. Those verses properly belong to the Solomon story, but they could well be incorporated into the present analysis as background information to 12:1–20,

since Solomon's death and Rehoboam's succession to the throne in Jerusalem are the background for the scene of Rehoboam's rejection at Shechem.

8. The account of Rehoboam's reign (12:21–31) follows immediately after that of Jeroboam; the account of the reign of Jeroboam's own successor, Nadab, comes later (see 15:25–28).

9. The horror of this curse is so unsurpassed that it enters the biblical tradition as a paradigm: see 1 Kgs. 16:4 and 21:24.

10. The narrator slips in a dig against the "youngsters" that is usually obscured in translation. The first group Rehoboam consults are literally "elders" or "old men," with a connotation that their age and experience may be a source of wisdom. The second group, however, are not "young men," despite the rendering in many translations, but "children" (*yĕlādîm*); in this way the narrator emphasizes not their age but their immaturity.

11. See chap. 3, n. 14 above for an explanation of this qualification. In versions that treat Jeroboam as absent before 12:20, of course, the reader would have no reason to expect Jeroboam to speak.

12. See the discussion above, pp. 135–36.

13. The beginnings of this line of interpretation were drawn by Karl Barth in his *Church Dogmatics*, II/2, *The Doctrine of God* (Edinburgh: T. & T. Clark, 1957), 393–409.

14. This does not necessarily mean biological sons. The phrase "prophet's son" was also used to describe the members of a group of prophets who gathered around and were led by a prophetic "father." See, for example, 2 Kgs. 2:3, 5, 7, where the NRSV translates "sons of the prophet" as "company of prophets."

15. Of course, this preference may also reveal something about me and my personal tendencies toward cynicism. As the literary maxim puts it, "the text reads the reader."

16. Here too my preferred reading may reflect my personal proclivities to cynicism.

17. The English text does not go any further than to leave this open as a possibility. The Hebrew text, on the other hand, makes it almost a certainty. In 12:18b, where the NRSV says that Rehoboam's flight to Jerusalem was subsequent to Adoram's death ("Rehoboam *then* hurriedly mounted his chariot . . ."), the Hebrew text implies that the two actions were simultaneous: "all Israel stoned him to death, while Rehoboam hurriedly mounted his chariot. . . ."

18. This question could also be treated in chap. 7 under "Gaps and Ambiguities." The narrator leaves a *gap* in the text: he does not reveal the old prophet's motives. Yet we cannot help but be curious about them, so we conjecture possible motives from the limited information the narrator does give us.

19. Since the narrator is willing to call the figure from Bethel a "prophet," his assertion that the prophet was lying refers not to his professional credentials but only to this specific oracle.

20. Joseph was one of Jacob's twelve sons, for whom most of the tribes were named. Joseph himself had two sons, Ephraim and Manasseh, who were adopted by Jacob (Gen. 48:8–20); these were the eponymous ancestors of the tribes of the "house of Joseph."

21. There is an element of omniscience, since I know things that have happened both at Jeroboam's palace (1 Kgs. 14:1–3) and at Ahijah's home (14:4–5), and especially since I hear Yhwh's very words to Ahijah (14:5). However, the narrator immediately undermines this omniscience by withholding the substance of Yhwh's speech and replacing it with generic language ("thus and thus you shall say to her," 14:5b).

22. At least, the old prophet's journey in 13:14 is not particularly significant. On the other hand, the man of God's journey in 13:19 is important because it too

is an explicit violation of Yhwh's command. Unfortunately this is obscured in the NRSV, which uses "return" in the command (13:17b) and "went back" in the disobedience (13:19). In Hebrew the same verb is used in both places. (We will look at some of the implications of this usage in the next section.) Perhaps the unnecessary phrase "with him" in 13:19 is a mild attempt to slow the phrase and underscore the verb.

23. Remember, these are the *narrator's* words, and the narrator is a creation of the author. They do not necessarily mean that the division continued up to the time of the *author*. They mean only that the author has situated the *narrative world* (the world in which the narrator tells the story) some time after Rehoboam's failure at Shechem and some time before the kingdoms were destroyed. The author may well have been writing after the destruction of the northern kingdom in the eighth century BCE or even after the destruction of the southern kingdom in the sixth.

24. The technique is called "breaking frame." I discuss the device in chap. 9 on the narrator.

25. However, the NRSV's identical clauses, "your father made our yoke heavy," are not identical in Hebrew; see the following note.

26. In 12:4 the NRSV's terms, though accurate, do not correlate exactly to the Hebrew words. The first "heavy" is *qšh*; "hard" is *kbd*; the second "heavy" is also *kbd*. In 12:9 Rehoboam uses neither word. In 12:10 the youngsters use *kbd*.

27. The wordplay, of course, disappears in translation, so it will be invisible to most readers of this book. It revolves around the noun "yoke" (*'ōl*) and the preposition "upon" (*'al*). In 12:4 the elders of Israel ask that "*our* yoke" (*'ullēnû*) be lightened, which Solomon placed "upon us" (*'ālēnû*). In 12:9 Rehoboam quotes them as speaking of "*the* yoke" (*hā'ōl*) that Solomon placed "upon us" (*'ālēnû*); because he drops the ending *-ēnû* ("our") on "yoke," the wordplay disappears almost entirely. In 12:10 the youngsters more accurately cite "our yoke" (*'ullēnû*) to match "from upon us" (*mē'ālēnû*).

28. The NRSV unaccountably introduces a variation not in the Hebrew. The verbs "place" (12:4) and "put" (12:9) are the same in Hebrew.

29. See the details in 4:7–19, where the northern half of Solomon's realm is divided into eleven or twelve (the Hebrew is not entirely clear) administrative districts, each of which was responsible for supporting the royal establishment for one month each year. The southern half of the realm, the tribe of Judah, would then have been responsible for only one month's supplies, or perhaps for no assessment at all.

30. In these passages I have modified the NRSV translation slightly to reflect the Hebrew more closely.

31. The change from "three days" to "on the third day" does not, to my mind, convey any layered meaning.

32. This is a recognized technique in Biblical Hebrew prose. After an interruption of some sort, the narrator will often repeat words that preceded the interruption as a way of resuming the story. The technical term for this device is "resumptive repetition."

33. The NRSV introduces a variation in the repetition by changing "did not listen" in 12:15 to "would not listen" in 12:16. In English that variation seems to me to add a nuance that the Israelite leaders perceived the king's refusal to be strong and irreversible. While nothing in the Hebrew warrants this variation, it strikes me as entirely appropriate in the context.

34. There is a major textual problem here, although fortunately it does not affect our analysis at all. The NRSV (and many, if not most, other English translations) inserts words intended to continue the Bethel/Dan parallel established

in 12:29 into 12:30. Both the ancient Hebrew manuscripts and the ancient translations do not support this insertion. Only one ancient Greek manuscript tradition has anything remotely similar, and even it is not similar enough to support the NRSV's insertion.

35. In these two verses I have emended the NRSV's translation slightly to reflect the wording of the Hebrew more precisely.
36. The repetition of "priests of the high places" from the immediately preceding line is striking, but it may be nothing more than a requirement of Hebrew syntax. The idiom "to fill the hand" (presumably with the implements of priestly office) in the sense of "to install [someone as priest]" occurs in three other places (Num. 3:3; Judg. 17:5, 12), and each time it specifies "as priest" or "to be priest." So, although our evidence is quite limited, the phrase may well be an indispensable part of the idiom.
37. Jeroboam's personal participation in the Bethel cult was already the theme of 1 Kgs. 12:32–33, where the king himself is portrayed acting as the priest in the inaugural ceremony for his new sanctuary at Bethel.
38. Although the condemnation implied in this shift from divine will to human will is not hard to grasp, it is a good index of the cultural differences between ancient Israel's worldview and that of modern, Western societies, in which freedom of choice and of self-determination ranks among the highest of values.
39. The NRSV changes "houses" and "cities" in 1 Kgs. 13:32b into "shrines" and "towns" in 2 Kgs. 23:19. But those changes are translator's choices; the Hebrew uses the same vocabulary in each passage.
40. In 1–2 Kings three such source documents are mentioned: the "Book of the Acts of Solomon" (as here in 11:41), the "Book of the Annals of the Kings of Israel" (as in 14:19, and regularly, following the reign of an Israelite king), and the "Book of the Annals of the Kings of Judah" (regularly, following the reign of a Judahite king). No ancient Israelite texts corresponding to these titles exist today.
41. Historical critics deem that the source documents did exist and that the author consulted them in writing 1–2 Kings. They are not sure, however, whether they represent official records from the royal archives of the two kingdoms or early, unofficial historical narratives. As explained above, for the literary critic these texts existed in the world of the narrative, but their existence in the world of the author and reader cannot be proven.
42. Consider how easily the narrator could have given this a strong negative turn ("how he warred against Judah") but did not. Given the narrator's generally negative attitude toward Jeroboam (13:33–34) elsewhere, the noncommittal tone of 14:19 is neutral by comparison.
43. In Hebrew it is even more bizarre: Jeroboam is standing *on* the altar. Strange as that sounds in English, in some ancient Near Eastern cultures the altar was a large platform atop which both priest and sacrificial victim were positioned for the act of sacrifice.
44. This effect could have been easily avoided, or at least minimized, if the narrator had chosen to summarize in different terms. For instance, "So the king continued to walk in the ways of his father Solomon" would have focused the narratee's attention on the past, and Rehoboam's continuity with it. The present text focuses the narratee's attention on the future and the question of how the Israelites will react to Rehoboam's intransigence.
45. On the other hand, it is not inconceivable that attention to popular opinion may have been more highly respected in Israel than in other polities. Note the apparent approval of Ahab's consultation of the "elders of the land" in 20:7–8.

46. It is also possible to see the remark in 12:20b as a frame break ("There was no one who followed the house of David, except the tribe of Judah alone"); but this sentence does not explicitly relate its information to the "today" of the narrator and narratee.
47. Unfortunately, the NRSV is misleading. In 11:26–27 it twice refers to Jeroboam "rebelling against the king." The echo with the word "rebellion" in 12:19 is a creation of the translator; in Hebrew the terms are completely different. The term in 12:19 is *pāšaʿ*, the common word for "revolt" or "rebel." The earlier passage, however, uses an idiomatic phrase, "to lift a hand [against]"; the idiom here certainly denotes some type of threat or opposition, but it may not carry the connotations of violence and schism implied in "rebel."
48. This phrase can be puzzling for the student. Despite its apparent inclusiveness, "all Israel" often refers specifically to the *northern* tribal territories that later became the kingdom of "Israel," as distinct from the "Israel" of David and Solomon, which included both those northern territories and the southern tribal territory that later became the kingdom of Judah.
49. The echo is even clearer in Hebrew than in my translation: "today" is literally in Hebrew simply "the day."
50. This repetition is much stronger in the Hebrew than in the NRSV. The Hebrew reads, "take the kingship from *the hand of* his son."
51. I have discussed this pattern at greater length in *Style and Structure in Biblical Hebrew Narrative* (Collegeville, MN: Liturgical Press, 2001), 41–43; and in *1 Kings* (Berit Olam: Studies in Hebrew Narrative and Poetry; Collegeville, MN: Liturgical Press, 1996), 144–46.
52. Jeroboam's dynasty, too, will fail after two generations (15:25–31).

Appendix 2

1. Notice, though, that this ending only partially resolves the arc of tension. Ahab's command included two parts: "Go through the land looking for water" and "perhaps we may find grass." The double departure notice signals that Ahab and Obadiah, between them, are "going through the land." But nothing is said here or elsewhere of them finding the water or fodder they seek. There is one bitterly ironic echo much later in the story. In 18:5 Ahab and Obadiah are looking for water in springs and wadis (*naḥal*, a small watercourse, usually one that peters out in the dry season). At the end of the story, there is a *naḥal* (the Wadi Kishon, 18:40), but the fluid that fills it is the blood of the prophets of Baal.
2. Here too the resolution is only partial. Yhwh gave Elijah two commands ("go," "show yourself to Ahab") and a purpose ("that I may send rain upon the earth"). At 18:2a Elijah has fulfilled the first command, but not yet the second; nor has the purpose yet been accomplished. These will not take place until 18:17 and 18:45, respectively.
3. Compare the discussion of 3:16–28 on pp. 15–16, where the tensive question suddenly changes in the middle of a scene.
4. The phrase "man of God" is used in the Hebrew Bible as a synonym for "prophet."
5. The narrator tells us that Elijah is a "Tishbite," but we have no idea what that means. The ancient Greek translators took it as a geographical term, and translated the next phrase "from Tishbe in Gilead"; and most modern English translations follow this conjecture. The Hebrew text tradition, however, simply calls him a "Tishbite" and says he was "one of the sojourners in Gilead" (that is, an Israelite originally from west of the Jordan River whose family

migrated across to Gilead on the east side). In any case, none of this points to Elijah as a divinely commissioned prophet.

6. A bit more precisely, 18:17–18 can be seen as ending the arc of tension begun by Yhwh's command in 18:1, "Go, present yourself to Ahab." In 18:17–18 Elijah does so. Then 18:19 opens a new arc with Elijah's command to Ahab to assemble the people and the prophets, and this arc is resolved in 18:20 when Ahab complies.

7. Most translations do not preserve the *purposive* nuance of the Hebrew here. The NRSV, for instance, renders, "I will send rain upon the earth." The Hebrew, however, implies intention: "*so that* I may send rain upon the earth."

8. For the historical critic, this is an almost sure sign that these two narratives were originally independent of their present context and that they were combined with the rest of the Elijah materials only later by an editor. The editor was probably also responsible for creating 18:18b–20 as a transition between the story of Elijah's conflict with Baal worship and the story of the drought, since this is the only place in chaps. 17–18 where the two themes converge.

9. Notice how this also draws a connection between the people of Israel in 18:21–40 and Obadiah earlier in the chapter: he too has access to water, with which he was able to provision the Yhwh prophets he had hidden in caves. We pursue this connection between Obadiah and the people of Israel further in the next section.

10. This suggests that, from a historical-critical point of view, 19:1 (like 18:18b–20), may be a later editor's attempt to smooth the transition between originally independent stories.

11. Commentators disagree on Elijah's intent in this dialogue. We look at the question more closely in the sections "Gaps and Ambiguities" and "Repetition and Variation."

12. This is based on the Hebrew text. In the NRSV, Obadiah is mentioned by name three times. But the translator supplied the name "Obadiah" in 18:7b; the Hebrew reads simply, "he recognized him."

13. The people's journey starts even before their silence. They are subtly accused of being partisans of Baal when Elijah claims that they "limp" with two different opinions (18:21), since "limping" will later prove to be characteristic of the prophets of Baal (18:26). Note also the word "you" in Elijah's speech addressed to the people (18:24), which seems to identify them with the prophets of Baal.

14. The language here is too rich for translation. The NRSV's "raved on" renders a specific form of the verb "to prophesy," used most often of prophesying in an altered state of consciousness, like a frenzy or a trance.

15. Unfortunately, this demand is completely and inevitably lost in translation. The sentence Elijah gives Obadiah to speak to Ahab ("Elijah is here," 18:8) has two quite distinct meanings in Hebrew. It means (a) "Here is Elijah!" (*hinnēh 'ēlîyāhû*) and (b) "Behold, Yhwh is my God!" (*hinnēh 'ēlî yāhû*). In view of Jezebel's pogrom, this confession of faith might well lead to Obadiah's martyrdom.

16. Whatever that means. See n. 5 above.

17. The Hebrew text says he is "over the house" (the NRSV renders it "in charge of the palace"). This is, in effect, a title for an office in the royal court. Note that I do not list as "telling" the narrator's remark that Obadiah "revered the LORD greatly," though this is one of those borderline cases between telling and direct showing. Nor do I take anything from 18:4, which is clearly direct showing, since it portrays Obadiah's actions without specific mention of the qualities they reveal.

18. Note that the narrator does *not* say that Yhwh was in the "still, small voice" (NRSV "sound of sheer silence").
19. We examine the significance of the verbatim repetition in the section "Repetion and Variation."
20. In the section "Structure and Symmetry" we see that the rhetorical shape of the speech heightens this sense of panic.
21. Baal was specifically the god of rain and storms. (One of his titles in nonbiblical literature is "Rider on the Clouds"—a title Israelite tradition claims for Yhwh in Ps. 68:4 [= Hebrew 68:5]). Since the Levant has few permanent rivers to supply water for irrigation (and Israel has none), the god who controls rain controls all crops and therefore all life; he is the supreme deity. Elijah's claim to withhold the rain in Yhwh's name is a direct affront to Baal because it establishes the rivalry precisely in the domain where Baal claimed supremacy.
22. The odd thing here is that the widow is a woman of *Zarephath*, which belongs to Sidon (17:9). In other words, she is not an Israelite, and therefore Yhwh is not her deity. She is no doubt a worshiper of one of the deities of Sidon, whose chief god was, ironically, Baal. Why Yhwh would presume to command her (remember, ancient Israel acknowledged the authority of other gods in other lands), and whether she would acknowledge his right to do so, are unclear.
23. See n. 15 above.
24. In Hebrew the text is quite clear that Elisha does not slaughter all twelve yoke of oxen, but only one, since "yoke" is plural in 19:19 and singular in 19:21.
25. We examine the technique of foreshadowing in chap. 6.
26. Note that this does not mean that Yhwh's enduring quality of benevolence is called into question. What is not certain, given that Elijah's reliability has not yet been established, is the claim that Yhwh will work a miracle to demonstrate that benevolence.
27. However unlikely it may be, it is theoretically possible that Ahab wishes to declare himself a faithful Yahwist in order to convince Elijah to end the drought. But once we get to Ahab's hostile greeting in 18:17 this reading is definitively ruled out.
28. This is a particularly interesting phrase. To "listen to the voice of" someone is the usual Hebrew idiom for "obey," at least when the one doing the listening is a human being. When *God* "listens to the voice of" a human being, however, translators render the phrase more literally in order to avoid saying that God is *obeying* a human being. In one passage, though, the author was clearly aware of—and uncomfortable with—the idiomatic force of the phrase: Josh. 10:14, where "heeded a human voice" (NRSV) is the same idiom, literally, "listened to the voice of a human being."
29. Though this is probably not true in terms of the origin of the traditions and the process of the text's gradual growth, in its present context the contest takes place during a three-year drought. That the people are willing to pour a large quantity of water out on the ground in obedience to the prophet of Yhwh testifies to their readiness to worship the God of Israel.
30. See the discussion on pp. 163–64.
31. See above, n. 28.
32. See the discussion above, p. 161.
33. See Exod. 16:8, where Moses tells the Israelites that Yhwh will give them "meat to eat in the evening and your fill of bread in the morning," and Exod. 16:12, where Yhwh promises "at twilight [literally, "between the evenings"] you shall eat meat and in the morning you shall have your fill of bread."
34. We will not pursue these parallels systematically in this book. For a more extended discussion, see my commentary *1 Kings* (Berit Olam: Studies in

Hebrew Narrative and Poetry; Collegeville, MN: Liturgical Press, 1996), 284–89.

35. And that claim already stands in tension with Obadiah's statement to Elijah that he, Obadiah, has managed to keep a hundred prophets of Yhwh alive (18:13).
36. See also 19:10 for Elijah's even more severe condemnation of "the Israelites."
37. On this translation, see n. 7 above.
38. The first mockery is Elijah's sarcastic remark about Baal himself ("Cry aloud . . . he is on a journey, or perhaps he is asleep," 18:27); the references are to Canaanite mythology, where Baal (the god responsible for rain and therefore crops) annually goes down to the realm of the god Death, who imprisons him until he is raised again to life in the new rainy season. But the narrator extends the mockery to the Baal prophets when he says that they obeyed Elijah's sarcastic order ("They cried aloud," 18:28). The gory details about the Baal prophets' behavior are calculated to scandalize and horrify the Israelite reader, for whom such self-mutilation was forbidden (see Lev. 19:28 and Deut. 14:1).
39. The narrator tells us only that Ahab reports to Jezebel "all that Elijah did," including his slaughter of the prophets of Baal. He does not say that Ahab reported the words Elijah spoke, nor the details of the contest itself.
40. Even the angelic caution that Elijah will need food "for the journey" (19:7) does not specify what journey the angel is referring to. Most readers take it as Elijah's journey to Horeb, but the angel says nothing so specific. It might equally well be Elijah's journey home to Israel and to the tasks that still await him there.
41. The first scholar to propose this reading seems to have been R. Breuil, *La puissance d'Élie* (Neuchâtel: Delachaux & Niestlé, 1945). It has since been accepted by a number of commentators.
42. Obadiah's apprehension that announcing this message to Ahab will get him killed does not require the second reading. Ahab has been seeking Elijah for three years, presumably with hostile intent. If Obadiah suddenly tells Ahab that he knows where Elijah is, the king may well suspect that Obadiah has been hiding him all along. It is not true, of course. But Obadiah *has* been hiding other prophets of Yhwh; and, even if Ahab overlooks it, Jezebel is not likely to leave such obstruction of her pogrom unpunished.
43. The NRSV captures that balance about as well as can be done, though the Hebrew is even closer. Both "one" and "another" in the NRSV translate identical words in the original.
44. It is wryly amusing to note that this contradiction is a sticking point for some translators who feel obliged to tame "sound of silence" into something that is a minimally audible sound (thus "whispering" or "murmuring"). The contemporary trouvère Paul Simon managed to communicate successfully with a whole generation by preserving the oxymoron.
45. The "ineffable" is literally "that which cannot be spoken." And the presence of the Divine in this *qôl* might (but only *might*) be implied by the absence of the repeated refrain, "But Yhwh was not in the. . . ."
46. The NRSV's "sheer" captures this physical nuance adequately; the KJV's "small" does so less well. A more forceful preservation of this nuance might be "a sound of slender silence."
47. The NRSV renders "which is east of the Jordan." That may be what the Hebrew means (though it is not certain), but in English it gives the misleading impression that the word "east" occurs twice in the verse. In fact, "eastward" (*qēdmāh*) and "east of" (*'al-pĕnê*, literally, "on the face of") are entirely different in Hebrew.

48. See above, n. 33.
49. I translate the Hebrew literally here.
50. It may even be a bit stronger than that. As there was in 17:5a, there is here an unnecessary line emphasizing Yhwh's response to Elijah's prayer: "Yhwh listened to the voice of Elijah." The phrase "to listen to the voice of [someone]" is also the usual Hebrew way of saying "to obey." See above, n. 28.
51. The NRSV leaves out the word "send," but it is in the Hebrew.
52. The variation is really another example of the use of repetition. The narrator's use of "cutting off" in 18:4 echoes with Ahab's unwillingness to "cut off" (*nakrît*, from the same verb; NRSV "lose") any of his animals (18:5). The echo points up the contrast between Ahab's worry about his livestock and his unconcern about Jezebel's depredations against his citizens. Obadiah's word "killing" in 18:13 echoes with his repeated protest that Elijah's command to him is a death sentence: "He will kill (*hārag*) me" (18:12, 14). Obadiah expects to suffer the same fate as the prophets Jezebel has already killed.
53. This reading can be pushed much further. Elijah chooses to remain "at the entrance to the cave." But in chap. 18 Elijah has implied that prophets who hide in caves (18:4, 13) do not really count as prophets (18:22). Now, in chap. 19, Elijah chooses to stay in the cave, and he no longer calls himself a "prophet." Compare 18:22 (literally, "I alone am left a prophet of Yhwh") with 19:10b, 14b (literally, "I alone am left").
54. This is a literal translation; the NRSV renders it "except by my word." The Hebrew is obviously idiomatic, and means "except when I say so."
55. In fact, the Hebrew is extraordinary. The idiom "listen to the voice of," which 17:22 uses to describe Yhwh's response to Elijah's intercessory prayer, regularly means "obey"—at least when the subject is a human being! See above, n. 28.
56. It is easy to overlook the fact that we know Obadiah's words *only because the narrator reports them to us*. So, in the last analysis, *both* readings are due to the narrator. As a consequence, the reliability of the narrator gets a bit muddied here. We can focus on the linear experience of hearing or reading the story, in which case we experience Obadiah's "from my youth" as a change from the narrator's earlier "greatly" (this is how I approached the variation in the preceding section). Or we can assume that the narrator has reliably reported Obadiah's words in 18:12 but changed them for his own reasons in the flashback of 18:3. This is the approach I take in this section.
57. I am leaving out the unqualified term "son" because it occurs so often in the passage that its repetition could support almost any structure one might wish. The phrase "*your* son," however, in 17:19a and 23d is an important repetition.
58. By translating "to cause the death of my son" in 17:18 the NRSV obscures this strong echo.
59. I must admit that this one does not really qualify as a "repetition" or as a "clear opposite." But if one understands "took" as "picked up," then the correlation is present conceptually, if not verbally.
60. There is also a repetition in 17:21–22, "let this child's life come into him again"/"the life of the child came into him again." I discussed this as a "command-and-compliance" structure above.
61. See *1 Kings*, 230–32.
62. Although it would take us much too far afield to pursue this issue, we must also consider the possibility that other factors may influence our readings over time. For instance, in the sole context of chap. 17, where Elijah's obedience to Yhwh is meticulous, the reading I have called "collaborative convergence" seems to fit best. In the larger context of the subsequent Elijah stories, where the prophet

seems unwilling to remain a prophet, the present passage may be the early sign of his later resistance.

63. See *1 Kings*, 271.
64. The NRSV has a repeated element in subunits *d* and *d'* (the word "go") that is not in the Hebrew. My linking of the two subunits is based on their *formal* similarity as divine commands (in the imperative mood) to Elijah. The English echo with the verb "go" is simply a happy coincidence.
65. I do not mean to imply that this interpretation is often proposed; I do not believe it is. I present it simply for its value to illustrate how reverse symmetry might point to a different interpretation.
66. See *Style and Structure in Biblical Hebrew Narrative* (Collegeville, MN: Liturgical Press, 2001), 104; *1 Kings*, 240.
67. This clause forms part of the first argument, not the second. The first argument centers on Ahab's frustrated search for Elijah and what will happen to Obadiah if he reawakens Ahab's frustration. The second argument (18:12c–13) rehearses information about Obadiah's character that the narrator already gave the narratee in 18:3b–4.
68. On the ambiguity of the message Elijah commands Obadiah to speak, see above, n. 15.

Appendix 3

1. Negative emotions like this constitute a rather precarious situation of stability, since they can so easily lead to hostile behavior. The words in Hebrew are even more precarious, since they do not connote the sort of cold, potentially resigned response implied by "resentful and sullen," but a hot, angry, and stubborn one. A somewhat more accurate rendering might be "fuming and furious."
2. There is some background to this exchange that would probably be familiar to the implied reader. Ben-hadad's demands are not unreasonable, if we assume that Ben-hadad was Ahab's overlord. Politically speaking, a vassal and all his property belonged, in theory, to the overlord. So in 20:2–3 Ben-hadad is asking Ahab for nothing more than a profession of continued loyalty as a vassal. Ahab's capitulation (not to mention the politeness with which he addresses Ben-hadad as "my lord") justifies the assumption that he was in fact Ben-hadad's vassal.
3. This would *not* have been an appropriate demand for an overlord to make of a vassal, unless the vassal had been guilty of rebellion. That is not likely the case, however, since Ben-hadad does not cite such a crime as justification for his demand.
4. On 22:28b see pages 189–90.
5. In 20:42 a prophet seems to predict Ahab's death, but that very general point is the only element common to 20:42 and 22:38b.
6. We consider the differences between 21:19 and 22:38b in more detail in the questions on "Manipulation of Time."
7. Notice, though, that this "refusal" is based on two principles. Naboth cites a legal reason why he is *unable* to sell his vineyard to Ahab (property that was "ancestral inheritance" could not be sold except in cases of dire emergency and then only temporarily). And Naboth interprets that legal constraint as a religious obligation ("The LORD forbid" is the NRSV's translation of a Hebrew phrase that reads, literally, "profanation to me from Yhwh").
8. Did you notice the description of Ahab in 21:4a? He is, in the NRSV's translation, "resentful and sullen"—exactly the same words used of him only five

verses earlier, in 20:43. Here too the connotations are not disappointment and resignation; they are anger and unwillingness to concede the issue. "Fuming and furious" is closer to the mark here too (see n. 1 above). The stability implied by Ahab's apparent acceptance of Naboth's decision is precarious indeed.

9. It is difficult to ascertain precisely where Elijah's words stop and the narrator's begin. Elijah clearly is speaking in 21:20b–22, and the narrator in 21:25–26. But the words in 21:23–24 could belong to either Elijah or the narrator. (There is nothing in Hebrew equivalent to quotation marks in English to indicate where direct discourse begins and ends.) We will examine this conundrum at greater length in the section "Voice(s) of the Narrator."

10. Jesse C. Long Jr. discusses the differences very insightfully in *1 & 2 Kings* (College Press NIV Commentary; Joplin, MO: College Press, 2002), 255–56.

11. Such a decree certainly does not accord with our contemporary notions of justice, but the implied reader would not be put off. For ancient Israel, the notion of transgenerational reward and punishment was standard. See, for instance, Exod. 34:6–7 and its citations in Exod. 20:5–6; Num. 14:18; Deut. 5:9–10; Ps. 103:8, 17–18; Jer. 32:18.

12. It will be resolved twice elsewhere, but in contradictory ways. In 22:38 Ahab's death is connected with a prophecy similar, though not identical, to Elijah's in 21:19, as if there had been no divine decree in 21:29 exempting Ahab from punishment (see pp. 196–97). In 2 Kgs. 9:24–26 Jehu justifies his assassination of Joram, Ahab's son (as decreed in 1 Kgs. 21:29), on the grounds of an oracle very close to that in 1 Kings 21:19.

13. Do "his servants" include Jehoshaphat? It is certainly possible to read 22:2–3 that way. This would strengthen the impression that Jehoshaphat's words in 22:4 are the reply of a vassal to his overlord.

14. Ramoth-gilead (literally, "Gilead Heights") was located in Gilead, a region east of the Jordan, lying roughly between the Sea of Galilee and the Dead Sea. The territory in this area was always contested among Israel to the west, Moab to the south, and Aram (also known as Damascus) to the north. Whoever was currently strongest held it. An inscription of Mesha, king of Moab from around the time of Ahab's sons, describes how Ahab's father, Omri, penetrated deep into Moabite territory and how Israel held that land until after Ahab's death.

15. Connecting these stories is not without some clear verbal basis in the text as well. The phrase "by the word of Yhwh" is quite rare in Biblical Hebrew, but it occurs repeatedly in 1 Kgs. 13 (vv. 1, 2, 5, 9, 17, 18, 32) and recurs here as well (20:35; NRSV "at the command of the LORD").

16. Textually this is true; chronologically it is not. Because of the way the author organizes 1–2 Kings, much of what follows the notice of Jehoshaphat's accession in 15:24 actually preceded it chronologically. But the *reader's linear experience of the text* means that, after meeting Jehoshaphat, the reader encounters several chapters of assassinations, coups d'état, and civil war in the story of Israel.

17. Some—but not all—of those questions receive brief answers in the account of Jehoshaphat's reign (22:41–46 [= Hebrew 22:41–47]) and the odd paragraph that is appended to his reign (22:47–50 [= Hebrew 22:48–51]). Jehoshaphat will also figure largely in 2 Kgs. 3.

18. The prophet Micaiah and the prophet Micah are two different people, but their names are, in effect, the same. Personal names in Hebrew are often compounded with a divine name, and can be shortened by leaving that element off. The -iah ending in many names is a form of the divine name Yhwh: "Micaiah" means "Who is like Yhwh?" (Compare "Michael": "Who is like El?") "Micah" is the shortened form: "Who is like . . . ?")

19. Many scholars suspect that, somewhere along the line, one copyist put a note in the margin of a manuscript pointing to the book of Micah—rather like an erudite footnote—and that subsequently a later copyist, thinking the marginal note represented something that had been inadvertently left out of the text, inserted it where he thought it belonged.
20. Or "fuming and furious"; see n. 1 above.
21. The unusual details would immediately alert the narratee and the implied reader that there is something significant about this description. We discuss this in greater detail in the section below on "Manipulation of Time."
22. What the NRSV translates as "Do not listen or consent" is somewhat stronger in Hebrew. A closer translation would run more like: "Do not listen and definitely do not consent!"
23. Another element here adds an even more positive note to the portrayal of Ahab. Compare 20:5 with 20:7 and see if you can identify it. I discuss it later in the section on "Repetition and Variation."
24. The "seal" was the ancient equivalent of a signature. In Israel it took the form of a cylindrical object that the owner could wear by means of a cord threaded through the long axis of the cylinder. The surface of the cylinder was inscribed with the owner's name (possibly including a title or a patronymic) and other characteristic designs. This was rolled across soft wax applied to a document, verifying that the owner of the seal had seen and approved the contents. In this case, however, Jezebel was using Ahab's seal, so there is no way to know whether Ahab knew about the letter or its contents.
25. We look at this example again in the section on the "Voice(s) of the Narrator."
26. There is an interesting ambiguity here. In Hebrew the word *'ĕlōhîm* is, in form, a plural, "gods." However, it is also the commonest word in the Hebrew Bible for Israel's (singular) "God." So, for the ancient Israelite implied reader, the Aramean advisers may be saying, "Their gods are gods of the hills" or "Their God is God of the hills." Pity the poor translator, however, who cannot preserve the ambiguity in English, and must choose to translate either according to the likely mind-set of the Aramean speakers ("gods") or the mind-set of the Israelite implied reader ("God").
27. Rhetorically, the claim is even stronger in Hebrew. The sentence is worded: *kî malkê bêt-yiśrā'ēl kî malkê ḥesed hēm*. The parallel structure of the two phrases (even though *kî* is used in two different senses) implies that "kings of the house of Israel" and "kings of mercy" are virtually synonymous.
28. The amount of ink expended by biblical scholars over the years to explain away this portrayal of Yhwh is enormous. The difficulty is alleviated slightly—but only slightly—if we remember that the "Yhwh" of the story world need not be a perfect duplicate of the "Yhwh" Israel worshiped. (See above, pp. 34–35.) The proper question to ask is, What response is the implied author trying to evoke from the implied reader that is so radical it requires a story about a Yhwh who lies in order to evoke it?
29. This is perhaps why readers easily miss a revealing modification Ahab makes in his reporting of Ben-hadad's command (see pp. 200–201).
30. The Hebrew is untranslatable. It is only four words but says, more or less, "Let-not one-who-is-buckling-his-armor-on boast like-one-who-is-taking-it-off." In other words, do not boast of your accomplishments before you have accomplished them.
31. Note that the prophet clearly manipulates the king in this direction by making his case singularly unconvincing. His plea is that the prisoner escaped while he was "doing this and that" (NRSV "busy here and there"). Hardly an argument calculated to justify the alleged malfeasance!

32. On the nature of these feelings, see n. 1 above.
33. And the escape is not only Jehoshaphat's. Ahab's decision to disguise himself and to have Jehoshaphat attract attention by wearing regalia also appears to have protected Ahab from the doom Micaiah predicted—at least until the random (and providential) arrow of 22:34.
34. In an interesting use of tempo, the narrator covers a relatively long period of time—"until at evening he died"—but by mentioning nothing that happens during that time except Ahab's death, he manages to focus our attention exclusively on Ahab's slow dying. It reminds me of a cinematic battle scene where the director lets surrounding noise and action fade out, so that all we see is a single wounded character's slow, painful last breaths.
35. This does not account for the detail about the two kings being clothed in their regalia, since nothing is said in Micaiah's speech about Yhwh's attire. (Contrast the similar vision in Isa. 6:1, which mentions that the "hem of his robe filled the temple.") The reason for this detail in 1 Kgs. 22:10 is probably to foreshadow the motif of royal clothing and disguise (*lack* of royal clothing) that will play such an important role in 22:30–34.
36. This difference could be trivial, since the corresponding foreshadowing in 21:19 is spoken by Yhwh, and we never hear Elijah deliver that oracle in so many words. On the other hand, it may also be significant that Elijah does *not* deliver Yhwh's threats in 21:19. Those divine threats envisage Ahab alone; Elijah, by contrast, unleashes a condemnation of Ahab's whole family. It is quite plausible to read Elijah's words here as going far beyond the mandate he received from Yhwh. See the remarks above on p. 186.
37. For the historical critic, who identifies meaning with the original author's intention, the problem is less challenging: the oracle came down in different forms through different oral traditions. The literary critic, unfortunately, cannot in principle avail herself or himself of this sort of explanation. The literary critic's task is to elaborate a plausible understanding of the text *as we have it*.
38. The English translation has to supply the direct object "scouts." The Hebrew merely says that "Ben-hadad sent." Is the drink starting to make him think and talk sloppily?
39. Here too Ben-hadad betrays his inebriation. See pp. 190–91 above for an analysis of his speech.
40. There are two vexing translation issues in 20:14. First, who are the "young men who serve the district governors"? It is difficult to identify precisely who is in view. Many commentators suggest specialized, elite shock troops (rather like ancient Israelite Green Berets). Recently, others have argued (more plausibly, in my opinion) that they were not military troops at all, but apprentice clerks! As different as those possibilities are, one's decision on the question will have no impact on the analysis above. The second issue is the meaning of the idiom used by Ahab, "Who shall bind the battle?" The NRSV, along with most translators and commentators, takes this to mean "Who shall *begin* the battle?" That is indeed possible, but it is not absolutely certain. A minority view would be that it refers to *ending* the battle. I have followed this view in the discussion above.
41. In the larger context of 1 Kgs. 17–19, however, this favorable picture of Ahab in chap. 20 is severely compromised by the unrelieved portrayal of Ahab in those chapters as a worshiper of Baal.
42. Note that in the following passage, where Micaiah reveals the divine plot, he does not deliver a divine oracle addressed by Yhwh to Ahab. Despite the NRSV's rendering of 22:19 ("Hear the word [Hebrew *dābār*] of the LORD"), what follows is no oracle but a story [which is also *dābār* in Hebrew] *about* Yhwh. "Hear a story of Yhwh" is an equally possible translation. While com-

mentators have spent much effort trying to explain away the text's clear assertion that God was responsible for the prophetic falsehood, surprisingly few commentators have wrestled with the fact that Micaiah divulged God's plans to Ahab *without any clear authorization to do so*. Ask yourself how the story would be different if Micaiah had *not* given Ahab this information. Would your evaluation of Ahab be any different?

43. It is possible to read this as simple abbreviation for the "fairest wives" of 20:3; but, given the more intense hostility of the second demand, it is equally plausible that Ben-hadad means "*all* your wives" in 20:5.
44. Whether these laws were already in effect at the time of Ahab and Naboth is unsure. However, they were almost certainly in effect in the days of the author and audience of the story as we have it, and the implied reader would no doubt have understood the story in the light of the laws of that day.
45. When Jezebel elaborates her plot later on in the chapter, she hews carefully to the requirements of Israelite law (two witnesses in a capital case, etc.). So if Ahab considered her ignorant of such issues, he was very wrong indeed!
46. Some translations (e.g., NAB, NJPS) avoid the problem by simply deleting the problematic words "and he said." In those renderings, it is not clear whether the repetition of Naboth's speech is done in the narrator's voice or in Ahab's.
47. Or, if one wishes to push even further, Ahab withholds this information from Jezebel so that the prospect of the legal impossibility of obtaining the vineyard will not stop her if she wishes to act on Ahab's behalf.
48. Throughout this discussion, I supply literal translations of the Hebrew text so that the precise nature and extent of the variations is apparent, and I italicize the variations I comment on.
49. The emphasis is just a bit stronger here in the English than in the Hebrew, where "as" and "just as" are the same word. It seems to me, though, that that is an effective way of capturing the emphatic force of the repetition in Hebrew, which in English (at least to my ear) only sounds verbose.
50. The term does vary slightly. In 21:9 and 21:13a, "scoundrels" translates a Hebrew phrase that reads literally, "men, sons of worthlessness" ("son of" in Hebrew idiom means "characterized by," so a "son of worthlessness" is a worthless person). The second "scoundrels" in 21:13 translates a slightly abbreviated phrase, "men of worthlessness." The meaning is approximately the same, comparable to English "good-for-nothing fellows" and "good-for-nothings."
51. In 1–2 Kings three such source documents are mentioned: the "Book of the Acts of Solomon" (as in 11:41), the "Book of the Annals of the Kings of Israel" (as here in 22:39, and regularly, following the reign of an Israelite king), and the "Book of the Annals of the Kings of Judah" (regularly, following the reign of a Judahite king). No ancient Israelite texts corresponding to these titles exist today.
52. Historical critics deem that the source documents really existed and that the author consulted them in writing 1–2 Kings. They are not sure, however, whether they represent official records from the royal archives of the two kingdoms or early, unofficial historical narratives. As explained above, for the literary critic these texts may have existed, but the possibility cannot be proven.
53. In the primary world of the implied author and implied reader, the effect of the remark would probably be approval. Archaeology has discovered truly spectacular ivory panels in the ruins of Ahab's palace; and some of the most impressive urban architecture in the northern kingdom is dated to the reign of Ahab. It is quite possible that the implied reader would have been familiar with these accomplishments and have taken 22:39 as praise of them. But that does not necessarily mean that in the secondary world of the narrator and

narratee Ahab's "ivory house" and "cities" were grounds for praise. The only building projects attributed to Ahab in the narrative of 1 Kings are idolatrous temples (16:32–33) and, perhaps (if Ahab sponsored it), Hiel's blasphemous reconstruction of Jericho (16:34). So, in the narrative world, the reference to "the cities he built" may be a subtle condemnation.

54. Since the whole account of Ahab's reign begins in 16:29 and includes the material I have called "the Elijah story" in chaps. 17–19 as well as "the Ahab story" of chaps. 20–22, all of this material must be considered in coming to a final judgment on Ahab.

55. There is another possible argument here based on historical-critical observation. The condemnatory language of 21:21–22 and 21:24 is drawn from a traditional prophetic oracle attested also in 14:10–11 and 16:2–4. This suggests that a single *source* lies behind 21:21–22, 24, and that 21:23 represents a secondary modification of the traditional formula. But this is a historical-critical conclusion, and says nothing about *literary* coherence. There is no doubt that the author of the text used a traditional prophetic oracle of condemnation; the literary question is *how* did the author use it? What effect is the present text intended to evoke in the reader?

56. On this, see the discussions above, p. 186 and n. 36.

57. There is an exception in 21:21, when Elijah says "I will cut off from *Ahab* every male. . . ." Here an appeal to historical criticism may be justified. As I mentioned above (n. 55), the wording of 21:21 is traditional; the author may have conformed to that traditional formulation by naming the condemned king instead of substituting a pronoun.

58. Note too that both 21:23 and 21:24 use "being consumed by dogs" as an image of the punishment Jezebel and Ahab will receive. This likewise binds the two verses into a self-contained unit.

59. This suggests that Elijah is quite aware that, as I mentioned just above, his condemnation goes far beyond what Yhwh authorized.

60. This also applies to the condemnation of Jezebel in 21:23. We know that 21:1–16 portrays Jezebel as an evildoer, but we also know that Yhwh makes no mention of Jezebel in 21:17–19. So we do not know why Elijah condemns her; in fact, the prophet does not cite any specific crime whatsoever in any of his condemnations.

61. See my *1 Kings* (Berit Olam: Studies in Hebrew Narrative and Poetry; Collegeville, MN: Liturgical Press, 1996), 308.

62. Technically, Ahab has left Naboth's vineyard in 21:4a, and is on his way home. I associate these words with 21:1–3 both for convenience and because the citation of Naboth's words in 21:4a supports the association.

63. See also my *Style and Structure in Biblical Hebrew Narrative* (Collegeville, MN: Liturgical Press, 2001), 28–29; *1 Kings*, 316–17; and "Methods and Meaning: Multiple Studies of 1 Kings 21," *Journal of Biblical Literature* 111 (1992): 194–96.

For Further Reading

(Each section is listed in chronological order.)

On Narrative and Narrative Criticism in General

1963. René Wellek and Austin Warren. *Theory of Literature.* Harmondsworth: Penguin. [This is a standard work and is available in many different editions and printings.]
1966. Robert Scholes and Robert Kellogg. *The Nature of Narrative.* London: Oxford University Press.
1978. Seymour Chatman. *Story and Discourse: Narrative Structure in Fiction and Film.* Ithaca, NY: Cornell University Press.
1983. Wayne C. Booth. *The Rhetoric of Fiction.* 2nd ed. Chicago: University of Chicago Press.
1997. Mieke Bal. *Narratology: Introduction to the Theory of Narrative.* 2nd ed. Toronto: University of Toronto Press.

On Narrative Criticism of the Bible

1977. David Robertson. *The Old Testament and the Literary Critic.* Philadelphia: Fortress.
1978. Jacob Licht. *Storytelling in the Bible.* Jerusalem: Magnes.
1981. Robert Alter. *The Art of Biblical Narrative.* New York: Basic Books.
1982. Northrop Frye. *The Great Code: The Bible and Literature.* Toronto: Academic Press Canada.
1983. Adele Berlin. *Poetics and Interpretation of Biblical Narrative.* Bible and Literature 9. Sheffield: Almond.
1984. Meir Weiss. *The Bible from Within: The Method of Total Interpretation.* Jerusalem: Magnes.
1987. Meir Sternberg. *The Poetics of Biblical Narrative: Ideological Literature and the Drama of Reading.* Indiana Studies in Biblical Literature. Bloomington: Indiana University Press.

1988. Robert W. Funk. *The Poetics of Biblical Narrative.* Sonoma, CA: Polebridge. [Primarily concerned with the New Testament.]
1989. Shimon Bar-Efrat. *Narrative Art in the Bible.* Bible and Literature 17. Sheffield: Almond.
1990. Mark Allan Powell. *What Is Narrative Criticism?* Minneapolis: Fortress.
1990. Jean Louis Ska. *"Our Fathers Have Told Us": Introduction to the Analysis of Hebrew Narratives.* Subsidia biblica 13. Rome: Pontifical Biblical Institute.
1990. Northrop Frye. *Words with Power: Being a Second Study of the Bible and Literature.* San Diego: Harcourt Brace Jovanovich.
1992. Robert Alter. *The World of Biblical Literature.* New York: Basic Books.
1993. David M. Gunn and Danna Nolan Fewell. *Narrative in the Hebrew Bible.* Oxford Bible Series. New York: Oxford University Press.
1996–1997. Helmut Utzschneider. "Text X Reader X Author: Towards a Theory of Exegesis: Some European Viewpoints." *Journal of Hebrew Scriptures* 1 [electronic journal, accessed 12 September 2008; http://www.arts.ualberta.ca/JHS/Articles/article1.htm.]
1999. Jan P. Fokkelman. *Reading Biblical Narrative: An Introductory Guide.* Louisville, KY: Westminster John Knox.
2001. Yairah Amit. *Reading Biblical Narratives: Literary Criticism and the Hebrew Bible.* Minneapolis: Fortress.
2002. Pamela Tamarkin Reis. *Reading the Lines: A Fresh Look at the Hebrew Bible.* Peabody, MA: Hendrickson.

On Stylistic (Symmetrical) Structuring in the Bible

1942. Nils W. Lund. *Chiasmus in the New Testament: A Study in Formgeschichte.* Chapel Hill: University of North Carolina Press; reprinted Peabody, MA: Hendrickson, 1992. [Despite the title, this work is at least as important for Hebrew Bible as it is for New Testament, and it does not have much to do with *Formgeschichte*.]
1981. Yehuda T. Radday. "Chiasmus in Hebrew Biblical Narrative." In *Chiasmus in Antiquity: Structures, Analyses, Exegesis,* edited by John W. Welch, 50–117. Hildesheim: Gerstenberg.
1997. Victor M. Wilson. *Divine Symmetries: The Art of Biblical Rhetoric.* Lanham, MD: University Press of America.
1999. David A. Dorsey. *The Literary Structure of the Old Testament: A Commentary on Genesis–Malachi.* Grand Rapids: Baker.
2001. Jerome T. Walsh. *Style and Structure in Biblical Hebrew Narrative.* Collegeville, MN: Liturgical Press.

On 1 Kings: Commentaries with Literary Emphasis

1983. Charles Conroy. *1–2 Samuel, 1–2 Kings.* Old Testament Message 6. Wilmington, DE: Michael Glazier.
1984. Burke O. Long. *1 Kings, with an Introduction to Historical Literature.* Forms of the Old Testament Literature 9. Grand Rapids: Eerdmans.
1985. Simon J. DeVries. *1 Kings.* Word Biblical Commentary 12. Waco: Word.
1987. Richard D. Nelson. *First and Second Kings.* Interpretation. Atlanta: John Knox.
1987. George Savran. "1 and 2 Kings." In *The Literary Guide to the Bible,* edited by Robert Alter and Frank Kermode, 146–64. Cambridge: Harvard University Press.
1995. Iain W. Provan. *1 and 2 Kings.* New International Bible Commentary on the Old Testament. Peabody, MA: Hendrickson.

1996. Jerome T. Walsh. *1 Kings*. Berit Olam: Studies in Hebrew Narrative and Poetry. Collegeville, MN: Liturgical Press.
2002. Jesse C. Long Jr. *1 & 2 Kings*. College Press NIV Commentary. Joplin, MO: College Press.

On 1 Kings: Commentaries with Historical-Critical Emphasis

1951. James A. Montgomery. *A Critical and Exegetical Commentary on the Books of Kings*, edited by Henry Snyder Gehman. International Critical Commentary. Edinburgh: T. & T. Clark.
1970. John Gray. *I & II Kings*. 2nd ed. Old Testament Library. Philadelphia: Westminster.
1984. Gwilym H. Jones. *1 and 2 Kings*. 2 vols. New Century Bible Commentary. Grand Rapids: Eerdmans.
2000. Walter Brueggemann. *1 & 2 Kings*. Smyth & Helwys Bible Commentary. Macon, GA: Smyth & Helwys.
2001. Mordechai Cogan. *I Kings*. Anchor Bible 10. New York: Doubleday.
2007. Marvin A. Sweeney. *I & II Kings: A Commentary*. Old Testament Library. Louisville, KY: Westminster John Knox.

Scripture Index

OLD TESTAMENT

Genesis
1:24–27	227n24
2:18–20	227n24
3	123
3:6	54
3:9–11	216n2
6:20	227n24
7:2	227n24
7:8	227n24
22	45
22:5	24
37–50	229–30n20
48:8–20	233n20
49	212n12

Exodus
16:8	176, 238n33
16:12	176, 238n33
20:5–6	242n11
20:7	89
24:9–11	177
34:6–7	37, 242n11

Leviticus
19:28	239n38
25:8–10	202
25:25–28	202

Numbers
14:18	242n11
22	123

Deuteronomy
5:9–10	242n11
6:5	220n9
14:1	239n38
17:5	204
17:16–17	58
17:22	190
32–33	212n12

Joshua
1:1	169
6:26	61, 223n9
10:14	238n28

Judges
2:11–19	61

1 Samuel
1:12–13	62
1:24–28	140
2:22–36	213n8
2:33	100
3:1–21	140
3:14	218–19n11
12:1–25	212n12
12:12–13	197
14:3	213n8
15:17–23	198
15:27–28	140
21:10 (= Hebrew 21:11)	230n29
22:20	213n8
25:1	212n12
27:1–4	212n9

2 Samuel
5:1–5	219n12
5:11	219n13
7	61
9–20	77
10:5–6	61
10:9–10	61
11	86
11:2	25, 92, 213n6, 217n19
11:2b	218n9
11:14–27	68
12:8	90
12:24	86
13:3	72
14:25	35, 57, 68, 92, 222n4
15–18	38
15:1	57, 68
15:2–6	77
15:32–37	26
16:5	230n29
17:15–22	26
19:16	230n26
19:23	220n11, 224n18
23:17	212n12
24	37

1 Kings
1	72
1:1	34, 50
1:1–4	14, 38–39, 73, 83
1:1–53	24, 27–28, 91, 228n5
1:1–2:11	25–26
1:1–2:12	113–14
1:1–2:46	16–18
1:1–11:43	229n14
1:3–4	28, 49–50
1:4	50, 92, 169, 213n6, 216n5, 217n20
1:4a	218n9
1:5	35, 38, 73, 92, 215n4
1:5–6	57, 100
1:5–7	68
1:6	34, 58, 67, 77, 98, 222n4
1:7	92
1:7–8	74
1:8	34
1:9	223n15, 224n17
1:9–10	47, 88–89
1:9b–10	74
1:10	221n24
1:11	34
1:11–14	35, 98
1:12–13	223n12

1 Kings (*continued*)

Reference	Pages
1:13	48, 59, 66–67, 89, 217n17, 224n19
1:15	50, 83, 86–87, 213n7
1:15–21	48
1:15–22	49
1:15–37	26, 116
1:16	35, 38
1:17	59, 217n17
1:17–18	89
1:17–19	77
1:18	38, 74, 224n19
1:19	88–89, 223n15
1:22–32	76–77
1:24–25	77
1:24–27	35, 110
1:25	74, 223n15
1:25–26	88–89
1:27	229n11
1:28	85
1:30	66, 68
1:33–34	67
1:33–35	87, 111–12, 117
1:36–37	28
1:38–40	24, 47–48, 55, 87, 112
1:41–49	47
1:43–46	112
1:43–48	48–49
1:46–48	217n18
1:49	35, 48
2:1–4	58
2:2–4	212n13, 220n8
2:2–9	48, 69–70, 213n16, 222n6
2:5–9	67
2:6	72
2:7	212n13
2:8	220n11, 224n18
2:8–9	117
2:9	72
2:11	219n12
2:12b	85–85, 110, 212n14, 222n5
2:13–18	46, 48, 68
2:13–46a	228n5
2:14–17	217n16
2:16–22	90–91
2:18	216n6
2:18–19	86, 223n10
2:19	38
2:25	28, 93, 224n20
2:26	226n11
2:26–27	212–13n15, 218–19n11
2:27b	100
2:28–34	110, 212–13n15
2:29	93
2:31	93
2:32	224n23
2:34	93
2:34–35	28
2:36	85
2:36–38	55
2:36–46a	14–15, 110, 112–13, 116–17
2:37	230n26
2:38b–41	118
2:39–41	218n4
2:42–44	126
2:42–45	213n16
2:46	85, 93, 212n7
2:46a	28
2:46b	84–85, 110, 212n14
3:1	60, 212n7, 212n14; 214n11, 219n16
3:3–15	45
3:3a	226n10
3:4	61, 109–10
3:5	37
3:7	215n5
3:10	34
3:11–14	36
3:12	57, 72, 101
3:12–13	61
3:15	109–10
3:16–24	50–51
3:16–28	15–16, 27, 46, 56, 75–76, 236n3
3:21	49
3:23	36
3:23–24	48
3:26	34, 221n28
3:27	214n10, 221n29
3:28	34, 72, 101, 214n1, 218n5, 221n20
4:1–19	56, 57
4:1–25 (= Hebrew 4:1–5:5)	110–11
4:7–19	234n29
4:7–21 (= Hebrew 4:7–5:1)	59
4:22 (= Hebrew 5:2)	226n17
4:29 (= Hebrew 5:9)	37
4:29–33 (= Hebrew 5:9–13)	56
4:29–34 (= Hebrew 5:9–14)	57, 221n19
5:1 (= Hebrew 5:15)	58
5:4 (= Hebrew 5:18)	59, 92, 215n6
5:7 (= Hebrew 5:21)	36, 215n5
5:10–12a (= Hebrew 5:24–26a)	101–2, 226n16
5:11 (= Hebrew 5:25)	226n19
5:12a (= Hebrew 5:26a)	37
5:13 (= Hebrew 5:27)	125
6	218n7
6–7	56, 60
6:1	60
6:9b–36	114–15
6:12–13	36
6:37–7:1	219n17
6:38	232n2
7:1–12	60
7:8b	60, 219n18
7:14	34, 72
8:1–11	55
8:2	232n2
8:4–7	221n22
8:8	100, 225n8
8:11–12	37
8:13–49	73
8:27	125
9:2	37
9:3–9	36
9:6–9	61, 125
9:10	219n17
9:10–11	102
9:10–14	109
9:15	60
9:16	59, 219n14
9:21–23	232n11
9:24	60
9:25b	60
9:26–28	69, 220n7
9:26–10:25	91
10:1–13	68–69, 109
10:4–9	56
10:5	34, 57, 215n2
10:11–12	220n7
10:21–29	57

10:22	69, 220n7	12:20b	236n46	15:25–28	233n8		
11:1–3	114	12:21	20, 147	15:25–31	236n52		
11:1–4	60	12:21–24	141–42	16:2–4	246n55		
11:2–3	222n7	12:21–25	232n1	16:4	233n9		
11:2–4	226n10	12:21–26	134	16:29–30	213n19		
11:3	57	12:21–31	233n8	16:29–19:21	195		
11:9	34	12:22–23	138	16:32–34	245–46n53		
11:11–13	36	12:26–27	139	16:34	61, 223n9		
11:14	37, 92, 215n6	12:29–30	234n34	17	21, 94		
11:14–22	28	12:30–31	93, 138, 140, 150–52	17:1	165, 178, 214n16, 222n31, 236n5, 240n54		
11:14–25	228–29n5						
11:23	37, 92, 215n6	12:30–13:34	118, 155				
11:26–27	236n47	12:31	235n35	17:1–24	160–61		
11:26–40	29, 51, 136, 141, 143, 228n5	12:32–33	235n37	17:1–19:21	21, 161–62		
		12:32–13:10	134–35	17:2–24	175–77		
11:26–14:18	20, 135–36	13	39, 242n15	17:3	229n6, 239n47		
11:27	232n6	13:1	139, 235n43	17:5–7	63		
11:28	137, 139	13:1–10	20, 29, 136–37	17:6	171		
11:29	78, 140, 147	13:2	139, 224n25	17:8–16	105, 179		
11:30–32	78, 147	13:2–6	93	17:9	167–68, 238n22		
11:31–39	119, 156–57	13:3	104, 153	17:14	168		
11:35	236n50	13:5	153	17:17–24	51, 63, 169, 171		
11:41	235n40, 245n51	13:6	224n24	17:18	240n58		
11:41–43	104, 152–53, 232n7	13:7	139–40	17:18–24	119, 180–81		
		13:11	139, 141	17:19a	240n57		
12	104	13:11–19	63, 145	17:20–21	166		
12:1	232n5	13:11–32	29, 51, 78, 138–39, 144–45, 147–48, 152, 187	17:21–22	240n60		
12:1–16	29, 137			17:22	240n50, 240n55		
12:1–20	29, 93, 118, 137, 148–50, 155			17:23d	240n57		
		13:14	233n22	18:1	237n6, 237n7		
12:2–3	214n14	13:17	233–34n22	18:1–6	20–21, 160		
12:3–16	51, 143–44	13:18	141, 213n17	18:2a	236n2		
12:4	234n26, 234n27, 234n28	13:19	233n22	18:3	240n56		
		13:27–30	63	18:3–6	29, 162–63		
12:6–19	138	13:28	122, 145	18:3–16	165		
12:7	118–19, 139, 155–56, 236n49	13:32b	235n39	18:3b–4	94, 105, 177–79		
		13:33	235n35, 235n36	18:4	168, 237n17, 240n53		
12:8	140, 233n10	13:33–34	93, 138, 140, 150–52, 235n42				
12:9	234n28			18:4–5	240n52		
12:9–10	234n26, 234n27	14:1–3	63, 146	18:5	236n1		
12:10b–11	139	14:1–5	233n21	18:6	79, 174, 239n43		
12:12	214n14	14:1–18	29, 51, 143	18:7–16	29, 163		
12:13b	140	14:1–20	139	18:7b	237n12		
12:14	139	14:5	78, 146	18:8	79, 174, 237n15, 239n42		
12:15	104, 138, 153–55, 189	14:5–6	217n21				
		14:10–11	246n55	18:9–14	119, 167, 181–82		
12:15–16	234n33	14:11	137				
12:16–19	63, 146–47	14:19	235n40, 235n42	18:10	168		
12:18	140	14:19–20	104, 152–53	18:12	240n56		
12:18b	233n17	14:21	111	18:12–13	241n67		
12:19	154–55, 236n47	14:29–31	111	18:12–14	240n52		
12:20	214n14, 232n5, 233n11	15:21–16:29	188	18:12b–13	94, 105, 177–79		
		15:24	31, 242n16				

254 Scripture Index

1 Kings (*continued*)

Ref	Pages	Ref	Pages	Ref	Pages
18:13	239n35, 240n53	20:1	190, 192, 200	21:4a	241n8
18:16	174	20:1–11	21, 184	21:5–7	205
18:17	167, 236n2, 238n27	20:1–12	52, 193–94	21:8–13	94–95, 203–4
		20:1–34	103–4, 198, 227n25	21:9	192, 245n50
				21:10	192–93
18:17–20	237n6	20:1–43	22	21:11	245n49
18:18b–20	237n8	20:2–3	241n2	21:13	195–96, 245n50
18:19	240n51	20:3	94, 200, 245n43	21:17–19	246n60
18:19–20	94, 177	20:4	190, 200	21:17–29	22, 186
18:21	237n13	20:5	94, 200, 243n23, 245n43	21:19	241n6, 242n12, 244n36
18:21–40	29–30, 51–52, 105, 164–65, 169–70, 187, 237n9	20:7	200–201, 243n23	21:19–25	206
		20:7–8	191, 235n45	21:19b	196–97
		20:9	190, 200	21:20b–26	242n9
18:22	177, 240n53	20:11	243n30	21:21	246n57
18:24	237n13	20:12	190	21:21–24	187, 246n55
18:26	237n13	20:12–34	184–85	21:23	246n60
18:26–35	63–64, 172	20:14	197, 244n40	21:23–24	105, 206–7, 246n58
18:27–28	239n38	20:15–21	64, 197		
18:29	237n14	20:16	190, 191	21:24	233n9
18:31b	179	20:17	244n38	21:24a	196
18:36–37	166	20:18	190–91, 244n39	21:25–26	52, 105, 195, 205
18:38	122	20:20a	119, 207		
18:40	236n1	20:23	193, 243n26	21:29	197, 242n12
18:41–42	94, 177, 225n26	20:26	192	22	31, 188–90, 199
		20:31	243n27	22:1	186
18:42	166	20:31–34	193	22:1–12	30, 187–88
18:45	236n2	20:32b	119, 207	22:1–38	22, 185
19:1	78, 237n10, 239n39	20:33	192	22:2–4	242n13
		20:33–43	207	22:3	186
19:1–2	167	20:33a	192	22:5–28	30, 187
19:1–8	52, 170	20:33b–34	74–75	22:8	190–91, 199
19:1–18	163–64, 172–74	20:34	186, 221n26, 221n27	22:9–12	64
19:2–18	29			22:10	190, 196, 244n35
19:3–4	79	20:35	242n15		
19:4	166	20:35–36	30, 187, 198	22:13–16	80, 199
19:5–7	52, 170–71	20:35–43	52, 103–4, 189, 194–95, 227n26, 228n28	22:13–23	187
19:7	239n40			22:14	191
19:9	178			22:15–28	30, 187–88
19:9–18	119, 181	20:36	204	22:19	196, 244n42
19:10	79, 94, 166, 178, 239n36, 240n53	20:38b–43	21, 184	22:19–23	193, 199
		20:40	243n31	22:23	191
		20:42	79, 198–99, 241n5	22:24	80, 190, 199–200
19:11a	241n64	20:43	190, 241–42n8		
19:12	79, 174–75, 178	21:1	190, 196	22:29–36	64, 196
19:13	178	21:1–4	246n62	22:30–34	244n35
19:13–14	240n53	21:1–16	22, 30, 120, 185–87, 201–2, 205–8, 246n60	22:32	40, 190
19:14	79, 94, 166, 178			22:34	80, 200, 244n33
19:15–16	214n15, 241n64				
19:18	63, 172	21:2	191	22:38	64, 122, 196–97, 242n12
19:19	168, 238n24	21:2–3	94		
19:21	168, 238n24	21:4	190, 195, 202, 245n46	22:38b	241n5, 241n6
20	189, 195			22:39	245n51, 245n53

22:39–40	105, 204–5, 213n19	9:25–26	197	**Isaiah**		
		23:15–16	232n3	6:1	73, 244n35	
22:41–46 (= Hebrew 22:41–47)	242n17	23:15–20	138–39	**Jeremiah**		
		23:19	235n39	32:18	242n11	
22:47–50 (= Hebrew 22:48–51)	242n17	23:19–20	93, 152			
		23:20	224n25	**NEW TESTAMENT**		
2 Kings		25:27–30	139			
1	26	**Job**		**Luke**		
1:3	190	2	215n6	10:30–35	216n13	
1:10	86	**Psalms**		**John**		
4:38–44	168	1:1	229n7	11:50–52	73	
6:24–7:2	219n20	68:4 (= Hebrew 68:5)	238n21	12:32–33	73	
6:24–7:20	168					
6:26–29	55	103:8	242n11	**Hebrews**		
7:8	55	103:17–18	242n11	4:12	129	
9:24–26	242n12					

Subject Index

Abiathar, 17, 18, 84, 88, 100, 110, 154, 212–13n15, 213n8, 219n11, 226n11
Abijah, 29, 137, 139
Abishag
    Adonijah's request for, 46, 68, 89–91, 110, 216n5
    Bathsheba and, 25, 26, 28, 50, 83
    beauty of, 25, 28, 29, 49–50, 83, 92, 213n6, 218n9, 224n21
    David and, 14, 25, 26, 28, 49–50, 73, 83, 113, 169, 212n5, 213n6, 216n5
    partisan of Adonijah, 92
    as virgin, 14, 216n5, 224n21
Abraham and Isaac story, 45, 210n4
Absalom, 34–35, 38, 57, 68, 77, 92, 222n4
Adam and Eve, 54, 216n2
Adonijah
    Abishag and, 46, 68, 216n5
    Absalom compared with, 34–35, 38, 57, 68, 77, 92, 222n4
    Bathsheba on, 38
    David's successor and, 16–18, 25, 38, 48–49, 57, 68, 73–74, 77, 100, 112
    death sentence against, 25
    En-rogel gathering of, 26, 47, 48–49, 74, 88–89, 113, 217n14, 217n18, 223n14, 224nn16–17
    execution of, 84, 93, 110, 216n5, 229n5
    as handsome, 34–35, 57, 98, 222n4
    number of references to, 25, 27
    purported conspiracy of, 35, 38, 73–74, 77, 88, 89, 224n20
    request for Abishag by, 46, 48, 68, 86, 89–91, 110, 216nn5–6, 217n16, 223nn10–11
    Solomon's judgment of, 28
    thoughts versus speech of, 215n4
Adoram, 137, 141, 233n17
Agag, 198
Ahab
    Aramean wars and, 21, 22, 40, 184–85, 189, 193–97, 200, 213n18, 244n40
    Ben-hadad and, 21, 22, 74–75, 79, 94, 103–4, 119, 184–86, 190–95, 200, 207, 241nn2–3
    building projects by, 245–46n53
    conversation between Naboth and, 94, 201–2
    description of, 190
    disguise of, 190, 244n33, 244n35
    drought and famine during reign of, 160, 161–62, 167, 238n27
    elders' advice to, 184, 191, 193, 200, 234n45
    Elijah and, 79, 161, 162, 167, 168, 174, 175, 177, 206, 213n18, 239n42, 244n36
    family of, 197, 200–201, 242n12
    fatal wounding and death of, 80, 185, 187, 189, 190, 193, 196–97, 200, 241n5, 242n12, 244nn33–34
    idolatry by, 167, 173, 205–6, 244n41, 246n53
    Jehoshaphat and, 188–89, 199
    Jezebel and, 78, 167, 170, 172–73, 192–93, 201–3, 207–8, 239n39
    Jezebel writing letters in Ahab's name, 192
    as main character, 30, 186–87
    Micaiah and, 185, 189, 191, 193, 196, 199
    Naboth's murder and, 185, 186, 204, 205–6, 208
    Naboth's vineyard and, 185–87, 191, 201–3, 207–8, 241–42nn7–8, 245n47
    negative attitudes toward, 103–4, 195, 205–7, 227n25, 228n28
    Obadiah and, 29, 79, 160, 162–63, 165, 168, 174, 181–82, 236n1, 237n15, 239n42, 240n52, 241n67
    positive attitudes toward, 103–4, 191, 200–201, 243n23
    prophetic condemnations of, 185, 187, 194–97, 198, 205–7, 244n36, 246n55, 246nn57–59
    and prophet's demand for Ben-hadad's death, 79, 103, 104, 198–99
    regalia of, 196, 244n35
    reign of, 103–4, 227n25, 246n54
    unnamed prophets and, 21, 22, 30, 79–80, 184, 187, 189, 194, 199
    wealth of, 200–201
    Yhwh's relationship with, 103–4, 173, 195, 198, 238n27
    See also Ahab story
Ahab story
    ambiguities in, 74, 79–80, 198–200

characterization in, 40–41, 190–93, 215n8
characters in, 30–31, 186–90
flashback in, 64, 196–97
gaps in, 79–80, 198–200
group characters in, 30, 188
internal monologue in, 215n8
main characters of, 30, 186–87
narrator in, 103–5, 195, 204–7
plot in, 21–22, 184–86
point of view in, 52, 193–95
questions on, 21–22, 30–31, 40–41, 52, 64, 79–80, 94–95, 105, 119–20
repetition and variation in, 93–94, 200–204
simultaneity in, 64
structure and symmetry in, 119–20, 207–8
tension in, 21–22, 184–86, 213n19
time manipulation in, 64, 196–97
See also Ahab; Ben-hadad, King; Jehoshaphat; Jezebel; Micaiah; Naboth

Ahijah
condemnation of Jeroboam by, 137
Jereboam's wife and, 78, 139, 146, 147, 217n21, 233n21
and Jeroboam's succession to Solomon's throne, 142, 143, 146, 147, 228n5
as main character, 29
monologues and speeches by, 20, 51, 135, 136–37, 143
on separation of ten tribes from house of David, 155
as Shilonite, 141
tearing of cloak by, 141, 147
allusion, 91–92
Alter, Robert, 222n1
alternating repetition, 115–17
ambiguities
in Ahab story, 74, 79–80, 198–200
definition of, 70
in Elijah story, 78–79, 172–75
Empson on, 220n12
in Jeroboam story, 78, 147–48
seeing double and, 76
semantic ambiguities, 71–74
in Solomon story, 72–77
syntactic ambiguities, 74–76
translation and, 70–71
working of, as narrative device, 76–77
Amnon, 72, 77
analepsis. *See* flashback
analogy, 91–92
angle of point of view, 44–46
apostrophe, 137
Aramean wars, 21, 22, 40, 184–85, 189, 193–97, 201, 213n18, 244n40
arcs of tension. *See* tension
Aristotle, 13–14
ark of the covenant, 55, 61, 100, 114–15. *See also* temple of Solomon
Asa, 31

asymmetry, 117–18. *See also* structure and symmetry
Auerbach, Eric, 210n4
author
implied versus real author, 6, 8, 9, 124, 125, 204, 210–11nn9–10, 215n3, 225n8, 231–32n10
narrator distinguished from, 100–102

Baal, 168, 169, 172, 173, 237n13, 238n21, 238n22, 239n38, 244n41
Baal prophets
Ahab's report to Jezebel on slaughter of, 78, 167, 170, 172–73, 239n39
contest between Elijah and, 51–52, 161, 162, 164, 167, 169–70, 172
Elijah on, 239n38
slaughter of, 164, 165, 167, 170, 172–73, 239n39
tempo of passages on, 63–64
Barth, Karl, 233n13
Barzillai's sons, 212n13
Bathsheba
Abishag and, 25, 26, 28, 50, 83
on Adonijah's gathering at En-rogel, 88–89, 223n14
and Adonijah's purported conspiracy, 38, 77, 88, 89
and Adonijah's request for Abishag, 46, 48, 68, 86, 89–91, 216nn5–6, 217n16, 223nn10–11
beauty of, 92, 213n6, 217n19, 218n9, 224n21
and conspiracy with Nathan for Solomon's kingship, 18, 25, 26, 35, 48, 59, 66–67, 74, 76–77, 86, 110, 113, 217n17
and David in his old age, 18, 25, 26, 35, 50, 72, 83, 85–89, 116, 217n17
David's desire for and adultery with, 25, 77, 86, 217n19, 221n21
and David's oath to put Solomon on throne, 25, 48, 59, 66–67, 79, 89, 228n29
language abilities of, 215n7
murder of husband of, 67–68, 77, 86
as Solomon's mother and queen mother, 25, 34, 38, 90
Benaiah, 26, 28, 85, 87, 92, 110
Ben-hadad, King
Ahab's relationship with, 22, 74–75, 185, 190, 192, 200, 207, 241nn2–3
Aramean wars and, 21, 22, 40, 184–85, 193–97, 200
description of, 190
drunkenness of, 190–91, 197, 244nn38–39
message of, to Ahab, 94, 119
peace treaty between Ahab and, 185, 186
Yhwh's intention toward, 79–80, 103, 104, 198–99, 207
Berlin, Adele, 44

Subject Index

Bethel prophet, 78, 135, 136, 138, 139, 142, 144–48, 152, 213n17, 233n22
Bible
    chapter and verse numbers in, 108, 228n3
    English translations of, 70–71, 211n11, 231n5, 243n26
    feminist criticism of, 4, 216n12
    form criticism of, 3
    historical criticism of, xii, 3–6, 209n1, 227n24, 227n26, 237n8, 244n37, 245n52, 246n57
    historicity of, 123, 231nn7–9
    ideological criticism of, 4–5
    literary criticism of, 210n3, 211n1
    narrative criticism of generally, xi–xii, 209n2
    Pentateuch in, 6, 227n24
    precritical interpretation of, 6, 209n1
    redaction criticism of, 3
    scenic style of, 124
    Septuagint and, 21
    source criticism of, 3, 210n3
    textual criticism of, 3
    translation of ambiguities in, 70–71
    See also Ahab story; Elijah story; Hebrew language and style; Jeroboam story; Solomon story; *and specific books of the Bible*
Black Beauty (Sewell), 226n13
breaking frame, 99–100, 104, 154–55, 179, 225n2, 236n46
Breuil, R., 239n41
Briggs, Richard S., 211n10

Caiaphas, 73
Calvino, Italo, xi
characterization
    in Ahab story, 40–41, 190–93, 215n8
    definition of, 33, 43
    direct showing technique of, 34, 35–37
    in Elijah story, 39–40, 165–69
    indirect showing technique of, 34, 37–39
    in Jeroboam story, 39, 139–43
    questions on, for exploring stories, 39–41
    in Solomon story, 33–39
    techniques of, 33–39
    telling technique of, 34–35
    See also characters; *and specific biblical characters*
characters
    of Ahab story, 30–31, 186–90
    anomalies in portrayal of, 27–28
    avoiding clutter regarding, 26–27
    description of, 57, 66
    in detective story, 27
    of Elijah story, 29–30, 162–65
    "flat" and "round" characters, 24, 213nn3–4
    Forster on, 24, 213n3
    group characters, 25, 26, 29–30, 118, 137, 164–65, 188
    indicators of importance of, 24
    internal monologues of, 35–36, 139–40, 215n8
    involved point of view and, 46
    of Jeroboam story, 28–29, 136–39
    monologues of, 20, 213n16
    narrator's repetition of, 85–87
    overdeveloped secondary character, 27, 28, 138
    point of view of, 46, 49–50
    prayer by generally, 36
    questions on, for exploring stories, 28–31
    reliability of, 87
    repetition of narrator by, 87–89
    secondary belief regarding, 23
    of Solomon story, 25–28
    thoughts of, 35–36, 215n4
    types of, 24–28
    underdeveloped main character, 27–28
    See also characterization; *and specific biblical characters*
Christianity, 127–28
Chronicles, Books of, 231n9
command and compliance/noncompliance, 18–19
communication, 2–3, 6. *See also* meanings
continuity, gaps of, 68–70
criticism
    definition of, 209n4
    See also historical criticism; literary criticism; narrative criticism
crucifixion of Jesus, 73

David, King
    Abishag and, 14, 25, 26, 28, 49–50, 73, 113, 169, 212n5, 213n6, 216n5
    Absalom's rebellion against, 38, 57, 68, 77
    Adonijah's purported conspiracy against, 35, 38, 73–74, 77, 88, 89, 224n20
    on anointing of Solomon, 87, 111–12
    Bathsheba and, 18, 25, 26, 28, 34, 35, 38, 48, 50, 76–77, 86–89, 116
    courtiers of, 38–39
    and Court Succession story, 77
    death of, 25, 114
    and desire for and adultery with Bathsheba, 25, 77, 217n19, 224n21
    Deuteronomistic theology and, 69–70
    dying advice and requests of, to Solomon, 16–18, 67, 69–70, 114, 212n13, 222n6
    failing health of, 14, 16, 17, 25, 38–39
    flight of, to Gath, 230n29
    God's relationship with, 37
    and murder of Uriah, 67–68, 77, 86
    Nathan and, 110, 116
    oath of, to put Solomon on throne, 25, 48, 59, 66–67, 79, 89, 228n29
    old age of, 14, 16–18, 25, 34, 35, 38–39, 50, 73, 83, 86–87, 92, 98, 217n20

sexual potency of, 14, 73, 113
successor of, 16–18, 59, 67, 72, 91, 100, 220n5
deconstruction, 210n5
detective story, 27
Deuteronomy, Book of
David and theology of, 69–70
Moses' dying in, 212n12
prophet's credentials, 190
requirements of covenant in, 220n9
on self-mutilation, 239n38
transgenerational reward and punishment in, 242n11
on wealth of kings, 58
dialogue, 18, 55–56
direct showing, 34, 35–37
disciples of Jesus, 213n9
distance and point of view, 47
drought and famine, 160, 161–62, 167, 238n27

echo, 92–93
eisegesis, 125
Elijah
Ahab and, 79, 161, 162, 167, 168, 174, 175, 177, 206, 213n18, 239n42
Ahab's murder of Naboth and, 186, 196–97
background information on, 214n16
complaints by, 79, 94
condemnation of Ahab's household and lineage by, 205–7, 244n36, 246nn57–59
contest between prophets of Baal and, 51–52, 161, 162, 164, 167, 169–70, 172
description of, 165–66, 236–37n5
flight of, to Horeb, 162–63, 166, 170, 173–74
identity of, 161, 165, 171, 179
Jezebel's threats against, 162, 166, 170, 173
messenger/angel from Yhwh to, 163–64, 170–71, 239n40
miraculous healing by, 160, 166, 169, 171, 180–81, 240n60
Obadiah and, 79, 161, 163, 167, 174, 177, 181–82, 237n15, 239n35
obedience of, to Yhwh, 160–63, 172, 174–77, 179, 186, 236n2, 240n62
prayers by, 40, 166–67, 169, 171, 176–77, 180–81, 240n50, 240n55
prophetic credentials of, 179, 214n16
rainfall and, 161–62, 172, 237n7
resignation of prophetic office considered by, 173–74, 175, 181, 240n53
resistance of, to Yhwh, 240–41n62
in Second Book of Kings, 86
theophany of, on Mount Horeb, 79, 162, 164–65, 174–75, 176
widow of Zarephath and, 165, 167–68, 176, 238n22
See also Elijah story

Elijah story
ambiguities in, 78–79, 172–75
breaking frame in, 179
characterization in, 39–40, 165–69
characters in, 29–30, 162–65
characters named but not appearing in, 214n15
dialogue in, 63
flashback in, 63, 168, 179
gaps in, 78–79, 172–75
group characters in, 29–30, 164–65
main characters of, 29
major units of, 161–62
narrator in, 104–5, 179
oxymoron in, 79, 222n33
plot in, 20–21, 160–62
point of view in, 51–52, 169–71
questions on, 20–21, 29–30, 39–40, 51–52, 63–64, 78–79, 94, 104–5, 119
repetition and variation in, 93, 175–78
structure and symmetry in, 119, 180–82
tension in, 20–21, 160–62
time manipulation in, 63–64, 171–72
See also Ahab; Elijah; Jezebel; Obadiah
Eli of Shiloh, 62, 100, 141, 197, 219n11
Elisha, 55, 168–69, 214n15, 238n24
Elkanah, 62
Empson, William, 220n12
Ephraim, 233n20
Ethbaal, 168
Eve and Adam, 54, 216n2
exegesis, 125
Exodus, Book of, 176, 177, 238n33, 242n11

fabula, 218n10
fact, gaps of, 66–67
famine. *See* drought and famine
feminist criticism, 4, 216n12
first-person narrator, 98, 99, 225n1, 225n5, 226–27n21
flashback, 58–59, 63, 64, 68, 146, 168, 179, 196–97
foreshadowing, 59–62, 146–47, 219n19
form criticism, 3
Forster, E. M., 24, 210n8, 213n3
forward symmetries, 114–15, 181, 229–30n20
frame break. *See* breaking frame

Galen, 212n4
gaps
in Ahab story, 79–80, 198–200
of continuity, 68–70
in Elijah story, 78–79, 172–75
of fact, 66–67
in Jeroboam story, 78, 147–48
of motivation, 67–68
physical descriptions of characters, 57, 66
seeing double and, 76
in Solomon story, 66–70, 76–77
working of, as narrative device, 76–77

Subject Index

Genesis, Book of
  Abraham and Isaac in, 45, 210n4
  Adam and Eve in, 54, 216n2
  creation in, 227n24
  "flat" characters in, 24
  Jacob in, 179, 212n12
  Joseph story in, 230n20, 233n20
  Noah's ark in, 227n24
  precreational chaos in, 175
  talking snake in, 123
God
  in Abraham and Isaac story, 45
  Ahab's relationship with, 103–4, 173, 195, 198, 238n27
  benevolence of, 238n26
  Ben-hadad's fate and, 79–80, 103, 104, 198–99, 207
  as character, and characterization of, 34–37, 57, 61, 163, 215n3, 216n2, 243n28
  David and, 37, 61
  disobedience of man of God against, 135, 138, 142, 145, 148, 233–34n22
  Elijah's obedience to, 160–63, 172, 174–77, 179, 186, 236n2, 240n62
  Elijah's prayers to, 40, 166–67, 169, 171, 176–77, 180–81, 240n50, 240n55
  Elijah's resistance to, 240–41n62
  Elijah's theophany on Mount Horeb, 79, 162, 164–65, 174–75, 176, 181
  falsehood of prophets and, 79–80, 103, 104, 193, 198–200, 243n28, 244–45n42
  and food for Israelites in Exodus, 238n33
  foreshadowing by, 61
  Job and, 37, 215n6
  Moses' theophany at Horeb/Sinai, 176, 177
  prayer to generally, 36
  punishment of Ahab by, for Naboth's murder, 186
  sacrifices to, by Solomon, 61, 109
  in Solomon story, 34–37, 57, 61
  in temple of Solomon, 73, 125, 232n12
  word of Yhwh, 129, 137, 179, 242n15, 244–45n42
  words and deeds of, 36–37
Good Samaritan parable, 216–17n13
Gray, John, 220n8
Green, Barbara, 227n22
group characters, 25, 26, 29–30, 118, 137, 164–65, 188. *See also* characters

Hadad the Edomite, 28, 92
Hannah, 62, 197
Hazael, 214n15
healing
  by Elijah, 160, 166, 169, 171, 180–81, 240n60
  of Jeroboam by man of God, 93, 134, 136, 140–42

Hebrew language and style
  characterization in, 36
  description of characters in, 57, 66
  of First Book of Kings, 8, 213n18
  forward symmetry in Hebrew poetry, 229n20
  inclusion and, 229n9, 229n11
  laconic nature of Hebrew narrative prose, 82
  markers of direct discourse not found in, 105
  meaningful verbal signals of structure in text, 228nn1–2, 228n4
  narrator remaining in background, 60, 104–5
  omission of written vowels in, 229n18
  parallelism in Hebrew poetry, 229n7
  point of view in, 49
  puns in, 72
  resumptive repetition in, 234n32
  scenic style, 124
  semantic ambiguities in, 71–74
  strict repetition and, 82, 83
  syntactic ambiguities in, 74–76
  tension in, 14
  time manipulation in, 54, 56
Hebrews, Letter to, 129
Hiram of Tyre, 34, 36, 58–59, 68–69, 92, 101–2, 109, 215n5, 219n13, 220n7, 226n17
historical criticism, xii, 3–6, 209n1, 227n24, 227n26, 237n8, 244n37, 245n52, 246n57

ideological criticism, 4–5
idolatry, 137, 151, 157, 205–6, 235n37, 246n53. *See also* Baal; Baal prophets
impersonal narrator, 98
implied author, 6, 8, 9, 124, 125, 204, 210–11nn9–10, 215n3, 225n8, 231–32n10
implied reader, 6, 8–9, 122–24, 171, 215n3, 225n8, 230n2, 231nn5–6
inclusion, 109–11
indirect showing, 34, 37–39
internal monologues, 35–36, 139–40, 215n8
involved point of view, 46
irony, 148, 155, 166, 168, 190, 215n5, 226nn14–15, 230n29, 232n5, 232n10
Isaac and Abraham story, 45, 210n4
Israel-Judah division, 138–39, 146–47, 188, 234n23, 234n29, 236n48

Jacob, 170, 179, 212n12, 233n20
Jehoiachin, 139
Jehoshaphat, 22, 30–31, 185, 187–90, 196, 199, 242n13, 242nn16–17, 244n33
Jehu, 197, 214n15, 242n12
Jeremiah, 242n11
Jeroboam
  Ahijah and succession of, to Solomon's throne, 137, 142, 143, 146, 228n5
  altar of, 20, 137, 140–42, 153, 232n2, 235n43

attempted rebellion by, 135, 136, 143, 147, 232n6, 236n47
changes in, 136–37
cult of golden calves and, 137, 151, 235n37
description of, 139, 143
escape of, to Egypt, 28, 135, 136
healing of, 93, 134, 136, 140–42
internal monologue of, 139–40
intransigence of, 151
kingship of, 20, 134, 137, 140, 142, 146–47, 153–57, 236n52
religious innovations instituted by, 135–36
silence of, 143
wife of, 29, 139, 143, 146, 147, 217n21, 233n21
See also Jeroboam story
Jeroboam story
  ambiguities in, 78, 147–48
  breaking frame in, 154–55, 236n46
  characterization in, 39, 139–43
  characters in, 28–29, 136–39
  flashback in, 63, 146
  foreshadowing in, 63, 146–47
  gaps in, 78, 147–48
  group characters in, 29, 118, 137
  internal monologue in, 139–40
  lion and donkey in, 122, 144–46, 152, 187, 204–5
  main characters of, 28–29, 136–37
  monologues in, 20
  narrator in, 104, 152–55
  plot in, 20, 134–36
  point of view in, 51, 143–45
  questions on, 20, 28–29, 39, 51, 63, 78, 93, 104, 118–19
  repetition and variation in, 93, 134, 148–52
  scenes in, 20
  structure and symmetry in, 118–19, 155–57
  tension in, 20, 134–36
  textual problem in, 214n14, 234–35n34
  time manipulation in, 63, 145–47
  See also Ahijah; Bethel prophet; man of God (Jeroboam story); Rehoboam; *and other specific characters*
Jeroboam's wife, 29, 139, 143, 146, 147, 217n21, 233n21
Jerusalem, destruction of, 61
Jesus, 73, 213n9
Jezebel
  Ahab's report to, on slaughter of Baal prophets, 78, 167, 170, 172–73, 239n39
  condemnation of, 205–7, 246n57, 246n60
  hirelings of, as scoundrels, 192–93, 195, 203–4, 245n50
  letters written by, in Ahab's name, 192, 243n24
  as main character, 186–87
  Naboth's vineyard and, 185–87, 192–93, 201–3, 207–8, 245n47
  narrator's negative attitude toward, 105
  plot by, against Naboth and his murder, 94–95, 185–87, 192–93, 203–5, 207–8, 245n45
  pogrom by, against Yahwist prophets, 163, 165, 178, 239n42, 240n52
  threats against Elijah by, 52, 162, 166, 170, 173
Joab
  Adonijah's gathering and, 47, 49, 88
  Benaiah as counterbalance to, 92
  characterization of, 25–26
  David's instructions for execution of, 16, 70, 213n16
  execution of, 16–18, 84, 93, 110, 213n16, 229n5
  murder committed by, 224n23
  story of, 212–13n15
Job, 37, 215n6, 224n22
John, Gospel of, 73
Jonadab, 72
Jonathan, 25, 26, 47–49, 112, 217n18
Joram, 242n12
Joseph story, 230n20, 233n20
Joshua, Book of, 61, 169, 223n9, 238n28
Josiah, 93, 232n3
Joyce, James, 218n1
Judah, 138–39, 146–47, 188, 234n23, 234n29, 236n48
Judaism, 127–28
Judges, Book of, 61, 235n36

Keegan, Terence J., 6, 210n6
Kings, First Book of
  ancient Hebrew as language of, 8
  English translations of, 211n11
  Greek versus Hebrew versions of, 213n18
  narrative criticism of generally, 10–11
  source documents for, 235nn40–41, 245nn51–52
  See also Ahab story; Elijah story; Jeroboam story; Solomon story
Kings, Second Book of
  on Ahab as king of Samaria, 190
  Aramean war in, 55
  Bethel prophet and, 152
  death of Ahab's son in, 197
  Elijah in, 86
  Elisha in, 55
  group characters in, 26
  Jehu in, 197
  Josiah in, 93, 232n3
  lepers in, 55
  prophecy in, 138, 152, 219n20
  source documents for, 235nn40–41, 245nn51–52

leitmotiv, 91
leitwort, 91

Leviticus, Book of, 239n38
liberation model. *See* ideological criticism
liberation theology, 5
limited narrator, 230n2, 231–32n10
linearity
   definition of, 15
   simultaneity and, 62, 64
   in Solomon story, 15–18
literary criticism, 4–9, 126–30, 210n3, 211n1. *See also* narrative criticism
Long, Jesse C., Jr., 242n10
Luke, Gospel of, 216–17n13

Manasseh, 233n20
manipulation of time. *See* time manipulation
man of God (Jeroboam story)
   Bethel prophet and, 135, 142, 144, 145, 147–48, 213n17
   characterization of, 139
   condemnation of Jeroboam's altar by, 20, 136, 137, 140–42, 153
   counterbalance between Jeroboam and, 136–37
   death and burial of, 136, 138, 139, 144, 147–48, 152
   disobedience of, 135, 138, 142, 145, 148, 233–34n22
   as foreigner in Bethel, 232n1
   healing of Jeroboam by, 93, 134, 136, 140–42
   Jeroboam's invitation to, 134–37, 140–41
   prophecy of, 134, 136, 138, 152, 153
   prophetic credentials of, 93
meanings
   authorial meaning, 102
   decoding the text for, 209n2
   historical criticism and, 3–5
   ideological criticism and, 4–5
   implied reader and, 124
   literary criticism and, 4–5, 209–10n2
   point of view and, 43–44
   reader-response criticism and, 210n2
   sample parable on, 1–3
   within communication, 2–3
Melville, Herman, 97–98, 100, 226n12
Mesha, 242n14
Micah, 189, 242–43nn18–19
Micaiah
   Ahab's death predicted by, 185, 193, 244n33, 244–45n42
   Ahab's hostility toward, 189, 191
   false prophecy by, 80
   on heavenly vision, 196, 244n35
   incarceration of, 185
   meaning of name, 242n18
   prophetic credentials of, 189–91, 199–200
   questions on, 31, 80
   as tool in narrative, 189
   visions of, 189
   Zedekiah and, 187–88, 199–200
miracles, 122, 123–24. *See also* healing
Moby-Dick (Melville), 97–98, 100, 226n12
monologues, 20, 213n16
Moses, 6, 169, 171, 176, 177, 212n12, 238n33
motivation, gaps of, 67–68
movies, 44, 48, 62
multiple narrative voices, 102–4, 226–27n21, 227n24

Naboth
   conversation between Ahab and, 94, 201–2
   description of, 190
   Jezebel's plot against, 94–95, 185–87, 192–93, 203–5, 207–8, 245n45
   as main character, 186–87
   murder of, 185, 186, 204–5, 208
   vineyard of, 21, 22, 120, 185–87, 191, 201–3, 207–8, 241–42nn7–8, 245n47
Nadab, 139, 233n8
narratees, 7, 9, 97–98, 99–100, 102, 122, 123, 124, 146–47, 153, 154, 170, 171, 179, 199, 207
narrative
   definition of, 7
   diagram of, 6
   of movies, 44, 48, 62
   painting compared with, 15, 62
   readers and, 122–24
   of stage plays, 62
   time line of, versus story time, 53
narrative criticism
   characterization, 33–41
   characters, 23–31
   complexities of generally, 9
   definition of, xii
   gaps and ambiguities, 65–80
   narrative and, 6, 7
   narrator, 97–105
   plot and tension, 13–22
   point of view, 43–52
   principles of, xii–xiii
   readers as narrative critics, 126–27
   reader's responsibilities, 121–30
   repetition and variation, 81–95
   scholars' interest in, for biblical criticism, xi, 209n2
   story and, 6–7
   structure and symmetry, 107–20
   structure of narrative text, 6–9
   text and, 6, 8–9
   time manipulation, 53–64
   See also Ahab story; Elijah story; Jeroboam story; Solomon story
narrator
   of Ahab story, 103–5, 195, 204–7
   attitude of, 98–99, 225n6, 226n10
   author distinguished from, 100–102

in background in biblical narrative, 60, 104–5
breaking frame and, 99–100, 104, 154–55, 225n2, 236n46
character's repetition of, 87–89
of Elijah story, 104–5, 179
first-person narrator, 98, 99, 225n1, 225n5, 226–27n21
functions of, 99–100
impersonal narrator, 98
of Jeroboam story, 104, 152–55
multiple narrative voices, 102–4, 226–27n21, 227n24
narratee and, 99–100, 225nn7–8, 226n20
narrator's repetition of, 83–85
qualities of, 98–99
questions on, for exploring stories, 104–5
reliable narrator, 83, 98, 222n3, 225n3, 225n6, 240n56
repetition of character by, 85–87
of Solomon story, 98, 100–102
third-person narrator, 98, 101, 225n2
understanding manipulations of, 122, 230n1
unreliability of, 230n2, 231–32n10
as voice telling the story, 97–104
See also point of view

Nathan
on Adonijah's gathering at En-rogel, 88–89, 223n14, 224nn16–17, 224n20
and anointing of Solomon, 87, 113
characterization of, 34
and conspiracy with Bathsheba for Solomon's kingship, 18, 25, 26, 35, 48, 59, 66–67, 74, 76–77, 86, 110, 113, 217n17, 228n5
David and, 110, 116
and David's oath to put Solomon on throne, 25, 48, 59, 66–67, 89, 228n29

Noah, 227n24
Numbers, Book of, 123, 235n36, 242n11

Obadiah
Ahab and, 29, 79, 160, 162–63, 165, 168, 174, 181–82, 236n1, 237n15, 239n42, 241n67
characterization of, 94, 177–78
divided loyalties of, 160, 165, 167, 168, 174, 181–82
Elijah and, 79, 161, 163, 167, 174, 177, 181–82, 237n15, 239n35
fears of Ahab's retribution against, 181–82, 239n42, 240n52
as main character, 29
as overdeveloped secondary character, 30, 167
responsibilities of, in Ahab's palace, 165, 168, 237n17
speech of, 119, 163
Yahwist loyalties of, 105, 160, 165, 168, 174, 177–79, 237n9, 237n17, 239n35

omniscient narrator, 44–45, 99, 169
Omri, 242n14
order, and time manipulation, 58
organization. *See* structure and symmetry
oxymoron, 79, 175, 222n33, 239n44

painting, 15
Peninnah, 62
Pentateuch, 6, 227n24. *See also* Bible
Peter, 213
plot
of Ahab story, 21–22, 184–86
approach for exploring, 19
Aristotle on, 13–14
and Bible's chapter and verse numbers, 211–12n3
definition of, 7, 210n8
dynamics of, 13–19, 211nn1–2
of Elijah story, 20–21, 160–62
of Jeroboam story, 20, 134–36
linearity in, 15–18, 62
questions on, for exploring stories, 19–22
scenes in, 18–19
of Solomon story, 14–19
tension in, 14–19, 211n2
See also characters; story

point of view
in Ahab story, 52, 193–95
angle of, 44–46
camera's eye and, 44–47
of character, 46, 49–50
dialogue and, 48–49
distance and, 47–48
in Elijah story, 51–52, 169–71
establishment of, 47–50
Hebrew technique for, 49
involved point of view, 46
in Jeroboam story, 19–22, 143–45
meaning and, 43–44
neutral external perspective, 45–46
omniscient narrator, 44–45, 99, 169
questions on, for exploring stories, 50–52
and showing what reader can see and hear, 47–48
in Solomon story, 45–50
of stage play versus movie, 44, 48

Polzin, Robert, 227n22
Porten, Bezalel, 230n24
prayer
characterization and, 36
in Elijah story, 40, 166–67, 169, 171, 176–77, 180–81, 240n50, 240n55
repetition of, 85, 86, 223n9
preaching, 128–30
precritical biblical interpretation, 6, 209n1
presence. *See* point of view
priests in Jeroboam story, 151–52, 235nn36–37
prolepsis. *See* foreshadowing

prophets
- of Baal, 63–64, 161, 164–67, 169–70, 172, 239nn38–39
- on Ben-hadad's fate, 79–80, 103, 104, 198–99, 207
- Bethel prophet in Jeroboam story, 78, 135, 136, 138, 139, 142, 144–48, 152, 213n17, 233n22
- condemnation of Ahab and Jezebel by, 185, 187, 194–97, 198, 205–7, 244n36, 246n55, 246nn57–60
- contest between Elijah and prophets of Baal, 51–52, 161, 162, 164, 167, 169–70, 172
- falsehood of, 79–80, 103, 104, 193, 198–200, 244–45n42
- foreshadowing by, 61–62
- fulfillment/nonfulfillment and prophecy, 19
- Jezebel's pogrom against Yahwist prophets, 163, 165, 178, 239n42, 240n52
- lion attack against, 187, 194
- repetition of prophecy, 85, 86, 223n9
- sons of the prophet, 233n14
- unnamed prophets in Ahab story, 21, 22, 30, 79–80, 184, 187, 189, 194, 199
- *See also* Elijah; man of God (Jeroboam story); Micaiah; Nathan; *and other specific prophets*

Psalms, 229n7, 238n21, 242n11

Queen of Sheba. *See* Sheba, Queen of

rain, 161–62, 172, 237n7, 239n38
reader-response criticism, 4, 210n2
readers
- as believers, 127–28
- characterization and, 33–35, 37–38
- choice by, of beginning and ending of reading passage, 218–19n11
- emotional reactions of, to story, 33, 126, 231n4
- implied versus real readers, 6, 8–9, 122–24, 171, 215n3, 225n8, 230n2, 231nn5–6
- narrative and, 122–24
- as narrative critic, 126–27
- narrator and, 99–100, 225nn7–8, 226n20
- as preachers, 128–30
- reader-response criticism, 4, 210n2
- roles of, 121–30
- story and, 122, 230–31n3
- text and, 124–26

redaction criticism, 3
Rehoboam
- Adoram and, 141, 233n17
- and dissolution of Davidic kingdom, 20, 154, 155
- elders' and youngsters' advice to, 93, 118, 137, 140, 141, 143–44, 148–49, 155–56, 214n14, 233n10
- flight by, from Shechem to Jerusalem, 20, 233n17
- Israelite leaders and, 150
- military strategy of, 134, 136, 142–43
- reign of, 233n8
- rejection of, as king at Shechem, 93, 134–36, 140, 155, 214n14, 232–33n7
- tension between Jeroboam and, 138

reliability
- of characters, 87
- of narrator, 83, 98, 222n3, 225n3, 225n6, 240n56

repetition and variation
- in Ahab story, 93–94, 200–204
- alternating repetition, 115–17
- analogy and allusion, 91–92
- character repeating character, 89–91
- character repeating narrator, 87–89
- definition of, 81
- echo, 92–93
- in Elijah story, 93, 175–78
- in Jeroboam story, 93, 134, 148–52
- leitwort and leitmotiv, 91
- narrator repeating character, 85–87
- narrator repeating narrator, 83–85
- organization and, 108–9
- questions on, for exploring stories, 93–95
- resumptive repetition, 234n32
- strict repetition, 82–91
- translation of, 109

resumptive repetition, 234n32
reverse symmetries, 111–14, 180
Rezon of Damascus, 28, 92

Samuel, First Book of
- David's flight to Gath in, 230n29
- Eli of Shiloh in, 62, 100, 141, 197, 219n11
- Hannah in, 62, 197
- Samuel's condemnation of Saul in, 198
- Samuel's dying in, 212n12
- Saul's tearing of Samuel's cloak in, 141
- simultaneity in, 62

Samuel, Second Book of
- Absalom in, 34–35, 57, 68, 77, 92, 222n4
- Bathsheba in, 25, 86, 213n6, 217n19
- on Court Succession story, 77
- David's inheritance of Saul's harem in, 90
- David's procrastination in, 67
- David's reign in, 219n12
- foreshadowing by prophecy in, 61
- God's relationship with David in, 37, 61
- Joab in, 25–26
- Jonathan in, 26
- rape of Tamar in, 72, 77
- Shimei in, 220n11, 230n29

Saul, 90, 141, 198, 212n9, 230n29
scenes
- beginning and ending of, 18–19
- command and compliance/noncompliance in, 18–19
- dialogue in, 18

prophecy and fulfillment/nonfulfillment in, 19
scenic style, 124
secondary world of the story, 7, 23, 122, 210n7, 230–31n3
semantic ambiguities, 71–74
Septuagint, 21
Sewell, Anna, 226n13
Sheba, Queen of, 34, 56, 57, 60, 68–69, 109, 215n2, 219n14, 219n16
Shemaiah, 138, 142
Shimei
    David's instructions for execution of, 16, 18, 70, 213n16, 230n27
    David's unconditional pardon of, 220n11
    execution of, 15, 17, 18, 84, 93, 110, 112, 117, 213n16, 229n5
    journey to Gath by, 15, 112–13, 117, 230n29
    Solomon's commands to, and Shimei's obedience, 14–15, 55, 85, 116–17, 218n4, 230n26
    Solomon's perjury against, 116–17, 126
    tribal leader of, 212n9
Simon, Paul, 239n44
Ska, Jean Louis, 44
Solomon
    adversaries of, 28
    beginning of reign of, 16–18, 26, 47, 212n14
    brutal use of power and executions ordered by, 17, 18, 84–85, 93, 110, 226n11, 228–29n5
    building projects of, 60, 102, 219nn17–18
    conspiracy between Nathan and Bathsheba for succession of, to kingship, 18, 25, 26, 35, 48, 59, 66–67, 74, 76–77, 86, 110, 113, 217n17
    David's dying advice to, 16–18, 67, 69–70, 114, 212n13, 222n6
    David's oath to put Solomon on throne, 25, 48, 59, 66–67, 79, 89, 228n29
    death of, 233n7
    dream of, 45, 61, 109, 110
    foreign wives of, 114, 222n7
    Hiram of Tyre and, 34, 36, 58–59, 68–69, 92, 101–2, 109, 215n5, 219n13, 220n7, 226n17
    inauguration ritual and anointing of, 24, 47, 48, 55, 87, 89, 111–12, 113
    kingdom of, 59, 84–85, 92–93, 110–11
    and legal case over mother of baby, 15–16, 27, 34, 36, 46, 49, 50–51, 56, 75–76, 214n10, 216n10, 221nn28–29
    marriage of, to Pharaoh's daughter, 28, 59, 60, 214n11, 219n14, 219n16
    mother of, 25, 34, 38, 90
    sacrifices to Yhwh by, 61, 109
    temple of, 55, 56, 60, 61, 73, 100, 114–15, 125, 218n7, 219n17, 221n22, 232n2, 232nn11–12
    and the succession to David, 16–18, 59, 67, 72, 91, 100, 220n5
    as underdeveloped main character, 27–28
    wealth of, 57–58, 61, 68–69, 91, 226n17
    wisdom of, 57, 61, 69, 70, 72, 91, 101, 102, 152–53, 221nn19–20
    See also Solomon story
Solomon story
    ambiguities in, 72–77
    beginning and end of, 228n5
    characterization in, 33–39
    characters in, 25–28
    chiastic pattern of entire story, 229n14
    flashback in, 58–59, 68
    foreshadowing in, 60–61
    gaps in, 66–70, 76–77
    God as character in, 34–37, 57, 61
    group characters in, 26
    linearity in, 15–18
    minor character ("extras") in, 26
    monologues in, 213n16
    narrator in, 98, 100–102
    neutral external perspective in, 46
    omniscient point of view in, 45
    order in, 58–61
    plot of, 14–19
    point of view in, 45–50
    structure and symmetry in, 109–17
    tension in, 14–18, 56
    time manipulation in, 55–61
    See also Abiathar; Abishag; Adonijah; Bathsheba; David, King; Joab; Nathan; Sheba, Queen of; Shimei; Solomon
source criticism, 3, 210n3
space. *See* point of view
stage plays, 62
Sternberg, Meir, 219n19
story
    approach for exploring, 19
    definition of, 209n3
    diagram of, 6
    fabula versus, 218n10
    narrative and, 7
    plot compared with, 7, 210n8
    purposes of, xi
    readers and, 122, 230–31n3
    secondary world of, 7, 23, 122, 210n7, 230–31n3
    time line of, versus narration time, 53
    two separate communication acts in, 9
    world of, in narrative criticism, 6, 7
    See also Ahab story; characterization; characters; Elijah story; Jeroboam story; narrator; plot; readers; Solomon story
strict repetition, 82–91. *See also* repetition and variation

structure and symmetry
- in Ahab story, 119–20, 207–8
- alternating repetition, 115–17
- asymmetry, 117–18
- in Elijah story, 119, 180–82
- forward symmetries, 114–15, 181, 229–30n20
- inclusion, 109–11
- in Jeroboam story, 118–19, 155–57
- questions on, for exploring stories, 118–20
- repetition and organization, 108–9
- reverse symmetries, 111–14, 180
- in Solomon story, 109–17
- symmetrical structures, 111–17
- thematic units, 108–9

Style and Structure in Biblical Hebrew Narrative (Walsh), 228n2

symmetry. *See* structure and symmetry

Tamar, 72, 77
telling, 34–35
temple of Solomon, 55, 56, 60, 61, 73, 100, 114–15, 125, 218n7, 219n17, 221n22, 232n2, 232nn11–12. *See also* ark of the covenant
tempo, 53–58. *See also* time manipulation
tension
- in Ahab story, 21–22, 184–86, 213n19
- and Bible's chapter and verse numbers, 211–12n3
- definition of, 14
- dynamic of, 13–14, 211n2
- in Elijah story, 20–21, 160–62
- in Jeroboam story, 20, 134–36
- monologues and, 20, 213n16
- in Solomon story, 14–18, 56

text
- implied versus real authors of, 6, 8, 9, 124, 125, 210–11nn9–10, 215n3, 225n8
- implied versus real readers of, 6, 8–9, 122–24, 215n3, 225n8, 230n2
- *See also* narrative; narrative criticism

textual criticism, 3
thematic units, 108–9
theophany
- of Elijah on Mount Horeb, 79, 162, 164–65, 174–75, 176, 181
- of Moses at Horeb/Sinai, 176, 177
- *See also* God

third-person narrator, 98, 101, 225n2
time manipulation
- in Ahab story, 64, 196–97
- description and, 57
- dialogue and, 55–56
- in Elijah story, 63–64, 171–72
- event and recital time taking equal lengths of time, 55–56
- events taking less time to transpire than to recount, 56–58
- events taking longer to happen than to read about, 54–55
- flashback and, 58–59, 63, 64, 68, 146, 168, 179, 196–97
- foreshadowing and, 59–62, 146–47, 219n19
- in Jeroboam story, 63, 145–47
- order and, 58
- questions on, for exploring stories, 63–64
- simultaneity and, 62, 64
- in Solomon story, 55–61
- story versus narrative time lines, 53
- tempo and, 53–58

Tolkien, J. R. R., 23, 210n7
translations of Bible, 70–71, 109, 211n11, 220n13, 220–21nn15–16, 231n5, 243n26

Ulysses (Joyce), 218n1
unreliable narrator, 230n2, 231–32n10
Uriah, 67–68, 77

vantage point. *See* point of view
variation. *See* repetition and variation
viewpoint. *See* point of view
voices of narrator. *See* narrator

wealth of Solomon, 57–58, 61, 68–69, 91, 226n17
wisdom of Solomon, 57, 61, 69, 70, 72, 91, 101, 102, 152–53, 221nn19–20

Yhwh. *See* God

Zadok, 26, 47, 87–89, 92, 110, 113
Zarephath, widow of, 165, 167–68, 176, 238n22
Zedekiah, 80, 187, 188, 190, 199–200

www.ingramcontent.com/pod-product-compliance
Lightning Source LLC
Chambersburg PA
CBHW081353290426
44110CB00018B/2365